DISCOVERING THE COMMUNITY

DISCOVERING
THE COMMUNITY

Comparative Analysis
Of Social, Political, And Economic Change

BERT E. SWANSON and EDITH SWANSON

IRVINGTON PUBLISHERS, INC., NEW YORK
Distributed by HALSTED PRESS, Division of
JOHN WILEY & SONS, INC.
New York • London • Toronto • Sydney

For information,
write to Irvington Publishers, Inc.,
551 Fifth Avenue, New York, New York 10017.
Distributed by HALSTED PRESS
A division of JOHN WILEY & SONS, Inc., New York

Library of Congress Cataloging in Publication Data

    Swanson, Bert E
      Discovering the community.

      1. Cities and towns—United States—Case
studies.   2. Municipal government—United States—
Case studies.   I. Swanson, Edith, 1926-
II. Title.
HT123.S84   301.36'3'0973   76-30488
ISBN 0-470-99060-0

Printed in The United States of America

To the memory
of
GEORGE PINKUS
An imaginative and good brother

ACKNOWLEDGMENTS

Our grateful appreciation to the many people without whose help and talent our work would be less complete

Christopher Lindley—as Co-director of the Consortium on Community Crisis Cornell University and Sarah Lawrence College, with whom the project began

Esther Raushenbush, President Emeritus of Sarah Lawrence College—for her early support in helping us bridge the gap between the college and community

Susan Ackiron—for her work in discovering her own community, New Rochelle, and conducting a feedback seminar there, "Consciousness and Commitment"

Charney Bromberg—for work on the original concept and format

New York State Department of Education, Title I of the Higher Education Act, and the Field Foundation—for early financial support

Helene Cooke and Joan Sherman—our first students to apply the   book to specific communities

Howard Pinkus and Marjorie Summers—for their artistic contributions

Sally Cravens and the staff of the Documents Room of the University of Florida—for their assistance in locating the appropriate data sources

Robert Lamm and **Francine Corton**—for their help with data collection

The Junior Leagues of Bronxville and Pelham, New York—for conducting the leadership studies in our two communities

Joseph A. McNamara and the **Westchester County Board of Canvassers**—for providing us an extensive account of the voting in our two communities

Susan Eddy, Patricia Reichert, and **Amy Corton**—for their patience and care in typing the manuscript

The many concerned citizens of Mount Vernon and New Rochelle—for sharing their insights with us

Irving Naiburg, our publisher—for his appreciation of innovations and for providing us an opportunity to develop not only this book but also encouraging us to continue this approach in our next ventures into local school systems

And finally, in advance—to you, the user—for engaging in community analysis with the hope that you will learn and with a request that you will provide us with feedback about your experiences using this book and write us:

Bert and Edith Swanson
1419 N.W. 48th Terrace
Gainsville, Fla. 32605

CONTENTS

NOTE TO THE READER

Throughout this book the word "Exercise" is synonymous with "Chapter."

Part I
AN APPROACH TO DISCOVERY

AN APPROACH TO DISCOVERY

INTRODUCTION

There is little question in the minds of most Americans that their communities are in trouble. It is not clear whether the trouble stems from social malaise, economic maldistribution of wealth and income, or political distrust. Since the end of World War II our cities have experienced population growth and social tension, increased personal income but taxpayer resistance to increased public expenditures, and improved professionalization of local government yet increased civil disorder and crime. Although these troubles may be developing as national phenomena, they are most dramatically expressed in the local community.

Critics of the urban scene have been most articulate. The anti-urban reaction to the rapidly evolving American City has long manifested fear and doubt about the city mob and the corrupt polity; distrust of commerce and industry; complaints about the bad air, the noise, the miserable crowding, the accumulated poverty, and the monotonous landscape; uneasiness about the destruction of social values where human communication has failed; and psychological reservations about the ability of people to withstand the tension and anxiety of urban life. We tend to forget that American cities have been in the making for a number of generations. Webber states that

> The course of city-building in America has been pursued
> without the aid of compass, map, rudder, or helmsman,
> and surely without a destination. Apparently it never
> occurred to anyone to do it otherwise. Until the new-
> town movement of recent days, cities were never con-
> ceived to be the designed-and-manufactured products of
> any corporation, public or private. Rather, they were
> but by-products of everyone's business—the residuals
> remaining from the conduct of the society's real busi-
> ness. Like other externalities of industrial processes,
> the clean-up job has been left to local governments to
> deal with as best they can—to tidy up the worst of the
> mess, possibly even to improve things a bit. But,
> because city-building is no one's affair, because cities
> develop as the consequences of billions of atomistic
> decisions, made by millions of deciders, over a long
> period of time, governments' efforts have typically been
> remedial and marginal. Their governance processes have

been inherently adaptive and evolutionary. Central
planning styles of the sorts that might fit an authori-
tarian organization do not match the structure of the
city development process. Neither the hierarchical
command-chain nor the goal-consensus of an army or that
of a small business firm can be found here.[1]

Although most of the attention has been focused on the "urban crisis,"
few communities of any size have been left untouched by the social, political, and economic problems of modernity and change. In the communities
directly affected and in those that wish to avoid turmoil, the propensity
to act prevails. However, effective action, we believe, should be pre-
faced by careful and extensive study to discover not only present conditions but some of the factors associated with the rapid change. Some
believe they can ill afford this luxury, as they experience "future shock"
—the result of acceleration, diversity, and novelty.[2] Many of us have
great difficulty perceiving the interconnections of diverse kinds of events
in different sectors of the community or discerning patterns of relationships, as we are trained as specialists. Still others resist close examination of their communities because they prefer to act before they think.

However, analysts and activists alike have begun to study their communities to understand sources of community problems and the variety of
social, political, and economic strategies and resources that might solve
them. Although many Americans' actions are based on personal experience,
others have begun to rely on the often unrelated perspectives of specialists
—historians, sociologists, political scientists, economists, psychologists,
anthropologists, planners, and geographers, whose approaches range from the
unsystematic "guesswork" of political scientist Banfield[3] in studying nine
big cities to the statistical factor analysis of Berry[4] in classifying 1,762
cities.

Our own experience in working with the problems of American communities
includes both theoretical and practical approaches. They include a comparative study of four communities;[5] policy studies of public education;[6] an intervention strategy to mobilize leadership for more effective community action;[7]
a study of social tensions among ethnic groups;[8] and, more recently, a framework for small-town revitalization.[9] Although each project has served its
immediate purpose, we have come to the point where we prefer a more comprehensive approach to understand collective action, change, and intervention.

Reflecting on our experiences, we now propose to engage in a discovery
of the community as part of any agenda for action and/or study. By community
discovery we mean taking apart the community into bits and pieces and putting them back together again into what should be a more meaningful whole.
That is, rather than take social phenomena as discrete data, we seek to
identify the connections between them and the political and economic facets
of community life. Individuals and groups express their social attainment, tastes, and preferences by moving to a city or selecting a particular
neighborhood, attaining a certain level of education, and/or adopting a particular family style of life. Likewise, voters make collective decisions

by the votes they cast in support of public authorities, by expressing
their preferences for possible forms of government, and by referenda for
selected policies. Similarly, consumers make dollar choices for the
house they own or rent, the taxes they pay and their indirect preferences
for certain kinds of public spending, which may reflect the income they
earn. The character of the community then is the product of the interaction of these many social preferences, voter decisions, and consumer
choices for public and private goods and services. Community discovery
can be seen as interested not only in each part—social, political, and
economic—but also in the whole record of a series of complex and interrelated decisions.

This book could have been prepared as a set of interrelated concepts
with little or no empirical data or specific places in mind. On the other
hand, the book could have compiled a data base on a particular community
without reference to the social sciences. We chose to interrelate concepts
and data to enhance the understanding of their application to a particular
place. We believe that the use of both also provides insight into patterns
of community behavior. Unfortunately, there is an enormous bureaucracy
collecting data without much reference to potential users and concept formation, as there is also an extensive amount of academic conceptualization
without reference to data. They not only pass each other, as ships in the
night, but each in its own way has made it difficult to utilize its work
to the advantage of all.

A few cautions are in order. In our attempt to be comprehensive
and concentrate on the social, political, and economic dimensions of the
community, we have had to sacrifice an in-depth investigation of each of
the dimensions and the variables within it. For instance, we have not
examined all the ramifications of population size or covered all the ground
a sociologist would. Second, although including a number of external factors, we have, by and large, treated the community as a relatively autonomous unit of analysis. No communities, however, are autonomous, self-
sufficient, or beyond state, regional, and national forces.[10] The boundaries of the community are "porous" in the sense that the community is
affected by the major issues of the time such as war and peace, depression
and inflation, or race relations. Third, in relying on readily available
data because it is accessible, cheap, and comparable, we are limited by
what officialdom has deemed worth collecting—which reveals its view of
the world and leaves many gaps in our current information about community
life. For example, voting behavior on local elections is missing from any
national data bank, except for Presidential elections for which it is given
on a county basis, meaning that local voting data must be collected locally.
Surveys of opinions and attitudes, significant in understanding human events,
are conducted essentially by private pollsters for their clients on a national
basis, and seldom examine a specific community.

A final caution is that one must be careful about the inferences
that can be drawn from aggregate data. Eulau has alerted us to two fal-
lacies. The first is the *fallacy of composition,* which "involves inference from the properties of the sub-units to the properties of the unit
they compose."[11] The second is the *fallacy of division* (the ecological

fallacy), which "involves inference from the properties of a whole to the properties of its parts."[12] We believe we have in Eulau's terms "constructed larger units out of smaller ones to permit comparative. . . analysis at a higher level."[13] For example, we have used the aggregate of wealth and income of one community's residents and compared it to the same aggregate measure for another community.

Our venture in community discovery is one of learning while doing. There are three objectives. The first is to familiarize the user with the sources, as well as the nature and limitations, of readily available data. At the same time, the user should become familiar with the accumulated body of knowledge about community affairs. For example, it is easy to speak loosely about the high level of municipal taxes; it is difficult to speak accurately about it. A comparative analysis of city budgets requires not only a common data source such as census reports but also a comparable set of cities that carry out more or less similar functions. The comparison is meaningless, for instance, if one compares New York City, which has a dependent school system with educational monies included in its municipal budget, with Chicago, which has an independent school system with a separate budget so that educational monies are excluded from the city's budget. For comparability, consideration also should be given to whether a city is carrying out what are normally considered county functions, such as public assistance programs, public health, and the like. Simultaneously, the existing body of knowledge on, for example, what socioeconomic and political factors are associated with varying levels of spending should be understood. Lineberry and Sharkansky have prepared a review of these factors and found some specific associations and others that were contradictory.[14]

The second objective is to engage in the analysis of data. This requires not only the collection of data and its assembly into meaningful patterns, but also its interpretation. Far too often community participants and/or analysts operate within the limitations of one of the following three approaches: the intuitive, the theoretical, or the empirical. Some generalize from one fact to many: Main Street is dead, and therefore the community is in decline. Such a conclusion is wrong, if in fact there are burgeoning shopping centers, office complexes, and industrial parks springing up elsewhere in the community. Some generalize from one setting to another: School desegregation worked in one community, and therefore it will work in any community. They ignore local variations in racial composition, prevailing ideologies, and patterns of influence. Some accept an abstract principle as reality without testing it out: Power elites control American communities. One should first determine whether the principle holds, i.e., whether in fact there is an elite and then whether or not that elite controls one's own community. To rely on intuition alone (gut reaction), on theory alone (abstractions), or on data alone (brute empiricism) is to limit the potentials of discovery. It is our aim in community discovery to use a more comprehensive approach, to challenge the assumptions of the intuitive by being explicit, of the theoretical by providing relevant data, and of the empirical by reviewing the available knowledge.

The third objective is to facilitate discussion and dissemination of the findings and insights gained by studying American communities. Seldom is there a discussion of the interplay of social, economic, and political factors in community affairs. Similarly, far too often those who live in communities never learn of the findings and recommendations of those who pursue systematic studies. Perhaps these insights could stimulate greater interest among citizens to learn about their town, to raise questions about the conduct of public affairs, and even to demand specific changes. For those with theoretical interests the findings could be useful in formulating hypotheses for future testing.

COMMUNITY STUDY DESIGN

To achieve these objectives several factors should be considered, the focus of the inquiry, how to approach the study, and which sites to select. We now will discuss each factor, as well as our own study rationale.

DECIDE THE FOCUS

Although one may think he wants to know everything there is to know about a community, it is important to select a task that is relevant to a topic and manageable, given the limitations of time and energy. This book, for example, covers some results of decisions, such as choices to move to or stay in town, the selection of who shall govern, and the adoption of a specific tax policy, rather than the decision-making process itself. It includes electoral preferences as reflected in actual voting results, rather than citizen attitudes or public opinion. It records federal and state financial aid, rather than exploring all the linkages to forces outside the community.

Jones suggests six criteria for the relative worth of topics for study:

> . . . include the importance of the topic for the
> development of scientific theory (Value: knowledge
> for its own sake); how increased knowledge of the topic
> will improve the social, economic, or political well-
> being of mankind (Value: maximizing some version of
> the good life); how many others are investigating the
> topic (Value: individuality); the amount of inconsis-
> tency in previous investigations (Value: clear up
> ambiguous areas of knowledge); and the ease with which
> the topic can be studied (Value: pragmatism, or hunt-
> ing where the ducks are).[15]

Some may wish to concentrate on the political or economic aspects of communities. Others may wish to select a few exercises from each section and examine more closely how they relate to each other. Another activity is to focus on a specific institutional area, such as the political parties, and select those exercises for study which are believed to be most closely associated with it, in this case social heterogeneity, party potential, and party effectiveness, for example. Whichever focus is selected, one should determine whether the resources are available to reach the desired objectives.

CHOOSE THE STUDY APPROACH

Social scientists have developed many approaches for studying American communities. In fact, the proliferation of ways to analyze cities has disturbed some analysts such as Long, as when he reacted to Sayre and Kaufman's assertion that "There are probably a hundred ways to write about the government and politics of New York City."[16] Long states that "While this amiable tolerance is in the best spirit of academic freedom, and analytically it may be true that there are a hundred or, equally plausibly, an infinity of ways. . ., one would hope there are not a hundred ways for competent political scientists to write an acceptable description of the government and politics of New York."[17]

The typology illustrated in Figure 1 illustrates some possible approaches, (1) the case study (noncomparative), (2) the uni-trend analysis, (3) the static comparative, and (4) the dynamic comparative. The first, *the case study*,[18] the most popular approach, selects one community to study, at one moment in time. An in-depth study of a single community provides a comprehensive view but cannot be generalized upon because any one community may be unique; its typicality is unknown.

The second approach is the *uni-trend analysis*.[19] A single community is studied over a number of time periods. This type of study helps us understand the reasons for persisting or changing patterns in a community and the probable effects of a specific change. However, the lack of comparisons with other places precludes an understanding of the differential effects of, say, certain forces.

FIGURE 1

TYPOLOGY OF COMPARATIVE ANALYTIC COMMUNITY STUDY APPROACHES

		NUMBER OF TIME PERIODS	
		One	*Two or More*
	One	Case study	Uni-trend analysis
NUMBER OF COMMUNITIES			
	Few/Many	Static comparative	Dynamic comparative

The third approach is the *static comparative*. A few or more communities are studied at one moment in time, often to develop a system of classification or to test a series of hypotheses. Classification studies using a few communities have yielded a wide range of community labels or types such as "caretaker," "affluent," "underdeveloped," and so on.[20] Unfortunately, such classifications are seldom used with continuity in further research because they have not been accepted widely enough to encourage general usage. Recently analysts have attempted to classify many communities by using factor analysis.[21] Social scientists have also begun to study a large number of cities by collecting identical data with comparable research methods at one moment in time in order to test comparative propositions or hypotheses.[22] The advantage in this approach is the ability to generalize findings based on statistical probability. However, because it is costly, these studies are limited to a narrow range of readily available data.

The fourth approach is the *dynamic comparative,* which involves study-ing two or more communities for two or more time periods. This more complex type of investigation has been referred to as an *experimental design,* and it may be one of two types: (1) the natural experiment or (2) planned inter-vention. The *natural experiment*[23] measures the effect of some specific change occurring over two or more time periods in several communities. Its advantage is that it permits the assessment of certain interesting and obser-vable changes in the community. Its difficulty lies in finding communities with similar sets of conditions at one moment in time. *Planned intervention*[24] attempts to probe how systems respond to very specific introduced stimuli. This type of study helps to formulate propositions concerning how different communities react to the same stimuli. However, for an outsider it is most difficult to secure a strategic position from which to induce change; even when it is possible, the outsider is accused of not having to live with the consequences of his acts.

Although the single case study is an enriching experience, it is clear that more can be learned from studying several places over more than one moment in time. However, each added community requires additional time to collect and analyze materials. Yet we believe the value of comparisons makes the effort worthwhile.

THE TIME FRAME
Whether the study covers one or more than one moment in time, what time period or specific moment is to be covered should be discussed and decided upon early. One may study the result of a specific election in November of 1968 or one may study election trends over a short or long period of time. City budgets are decided upon annually, and mayors are elected every two or four years. The time frame selected is in part deter-mined by readily available data reports and in part by the events that are of interest. The U.S. Bureau of the Census is the source of most nationally collected data and provides information every ten years on population charac-teristics and housing conditions (beginning in 1985 this information will be published every five years). Every five years it also provides reports on business and government, with some annual reports available on city and county finance.

If a community is to be studied at one moment in time, it would be best to pick a year when the amount of available data can be maximized;

i.e., the year 1960 provides coordinated data on population as well as on
the Presidential election. If an experimental approach is taken on the
effects of fiscal policy, then a decade such as 1960 to 1970 might best
illustrate changes in taxation and turnover of public officials. It is
also possible to plot increments of change on a broader sweep of history
by including several decades.

SELECT THE SITE

Which community or communities to study depends on what is expected.
A city may be selected because (1) it is convenient and holds personal
interest or familiarity, (2) it is undergoing important changes or has
experienced a significant change, or (3) it is useful for a follow-up or
supplement to a previous study.

Each analyst seems to have his/her own special reasons for studying
a particular community. Perhaps the most provocative stimulus is an issue
that has developed into a community controversy or conflict. Analysts,
like bees drawn to flowers, are often attracted to communities where controversies over such issues as fluoridation of the water supply, desegregation of the public schools, urban renewal, annexation or consolidation,
or the establishment of the city manager form of government have occurred.
Others are attracted to communities with unusual reputations established
by historical events, successful performances in problem solving, or some
dynamic or enigmatic public personality. Still others prefer to examine
certain types of places such as industrial, suburban, or metropolitan
areas or small towns.

One often-overlooked decision is the definition of the community as
a unit of analysis. The definition of community seems to vary according to
its use. Definitions range from a social psychological feeling or sense
of community to a municipal corporation or an economic trade area. Perhaps the most familiar is the statistical definition developed by census
takers who collect data on such aggregates of population as city, county,
urban places, and standard metropolitan statistical areas (SMSA).

The area of interest should guide the choice of an appropriate
unit, whether it be a social network, an economic trade area, a governmental jurisdiction, or any combination of these. We suggest that a
decision-making or policy-formulating system be chosen, that is, such legally
based systems as municipalities, counties, school districts, autonomous
special districts, metropolitan public authorities, or quasi-governmental
regional planning councils. We further recommend that, to maximize financial data sources, cities of 10,000 population or over be selected. If one
prefers annual budget records, however, then cities of 50,000 or more should
be chosen. Finally, the local library should be checked to see whether
there are adequate data available for the places under consideration.

Comparative Settings The selection of two or more communities for comparative purposes may be based on the criterion that on some one or few characteristics and changes in those characteristics they are similar or dissimilar.

They may be alike or different on a social characteristic such as city type (central city, suburb, small town) or population size, a political characteristic such as form of government (strong mayor, city manager) or degree of political competition, or an economic characteristic such as economic function (manufacturing, retail) or level of expenditures, and the changes they manifest in that characteristic may be similar or dissimilar, i.e., expenditures have increased 10 percent in a decade for one place and 50 percent for another. Four types of comparative settings are suggested by the typology shown in Figure 2. One is a *congruent* setting, where communities have a smiliar characteristic (or characteristics) changing in the same direction and to the same degree. The second is a *divergent* setting, where a smiliar characteristic is changing either in a different direction or to a greater degree. The third is a *convergent* setting, where a dissimilar characteristic is changing in a direction and to a degree that it becomes relatively the same at t_2 (the second time period). The fourth is an *incongruent* setting, where the communities are different on some characteristic and the direction and degree of changes in that characteristic are different.

FIGURE 2

TYPOLOGY OF COMPARATIVE COMMUNITY SETTINGS

		CHANGE IN COMMUNITY CHARACTERISTIC(S)	
		Similar	*Dissimilar*
		Congruent	Divergent
COMMUNITY CHARACTERISTIC(S)	*Similar*		
	Dissimilar	Convergent	Incongruent

OUR STUDY RATIONALE

To illustrate the considerations for designing a study, let us discuss some of the factors that influenced our selection of Mount Vernon and New Rochelle, both in New York State. Our interest was stimulated when we were called into Mount Vernon to participate in resolving a number of community problems and controversies. These included the desegregation of the public schools,[25] the implementation of an urban renewal program, and the coordination of an Urban Tension Seminar involving community dialogue, study, and action. To carry out these assignments we conducted a citizen's attitudinal survey for the Human Rights Commission, a population projection for the Board of Education, a family survey for the Jewish Community Council, and a wide variety of tasks for the Black Ad Hoc Council.

Although these individual projects gave us some valuable insights into the characteristics and changing nature of Mount Vernon, we soon realized that we needed to undertake a more comprehensive study of the community. We set up an *experimental* design (natural) and decided to use a *congruent* set of two communities for two time periods. Our task then was to find a comparable city. We chose New Rochelle because it had similar characteristics in its suburban location and population size. Our interest, therefore, was to discover whether these *congruent* communities displayed consistently similar social, political, and economic patterns or whether there were some significant differences and, if so, in which ways were they different. We chose basically the 1960 to 1970 decade as our time frame because it was the period in which we were active in the community.

OPERATIONAL PROCEDURES

Once the users have decided on the focus, chosen the study approach, and selected the study sites, they still must make a number of critical decisions to complete the exercises. These include where and how to collect data, how to assemble it, and what relevant findings and implications to draw out. They should also explore ways to disseminate the insights gained and to discuss broader implications.

THE EXERCISE FORMAT

We have chosen to present our material in the format of a workbook divided into three major parts—social, political, and economic. Each part includes a number of theoretical and practical exercises, each with the following features:

1. Orienting question
2. Concept
3. Typology
4. Sources and caveats
5. Profile examples
6. Operational definitions
7. Classification indicators
8. Findings and suggested implications
9. Speculations
10. Community data profile
11. Discussion
12. Notes

An *orienting question* has been posed to shape the focus of the exercise, that is, what in essence do we want to know? In the *concept* the main ideas are defined, discussed, and related to some selected insights, statements, or propositions as well as to empirical data gathered from either systematic or speculative studies.

In order to set communities within the larger framework of the nation's cities, we have made an effort to provide a series of *typologies* by which communities can be classified. We have chosen to use national averages on municipalities wherever possible as a cutting-point or standard to determine a city's placement as above or below the average for the nation's cities. If such data are not available, alternative cutting points have been developed. This approach was selected as the one which would generally serve the widest variety of cities. But inherent in this approach is the loss in most instances of the refinement of comparing cities of approximately the same size and type. If a number of cities in one state were to be studied, our approach could easily be modified by using state averages rather than national ones. Wherever possible, cutting points based on national averages (per capita figures, percentages, and/or degrees of change) have been established and presented in a table of *classification indicators* along with the comparable measures for our two communities. The resulting classifications, of course, are limited to a specific aspect of the community and are not intended to label the community as good or bad, efficient or inefficient, successful or unsuccessful. Our labels are not immune to attack. It should be noted that they are intended to place communities in a position relative to that of other communities.

Each exercise in turn has recognized *sources* wherein data can be found. Also included are a number of *caveats*, or warnings about the comparability of measures, the reliability of the data, and possible difficulties and complexities in acquiring some data. The *profile examples* are a set of tables and occasionally graphs or charts that provide the array of empirical data and illustrate change over a decade or some other indicated period of time for our two cities, Mount Vernon and New Rochelle, and where possible for the nation. Each profile example is followed by the appropriate *operational defintions* to assist in computing the components of the tables. The section on *findings and suggested implications* begins with a classification, describes the particular characteristics under study, and points up changes and trends. In addition, we present *speculations* on the implications of possible findings when related to other variables, and we suggest their possible linkages to policy alternatives.

Community data profile for each exercise follows the profile examples, providing space for compiling and organizing the data that the user collects on his own community. A discussion sheet facilitates the exchange of ideas about conditions and trends pertaining to the specific data and concepts. At the same time, we encourage the exploration of the effect of these variables upon major areas of community life. Although the questions in the discussion sheet are directed toward the primary community, they can be adapted for comparative purposes by repeating them for two or more communities. We have also supplied relevant notes so that the reader may refer to the original work for more detail.

IMPLEMENTING THE EXERCISES

Identify the sources and collect data. Having selected the place, the area of interest, and the relevant exercises, it is now time to list the data needs and their sources and the specific dates required. Much of the data is found in a wide variety of census publications on population, business, and governments.[26] A condensed source of much data for cities of 50,000 or more can be found in the *County and City Data Book* as well as the *United States Summary* of the *General Social and Economic Characteristics*. Other reports also are compiled by federal, state, and local agencies, both public and private. Consult the *sources* and *caveats* for each exercise as well as your library, and check off the available items.

There may be gaps to fill that require a field trip. The following is a suggested itinerary for a field trip that would facilitate collecting most of the data needs of this workbook. There are a number of key places where data are kept.

1. *City Hall:* Most local government officials are located at City Hall, such as the city clerk, the comptroller, the tax assessor, and the planner. From these officials may be obtained municipal budgets, reports on general revenue-sharing, lists of the number and kinds of government employees and elected officials, master plans, and special studies.

2. *County Courthouse:* Most election and registration data—certainly for national, state, and county elections—can be found here. Some city election data are located at City Hall. Be sure to secure precinct maps along with your election data. Generally, tax assessment materials are found here.

3. *Chamber of Commerce:* The Chamber is a source for such economic information as the number and size of business firms, levels of business activity, market analysis, labor-force statistics, future city growth and population projections, and community organizations. It should also have a good selection of maps of the community.

4. *Newspapers:* The local newspaper is a good source from which to acquire a sense of community problems and issues, especially if the paper has an annual review of community events. Often biographical sketches of public figures are kept on file here.

Assemble and transform data. Having collected the data, use the community data profile for the proper form of data assembly. The profile examples and the operational definitions provide a guide to the assembly of data into tables and diagrams (maps, charts, and graphs).[27]

Generally we have used four data transformations. The first is to compute simple *percentages* or proportions—the easiest measure to understand and perform:

$$\text{Category Percentage} = \frac{(\text{Category } N)\ (100)}{\text{Total } N}$$

The second is *percentage change* as a way of looking at change over time:

$$\text{Percent Change } t_1 \text{ to } t_2 = \frac{[(\text{Category } N \ t_2) - (\text{Category } N \ t_1)]\ (100)}{(\text{Category } N \ t_1)}$$

The third is *per capita* figures generally used for measures of wealth, income, revenues, and expenditures when making comparisons between communities of different size:

$$\text{Per Capita Category} = \frac{(\text{Category } N)}{\text{Total Population}}$$

The fourth is an *index* or a combination of several measures into one. These indexes vary according to the concept being operationalized. For example, a *metric index*[28] requires first a translation of unlike measures that are going to be combined into like terms, such as the Socioeconomic Status Index, which combines occupation, income, and education. As occupation is expressed in job categories, income in dollars, and education in years of schooling, each must be given a score ranging from 1 to 100 before they can be added:

$$\text{SES Index} = \frac{\text{Occupation Score} + \text{Income Score} + \text{Education Score}}{3}$$

An *ordinal index* is one in which all categories that are to be combined are comparable, such as number of people, and categories may be weighted:

$$\text{Heterogeneity Index} = \frac{[(\text{Foreign Born}) \times 2(\text{Negroes})]\ (100)}{\text{Total Population}}$$

Draw Out Findings and Implications. Discovering the community through analysis requires that the data, whether tabular or graphic, be examined systematically for relationships. A guide suggested by Benson includes looking for (1) the greatest range of variation, (2) the overall consistency of the pattern, (3) the intermediate ranges of variability, and (4) inconsistencies and abnormalities.[29] The following analytic design is suggested as a guide to the interpretation of tables and diagrams for two communities for two time periods (see Figure 3). The following logical sequence is suggested.

1. Classify community according to typology.
2. Trend community A, t_1 to t_2.
3. Compare community A, t_2, to community B, t_2, and to a comparable U.S. statistic.
4. Trend community B, t_1 to t_2.
5. Compare the trend of community A to that of community B.

FIGURE 3

GUIDE TO COMPARATIVE ANALYSIS

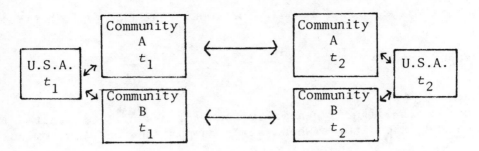

With the use of this design and the questions in the discussion sheets, statements can be made describing comparative conditions and changes. To explain certain phenomena, differences, or changes that have occurred, the search for other relevant variables through knowledge or intuition should be developed. The process described is repeated for each relevant variable, and parallel or unusual variations are noted that suggest tentative explanations and implications. Of course, if a few cases form the basis of analysis, the statement will be the outcome of more subjective than objective probability.

Findings and implications can be put into descriptive, explanatory, predictive, and/or prescriptive statements. The *descriptive* form is expressed in the factual details of the social, political, and economic profiles of the community. An *explanatory* statement attempts to identify the cause and effect of a particular fact or phenomenon. A *predictive* statement, on the other hand, projects what will happen on the basis of past trends or some theory of what makes the system behave the way it does. *Prescriptive* statements imply some normative preferences, objectives, or goals of what *ought* to be and often require some strategy interventions or policy changes if predictions are determined to be unacceptable. The following statements on racial change in a community illustrate the distinction between these four kinds of statements:

Descriptive: Blacks comprise one-third of the population and are a growing proportion of the population.

Explanatory: The "tipping point" phenomenon has been reached, stimulating whites to leave the community and blacks to move in.

Predictive: All things remaining equal, the community will become half black and half white in the next decade.

Prescriptive: *Option A:* If the preference is to regain a white-dominated community, one might prescribe that public education ought to be improved to encourage whites to stay and housing codes be strictly enforced to discourage low-income families, often blacks, from moving in.

Option B: If the preference is for a black-dominated community, blacks could enunciate their strategies in preparation for assuming power, which generally triggers anxiety in the whites that would stimulate them to move out while serving to attract a new wave of black in-migration.

Option C: If the preference is for an integrated community, blacks and whites would have to formulate mutually agreed-upon policies that would provide for equality of opportunity and/or achievement.

Transmit findings and explore implications. Sharing the results of the project with others can be a rewarding challenge or a problem in communications. Dissemination can take several forms. One is a *written report,* which should cover: (1) the focus, (2) the display of pertinent data, and (3) the major conclusions. The report can focus on the community as a whole, a major social, political, or economic dimension, or a set of relevant variables. The report can be a descriptive narrative with selected tables and diagrams; or it can be a set of propositional statements that attempt to explain, predict, or prescribe something about community affairs. Although most will use this workbook only for the classroom, to reach a wide audience the report or reports generated in the classroom could be disseminated through local newspapers or community organizations.

A *feedback seminar* is a second means of sharing the findings of community discovery.[30] Such a seminar would bring together a group of concerned citizens to participate in an exploration of the meaning and implications of the project report. The seminar may use the *discussion sheet* as a format that considers community conditions and trends, what contributes to them, and what the consequences are for major areas of community life. The discussion should explore the preferred community changes and how to accomplish them through alternative policy changes.

A number of seminar objectives can be achieved, including stimulating an interest in a more comprehensive community analysis, clarification of the findings and implications, and the identification of community problems and priorities for community action. A variety of persons can be selected to participate, including public authorities, civic leaders, and concerned citizens. We have found it useful to select fairly homogeneous participants when controversy is intense and a change-oriented group requires an opportunity to discuss openly the broader implications of their findings. On the other hand, a more representative heterogeneous group is advisable if the mobilization of broad support for community action is the objective. The agenda of the seminar should be designed with specific objectives and tasks in mind.

A third way of using the findings and suggested implications is for the individual student or participant to explore such specific questions as whether he/she should or would: stay in the community or leave, vote for the incumbents or their opponents, and/or support present tax policies or work for change. Another aspect of the individual approach is for each person to assume a key community role and interpret findings from that point of view. Such roles might include: (1) the mayor, (2) a political party leader, (3) the city manager, (4) an advocate or watchdog, (5) a community organizer, (6) a religious leader, (7) a corporate executive, (8) a newspaper publisher, (9) a civil-rights leader, (10) a taxpayer, (11) a candidate for office, (12) a planner, (13) a labor leader, and (14) an elected representative to the state or federal legislative body.

NOTES

1. Melvin M. Webber, "A Reexamination of Centrally Planned Change" in *Centrally Planned Change* edited by Robert Mayer, Robert Moroney, and Robert Morris (University of Illinois Press, 1974), pp. 18-19.

2. Alvin Toffler, *Future Shock* (Random House, 1970).

3. Edward C. Banfield, *Big City Politics* (Random House, 1965), p. 5.

4. Brian J. L. Berry (ed.), *City Classification Handbook* (John Wiley & Sons, 1972).

5. Robert E. Agger, Daniel Goldrich, and Bert E. Swanson, *The Rulers and the Ruled: Political Power and Impotence in American Communities* (Duxbury, 1972).

6. Bert E. Swanson, *The Struggle for Equality* (Hobb-Dorman, 1966) and *Desegregation-Decentralization Controversies in the Public Schools of New York City* (Institute for Community Studies, Sarah Lawrence College, 1968).

7. Bert E. Swanson, *Concern for Community in Urban America* (Odessey Press, 1970) and Bert and Edith Swanson, *The Tenuous Bonds Between Town and Gown* (forthcoming).

8. Louis Harris and Bert Swanson, *Black-Jewish Relations in New York City* (Praeger Publishers & Co., 1970).

9. Bert E. Swanson and Richard Cohen, *The Small Town in America: A Guide for Study and Community Development* (U.S. Office of Education, 1976).

10. Rolland Warren, *The Community in America* (Rand McNally & Co., 1963), pp. 237-266.

11. Heinz Eulau, *Micro-Macro Political Analysis* (Aldine Publishing Co., 1969), p. 5.

12. *Ibid.*, p. 5.

13. *Ibid.*, p. 8.

14.   Robert L. Lineberry and Ira Sharkansky, *Urban Politics and Public Policy* (Harper & Row Publishers, 1971), pp. 218-277.

15.   E. Terrence Jones, *Conducting Political Research* (Harper & Row, 1971), pp. 12-13.

16.   Wallace Sayre and Herbert Kaufman, *Governing New York City* (Russell Sage Foundation, 1960), p. XXV.

17.   Norton Long, *The Polity* (Rand McNally, 1962), p. 217.

18.   For example, see Floyd Hunter, *Community Power Structure* (Doubleday Anchor Books, 1964).

19.   See the follow-up of Robert and Helen Lynd, in their *Middletown* (Harcourt, Brace & Co., 1929), and *Middletown in Transition* (Harcourt, Brace & Co., 1937).

20.   For example, see Oliver Williams and Charles Adrian, *Four Cities* (University of Pennsylvania Press, 1963).

21.   Berry.

22.   Terry N. Clark, "Community Structure, Decision-making, Budget Expenditure and Urban Renewal in 51 American Communities," in *Community Politics* edited by C. N. Bonjean, T. N. Clark, and R. L. Lineberry (New York: The Free Press, 1971), pp. 293-313.

23.   Agger, Goldrich, and Swanson, see Chapters 9 and 10, pp. 189-250; and Heinz Eulau and Kenneth Prewitt, *Labyrinths of Democracy* (The Bobbs-Merrill Co., 1973), Chapter 29.

24.   Robert E. Agger and Marshall Goldstein, *Who Will Rule the Schools?* (Wadsworth Publishing, 1971).

25.   Bert E. Swanson, "Psycho-Political Patterns of School Desegregation, *Education and Urban Society,* Vol. 1, No. 2, Feb. 1969, pp. 193-230.

26.   For several helpful guides see, guide to *Recurrent and Special Governmental Statistics* (U.S. Department of Commerce, Bureau of the Census), *Directory of Non-Federal Statistics for States and Local Areas* (U.S. Department of Commerce, Bureau of the Census), and *Bureau of Census Catalogue of Publications, 1790-1972* (annual publication).

27.   For a detailed discussion on the preparation of tables and diagrams consult Oliver Benson, *Political Science Laboratory* (Charles E. Merrill Publishing Co., 1969), Chapters 2 and 3, pp. 22-109.

28.   Jones, pp. 33-37.

29.   Benson, p. 23.

30.   For a detailed discussion of a similar approach, the decisional seminar, see Harold D. Lasswell, *The Future of Political Science* (Atherton Press, 1963), pp. 125-140.

Part II
THE SOCIAL DIMENSION

SI. COMMUNITY LOCATION

WHERE IS YOUR COMMUNITY IN ITS GEOGRAPHIC ENVIRONMENT?

CONCEPT

In the beginning there were those who decided where to locate the community. Today, how a city functions depends in part on where it is located: within a metropolitan area, on the coast as a seaport, in a farm belt serving as a retail center, and so on. A number of efforts have been made to delineate the factors associated with the location of communities. One is the "break-in-transportation" theory, which identifies the types of economic activities of a place by the reasons certain kinds of people settle there, as in a seaport or along waterways, railways, or major highway intersections. Another is the "central-place" theory, which describes the geography of economic regions as a function of distance, mass production, and competition. This may lead to perceiving a system of cities as an urban hierarchy, based on "rank size," and to classifying centers according to their place in the hierarchy and/or according to the functional correlates of city size.

Other theories are based on situational or specific site factors. Geographers differentiate between site and situation. The former is based on the precise features of the terrain on which a settlement began and over which it has spread, whereas the latter is based on human characteristics as they affect the character and fortunes of the settlement. Finally, there are location theories which take into account "city-founders" and "city-fillers," that is, distinguish between activities that establish a community and those that persist because the city continues to exist.[1]

Some would maintain that once a city has been established its location continues to affect its growth, its economic development, the kinds of populations it attracts, its degree of in-and-out migration, and the attitudes and participation of its residents. In fact, Cox makes the case that, "Racial tension and riots, the virtual bankruptcy of many municipalities, inequalities of wealth, and the increasing role of the government in the urban economy have brought the city into the political forum. . . . [and] that many of these political issues have a very strong locational component."[2] Verba and Nie found that citizen

23

participation is higher for isolated villages, towns, and cities but lower
for suburbs.[3] They also found participation about average for the core
cities.

To locate a community in its physical environment one should look to
its geographic setting. Here one should consider the location relative to
major arteries—water, highways, rail, or air—and if appropriate to major
sites of natural resources—oil, coal, farm land, electric power, and the
like. The physical environment is important for understanding a community's
past and future growth as well as its present and future problems. Geographic
location is believed to affect social, economic, and political conditions,
which in turn affect the resource base available to a community. Raw materials, transportation facilities, markets, and the labor supply all contribute to the community's attractiveness to manufacturing and commercial interests and help determine what kinds of people move in and continue to
live there.

The concept of "relative location" considers several related factors
in the original location of a community and its attraction for economic firms
and certain kinds of people to reside there. As Yeates and Garner point out,
"Many decisions are made to maximize the advantages of relative location
and accessibility."[4]

Once a community has been located, one should be aware that there are
various types of data about cities which appear organized according to
size, proximity to other cities, relationship to a greater metropolitan
area, and the like. One of the more commonly used sources of data about
various communities is the *Census of Population*. Here the data are presented
in accord with various ways of looking at a community, that is, from a part
of a Standard Metropolitan Statistical Area (SMSA) to the individual place.
One organizing principle is the SMSA which is a county or group of contiguous counties containing at least one city of 50,000 inhabitants or more, or
"twin cities" with a combined population of at least 50,000. In addition to
the county, or counties, containing such a city or cities, contiguous counties
are included in an SMSA if, according to certain criteria, they are socially
and economically integrated with the central city. In the New England states,
SMSAs consist of towns and cities instead of counties. In 1970 there were 261
SMSAs identified. Data within an SMSA are recorded for the *central city(s)*
and the *urban balance*. As stated before, the central city is any city with
a population of 50,000 or more. The *urban balance* is the remaining population within the SMSA that is neither within the central cities nor classified
as rural—farm and nonfarm. Data are also recorded for *urbanized areas* which
report on the central city together with the population contiguous to the
central city which meets certain criteria as specified in the census definitions. Another reporting unit is the *place* which is any incorporated unit
such as a city, borough, town, and village as well as an unincorporated
unit with a closely settled population center but without corporate limits.
Data are also reported for *counties*. Using census reports one can identify

suburban populations by one of three methods: (1) the population in the urban balance, (2) subtracting the population in the central city from that in the urbanized area, and (3) subtracting the population in the central city from the total population of the SMSA. The two sets of data in the last method are generally referred to as data pertaining to the central city (CC) and outside the central city (OCC). It should be noted that of the above kinds of units only places (including central cities) and counties are legal decision-making units. An illustration of the differences between those living in the central city and those living outside the central city is found in the following figure prepared by the Advisory Commission on Intergovernmental Relations (ACIR)[5]

FIGURE SI-1.   POPULATION CHARACTERISTICS BY METROPOLITAN LOCATION
              (In SMSAs in General, All Regions and Sizes)

Central City Proportion Higher	*Equivalent Proportions*	*Suburban Higher*
Elderly	Ages 10-44 total and nonwhite	Young children
Unrelated individuals		Migrants—total and nonwhite
Broken families with children	Nonwhite craftsmen	
	Education	Families with children
Clerical and sales workers	Dropouts	
		Craftsmen
Household and service-total and nonwhite		Upper middle rentals
Working wives		Commuters
Unemployed		Highest nonwhite housing values (except South)
Nonwhite movers		
Nonwhites		

    Several ways of classifying cities according to their metropolitan location have been developed. Jones, Forstall, and Collver classify cities with populations over 10,000 according to their metropolitan status based on the 1960 Census of Population. They classify as Central Cities (C) the largest cities in SMSAs; other urban places over 10,000 located within SMSAs are classified as Suburbs (S), and Independent Cities (I) are all urban places with populations over 10,000 but located outside SMSAs.[6] You may find your community in their listings.

Vernon developed for the New York metropolitan area a fourfold classification: central city (Core area), suburbs (Inner Ring), rural nonfarm area (Intermediate Ring), and rural farm area (Outer Ring).[7] The Core usually contains a majority of the region's population and an even larger percentage of its jobs. The Inner Ring can be characterized by less extensive land usage and contains the next largest percentage of population and jobs. In this ring are the suburbs, largely homes of commuters who work in the Core. The Inner Ring, with the exception of towns closest to large cities, contains fewer apartment houses than one-family homes, and with few exceptions is the home of middle and upper income families. The Intermediate Ring is still further out from the Core and contains rural but not farm land. Homes are generally on large plots of land and surround small villages. In a densely settled metropolitan region, the Intermediate Ring may include small cities with a variety of industrial, commercial, and service activities. The Intermediate Ring contains an even smaller population and fewer jobs than the Inner Ring. Finally, the Outer Ring contains farm land and often vacation areas. Residents of the Outer Ring may work in the Core, while others may look to it as recreationally attractive.

Another taxonomy of cities which we prefer was developed by Rossmiller, Hale, and Frohreich for a national study of school finance (see Figure SI-2). Their classification scheme offers more distinctions than the previously noted ones, and we have modified it for general city classification. Following are their seven major types:[8]

> 1. *Major urban core city*—a city located in a standard metropolitan statistical area (SMSA), named in the title of the SMSA and having a population of 250,000 or more persons in 1970.
>
> 2. *Minor urban core city*—a city located in an SMSA, named in the title of the SMSA, and having a population of less than 250,000 persons in 1970.
>
> 3. *Independent city*—a city not located in an SMSA and having a population of 25,000 or more persons in 1970.
>
> 4. *Established suburb*—a city or village located in an SMSA that is not one of the core cities, which has experienced a population increase averaging less than 2 percent annually over the past ten years.[9]
>
> 5. *Developing suburb*—a city or village located in an SMSA, which is not one of the core cities and which has experienced a population increase of at least 2 percent annually over the past ten years.[10]
>
> 6. *Small city*—a city, village, or other incorporated municipality not located in an SMSA and having a population of from 10,000 to 24,999 in 1970.
>
> 7. *Small town* or agricultural service center—an area not located in an SMSA in which the largest populated place had a population of less than 10,000 persons in 1970.

FIGURE SI-2. TAXONOMY OF CITIES

	In an SMSA	*Not in an SMSA*
CITY/TOWN POPULATION		
Over 250,000	Major urban core	
Under 250,000	Minor urban core	
Over 25,000		Independent city
10,000-24,999		Small city
Under 10,000		Small town
SUBURB		
Average annual population growth 2% or more during past decade	Developing suburb	
Average annual population growth less than 2% during past decade	Established suburb	

SOURCES AND CAVEATS

Local planning commissions often have maps delineating legal boundaries, regional setting, major arteries, and economic areas. Your local Chamber of Commerce is another source for maps as well as data on transportation, industry, and commerce. Road maps can also provide valuable information about major community arteries. Standard metropolitan statistical areas (SMSAs) can be found in the Bureau of the Budget publication, *Standard Metropolitan Statistical Areas* (U.S. Government Printing Office, Washington, D.C.).

To learn about your community's location secure a map of your area. Locate your community on major highways, parkways, and thruways as well as on bodies of water (ocean, gulf, lake, river or canal). Determine if the community has a railroad line linked to other cities and a mass transit system within a metropolitan area. Next find the legal boundaries of your city. (We focus on legal boundaries because most census data—demographic, labor force, and public finance—and voting data have been assembled for various legal governmental units.) Locate it in terms of its relationship to a central city or suburban towns and villages.

Find out if it is in one of the more than 261 Standard Metropolitan Statistical Areas (SMSAs). Classify your city according to one of the previously suggested schemes. If you choose the Rossmiller *et al.* taxonomy, you must know your city's population (see Exercise SII), SMSA status, and if it is a suburb, its population change for the past decade.

PROFILE EXAMPLE

FIGURE SI-3. LOCATION OF MOUNT VERNON AND NEW ROCHELLE IN THE METROPOLITAN AREA

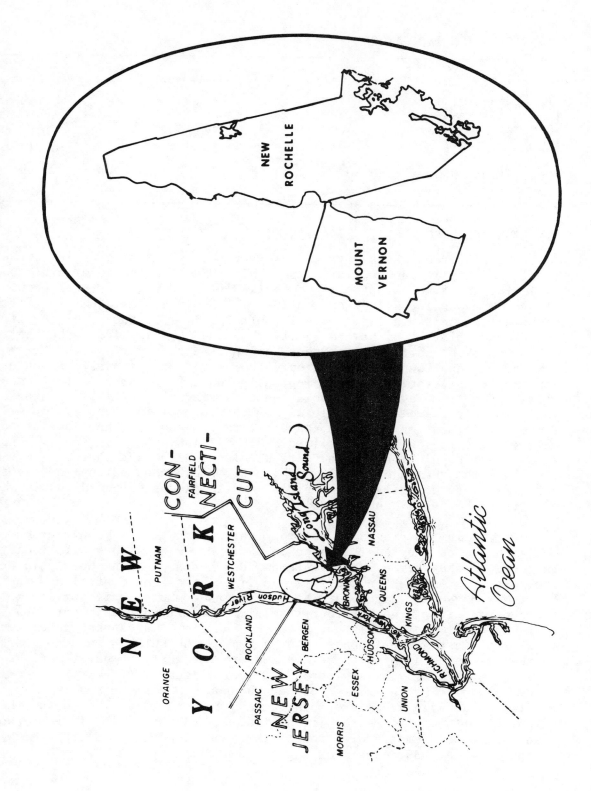

CLASSIFICATION INDICATORS

	Mount Vernon	New Rochelle
In an SMSA?	Yes	Yes
Core city?	No	No
Population, 1970	72,778	76,812
Population change, 1960-70 (See Exercise SII, Table 1)	-4.3	-1.9

FINDINGS AND SUGGESTED IMPLICATIONS

Mount Vernon is an *established suburb* in the southern tier of Westchester County in the New York SMSA. This SMSA is composed of nine counties including the five boroughs of New York City. In 1960 the total population of the SMSA was 10,694,632 and in 1970, 11,528,649. In 1960 three fifths of Mount Vernon's dwellings were in multifamily structures, giving it more the characteristics of New York City than the more spacious suburban communities to the north of it. Mount Vernon is also a part of the New York, New Jersey, and Connecticut region. According to the classification of the Regional Plan Association this region includes 22 counties with 19 million people. Some time ago the Association estimated that by 1985 the region would include 25 million people and by the turn of the century, 30 million.[11] These earlier estimates have been drastically reduced. The Association now believes the region has stabilized at 20 million, which virtually constitutes "zero population growth." Its studies indicate "a sharp rise in migration into the region of people of Hispanic background during the 1970s, a sharp fall-off of entry of nonwhites, and an exodus of non-Hispanic whites even from the nearer suburbs."[12]

It is in this regional setting that one must view Mount Vernon and New Rochelle as they are situated in the Inner Ring with New York City as the Core of the region. Mount Vernon, just north of Bronx County in New York City, is located on two railroad lines, the Penn Central and the New York, New Haven and Hartford, which serve as commuter rail service into the central city. Nine bus routes service the city and adjacent areas, but only one bus route travels north to the industrial areas and governmental complex of Westchester County. Two parkways, the Hutchinson River Parkway to the east and the Bronx River Parkway to the west, border the city. The Cross-County Parkway passes through the city from east to west approximately one mile south of its northern boundary. Mount Vernon is also located on a barge canal providing access to Long Island Sound and the shipping ports of the metropolitan area. Its elevation is 115 feet above mean sea level. Temperatures range from about 20 degrees during the winter to approximately 85 degrees during the summer.

New Rochelle, also classified as an *established suburb,* like Mount
Vernon is located in the southern tier of Westchester County in the Inner
Ring of the region. The city has one railroad line, the New York, New Haven
and Hartford. Three bus companies service the city. Two parkways cross the
city, the Hutchinson River Parkway on the west and the New England Thruway
in the south. New Rochelle has direct access to the Long Island Sound, bordering the Sound along its southeastern boundary. The Sound not only provides access to metropolitan ports but also provides recreational facilities—
swimming and boating—for its residents.

Mount Vernon's location, close to New York City with two railroads and
accessible parkways, makes it a convenient bedroom community for commuters.
Its proximity to New York City draws away a number of professional and
business people from community affairs. Its location on a barge canal and on
the railroads makes it a good location for industrial activity. However, it
lacks good mass transit to industrial areas within the county where there
are more job opportunities for its blue-collar workers. Like Mount Vernon,
New Rochelle is largely a bedroom community. However, unlike Mount Vernon,
it has developed commercially rather than industrially. New Rochelle contains one of the four major shopping malls in the immediate area. These
shopping centers have attracted retail trade away from Mount Vernon, leaving
its main business street in decline and encouraging civic leaders to seek
light industry to support its tax base.

In part the economic future and development of a community depend on
the imagery held by those outside who make important decisions affecting
the city. Figure SI-4 indicates some of our speculations on the social,
political, and economic images associated with various community locations.

FIGURE SI-4. SPECULATIONS ON IMAGES ASSOCIATED WITH TYPES OF COMMUNITY LOCATIONS

Social Images	*Political Images*	*Economic Images*
MAJOR URBAN CORE		
Very heterogeneous population	Strong mayor form of government	Diversified economic base
Stable or declining in size	One-party system	Great property wealth
Great social disparities	Moderate electoral participation	Extremes of income
High proportion of females in the labor force		High levels of revenues and expenditures
Many attenuated families		Dependent school systems
MINOR URBAN CORE		
Growing population size	City manager form of government	Moderate wealth and income
Younger population	Moderate electoral participation	Diversified tax base
		Growing expenditure levels
INDEPENDENT CITIES		
Moderately heterogeneous	Limited electoral options	Economically independent
Stable population size	Consensual politics	Moderate wealth and income
	High electoral participation	High expenditure levels
SMALL CITIES		
Moderately heterogeneous	City manager form of government	Moderate levels of revenues and expenditures
Moderate social disparities	Nonpartisan politics	High utility revenues
	Moderate electoral participation	High retail sales
SMALL TOWNS		
Homogeneous populations	Minimal scope of government	Dependent economic base
Stagnant growth	Low rate of electoral participation	Low levels of revenue and expenditures
Older populations	Personalized politics	Low tax ideology
Lower degree of social disparities	Elites control	
DEVELOPING SUBURBS		
Homogeneous populations	Nonpartisan politics	Very limited economic base
Younger populations	Low electoral participation	Low levels of revenues and expenditures
Little social disparity	Limited electoral options	Low taxes
ESTABLISHED SUBURBS		
Growing heterogeneity	High electoral participation	Diversifying economic base
Population growth leveling off	Many electoral options	High levels of wealth and income
	Highly competitive elections	High levels of revenue and expenditures

DISCUSSION

1. In what classification is your community? (a) major urban core, (b) minor urban core, (c) independent city, (d) small city, (e) small town, (f) developing suburb, (g) established suburb.

2. Where is your community geographically? (a) what region in the United States, (b) what region of the state, (c) on a major artery, (d) at the site of some natural resource, (e) in a preferable climate or scenic site.

3. Is your community a relatively autonomous one? (a) What is its proximity to another major community? (b) Is it the center for other communities economically or culturally, for medical services and the like, or is it dependent on another city? (c) From what area does your community draw its foodstuffs, raw materials, and labor force?

4. Does its location affect the kind of migration into and out of the community? (a) Is it a port of entry for those coming from foreign countries? (b) Is it the site of a particular kind of work drawing persons with certain skills? (c) Does it have the kind of climate or conditions to draw retirees or older persons? (d) Is it a place that attracts people from rural areas and small towns?

5. What are the major transportation linkages with other communities? (a) air, (b) highways, (c) rivers, (d) canals, (e) railroads.

6. What are some likely future problems with the physical environment of your community? (a) land use, (b) air and water pollution, (c) planned use of natural resources.

7. Does its location encourage or discourage a sense of community? (a) Are the majority of your residents commuters with split loyalties? (b) Are the cultural and social activities sufficient to keep your residents interested in the community? (c) Do your residents take an active part in social and political matters?

8. Speculate on the consequences of your community's location on the following major aspects of community life: (a) education, (b) housing, (c) crime, (d) health, (e) welfare, (f) economic opportunities, (g) cultural activities, and (h) social tensions.

NOTES

1. Otis Dudley Duncan *et al.*, *Metropolis and Region* (Johns Hopkins Press, 1960), pp. 28-32.

2. Kevin R. Cox, *Conflict, Power and Politics in the City* (McGraw-Hill Book Co., 1973), p. xi.

3. Sidney Verba and Norman H. Nie, *Participation in America* (Harper & Row Publishers, 1972), p. 236.

4. Maurice H. Yeates and Barry J. Garner, *The North American City* (Harper & Row Publishers, 1971), p. 12; see also Chapter IV, pp. 88-117.

5. For a more comprehensive list of population characteristics by size and region see Advisory Commission on Intergovernmental Relations, *Metropolitan America: Challenge to Federalism* (U.S. Government Printing Office, 1966), pp. 27-30.

6. Victor Jones, Richard L. Forstall, and Andrew Collver, "Economic and Social Characteristics of Urban Places (International City Management Association, 1967), in *The Municipal Yearbook,* 1967, pp. 30-65.

7. Raymond Vernon, *Anatomy of a Metropolis* (Harvard University Press, 1959), pp. 1-20.

8. Richard A. Rossmiller, James A. Hale, and Lloyd E. Froehreich, *Fiscal Capacity and Educational Finance* (University of Wisconsin, 1970), p. 28.

9. The authors used a school enrollment increase of less than 5 percent annually over the most recent five-to-seven-year period for which data are available. Since we are interested in total population, we have calculated that a comparable increase for the past ten years is 2 percent.

10. The authors used a school enrollment increase of at least 5 percent annually over the most recent five-to-seven-year period. We have used a total population increase of at least 2 percent annually over the past ten years.

11. Regional Plan Association, *The Second Regional Plan,* November, 1968, p. 12.

12. *New York Times,* January 30, 1975, p. 37.

COMMUNITY SIZE, DENSITY, AND CHANGE

IS THE POPULATION OF YOUR COMMUNITY GROWING OR DECLINING?

CONCEPT

Demographers say the simplest way to get the sense of a city is to count heads and see how closely crowded they are. The rationale for studying community size is that "size is objective, capable of being measured, and sociologically relevant."[1] Population size is the count of the residents of a place, not including those who merely work, shop, or play there. Density is the relationship between the number of residents and the land area in square miles. Density figures are an average for the community as a whole. Thus part of a community might be more densely populated by a concentration of high-rise apartments while another part of town might include more single-family homes or industrial areas where fewer people per square mile live. The density of cities varies considerably. For instance, among cities of 100,000 or more persons in 1970, the range in density was from 576 persons per square mile in Oklahoma City to 26,343 in New York City.

The dynamic aspect of size and density is change, that is, growth or decline over time (see Table SII-1). Population changes may occur through such causes as births and deaths or through in-or out-migration. Density changes may occur as a result of population changes and/or changes in land area. Annexation is the major means by which the land area of a community is increased. However, since World War II many suburbs have resisted being annexed into the central city.

Although there is nothing magical about the size of a city, the concept is important because state governments classify cities by size for the allocation of authority, taxing powers, and financial aid. Occasionally density is included as part of state aid formulas as a more realistic basis of differentiation between community problems and resources to meet those needs. The U.S. Census Bureau also classifies places by size in collecting and reporting selected characteristics.

Analysts such as Munson have used population size as part of an index of urbanism.[2] Reissman, however, points out the limited potential of using population size alone. He maintains that the differences between cities are more than simply the matter of numbers. Other factors affect the

TABLE SII-1

POPULATION AND CHANGE BY CITY SIZE
(Population 1,000's)

	1960	1970	% Change
United States	179,323	203,212	16.1
Urban	125,269	149,325	19.2
1,000,000 or more	17,484	18,769	7.3
500,000 - 1,000,000	11,111	12,967	16.7
250,000 - 500,000	10,766	10,442	-3.0
100,000 - 250,000	11,652	14,286	22.6
50,000 - 100,000	13,386	16,724	20.9
25,000 - 50,000	14,951	17,848	19.4
10,000 - 25,000	17,568	21,415	21.9
5,000 - 10,000	9,780	12,924	32.1
2,500 - 5,000	7,580	8,038	6.0
Places under 2,500	690	727	5.4
Unincorporated parts of urbanized areas	9,851	15,186	54.2
Rural	54,054	53,887	-0.3
1,000 - 2,500	6,497	6,656	2.4
Under 1,000	3,894	3,852	-1.1
Other rural	43,664	43,379	-0.7

Adapted from *The Statistical Abstract of the U.S. 1974*, Bureau of the Census, Table 17, p. 18.

significance of population size, such as the distance the city is from a larger
metropolis (see Exercise SI), the amount of political power it wields, its economic resources (see Exercise EI), and its social status (see Exercise SV).
Size may be most useful when comparing extremes, the large city and the small
town. Yet as imperfect as population size is, Riessman uses it as one measure
in constructing the first of four variables (urban status, industrial status,
prevalence of a middle class, prevalence of nationalism) in his development of
a typology of urbanism and change.[3]

Yeates and Garner develop the relationship between population density
and population growth rates. They suggest that areas of high population density
have lower population growth rates than areas of low population densities.
That is, the inner city, which is the most dense, displays lower growth rates
(even declining ones) when compared to the periphery of the city, where there
are low population densities. They write, "not only is the population growth
rate related in a systematic fashion to distance from the center of the city,
but also to the density of population itself."[4]

Among the implications of population size are those advanced by Duncan
and Reiss that size produces differences according to selected migration, family organization, and economic structure and function. They found that long-
distance migrants were more attracted to large cities than to small ones and
therefore large cities contain disproportionately more females and young people
than do small cities and have greater ethnic diversity than smaller cities.
Second, the larger the city, the greater the proportion of working women, the
smaller the proportion of those married, and the greater the number of secondary
institutions carrying out the usual family functions. Third, Duncan and Reiss
found, the larger the city, the greater the proportion of those in white-collar
jobs, the higher the median income, the higher the median rent, and the more
similar the occupational distribution between males and females.[5] In addition
to these social and economic associations with size, political analysts such
as Plato, Aristotle, and Rousseau believed that a small-sized polity would enhance the opportunities for citizen participation in and control of government.
Dahl and Tufte, however, can find no optimal size place that enhances a citizen's
effectiveness to control its government and a system capacity to respond fully
to the collective preferences of its citizens. They suggest instead that
". . . we need some very small units and some very large units."[6]

It has been stated that a difference in size can amount to a difference
in kind. Swanson and Cohen maintain that small towns "offer particular life
styles and residential environments which are alternatives to city living.
Small towns may represent a slower pace of life, a chance to know your neighbors, a community which one can identify and define, a place where a resident's
contribution to the quality of life may be more readily noticed and appreciated."[7]

Like size, density has social, economic, and political implications.
For instance, Warren states, "the higher the concentration of people in a given
area, the greater the degree of specialization which must take place for them
to subsist."[8] He continues by saying that the anonymity of people in the large
city "necessitate[s] the various secondary controls on behavior which include
complicated police systems and courts. The business of everyday living is carried on to a large extent with people whom one does not know."[9]

Some of the public service and cost implications of growth were stressed by the Kerner Commission studying the urban riots of the 1960s:

> growing municipalities have been hard pressed for services generated by population increase. On the other hand, stable or declining cities have not only been faced with steady cost increases, but also with a slow-growing, or even declining, tax base.
>
> As a result of the population shifts of the post-war period, concentrating the more affluent parts of the urban population in residential suburbs while leaving the less affluent in the central cities, the increasing burden of municipal taxes frequently falls upon that part of the urban population least able to pay them.
>
> Increasing concentrations of urban growth have called forth greater expenditures for every kind of public service: education, health, police protection, fire protection, parks, sewage disposal, sanitation, water supply, etc. These expenditures have strikingly out-paced tax revenues.[10]

Although migration remains an important factor in urban growth, Yeates and Garner point out that recent improved health conditions have resulted in a natural increase in city population unlike that of the past. Gibbs found that in recent decades migration from small cities to larger ones has become more important in population growth than rural-urban migration.[11] By the middle of the seventies, however, a reversal in this trend appeared when population began to shift from many of the large central cities to small cities and towns. A survey conducted for the Commission on Population Growth and the American Future indicates the preference among Americans for small towns and farms.[12] Only the black population is nearly evenly divided in its preference for the three scales of places (see Table SII-2).

TABLE SII-2

RESPONSES TO SURVEY QUESTION,

"WHERE WOULD YOU PREFER TO LIVE?"-1972

(In percent)

	Rural or Small town	Small Urban	Large Urban	No Opinion
National......................	53	33	13	1
Residence:				
Rural or small town.........	88	10	2	
Small urban.................	39	55	6	
Large urban.................	34	26	39	2
Region:				
Northeast...................	58	28	14	
South.......................	57	30	12	
North central..............	46	37	17	
West........................	50	38	12	
Age:				
Under 30 yr.................	56	28	15	
30 yr and over.............	52	34	13	1
Color:				
White.......................	54	33	11	
Black.......................	33	34	33	
Education:				
Less than high school.......	57	30	12	1
High school complete........	54	32	13	1
Some college................	47	38	14	1
College complete............	40	38	22	
Income:				
Under $5,000................	57	32	10	1
$5,000 to $9,999............	53	34	12	
$10,000 to $14,999..........	45	29	11	
$15,000 or more.............	45	34	21	

Note: Rural or small town includes the farm, open country, or smalltown responses. Small urban represents small city, or medium size city, and suburb. Large urban includes the large city and its suburbs.

Source: Population Commission (1972), p. 605.

The following is the Commission's summary of its findings on the relationship between city size and public attitudes, social consequences, behavioral properties of large urban systems, limits to democracy, and the economics of scale.[13]

Public Attitudes Toward City Size
There exists a strong and pervasive preference for smaller scale living environments--typically, in national polls regarding preferred residence, an absolute majority of Americans indicated they would prefer to live in a small town or rural environment.

There exists considerable dissatisfaction with the large urban environments relative to the small town/rural environments.

The preference for smaller scales seems to be a long-standing one--opinion polls back to 1948 register a majority preference for smaller scales.

These preferences are not merely nostalgic yearnings-- a larger percentage of the young (under 30 years of age) now indicate a preference for smaller scales.

These preferences are not simply a part of an American myth that views the good life as being found in the country--polls show real increases in expressed satisfaction with place of residence as scale decreases.

These preference patterns are supported by related survey data which show that people's perception of past and expectations of future community change are most negative in the larger cities and most positive in the small towns and rural areas.

Two state studies (in Wisconsin and Washington) suggest that, although many people prefer a smaller scale of living, they would like to live within commuting distance of a larger city.

National preferences extend to support for a national distribution policy that would limit population growth in larger urban areas and stimulate growth in smaller towns and rural areas.

Social Consequences of Increasing City Size
Large urban environments offer desirable social attributes for many people--economic diversity, cultural opportunities, anonymity, free expression of diverse life-styles, and opportunities for personal achievement. For others, these same environments have undesirable attributes along similar dimensions--an underlying homogeneity yielding a superficial diversity, cultural breakdown, alienation, too much competition.

To a considerable extent, urban places are primarily economic entities in their structures and functions and, as such, larger urban places represent the further articulation of economic functions and structures. To the extent that these economic functions are maximized, it is doubtful that non-economic aspects of urban existence-- i.e., social aspects--are simultaneously maximized.

Rates of violent crime are correlated with increasing urban scale even after accounting for socioeconomic differentials between larger and smaller urban places.

Larger scale environments seem to be premised to a greater degree upon the aesthetics of simplicity, economy, and efficiency and this, in turn, diminishes perceptual diversity.

Larger scales are less comprehensible and more difficult to relate to. Further, their size seems to diminish the sense of relative significance of individuals.

Larger scale urban places often allow a lesser degree of access to the natural environment since greater distances must usually be traveled to escape the urban region.

All contemporary trends associated with the emergence of alienation are directly or indirectly tied to the growth of very large urban environments; e.g., the enlargement of living scale beyond human comprehension, the decline of kinship ties, increased geographic mobility, increased social differentiation, and the decline of more traditional social forms.

As the scale of social systems increases, the form of social "glue" that makes the system cohesive changes. Family based ties in smaller urban systems give way to role-related ties in our larger urban systems as primary sources of social elasticity. The emergence of even larger scale systems may require new forms of social cohesion--highly formalized and rationalized external social controls may emerge under conditions of social stress.

A relative absence of social pathology is not a good indicator that things are alright. Man's adaptability allows him to tolerate, and thereby mask, the warning signals of social pathology. Further, we confuse the tolerability of an environment with its desirability.

Behavioral Properties of Large Urban Systems
Larger systems may grow to a point where they yield diminishing returns to scale--particularly when considered from an overall socioeconomic perspective; however, since we do not have the indicators to measure this expectable outcome of systems growth, we behave as if it would not occur.

Successful systems, when premised upon plentiful resources, can become unsuccessful when premised upon scarce resources.

The highly specialized work roles implied by the division of labor found in large urban systems may contribute to worker boredom, absenteeism, lowered productivity, and lowered product quality.

As system size increases, interdependence increases and, in turn, vulnerability of the system to damaging perturbations increases.

Larger systems are more complex, and that complexity makes the system less comprehensible and less amenable to effective regulation/control.

Growth of a system creates form but that form, in turn, inhibits the nature of future growth, thereby locking us into a relatively inflexible physical form.

Larger systems tend toward conditions of low performance.

City Size and the Limits to Democracy

Large systems are generally complex and that complexity, in turn, limits the rate of effective acquisition and use of knowledge, which makes the maintenance of "relative political maturity" more difficult for all constituents in the political process.

As effective political participation of the average citizen is diminished by lack of relative political maturity, and as the effective comprehension of highly complex issues becomes more difficult for the politician and civil servant, increasing reliance is placed upon specialist/experts--persons who are essential to the system but outside of the usual checks and balances of American political processes.

For those who cannot specialize, given their mandated broad focus of concern (e.g., the mayor), complexity reduces the comprehensibility of the system being governed and increases the likelihood of attempting to employ simple solutions to solve difficult problems which, in turn, increases the likelihood that the system will tend towards conditions of relatively low performance.

Large systems are generally interdependent which, in turn, implies the need for a broad focus of regulation and control. Interdependent systems are generally more vulnerable, and this reinforces the need for effective regulation and control.

Large systems are also increasingly rigid since no part can be changed without affecting the other components

of the system. Larger systems are therefore more inflexible and resistant to change.

As scale increases, the number of constituents
generally increases at a much faster rate than the number of governing officials; the result is that the amount
of time an official can spend with any one person or
group is proportionately diminished.

As scale increases, the impact of any one individual upon the outcome of an election is diminished since
the individual is but one among millions. The payoff
to participating knowledgeably under such circumstances
is small. Participation in very large systems becomes
"trivial" through the media of voting; participation in
the subsystems of a large system (where the individual
could presumably "make a difference" since he is not
overwhelmed numerically) also becomes "trivial" since
the issues are generally not of substantial significance.
Large systems, then, trivialize political involvement.

City Size and Environmental Quality

Overall, environmental quality seems to deteriorate
as city size increases.

Air pollution is strongly correlated with increasing
city size.

There is suggestive evidence that mortality rates
increase as city size increases owing to increased concentration of air pollutants.

Increased noise pollution is correlated with increasing city size.

Increasing commuting time is correlated with increasing city size.

Significant man-made changes in local climate are
correlated with increasing city size.

Increased garbage collection and waste treatment
costs are tentatively associated with larger city size
but the cost differences relative to smaller cities are
trivial.

Larger cities seem to be better innovators.

The Economics of City Size

In general, economic forces seem to favor the continued growth of larger--though perhaps not the largest--
urban areas.

With respect to an individual company, economic
incentives seem to be either neutral or slightly favorable to the largest urban places. Although the suburbs
of large urban areas seem to be growing due, in some
substantial part, to the movement of manufacturing

employment to the urban periphery, this still contributes to the overall growth of larger urban places.
Recent movement of white collar employment beyond the
largest urban areas suggests that there may be some dis-
economies of scale for the very largest urban places
but, in general, across a large city size range, there
do not seem to be substantial economic incentives which
favor one particular urban size class.

With respect to the individual employee, the larger
urban places offer significant economic advantages to
those most interested in developing a specialized field
of professional competence and in obtaining higher economic rewards. The higher net income associated with
larger urban places may, for many, compensate to some
unknown degree for the disamenities of urban living.

With respect to public sector economics, it appears that the cost of public services may generally be
somewhat higher in the largest urban places. Differences
in the quality of public services are difficult to estimate. Nevertheless, the higher costs of public services
may be more than offset by higher incomes in larger urban environments. Overall, differences in the cost of
public services seem of marginal economic significance
in proportion to the average family budget.

In order to determine whether population change is due primarily to
natural causes or to migration we examined the various components of change
such as births and deaths and their relationship to total population change.
A community's increase in population may be due to natural causes if its
births exceed deaths, or the population may decrease through natural causes
if deaths exceed births. Population increase or decrease may be due to
in- or out-migration. Most often it is a combination of both natural
causes and migration that affects population change. Most people move
because of job opportunities; other considerations are climate, friends and
relatives, availability of housing, and education. Those who move tend to
be above average in education and occupational skill and are more energetic.
Tilly refutes the common argument used to explain migration into a community,
"that if a town improves its living conditions and public services too
energetically, it will simply see its resources consumed by a rush of new,
poor, dependent migrants-drifters, welfare chiselers, and problem families."[14]
He believes that living conditions and public services play only a small
part in the movement of the favored or more advantaged persons. Thus, as
Burgess suggests, growth and rates of expansion

may be studied not only in the physical growth and business development, but also in the consequent changes in
the social organization and in personality types. How
far is the growth of the city, in its physical and technical aspects, matched by a natural but adequate readjust-
ment in the social organization? What, for a city, is a
normal rate of expansion, a rate of expansion with which
controlled changes in the social organization might successfully keep pace?[15]

Therefore, some analysts and practitioners want to know something about future population changes and whether a community will grow in size, stabilize, or decline. To project or estimate future population trends requires knowledge of past trends and noting the causes associated with such factors as the sex-age profile (see Exercise SIV) and other social, economic, and political considerations. Population estimates are sometimes available from local planning agencies, Chambers of Commerce, or some university study groups.

A major issue developed in the 1970s over growth, especially because of those who advocate zero population growth (ZPG). Americans, "hell-bent" on progress, have begun to question the cost of economic growth and have put forth proposals for a no-growth society with a "steady-state" economy. The proponents believe that the exponential rate of population growth threatens present standards of living, as there is a fixed amount of natural resources and the spill-over effects of pollution are too costly to the quality of life to which we have become accustomed. Olson, Landsberg, and Fisher have identified four types of advocates and their extremely strong arguments. One, *ecofreaks* who believe that ". . . economic growth should be stopped now before biosuicide is at issue simply because the pollution and other assaults on our aesthetic sensibilities it brings in its wake make growth unpleasant on balance."[16] Two, *sociofreaks* who are concerned about the social disruptions brought by urbanism and geographic mobility and who believe that economic growth ". . . inevitably means change and presumably requires incentives which permit some to rise while others fall and which induces others to move away from their communities, friends, and even families."[17] Three, *psychofreaks* sense that when "wealth accumulates, men decay" and therefore "abhor the motives, consciousness, and habits of mind of economic growth."[18] Finally, the *safety-freaks* would go to great lengths to avoid risk that stems from unfathomed complexity and the uncertainty ". . . that will result from any major new use of the environment" and fear that the "environmental side effects may be very difficult, sometimes even impossible, to reverse or undo."[19]

Although some communities attempt to pass restrictive zoning, limiting housing permits, and the like, such activities are generally unsuccessful as no city is an island, entire unto itself.[20] McKean suggests an alternative approach to concern about the depletion of nonrenewable resources, that is, that governmental tax policy should be used to deter consumption with the collected revenues used to reduce other taxes. Concerning the adverse spill-over effects from economic growth, he would minimize the government's role and use pricing mechanisms such as ". . . effluent charges, liability reassignments (to fasten external costs on those activities that generate them), congestion fees, external-cost taxes on common-pool resources like fish and other spill-over charges."[21]

TYPOLOGY

We have used both population change and the major cause of that change in a typology to classify each community. *Natural growth* communities represent an increase in population primarily due to an excess of births over deaths rather than due to in-migration. These communities are generally youthful places with a relatively stable economy. A community undergoing *natural decline* is one where the excess of deaths over births exceeds any out-migration and most often appears with an aging population and a declining economic base. A growing community experiencing *in-migration* is one in which the increment of growth exceeds the excess of births over deaths. Such communities are found in exclusive suburbs and cities undergoing considerable economic development. Finally, *out-migration* represents a decrease in population that exceeds the excess of deaths over births and is mainly due to the departure of young adults who leave to find jobs and homes and to develop their families elsewhere. Central cities with increasing heterogenity most often experience selective out-migration patterns.

FIGURE SII-I.   TYPOLOGY ON POPULATION GROWTH AND DECLINE

POPULATION CHANGE

	Increase	*Decrease*
Less	Natural Growth	Natural Decline
NET MIGRATION RELATIVE TO POPULATION CHANGE		
More	In-Migration	Out-Migration

SOURCES AND CAVEATS

Population data can be found in U.S. Bureau of the Census, *Census of Population:* Vol. 1, *Characteristics of the Population,* Part A, *Number of Inhabitants,* published every ten years. In addition, the Bureau of the Census also conducts special censuses on off years. Statistics and tables in these documents are classified according to the size and nature of the community: urban places with populations over 50,000, counties and towns with populations between 2,500 and 10,000, and so on. Land area data appear in the U.S. Bureau of the Census, *County and City Data Book* for the years 1962 and 1972. For annexations see Census of Population and Housing, *General Demographic Trends for Metropolitan Areas, 1960 to 1970,* PHC(2) for the specific state(s) in which your communities are located. Be certain that you use one reference consistently for one kind of data, as different volumes of the Census report different totals for the same community.

The birth and death statistics used as components of change are estimates based on reported births and deaths by place of residence, 1960 through 1969. They appear in *Vital Statistics of the U.S.,* Vol. 1, *Natality,* and Vol. 2, *Mortality,* published annually by The Division of Vital Statistics, National Center for Health Statistics. If your community is in an SMSA, net migration figures can be obtained from the census series, *General Demographic Trends* which includes individual reports for each state.

The process of computing net migration includes computing the total population change from 1960 to 1970 and then subtracting from the change the difference between the births and deaths that occurred during the 10-year period. Therefore, in a community with an increasing population any excess of births over deaths results in a net in-migration figure smaller (by the amount of the excess) than the total population increase. On the other hand, in a community with a decreasing population, any excess of births over deaths results in a net out-migration figure larger (by the amount of the excess) than the total population decrease. It should be noted that population changes may be due to annexations, which must be taken into account when computing migration figures.

If a community has substantially changed its population size within the time frame of study by changing its legal boundaries—annexation or consolidation—one should expect this to affect all the other aspects of change. In the last analysis, the shift has brought about a new community which then must be analyzed with changes in the number and kinds of residents, constituents, and taxpayers in mind.

PROFILE EXAMPLE

TABLE SII-3. POPULATION SIZE AND CHANGE, 1900 - 1970

POPULATION	MOUNT VERNON		NEW ROCHELLE	
	Number	% Change	Number	% Change
1900	21,228		14,720	
1910	30,919	+45.6	28,867	+96.1
1920	42,726	+38.1	36,213	+25.4
1930	61,499	+43.9	54,000	+49.1
1940	67,362	+ 9.5	58.408	+ 8.2
1950	71,899	+ 6.7	59,725	+ 2.3
1960	76,010	+ 5.7	76,812	+28.6
1970	72,778	- 4.3	75,385	- 1.9

TABLE SII-4. POPULATION DENSITY, 1960 and 1970

	MOUNT VERNON		NEW ROCHELLE	
	Square Miles	Density	Square Miles	Density
1960	4.3	17,677	10.4	7531
1970	4.3	16,925	10.4	7249

TABLE SII-5. COMPONENTS OF POPULATION CHANGE, 1960 - 1970

	POPULATION		CHANGE		COMPONENTS OF CHANGE		Net Migration	
	1970	1960	Number	Percent	Births	Deaths	Number	Percent
MOUNT VERNON	72,778	76,010	-3232	-4.3	13,891	9,102	-8021	-10.6
NEW ROCHELLE	75,385	76,812	-1427	-1.9	12,435	7,401	-6461	-8.4
UNITED STATES (in 1000's)	204,335	180,007	24,328	13.5	38,003	18,263	3,557	2.0

OPERATIONAL DEFINITIONS

Population Change (1960 to 1970) = Population (1970) - Population (1960)

% Population Change (1960 to 1970) = $\frac{\text{Population Change}}{\text{Population (1960)}}$

Density = $\frac{\text{Population}}{\text{Square Miles}}$

Net Migration = (Population 1970 - Population 1960) - [Births - Deaths, (1960-1969)]

% Net Migration = $\frac{\text{Net Migration}}{\text{Population, 1960}}$

CLASSIFICATION INDICATORS

	Mount Vernon	New Rochelle
% Population Change (1960-70) (See Table SII-5)	-4.3	-1.9
% Net Migration (1960-70) (See Table SII-5)	-10.6	-8.4

FINDINGS AND SUGGESTED IMPLICATIONS

Both Mount Vernon and New Rochelle in 1970 were experiencing net *out-migration*. Other cities of similar size in the nation increased (20.9 percent) on the average, while these two cities decreased (see Tables SII-1 and SII-3). The major growth of both cities occurred from the turn of the century and continued until the Depression (see Table SII-3). Mount Vernon's growth began to slow down after 1930, and by 1960 it began to lose population. Similarly, New Rochelle's growth tapered off beginning in 1930, but it experienced a sharp spurt from 1950 to 1960 and leveled off by 1970.

Both communities, with populations over 70,000, are classified as cities by the state of New York (see Table SII-3), which allows them to enjoy relative autonomy in running their affairs. They maintain most of their own public services other than the health, education, and welfare functions. Moreover, the limits on their taxing and debt-raising authority are almost the same as those of the major cities in the state.

Mount Vernon is one of the most densely populated cities in the state and has nearly three times the density of New Rochelle (see Table SII-4). This density is unequally distributed, with the area south of the railroad tracks being more densely populated than that in the north.

Although both Mount Vernon and New Rochelle are considered suburban communities bordering New York City, Mount Vernon with its higher density more closely resembles an urban place than does New Rochelle. The scarcity of open space and an aging housing supply incurred from the peak of growth early in the century suggest at least two possible consequences for Mount Vernon's future: the decline in value of its old houses might attract and permit an increased influx of lower-income persons into the community, and a replacement of the aging single-family residences with high-rise apartments might increase the density. New Rochelle, on the other hand, with lower density and more open space provides a potential for new housing to be built and may be better able in the near future to maintain its suburban character and continue to attract populations similar to those of the past.

Although both communities in 1970 appeared relatively stable, in that the decline in population was small, this decline may have affected

the mood of the people as they noted both the continual growth of the
nation and the substantial exodus of their neighbors. It is important
to learn who moved out and why they decided to leave town. Young adults
may have left because there was no acceptable way to earn a livelihood,
or families with school-age children may have left because the schools
did not offer an adequate education. One ethnic group or socioeconomic
class may have moved to other preferred places. The Regional Plan Association, for example, commenting on the New York metropolitan region
stated that current population trends will leave the central city and
older cities of the region ". . . primarily with the unemployed and the
retired poor."[22] As people leave, the marketplace as a sensitive baro-
meter reflects the change. Some businesses move out, fearing the competition from the four shopping malls that surround Mount Vernon; other
businessmen resort to a conservative strategy commensurate with a no-
growth policy; and still other businessmen join in a concerted Chamber
of Commerce effort to boost the economic attractiveness of the community.
The mobility of its citizens tends to loosen the political bonds of the
community, thus potentially changing the competitive struggle between
the political parties for the favor of the voters. The patterns of power
may also shift as the population changes.

We offer the following speculations on the possible consequences
of various population conditions—populations that are growing, stable,
or declining. Our focus is on the total number of people, not on changing
population composition or economic conditions. Thus, by a growing population we mean the number of people has increased by at least 1 percent
a year or 10 percent for the decade; a declining population is one in
which the number has decreased by at least 1 percent per year or 10 percent in the decade; and a stable population lies in between with growth
or decline of less than 10 percent for the decade.

FIGURE SII-2. SPECULATIONS ON THE CONSEQUENCES OF VARIOUS POPULATION CONDITIONS

Social	*Political*	*Economic*
GROWING		
Increased population density	Increase in competitive demands	Increased costs for public services
Change in stratification patterns	Introduction of political instability	Changing forms of income
Declining sense of community	Need to expand local boundaries	Increased property value
	Elected officials become development oriented	Increased tax revenues
		Increased economies of scale
STABLE		
Loss of young people	Becomes more consensual	Limited renewal of physical facilities
Residents become more parochial	Less turnover of leadership	Costs increase but revenues do not keep pace
Residents become more accepting of conditions	Less participation and controversy	Property values level off
		Less attractive for investments
DECLINING		
Residents with high socio-economic status tend to leave	Pressure to increase scope of government	Some economic firms leave; new firms not attracted
Increased dependent populations	Rhetoric polarizes progressives and conservatives	Property values decline
	Controversy develops over less significant matters	Public service needs and costs increase
	Residents become politicized	Tax pressures increase
	Increased turnover of elected officials	

DISCUSSION

1. What is your community's growth or decline classification?

2. What are the present size, density, and growth rate of your community's population and to what extent have they changed during the decade?

3. To what do you attribute your community's population growth or decline? (a) availability of open land, (b) expanding/contracting economic opportunity, (c) quality of educational and social services, (d) proximity to burgeoning central city, (e) development of more attractive areas nearby, (f) "boosterism" of community leaders, (g) aging housing supply, (h) desire by those throughout metropolitan area to avoid living with others of different class, ethnic, and/or racial groups, (i) community controversy.

4. Speculate on the ways in which the size, density, and growth or decline of your community's population affect the following major areas of community life: (a) education, (b) housing, (c) crime, (d) health, (e) welfare, (f) economic opportunity, (g) cultural activities, and (h) social tensions.

5. Do you think it is important for your community to change the direction of its population growth pattern? If so, in what direction? What social, economic, and/or political strategies might you employ to bring about the desired change?

NOTES

1. Leonard Reissman, *The Urban Process* (The Free Press of Glencoe, 1964), p. 73.

2. Byron E. Munson, *Changing Community Dimensions* (Ohio State University Press, 1968), p. 25.

3. Reissman, pp. 202-3.

4. Maurice H. Yeates and Barry J. Garner, *The North American City* (Harper and Row, 1971), p. 273. Also see their Chapter 8, pp. 213-22, and Chapter 10, pp. 262-85.

5. Otis Dudley Duncan and Albert Reiss, *Social Characteristics of Urban and Rural Communities, 1950* (John Wiley and Sons, 1956), pp. 2-5.

6. Robert A. Dahl and Edward R. Tufte, *Size and Democracy* (Stanford University Press, 1973), p. 140.

7. Bert E. Swanson and Richard A. Cohen, *The Small Town in America, A Guide for Study and Community Development,* forthcoming.

8. Roland L. Warren, *Studying Your Community* (Russell Sage Foundation, 1955), p. 7.

9. *Ibid.,* p. 7.

10. *Report of the Advisory Commission on Civil Disorders* (A Bantam Book, 1968), p. 393.

11. Jack Gibbs, "The Evaluation of Population Concentration," *Economic Geography,* 39, 1963, pp. 119-129.

12. The Stanford Research Institute, *City Size and the Quality of Life* (U.S. Government Printing Office, 1975), p. 18.

13. *Ibid.,* pp. 6-10.

14. Charles Tilly, "Race and Migration to the American City," in *The Metropolitan Enigma* edited by James Q. Wilson (Anchor Books, 1970), p. 150.

15. E. W. Burgess, "The Growth of the City," in *The City* edited by Murray Stewart (Penguin Books, 1972), p. 122.

16. Mancur Olson, Hans H. Landsberg, and Joseph L. Fisher, "Epilogue," in *The No-Growth Society* edited by M. Olson and H. Landsberg (W.W. Norton and Co., 1973), p. 231.

17. *Ibid.,* p. 234.

18. *Ibid.,* p. 235.

19. *Ibid.,* p. 237.

20. William Alonso, "Urban Zero Population Growth," in *Ibid.,* p. 204.

21. Roland N. McKean, "Growth vs. No Growth," in *Ibid.,* p. 223.

22. Reported in *The New York Times,* January 30, 1975, p. 37.

COMMUNITY DATA PROFILE SII-A

(SII-3) POPULATION SIZE AND CHANGE, 1900 - 1970

Population	Your Community	% Change	Comparison City	% Change
1900				
1910				
1920				
1930				
1940				
1950				
1960				
1970				

(SII-4) POPULATION DENSITY, 1960 and 1970

Density	Your Community		Comparison City	
	Square Miles	Density	Square Miles	Density
1960				
1970				

(SII-5) COMPONENTS OF POPULATION CHANGE, 1960 - 1970

	Population		Change		Components of Change			
							Net Migration	
	1970	1960	Number	Percent	Births	Deaths	Number	Percent
Your Community								
Comparison City								

CLASSIFICATION INDICATORS (SEE TABLE SII-5)

	Your Community	Comparison City
% Population Change (1960-1970)		
% Net Migration		
CLASSIFICATION		

SIII. ETHNIC DIVERSITY

HOW HETEROGENEOUS IS YOUR COMMUNITY AND IN WHAT DIRECTION
IS IT CHANGING?

CONCEPT

It has long been assumed that as the size of a city increases the
degree of diversity of its population increases. In fact, heterogeneity
has become one of the characteristics most frequently associated with urbanism. Wirth argues that large numbers of people permit a greater range of
individual variation as well as greater potential differentiation among
them:

> The city has thus historically been the melting-pot
> of races, peoples, and cultures, and a most favor-
> able breeding-ground of new biological and cultural
> hybrids. It has not only tolerated but rewarded in-
> dividual differences. It has brought together people
> from the ends of the earth because they are different
> and thus useful to one another, rather than because
> they are homogeneous and like-minded.[1]

This theory, deductively arrived at, has been criticized by Reissman, who
questions the relationship between size, density, and heterogeneity,
". . . if size does 'cause' the rise of segmentalized relationships between
urban dwellers, precisely how does it affect the economy of the city or the
accepted cultural values in urban society or the function of political institutions?"[2]

In another approach to heterogeneity, Gordon has proposed that the
subcultures of our society represent a sense of "peoplehood" or ethnic group
based on race, religion, and national origin. One's ethnic identity

> . . . serves psychologically as a source of group self-
> identification . . . it provides a patterned network
> of groups and institutions which allows an individual
> to confine his primary group relationships to his own
> ethnic group throughout all stages of the life cycle
> . . . it refracts the national cultural patterns of
> behavior and values through the prism of its own cul-
> tural heritage.[3]

He notes that there are variable roles of adaptation and types of assimilation by the different ethnic groups to the core dominant culture.[4] The
persistence of ethnicity among newcomers and the actions of native residents not only have implications for prejudice and discrimination and demands for desegregation and integration but also provide a reservoir of
built-in differences, tensions, and conflict that shape our social, economic, and political institutions as well as challenge the viability of
our society. Not only do various ethnics tend to separate themselves so
that they live and interact among "their own kind," but there are persis-
tent in our society a wide variety of discriminatory practices associated
with selecting a home, securing employment, education, and so forth which
keep out various ethnics. These discriminatory practices have implications
for public policy and pose major differences in policy preferences, problem solving approaches, and quality of life outcomes. (See Exercises
PVI and PVII for a discussion of ethnic voting behavior.)

There are a number of ways to measure the degree of heterogeneity in
American communities. Angell in his study of moral integration developed
a *heterogeneity index* based on the number of foreign born and nonwhite residents in the city.[5] This is a rather arbitrary measure using white foreign-born and assigning a weighting factor of 2 to nonwhites. Jonassen,
on the other hand, assigned a weight of 3 for blacks.[6] The Taeubers, more
concerned with the degree of spatial distribution of diverse populations,
have formulated a residential *segregation index* that measures the degree of
racial segregation in the metropolitan areas of the country. The underlying rationale of the Taeuber index is that if race made no difference in
residential patterns, then every neighborhood would have blacks and whites
in approximately the same ratio as they appear in the city as a whole.
Thus, if in a community blacks constitute 20 percent of the households,
then that proportion of households in each city block should be black. If
such a situation occurred, the index would equal zero, and there would be
no racial residential segregation. In the opposite situation, where there
is no intermixture but each city block comprises either only white or only
black households, the index would be 100 or total segregation. Thus the
index can be anywhere from 0 to 100—the lower the index, the less the
segregation. The Taeubers, therefore, interpreted the index as showing the
minimum percentage of blacks who would have to move around in the community
in order to produce an integrated community in which the percentage of
blacks living on each block is the same throughout the city (0 on the index).
In a study of 207 cities in 1960, the mean index values were: central cities
86.8, suburbs 82.3, and independent cities 89.5. A high residential segregation index will be reflected in segregated neighborhood schools unless
efforts such as open enrollment and other measures have been instituted to
desegregate the schools. You may find the segregation index of your community for the years 1940, 1950, and 1960 in the Taeuber study.[7]

We have chosen to delineate the potential ethnic cleavages in the
community by looking at as wide a spectrum of racial and nativity groups
as data permit. This includes: (1) native white of native white parents,

(2) native white of foreign or mixed parents, (3) foreign-born whites, (4) blacks, whether native or foreign-born, and (5) other races. A homogeneous community is one in which residents are primarily of one of these categories, i.e., essentially native white of native white parents as commonly found in upper-income suburbs. A heterogeneous community would comprise an admixture of some or all five of the categories as it is commonly found in the Northeast. In the South, the population is generally dichotomized into blacks and whites although occasionally the combination is "Anglos," "Latinos," and blacks. The more evenly balanced the racial or ethnic groups in a community, the more likely coalition politics will develop.

It should be noted that the 1970 census publications did not break down nativity group data by race. Therefore, in order to provide data for as broad a spectrum of diversity as possible, we have taken the liberty of making two assumptions: (1) persons of nonwhite races other than Negroes were native born and (2) all natives of foreign or mixed parents were white. We do not believe that this unduly distorts the data since persons of "other races" constitute a very small proportion of the population in most communities and nonwhites nationwide (data are available for the U.S.) constitute a very small proportion of native persons with foreign or mixed parents. In addition, throughout this manuscript we have chosen to use the popularly accepted word "black" when referring to Negroes. Data in the census reports, however, appear under the label Negro. Our use of the term "nonwhite" is consistent with its use in the census reports and refers to Negroes and those of other nonwhite races.

Aside from the five major categories discussed above, we look at persons of foreign stock (those either foreign-born or of foreign-born parents) by national origin and list the three largest groups in order to provide a sense of the diversity among this population segment. In addition, we include persons of Spanish language because they constitute a population group of special significance in many communities. It should be noted that the census reports provide data on persons of Spanish heritage in three different ways: (1) in 42 states and the District of Columbia this population is identified as "Persons of Spanish language," that is, all persons in families in which the head or wife reported Spanish as his or her mother tongue, (2) in 5 southeastern states as "Persons of Spanish language or Spanish surname," and (3) in 3 Middle Atlantic states, as "Persons of Puerto Rican birth or parentage."

Of growing interest is the racial change of American cities. Since 1960 the black population of a number of central cities has increased much faster than the white. In 1970, blacks constituted one-third or more of the population in six of the ten largest cities. (Blacks have been elected mayor in four—Los Angeles, Detroit, Cleveland and Atlanta—of the ten largest cities.) The suburbs, on the other hand, grew with increasing white in-migration. Grodzins,[8] one of the first to perceive this change, described the development of a white "noose" around the black central city or, as Tilly explained, the

process was the bleaching of the suburbs through the
addition of huge numbers of whites and almost no Negroes.
Some of the bleaching occurred because of the flight
of whites from the problems and people of the central
city, some of it because jobs and housing attracted new
white migrants directly to the suburbs rather than to
central cities, more of it because, in the normal process
of moving around and out toward the sites of new housing,
low incomes and organized discrimination barred Negroes
from taking part.[9]

Part of the explanation for racial change can be found in studying
migration patterns. The reasons whites and blacks move should be examined
separately, as they may reveal a common or a different dynamic that may be
based partially on reaction to each other. White out-migration in a racially
changing town has been explained as part of a "tipping-point" dynamic that
begins to operate when the tolerance for interracial living has been exceeded
as far as whites are concerned, and they begin to leave at an accelerated
rate. White exodus may result from two factors, one which pushes (unattrac-
tive features) whites out of their community and the other which pulls (favorable features) them toward the ample opportunities elsewhere. Similarly
blacks may have forces pushing them out· of rural, southern, or northern
inner-city ghettoes and features pulling them towards the more attractive
cities, especially northern cities or their suburbs.

While the black migrants of the past were believed to be of lower
social and economic status than other residents, more recent developments
led the Taeubers to conclude that "There is a large and increasingly important high-status intermetropolitan migration in the total movement of Negro
populations."[10] In fact, black migrants to northern and border cities are
educationally similar to the resident whites and superior to the resident
blacks. This led Tilly to speculate on strategic implications:

These complicated comparisons hold an ironic implication for those city fathers who wish they could speed
the departure of Negroes from their towns and keep new
Negro migrants from coming in. Such a strategy would
be a very good way to depress the average level of quali-
fications of the city's Negro population. It would
probably increase the proportion, if not the absolute
number, of the Negro population heavily dependent on
public services. The way to insure a young and skilled
Negro population would be to attract new migrants and
be sure that the mobile people already in the city were
too satisfied to depart.[11]

We recommend tracing the racial change over the past few decades and,
if possible, obtaining a population projection prepared by a local planning

commission, Chamber of Commerce, or university research group. It is also sometimes useful to compare the racial change of your community with that of other neighboring communities, or with your county and/or state. A population projection including both ethnic and total population trends should suggest potential community problems and opportunities for change.

TYPOLOGY

     We offer the following typology on ethnic heterogeneity based on the proportion of native whites of native white parentage on the one hand, and the change in the heterogeneity index (using Angell's measure) from 1960 to 1970, on the other hand. Both have been computed for the nation and are the basis of classifying a city according to its ethnic characteristics. This typology not only distinguishes between the diversity of population but indicates the degree of change. Thus a community may be in the process of *increasing heterogeneity* as found when the proportion of native white population is below that of the nation and the degree of heterogeneity is changing more than the nation's, which is increasing slightly. Actually many of our central cities and more mature suburbs are increasing their diversity with the influx of blacks. A number of middle-sized cities are experiencing *declining heterogeneity* as the waves of immigration from abroad have ceased and the proportions of blacks are not increasing. Small towns and the more affluent suburbs are experiencing *increasing homogeneity* with the proportion of native whites above that of the nation as the grandchildren of immigrants become third generation Americans and the heterogeneity index increases less than the nation's or in fact declines. Some middle- and lower-income suburbs are experiencing *declining homogeneity* as they attract some foreign born and a few blacks who are moving out of the central cities into the suburban communities most accessible to them.

FIGURE SIII-1. TYPOLOGY OF ETHNIC HETEROGENEITY AND CHANGE

(Relative to Nation)

PERCENTAGE NATIVE WHITE OF NATIVE WHITE PARENTAGE

		Above	*Below*
	More	Declining Homogeneity	Increasing Heterogeneity
HETEROGENEITY INDEX CHANGE			
	Less	Increasing Homogeneity	Declining Heterogeneity

SOURCES AND CAVEATS

Statistics on nativity and parentage, race, and country of origin of foreign stock can be found in two census publications: the U.S. Bureau of the Census, *Census of Population: General Social and Economic Characteristics,* Series PC (1) for your state for the years 1950, 1960, 1970 and in *General Population Characteristics* for the same years. To calculate the categories of persons for Table SIII-1 for 1970, two tables need to be used: Table 81 which includes data for the total population and Table 91 for data on the Negro (black) population in *General Social and Economic Characteristics*. In *General Population Characteristics,* Table 23 contains the data for "other races." In 1960 the number of persons in the categories "native white of native white parents," "native white of foreign or mixed parents," and "foreign born whites" are given in the publication *General Social and Economic Characteristics, 1960,* Table 72. The Negro (black) population is given in Table 21 of *General Population Characteristics*. The number of persons of "other races" excluding Negroes must be calculated (see Operational Definitions, Table SIII-1). Racial segregation indices can be found in Karl E. and Alma F. Taeuber, *Negroes in Cities* (Aldine Publishing Co., 1965), pp. 31-43 and pp. 235-238. For those who wish to compute their own segregation index, racial housing statistics can be found in the U.S. Bureau of the Census, *U. S. Census of Housing, Block Statistics, Series HC (3)*. Population projections may be obtained from the Planning Board, Chamber of Commerce, university, or college in your community. If your community has a master plan, a population projection may appear as part of that document.

Note that the population projection table for Mount Vernon uses data on nonwhites rather than blacks. Since it was conducted in 1965, the 1970 figures in the table were estimates and therefore differ from the actual 1970 population figures. A projection, it should be remembered, *estimates* future population of a community and *assumes* that the community is following and will follow relatively the same course it had been following. If substantial change occurs in community policy or action and/or population behavior changes, the estimates may not materialize.

PROFILE EXAMPLE

TABLE SIII-1

ETHNIC HETEROGENEITY BY NATIONAL ORIGIN AND RACE

	MOUNT VERNON				NEW ROCHELLE				UNITED STATES			
	1960 Number	%	1970 Number	%	1960 Number	%	1970 Number	%	1960 Number	%	1970 Number	%
Total Population	76,010	100.0	72,796	100.0	76,812	100.0	75,385	100.0	179,325,671	100.0	203,210,158	100.0
Native White of Native White Parents	27,904	36.7	20,505	28.2	33,543	43.7	33,890	45.0	125,759,291	70.1	146,231,286	72.0
Native White of Foreign or Mixed Parents	22,778	30.0	17,628	24.4	22,885	29.8	20,736	27.5	23,784,347	13.3	23,154,165	11.4
Foreign Born White	10,274	13.5	8,354	11.3	9,947	12.9	9,158	12.0	9,294,033	5.2	8,733,770	4.3
Black (total)	14,918	19.6	25,778	35.4	10,103	13.2	10,657	14.1	18,872,000	10.5	22,539,362	11.1
Other Races	136	0.2	531	0.7	334	0.4	944	1.3	1,616,000	0.9	2,551,572	1.3

OPERATIONAL DEFINITIONS

1970

Native, other than Negroes = [(GSE Table 81)] - [Native Negroes (GSE Table 91)]

Native White = [Native, other than Negroes] - [Other Races   (Not Negroes) (GP Table 23)]

Native White of Native White Parents = [Native White] - [Native White of Foreign of Mixed Parents]

Foreign Born Whites = [Foreign Born (GSE Table 81)] - [Foreign Born Negroes (GSE Table 91)]

Blacks = All Negroes (GSE Table 91)

1960

Other Races   = [Total Nonwhites (GP Table 21, bottom of page) -
                Negroes (Male and Female) (GP Table 21)]

PROFILE EXAMPLE

TABLE SIII-2

MAJOR NATIONAL ORIGIN GROUPS

| | MOUNT VERNON | | | | NEW ROCHELLE | | | | UNITED STATES | | | |
| | 1960 | | 1970 | | 1960 | | 1970 | | 1960 | | 1970 | |
	Number	%	Number	%	Number	%	Number	%	Number	%	Number	%
Total Population	76,010	100.0	72,796	100.0	76,812	100.0	75,385	100.0	179,325,671	100.0	203,210,158	100.0
Persons of Spanish Language	NA	NA	1,780	2.4	NA	NA	1,937	2.6	NA	NA	9,589,216	4.7
Foreign Stock	34,064	44.8	27,345	37.7	33,799	44.0	30,402	40.3	34,050,406	19.0	33,575,232	16.5
Italian	13,369	39.2	10,889	39.8	9,867	29.2	10,220	33.6	4,543,935	13.3	4,240,779	12.6
USSR	3,739	11.0	2,195	8.0	4,053	12.0	3,394	11.1	432,664[a]	12.7	3,622,035[a]	10.8
German	3,629	10.7	1,862	6.8	3,099	9.2	2,229	7.3	3,181,051[b]	9.3	3,034,556[b]	9.0

[a]Second largest national origin group in the U.S. was German

[b]Third largest national origin group in the U.S. was Canadian

OPERATIONAL DEFINITIONS

Foreign Stock = Native of Foreign or Mixed Parents + Foreign Born

$$\% \text{ Foreign Stock} = \frac{\text{Foreign Stock}}{\text{Total Population}}$$

$$\% \text{ National Origin Group} = \frac{\text{Number in National Origin Group}}{\text{Total Foreign Stock}}$$

PROFILE EXAMPLE

TABLE SIII-3.   HETEROGENEITY INDEX

	MOUNT VERNON		NEW ROCHELLE		UNITED STATES	
	Index	% Change	Index	% Change	Index	% Change
1940	343.5		405.0			
1950	420.5	22.4	409.6	1.1		
1960	531.3	26.3	401.3	-2.0	280.0	
1970	837.5	57.6	429.3	7.0	289.9	3.5

TABLE SIII-4.   RACIAL SEGREGATION INDEX

Year	MOUNT VERNON	NEW ROCHELLE
1940	78.9	80.6
1950	78.0	78.9
1960	73.2	79.5
1970	77.8	74.3
Change		
1940 to 1960	-5.7	-1.1
1960 to 1970	4.6	-5.2

TABLE SIII-5.   COMPONENTS OF POPULATION CHANGE BY RACE: 1970 and 1960

	Population		Change		Components of Change		Net Migration	
	1970	1960*	Number	Percent	Births	Deaths	Number	Percent
MOUNT VERNON								
Total	72,796	76,010	- 3,214	-4.2	13,891	9,102	- 8,003	-10.5
White	47,018	60,956	-13,938	-22.9	8,481	7,220	-15,199	-24.9
Black	25,778	14,918	10,860	72.8	5,410	1,882	7,437	49.8
NEW ROCHELLE								
Total	75,385	76,812	- 1,427	-1.9	12,435	7,401	-6,461	- 8.4
White	64,728	66,375	- 1,647	-2.5	9.983	6,278	-5,352	- 8.1
Black	10,657	10,103	554	5.5	2.452	1,123	- 775	- 7.8

    *
     Total includes other races

OPERATIONAL DEFINITIONS

$$\text{Heterogeneity Index} = \frac{\text{Foreign Born White} + 2(\text{Nonwhites})}{.001 \ (\text{Total Population})}$$

$$\% \text{ Change in Heterogeneity Index} = \frac{\text{Index, 1970} - \text{Index, 1960}}{\text{Index, 1960}}$$

$$\text{Net Migration} = \text{Net Change (1960 to 1970)} - (\text{Births} - \text{Deaths})$$

$$\% \text{ Net Migration} = \frac{\text{Net Migration}}{\text{Population, 1960}}$$

PROFILE EXAMPLE

TABLE SIII-6.   TREND OF BLACKS AS PROPORTION OF TOTAL POPULATION

	MOUNT VERNON			NEW ROCHELLE		
	Number	%	% Change	Number	%	% Change
1940	5,103	7.6		6,228	10.7	
1950	7,850	10.9	53.8	7,403	12.4	18.9
1960	14,918	19.6	90.0	10,103	13.2	36.5
1970	25,778	35.4	72.8	10,657	14.1	5.5

TABLE SIII-7.   POPULATION PROJECTION OF MOUNT VERNON, BASED ON 1960 - 1965 RATES OF SURVIVAL, BIRTH, AND MIGRATION, CONDUCTED IN 1965

Year	Total Population	Total Non-Whites	Percent Non-Whites
1950	71,899	7,929	11.0
1957	75,425	12,151	16.1
1960	76,010	15,111	19.8
1965	72,918	19,948	27.3
1970*	73,731	27,502	37.3
1975*	77,211	37,079	48.0
1980*	84,825	50,579	59.6

*Estimated

TABLE SIII-8.   PERCENT BLACK OF TOTAL POPULATION: MOUNT VERNON, NEW ROCHELLE, WHITE PLAINS, YONKERS, AND WESTCHESTER COUNTY, 1950 - 1970

	MOUNT VERNON	NEW ROCHELLE	WHITE PLAINS	YONKERS	WESTCHESTER COUNTY
1950					
Total Population	71,899	59,725	43,466	152,798	625,816
Number of Blacks	7,850	7,403	4,293	4,955	38,061
% Blacks	10.9	12.4	9.9	3.2	6.1
1960					
Total Population	76,016	76,812	50,485	190,634	808,891
Number of Blacks	14,918	10,103	5,880	7,663	60,455
% Blacks	19.6	13.2	11.6	4.0	7.5
1970					
Total Population	72,796	75,385	50,125	204,297	891,409
Number of Blacks	25,778	10,657	7,250	13,003	85,041
% Blacks	35.4	14.1	14.5	6.4	9.5
Percent Change 1950 - 1970					
Total Population	1.2	33.6	15.5	26.2	42.6
Blacks	228.4	44.0	68.9	162.4	123.4

OPERATIONAL DEFINITIONS

$$\% \text{ Black Change, Time}_1 \text{ to } t_2 = \frac{\text{Number Blacks, Time}_2 - \text{Number Blacks, Time}_1}{\text{Number Blacks, Time}_1}$$

$$\% \text{ Black} = \frac{\text{Number of Blacks}}{\text{Total Population}}$$

$$\% \text{ Change 1950 - 1970} = \frac{\text{Number of Blacks, 1970} - \text{Number of Blacks, 1950}}{\text{Number of Blacks, 1950}}$$

PROFILE EXAMPLE

FIGURE SIII-2

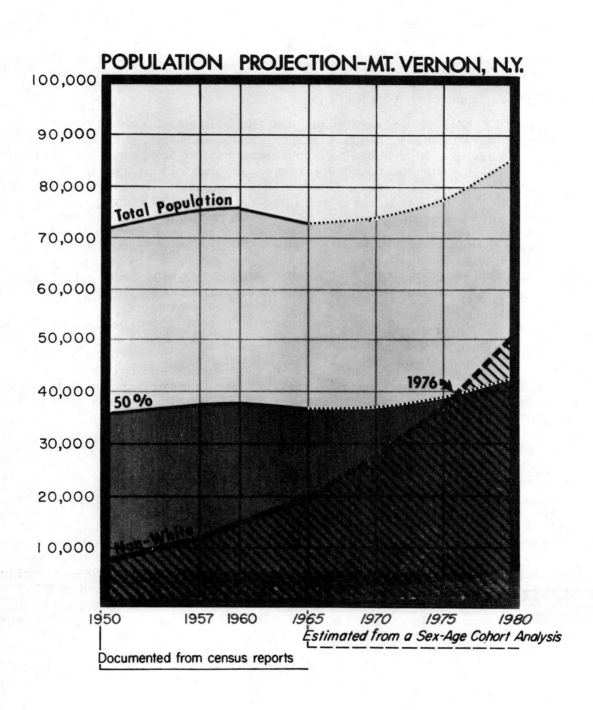

CLASSIFICATION INDICATORS

	United States	Mount Vernon	New Rochelle
% Native of Native White Parentage, 1970 (See Table SIII-1)	72.0	28.2	45.0
Degree Change in Heterogeneity Index, 1960 to 1970 (See Table SIII-2)	3.5	57.6	7.0

FINDINGS AND SUGGESTED IMPLICATIONS

In 1970 both Mount Vernon and New Rochelle were communities with *increasing heterogeneity*. Mount Vernon, however, had a more diverse population with only one fourth of its population native born whites of native white parentage compared to the nearly three quarters at the national level (see Table SIII-1). At the same time, Mount Vernon's heterogeneity index (837.5) was three times greater than the nation's, and during the decade its index increased substantially more (57.6 percent) than the nation's (3.5 percent) (see Table SIII-3). The dramatic change in Mount Vernon's heterogeneity index was primarily due to the increase in the black population and a decrease in native-born whites of native white parentage. Foreign stock comprised two-fifths of the population with Italians as the largest component—39.8 percent in Mount Vernon (see Table SIII-2).

New Rochelle, although a community with *increasing heterogeneity,* was increasing its diversity much less than Mount Vernon was. It is significant that New Rochelle's index has remained relatively constant for 30 years. In 1940 its index was greater than Mount Vernon's whereas in 1970 it was less than half of it. As New Rochelle grew in size, the proportions of native whites of native white parents, foreign born, and black remained relatively constant.

Although both communities were less residentially segregated than most of the nation's suburban places, New Rochelle, which was more segregated in 1940 than Mount Vernon, had become less so by 1970 (see Table SIII-4). The steady decline of segregation in New Rochelle may be due in part to the smaller number of blacks—less than one half as many as in Mount Vernon— and the conscious effort of the community to develop and maintain a few integrated neighborhoods. Mount Vernon, on the other hand, has experienced a rapid increase in its black population, concentrated in the part of town south of the railroad tracks. This segregated pattern in 1970 was reflected in the racial composition of the schools, as all the south-side schools (six of the eleven in town) had black enrollments of 95 percent or more (one school was 99.8 percent black). Although the New York State Education Department mandated desegregation of the school system, the community has been able to resist it since 1963.

With regard to racial change, again Mount Vernon began the period 1940 with a smaller black population than New Rochelle, but by 1970 it had gained significantly and dramatically more blacks (see Table SIII-8). In fact, the black population increase exceeded that of all other county towns and the county as a whole. Blacks in Mount Vernon increased more than fivefold, from 5,103 people or 7.6 percent of the population in 1940 to 25,778 or 35.4 percent in 1970. A widely used explanation for this development is that New Rochelle underwent major civic improvements and urban redevelopment of black neighborhoods that resulted not only in the dislocation of blacks but even in the use of Mount Vernon as one of its relocation sites. In fact, Mount Vernon officials associate the increase in blacks in their town with the location of publicly assisted families by the county welfare department. They complained to county officials that their city had become the "dumping ground" for welfare clients. County officials denied the charge.

A close examination of the components of population change reveals that about two thirds of the black newcomers to Mount Vernon were in-migrants (see Table SIII-5) and the other third were born in town. New Rochelle, on the other hand, experienced a net out-migration of blacks for the decade. Perhaps the most important factor in the changing population of both communities was the net out-migration of whites. While New Rochelle had an almost equal proportion of blacks and whites leaving (approximately 8 percent), Mount Vernon experienced a massive exodus of whites (15,199 persons or 28.9 percent). The white exodus, three times greater in Mount Vernon than New Rochelle, led us to conduct a population projection through the use of a sex-age-cohort analysis in 1965. We estimated that Mount Vernon would become a half-black, half-white community during the 1970s if little or nothing occurred to modify this trend (see Table SIII-7). However, whether this projection is fulfilled or not depends upon how the community leaders and citizens perceive and respond to these trends and projections. They may accept them as inevitable and do nothing; they may accelerate the change by adopting policies that affect whites adversely, stimulating them in increasing proportions to leave town; or they may resist the change by formulating racially oriented policies and programs to return or increase the white population by selectively encouraging some persons to move in while discouraging others. The fact that our population estimates were conducted in 1965 on relative proportions of blacks and whites overestimated the proportion of blacks for 1970 by 1.9 percent. This overestimate could be due to one or more of the following conditions: (1) the unexpected total population decrease; (2) public officials began to formulate policies and programs on urban redevelopment that reduced the resident black population and discouraged the in-migration of blacks (the public works commissioner even proposed a local immigration policy prohibiting blacks from moving in); (3) blacks became less and less attracted to the city, or younger white families were attracted to the community as real estate prices declined or as they sought the challenge of the struggle for integration.

Figure SIII-3 contains our speculations on some of the factors which native whites, white ethnics, and blacks may consider as they decide to move in, move out, or stay in a specific community. Each person or family moving generally takes a number of these factors into account. Their socio-economic class position may drastically affect the decision. However, it should be noted that some people are unaware and unknowing about specific facts and may often have little to choose from as they seek a home close to their job.

FIGURE SIII-3. SPECULATIONS ON REASONS PEOPLE MOVE

	IN-MIGRATION		OUT-MIGRATION	
	Pull	Repell	Stay	Push
NATIVE WHITE	Homogeneous population	Heterogeneity (ethnics/blacks)	Restrictions against others	Community controversy/conflict
	Economic growth	Diverse life styles	Controlled growth	Uncontrolled change
	Limited scope of government	High cost and inefficient government	Stability	Increased scope of government
	High status	Competitive elite leadership	Reform government	Declining community
	Individualistic orientation		Consensual elite leadership	Corrupt government
	Jobs		Quality schools	Lax code enforcement
	Elite leadership		Efficient public services	Visible relative deprivation
				Competitive mass politics
WHITE ETHNICS	"Kith and kin"	Prejudice against their nationality	Communal opportunities	Ethnic discrimination
	Opportunity for upward mobility	Low levels of public services	Private regardingness	Increasing black population
	Youth service orientation	Blacks	Strict code enforcement	Decline of property values
	Machine politics	High taxes	"Law and order"	Family disorganization
	Competitive mass politics	Consensual elite leadership	Increased scope of government	Rapid increase in crime
	Acceptance of diverse life styles	Community controversy/conflict	Machine politics	Increased welfare burden
	Multi-strata (classes)	Public housing	Competitive elite leadership	Consensual mass politics
			Urban renewal	Neighborhood "tipping-point," "blockbusting"
BLACKS	Family and friends	Discriminatory against blacks	Ability to survive economically	Established caste system
	Jobs	High cost of living	Tolerance	Urban renewal
	Availability of housing (cost/nondiscrimination)	High taxes	Competitive elite leadership	Tightened code enforcement
	Expanded scope of government	Obvious relative deprivation		Illegitimate sanctions
	Extensive public transportation	Poor public transportation		Anti-black consensual mass politics
	Public housing			

DISCUSSION

1. What is the ethnic heterogeneity classification of your community?

2. What are the heterogeneity index, the segregation index, and the relative proportions of native whites of native white parents, foreign born whites, blacks, and other races in your community? To what extent have these factors changed during the decade?

3. To what do you attribute your community's changing heterogeneity? (a) change in the foreign born, (b) change in the native whites, (c) change in the blacks (d) change in other races, (e) a selective change in the relationship between birth and death rates, (f) a total population change.

4. Speculate on the ways the amount of diversity and its change in your community affect the following major areas of community life: (a) education, (b) housing, (c) crime, (d) health, (e) welfare, (f) economic opportunity, (g) cultural activities, (h) social tensions.

5. Do you think it is important for your community to change its heterogeneity trend? If so, in what direction? What social, political, and/or economic strategies might be employed to bring about the desired change?

NOTES

1. Louis Wirth, *Community Life and Social Policy* (University of Chicago Press, 1956), p. 119.

2. Leonard Reissman, *The Urban Process* (The Free Press, 1964), p. 144.

3. Milton M. Gordon, *Assimilation in American Life* (Oxford University Press, 1964), p. 38.

4. See Gordon's Paradigm of Assimilation, *ibid.,* p. 76.

5. Robert Angell, "The Moral Integration of American Cities," *Cities and Society* edited by Paul Hutt and Albert Reiss (The Free Press, 1957), p. 624.

6. Christen Jonassen, *The Measurement of Community Dimensions and Elements* (Ohio State University, 1959), p. 6.

7. See the segregation index for a list of American cities in Karl Taeuber and Alma Taeuber, *Negroes in Cities* (Aldine Publishing Co., 1965), p. 39-41.

8. Morton Grodzins, *The Metropolitan Area as a Racial Problem* (University of Pittsburgh Press, 1959).

9. Charles Tilly, "Race and Migration to the American City," in
The Metropolitan Enigma edited by James Q. Wilson (Doubleday and Co., 1970),
p. 148.

10. Taeuber and Taeuber, p. 144.

11. Tilly, p. 153.

COMMUNITY DATA PROFILE SIII-A

(SIII-1) ETHNIC HETEROGENEITY BY NATIONAL ORIGIN AND RACE

	Your Community 1960 #	%	1970 #	%	Comparison City 1960 #	%	1970 #	%
Total Population								
Native White of Native White Parents								
Native White of Foreign or Mixed Parents								
Foreign Born White								
Black								
White								

(SIII-2) MAJOR NATIONAL ORIGIN GROUPS

	Your Community 1960 #	%	1970 #	%	Comparison City 1960 #	%	1970 #	%
Total Population								
Persons of Spanish Language								
Foreign Stock								
1.								
2.								
3.								

(SIII-3) HETEROGENEITY INDEX

Year	Your Community Index	% Change	Comparison City Index	% Change
1940				
1950				
1960				
1970				

(SIII-4) RACIAL SEGREGATION INDEX

Year	Your Community	Comparison City
1940		
1950		
1960		
1970		
Change 1940-60		
Change 1960-70		

(SIII-5) COMPONENTS OF POPULATION CHANGE BY RACE

	Population 1970	1960	Change Number	%	Births	Deaths	Net Migration Number	%
Your Community								
Total								
White								
Black								
Comparison City								
Total								
White								
Black								

COMMUNITY DATA PROFILE SIII-B

(SIII-6) BLACK PROPORTION OF TOTAL POPULATION

	Your Community			Comparison City		
	Number	%	% Change	Number	%	% Change
1940						
1950						
1960						
1970						

(SIII-8) COMPARATIVE BLACK PROPORTIONS OF TOTAL POPULATION

	Your Community	Comparison City	City #1	City #2	Your County
1950					
Total Population					
Number of Blacks					
% Blacks					
1960					
Total Population					
Number of Blacks					
% Blacks					
1970					
Total Population					
Number of Blacks					
% Blacks					
Percent Change 1950 to 1970					
Total Population					
Blacks					

CLASSIFICATION INDICATORS
(Table SIII-1 and SIII-2)

	Your Community	Comparison City
% Native of Native White Parentage		
% Change in Heterogeneity Index, 1960-1970		
CLASSIFICATION		

SIV. SEX-AGE AND RELATED FAMILY CHARACTERISTICS

WHAT IS THE STATUS AND BURDEN OF YOUR LABOR FORCE?

CONCEPT

Most communities would like to think they have a distinctive social setting and cast a unique shadow. Part of this distinction can be attributed to the prevailing cultural values, the projected imagery, and what is in the eye of the beholder. It is important to note that there are certain agreed-upon features that distinguish central cities from suburbs, old cities from newer ones, busy bustling places from quiet towns, manufacturing centers from retirement or resort towns. New York City differs from suburban Scarsdale, Boston from Houston, Seattle from Tacoma, and Detroit from St. Petersburg. We will examine some less visible differences which are found in the sex-age profile, labor force status, vital statistics, and family structure.

The *sex-age* profile is a useful means of illustrating the ratio of males to females within each age group. According to Taeuber, predominance and change of specific age and sex groups reflect mortality as well as migration and provide a useful indicator of major social change.[1] Information about age and sex distributions, in turn, provides the basis for computations of other widely used rates or ratios. One is the *nonworker-to-worker ratio,* or the ratio comparing those persons 16 years old or older not in the labor force to those who are in it. For urban America the ratio is 1.36 nonworkers for every worker. The higher the ratio, the greater the burden on those in the labor force. One important age group is youth, those 18 years old and under who are expected to be in school or who soon will be. They comprised 34.3 percent of the nation's population in 1970. Another group considered dependent on those that work are persons 65 years or older, who in 1970 made up 9.9 percent of the total population.

An important group affecting population growth is that of women 15 to 44 years old considered to be in their childbearing years. These women comprised 40.4 percent of the nation's female population. Among them it is important to note the *cumulative fertility rate,* or the number of children ever born per 1,000 women ever married of childbearing age. In 1970, the cumulative fertility rate was 2,452 for the U.S. Obviously, a relatively large female cohort in the childbearing age combined with a high fertility rate indicates not only a community that is youthful but one that has a great population growth dynamic.

77

Berelson indicates that, although the fertility rate is ultimately dependent on the capacity to have children, which in turn depends on the general state of health as well as on the conditions specifically associated with childbearing,[2] it is even more dependent upon individual decisions to have or not to have children than on any ethnic or class differences in regard to capacity. Deliberate control of fertility has become a strong factor in national policy and includes such practices as postponing marriage, enforcing celibacy, sexual abstinence, preventing marriage, and practicing contraception, abortion, sterilization, or in some cultures even infanticide. Among the major differentials in human fertility cited by Berelson are those which relate to historical periods and cultural patterns. The historical relationships are: (1) higher fertility in stable times than in periods of sharp social change and (2) higher fertility in times of prosperity. Relationships that are based on cultural patterns include: (1) higher fertility among descendants of large families; (2) higher fertility in lower socioeconomic groups (however, the topmost socioeconomic group has higher fertility rates than the middle or middle-high group); (3) higher fertility among stable families than among those who move either geographically or socially; (4) higher fertility in rural settings than in urban, and higher fertility in small cities than in large ones; (5) higher fertility among Catholics than among Protestants, higher among Protestants than among Jews, and (6) higher fertility among national and racial minorities low in socioeconomic status (Negroes and Puerto Ricans) than those high in status.[3]

Related to fertility rates is the *birth rate,* the number of live births by place of residence per 1,000 of total population. The birth rate reflects the same associations as those findings for fertility cited by Berelson. In addition the *death rate* or the number of deaths by place of residence per 1,000 of total population provides some indication of the dynamics of a community's population growth or decline due to natural causes. Another important measure in this connection is the *infant mortality rate,* the number of deaths of infants under one year per 1,000 live births. Infant mortality was once regarded as the most sensitive index of the quality of health care, nutrition, and sanitation. However, Moriyama states that as infant mortality rates decrease, they provide less information largely because of two factors, the deceleration in the rate of decline in the death rate for pneumonia and the unyielding course of mortality among neonates (infants under 28 days of age). The latter refers to little change "in the prevention of deaths from factors relating to the birth process such as birth injuries, postnatal asphyxia, congenital malformations, and prematurity."[4]

A significant development of the American labor force is its increasing proportion of women. Two fifths of all women 16 years old or older in the nation were in the labor force in 1970. Scammon and Wattenberg note that this remarkable increase reflects a radical change in a way of life, from the cliche of "a woman's place is in the home" to her place in the office, factory, or school. They note that a woman who works is exposed to: (1) an inside look at the business world; (2) to men, not her husband, in a place not her home; and (3) some feelings of economic independence. For possible consequences they ask whether women change in regard to: (1) becoming tougher consumers, (2) having changed attitudes towards business life, (3) having opened up new horizons, and (4) their sense of independence leading to divorce and marital infidelity.[5] Yet some studies indicate that juvenile delinquency is lower and students receive better grades when the mother works.

All these natural processes and their associated factors obviously affect the sex-age profile of the community. The sex-age patterns in turn affect the kinds of family patterns that develop, especially in regard to the proportions of females in the labor force. Although there are many schemes to classify families, such as achievement-oriented, non-supportive, achievement-conflict, and low aspiration as suggested by Strauss,[6] we use simply "nuclear" and "attenuated" families. The former is the traditional two-parent or husband-wife family. The latter is the one-parent household, generally thought of as a "broken" family. Most often the attenuated family is headed by a female and generally has greater need for public assistance such as that provided by Aid to Families with Dependent Children (AFDC). In 1960, 10.8 percent of white families were one-parent families whereas 25.9 percent of black families were attenuated. By 1970, the percentage of attenuated white families stayed the same while the attenuated black families increased to 33.0 percent.

The importance of family structure was pointed up by President Johnson in a speech at Howard University on June 4, 1965 when he stated, "When the family collapses, it is the children that are usually damaged. When it happens on a massive scale, the community itself is crippled."[7] The President making these remarks in the context of a diagnosis of the problems facing blacks living not just in the rural South but also, and especially, in the urban North, emphasized the importance of the breakdown of the black family structure as its influence radiates to every part of community life.

President Johnson's speech was based on the findings of what has become known as the "Moynihan Report" which attempts to build the case that government antidiscrimination action was in itself not enough to assure blacks of equality. Moynihan believed that the treatment of blacks by the American society made it highly improbable that blacks could achieve equal results even granted new opportunities emanating from the civil rights legislation. He stated, "at the heart of the deterioration of the fabric of Negro society is the deterioration of the Negro family."[8] His evidence of the breakdown of the black family was that:

1) Nearly a quarter of urban black marriages were dissolved.

2) Nearly one quarter of black births were illegitimate.

3) Almost one fourth of black families were headed by females.

4) The breakdown of the black family had led to a startling increase in welfare dependency.

The report continues that the roots of the problem were slavery, hostility toward the black male during reconstruction, disorganizing effects of a rapid transition by blacks from rural areas to urban ones, higher incidence of unemployment and its long-run rising trend among black males which is associated with widespread poverty among black families, and the failure of the American wage system to provide enough for family needs. All of these produced instability for many black families resulting in a "tangle of pathology." The strands of the pathology include: (1) the "matriarchical" structure of the family (the wife dominates the family generally because the black woman is better educated, holds more white collar and professional jobs, and, in fact, often earns more than her husband); (2) the failure of black youth to learn in school as much as white children and their high drop out rate; (3) high delinquency and crime rates among black youth; (4) the high failure rate of the Armed Forces Mental Test among black young men indicating "an inadequate preparation for life"; and, (5) the widespread alienation or withdrawal of black men from family life and society.[9]

According to Moynihan, these strands intertwine and produce a recurring cycle—black men are discriminated against by the economic system and do less well than black women. They therefore do not play a dominant role in the family and some leave home. Women are left to support and rear the children. Children growing up in an unstable home cannot do well in school, drop out, do not qualify for well-paying jobs, and the cycle repeats itself. Moynihan suggested that the cycle needed to be broken. The report closed with a statement of national effort: "The policy of the United States is to bring the Negro American to full and equal sharing in the responsibilities and rewards of citizenship. To this end the programs of the Federal government bearing on this objective shall be designed to have the effect directly or indirectly, of enhancing the stability and resources of the Negro American family."[10]

Although the Moynihan Report engendered numerous angry reactions, especially by civil rights leaders, no one denied the extent of the one-parent home in the black community. By and large the Report was attacked for its methodology (e.g. for not comparing blacks and whites within an income group) and especially for the impression it left that whatever the causes, the "pathology" was now self-generating and that the dynamic pertained to almost all black families. Whitney Young, Jr. wrote, "family instability has been presented in the press and elsewhere as being the cause of Negro failure to achieve equality. This is a gross distortion. It is instead the result of patterns of discrimination which deny to Negro citizens the same chance to hold a job and earn a decent living that the white American has."[11]

Prevailing sex-age and family patterns affect both private and public decisions on housing, education, and recreation as well as attitudes toward those who migrate in or out. Among the possible implications for a community of an aging population are: (1) growing political conservatism; (2) economic drain (from people living from savings accounts and the like); (3) increased use of special services (such as senior citizen housing, medical care, and mass transportation); and (4) the need for planned activities because the aged have difficulty finding friends.[12] Communities with very young populations face different problems and generally emphasize the need for extensive educational facilities, recreation programs, and child-care centers. As the ratio of dependent population grows, the burden on the productive part of the population increases. That is, taxes need to be increased to meet the needs for special public services—schools, day-care centers, health care, homes for the aged, and so on. Even an age-balanced community, which may on the surface appear ideal, has its problems. It may engender many competing demands. If these demands are not fulfilled to the satisfaction of each group, tension or controversy may cause the community to experience policy paralysis.

TYPOLOGY

We offer the following typology as one way of characterizing the labor force data presented here. On the one hand, the nonworker-to-worker ratio is used to distinguish those who are in the labor force and carry the burden of supporting the nonworkers. On the other hand, the proportion of females in the labor force is presented. Both measures are used relative to the national average.

FIGURE SIV-1.   TYPOLOGY OF THE LABOR FORCE BURDEN

(Relative to the Nation)

		NONWORKER-TO-WORKER RATIO	
		Higher	*Lower*
		Female Sharing Burden	Voluntary Female Participatory
% FEMALES IN LABOR FORCE	*Higher*		
	Lower		
		Burdened Male	Traditional Female-Dependent

A community where the proportion of females in the labor force is less than that of the nation and the nonworker-to-worker ratio is lower than the nation's is considered a *traditional female-dependency* place. We use the terms traditional and dependency to convey the sense that females have not left their homes to enter the labor market but rather are engaged primarily in running the home and rearing the children. The burden here is lower than the national average as families here are not large and the aged and poor are fewer. These places are less-urbanized smaller communities. The *burdened male* community has a higher nonworker-to-worker ratio with fewer females in the labor force. This type occurs in older and more industrialized communities where families are larger and the aged and poor are more numerous.

There are two situations in which females enter the labor force more frequently than the national average. One is when the *female shares the burden,* more or less because she must supplement the family's income. This occurs primarily in communities with a large proportion of blacks, among whom women have traditionally been in the labor force. The other situation is a *voluntary female-participatory* community where women are better educated and choose to be gainfully employed. Such places are mainly larger central cities and their suburbs.

SOURCES AND CAVEATS

The Census Series PC(1)-C, *General Population Characteristics* provides statistics on median age and age by category. Labor force and family structure data can be found for both 1960 and 1970 in the U.S. Bureau of the Census, Census of Population, *General Social and Economic Characteristics,* Series PC(1)-C, for each state and the United States. Vital statistics (birth, death, and infant mortality rates) can be found in the U.S. Department of Health, Education, and Welfare, *Vital Statistics of the United States,* Vol. 1, *Natality,* and Vol. II, Part B, *Mortality.*

Note that in 1960 few data were reported for the black population separately; blacks were included in a category called "non-whites." For Mount Vernon persons of other races constituted only .25 percent and for New Rochelle .49 percent. For the U.S., limited data on blacks is available in the U.S. Census of Population: 1960, *Subject Reports, Non-White Population by Race,* Final Report PC(2)-1C.

The basis for labor-force statistics was changed from 14 years old and older in 1960 to 16 years old and older in 1970. Therefore, data for the two years should be compared with caution. Note that we include the percentage of persons under 18 years old who do not live with both parents, rather than the percentage living with both parents as do the census reports, because our emphasis is on young people growing up in "broken homes" with generally a different life style.

PROFILE EXAMPLE

TABLE SIV-1. POPULATION BY SEX, AGE, AND RACE

<u>1960</u>

	MOUNT VERNON					NEW ROCHELLE			
	Males		*Females*			*Males*		*Females*	
	Total	Black	Total	Black		Total	Black	Total	Black
-5	3558	883	3436	905		3674	499	3483	487
5-9	2977	744	2909	751		3526	427	3406	461
10-14	2939	617	2840	641		3241	415	3137	399
15-19	2194	430	2408	504		2184	265	2688	331
20-24	1908	438	2374	664		1836	278	2555	499
25-29	2216	496	2453	620		2028	287	2487	483
30-34	2434	472	2780	726		2401	327	2924	468
35-39	2356	544	2832	701		2630	372	3027	514
40-44	2277	498	2865	692		2459	318	2903	486
45-49	2501	411	3194	607		2582	309	2944	473
50-54	2578	394	2873	464		2479	259	2836	438
55-59	2298	307	2592	353		2254	255	2390	335
60-64	1931	205	2089	248		1679	154	1955	261
65-69	1413	129	1760	208		1224	145	1485	149
70-74	944	85	1339	135		789	66	1136	112
75+	1082	106	1660	133		922	73	1548	134

<u>1970</u>

	Total	Black	Total	Black		Total	Black	Total	Black
-5	2832	1307	2744	1301		2857	468	2675	421
5-9	2910	1341	2835	1391		3153	541	3073	539
10-14	2945	1217	2903	1287		3299	483	3149	485
15-19	2663	1042	2664	1027		2868	351	3265	465
20-24	2338	793	2994	1199		2160	307	3118	413
25-29	2307	885	2532	1136		2210	291	2585	431
30-34	1927	792	2207	1100		1916	251	2272	428
35-39	1798	757	2070	924		2005	273	2251	396
40-44	2048	704	2463	971		2199	319	2688	458
45-49	2117	674	2601	912		2370	311	2718	444
50-54	2094	604	2720	863		2160	252	2492	393
55-59	2117	475	2612	649		2111	214	2531	344
60-64	1998	390	2283	538		1892	199	2315	359
65-69	1285	285	1931	432		1393	155	1860	270
70-74	949	155	1533	256		955	100	1419	180
75+	1190	169	2168	307		1178	100	2248	206

PROFILE EXAMPLE

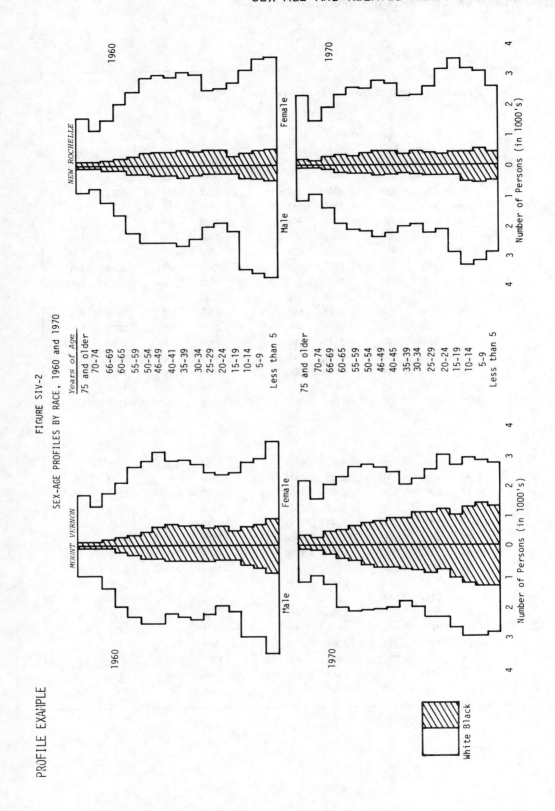

FIGURE SIV-2

SEX-AGE PROFILES BY RACE, 1960 and 1970

PROFILE EXAMPLE

TABLE SIV-2. AGE SEGMENTS AND FERTILITY BY RACE, 1960 and 1970

| | MOUNT VERNON 1960 | | | MOUNT VERNON 1970 | | | NEW ROCHELLE 1960 | | | NEW ROCHELLE 1970 | | | UNITED STATES 1960 | | | UNITED STATES 1970 | | |
	Total	White	Black	Total	White	Black	Total	White	Black	Total	White	Black	Total	White	Black	Total	White	Black
Median age	35.6	M=35.8 F=38.8	M=27.7 F=30.6	34.5	M=37.2 F=43.2	M=30.8 F=33.8	33.9	M=33.4 F=34.8	M=30.8 F=33.8	33.9	33.0 36.0	27.7 34.2	29.5	28.5	23.5	28.1	28.9	22.4
Percent population under 18 years	28.6	27.3	33.8	28.1	24.1	35.4	30.6	31.1	28.6	29.2	28.6	32.7	35.8	35.0	NA	34.4	33.4	42.3
Percent population over 65 years	10.8	12.2	5.3	12.4	15.9	6.4	9.2	9.7	6.5	12.3	12.9	9.1	9.2	9.7	6.2	9.9	10.3	7.0
Percent females 15 to 44 years	38.9	36.8	46.8	38.0	34.5	44.2	40.5	39.6	46.1	39.8	39.6	41.1	39.7	39.5	40.3	40.4	40.1	41.4
Cumulative Fertility Rate*	2127	NA	2174	2452	NA	2532	2176	NA	1837	2526	NA	2488	2627	2575	3049	3132	3047	3817

*Children ever born per 1000 women ever married (35-44 years old)

TABLE SIV-3. VITAL STATISTICS BY RACE, 1960 and 1970

| | MOUNT VERNON 1960 | | | MOUNT VERNON 1970 | | | NEW ROCHELLE 1960 | | | NEW ROCHELLE 1970 | | | UNITED STATES 1960 | | | UNITED STATES 1970 | | |
	Total	White	Black	Total	White	Black	Total	White	Black	Total	White	Black	Total	White	Black	Total	White	Black
Birth Rate	20.5	18.6	28.4	15.7	11.6	25.8	18.4	17.6	23.5	12.1	10.4	19.7	23.7	22.7	31.9	17.8	16.9	24.0
Death Rate	10.0	10.5	8.0	11.3	12.7	8.8	9.9	9.6	11.4	9.7	9.5	10.0	9.5	9.5	10.1	9.5	9.5	9.6
Infant Mortality Rate	21.9	17.7	32.9	24.2	16.5	31.5	30.5	18.9	85.4	27.4	23.8	42.9	26.0	22.9	43.2	20.0	17.8	30.9

OPERATIONAL DEFINITIONS

% Under 18 yrs. Old = $\dfrac{\text{Number of Residents under 18}}{\text{Total Population}}$

% 65 yrs. or Older = $\dfrac{\text{Population 65 Years and Older}}{\text{Total Population}}$

% Females 15 to 44 yrs. = $\dfrac{\text{Number of Females 15 to 44}}{\text{All Females}}$

Cumulative Fertility Rate = $\dfrac{\text{Number of Children Ever Born to Women Ever Married, 35-44 yrs.}}{.001 \ (\text{Number of Women Ever Married, 35-44 years})}$

Birth Rate = $\dfrac{\text{Number of Live Births}}{.001 \ (\text{Total Population})}$

Death Rate = $\dfrac{\text{Number of Deaths}}{.001 \ (\text{Total Population})}$

Infant Mortality Rate = $\dfrac{\text{Number of Infant (under 1 yr.) Deaths}}{.001 \ (\text{Number of Live Births})}$

PROFILE EXAMPLE

TABLE SIV-4. LABOR FORCE STATUS BY RACE AND SEX, 1960 and 1970

	1 9 6 0						1 9 7 0					
	Total	%	White	%	Non-White	%	Total	%	White	%	Black	%
MOUNT VERNON												
Population, 16 yrs. and over*	58,382		47,783	81.8	10,599	18.2	54,409		36,894		17,515	
Males	26,608	45.6	22,071	46.2	4,537	42.8	24,104	44.3	16,710	45.3	7,394	42.2
Females	31,774	54.4	25,712	53.8	6,062	57.2	30,305	55.7	20,184	54.7	10,121	57.8
In Labor Force*	34,546	59.2	27,381	57.3	7,165	67.6	33,715	62.0	21,946	57.5	11,769	67.2
Males	21,757	81.8	18,017	81.6	3,740	82.4	18,964	78.7	13,087	78.3	5,877	79.4
Females	12,789	40.2	9,364	36.4	3,425	56.5	14,751	48.7	8,859	43.9	5,892	58.2
Ratio non-workers to workers	1.20		1.22		1.11		1.16		1.14		1.19	
NEW ROCHELLE												
Population, 16 yrs. and over*	57,385		49,471	-	7,914	39.8	55,824		48,205		7,619	
Males	26,036	45.4	22,885	46.3	3,151	46.3	24,685	44.2	21,682	45.0	3,003	39.4
Females	31,349	54.6	26,586	53.7	4,763	60.2	31,139	55.8	26,523	55.0	4,616	60.6
In Labor Force*	33,462	58.3	27,909	56.4	5,553	70.2	32,851	58.8	27,947	58.0	4,904	64.4
Males	21,586	82.9	19,076	83.4	2,510	79.7	19,763	80.0	17,475	80.6	2,288	76.2
Females	11,876	37.9	8,833	33.2	3,043	63.9	13,088	42.0	10,472	39.5	2,616	56.7
Ratio non-workers to workers	1.30		1.38		.89		1.29		1.32		1.17	
UNITED STATES												
Population, 16 yrs. and over*	126,276,516		113,122,871	-	13,153,645		141,087,270		125,367,127		14,015,283	
Males	61,315,353	48.6	55,036,172	48.7	6,279,181	47.7	67,235,510	47.7	59,946,581	47.8	6,449,469	46.0
Females	64,961,163	51.4	58,086,699	51.3	6,874,464	52.3	73,851,762	52.3	65,420,546	52.2	7,565,814	54.0
In Labor Force*	69,877,476	55.3	62,478,137	55.2	7,399,339	56.3	82,048,781	58.2	72,954,518	58.2	8,092,391	57.7
Males	47,467,720	77.4	42,939,887	78.0	4,527,833	72.1	51,502,114	76.6	46,388,804	77.4	4,501,560	69.8
Females	22,409,756	34.5	19,538,250	33.6	2,871,506	41.8	30,546,667	41.4	26,565,714	40.6	3,590,831	47.5
Ratio non-workers to workers	1.57		1.54		1.39		1.48		1.44		1.79	

*In 1960, those 14 years old and older were included as potentially in the labor force.

OPERATIONAL DEFINITIONS

% Males in Labor Force = $\dfrac{\text{Number of Males in Labor Force}}{\text{Number of Males 16 yrs. and Older}}$

Ratio of Non-workers to Workers = $\dfrac{(\text{Total Population} - \text{Number in Labor Force})}{\text{Number in Labor Force}}$

PROFILE EXAMPLE

TABLE SIV-5. FAMILY STRUCTURE BY RACE, 1960 and 1970

	1960						1970					
	Total	%	White	%	Black	%	Total	%	White	%	Black	%
MOUNT VERNON												
All Families	20,526		17,130		3,396		19,265		12,966		6,299	
Husband-Wife	17,447	85.0	14,903	87.0	2,544	74.9	15,429	80.1	11,191	86.3	4,238	67.3
Attenuated	3,079	15.0	2,227	13.0	852	25.1	3,736	19.9	1,675	12.9	2,061	32.7
Male Head	NA		NA		NA		696	3.6	394	3.0	302	4.8
Female Head	NA		NA		NA		3,140	16.3	1,381	10.7	1,759	27.9
Persons Under 18	21,811		16,572		5,239		20,485		11,193		9,137	
% Not Living with Both Parents	15.3		9.2		33.8		26.2		13.1		42.7	
% Living in Female-Headed Households	NA		NA		NA		16.3		7.3		27.5	
NEW ROCHELLE												
All Families	19,518		17,443		2,075		19,590		17,137		2,453	
Husband-Wife	16,993	87.1	15,460	88.6	1,533	73.9	16,782	85.7	15,130	88.3	1,652	67.3
Attenuated	2,525	12.9	1,983	11.4	542	26.1	2,808	14.3	2,007	11.7	801	32.7
Male Head	NA		NA		NA		545	2.8	450	2.6	95	3.9
Female Head	NA		NA		NA		2,263	11.5	1,557	9.1	702	28.8
Persons Under 18	23,470		20,509		2,961		21,991		18,507		3,484	
% Not Living with Both Parents	10.4		6.5		37.6		14.2		9.3		40.4	
% Living in Female-Headed Households	NA		NA		NA		8.7		5.8		24.6	
UNITED STATES												
All Families	45,128,393		40,872,872		3,950,316		50,968,827		45,770,351		4,863,401	
Husband-Wife	39,640,999	87.8	36,455,196	89.2	2,929,091	74.1	44,062,376	86.4	40,747,042	89.0	3,260,172	67.0
Attenuated	5,487,394	12.2	4,417,696	10.8	1,021,225	25.9	6,906,451	13.6	5,023,309	11.0	1,603,229	33.0
Male Head	1,293,634	2.9	1,112,962	2.7	163,588	4.1	1,402,347	2.8	884,553	2.0	269,026	5.6
Female Head	4,193,760	9.3	3,304,714	8.1	857,637	21.8	5,504,104	10.8	4,138,756	9.0	1,334,203	27.4
Persons Under 18	64,309,881		55,586,283		NA		69,644,081		59,446,070		9,508,346	
% Not Living with Both Parents	13.2		10.0		NA		17.9		13.7		43.8	
% Living in Female-Headed Households	NA		NA		NA		10.0		7.3		26.6	

OPERATIONAL DEFINITIONS

% Attenuated Families = (All Families – Husband/Wife Families) / All Families

% Persons Under 18 Not Living with Both Parents = 100 – % Persons under 18 Living with Both Parents

CLASSIFICATION INDICATORS

	United States	Mount Vernon	New Rochelle
Nonworker-to-Worker Ratio, 1970 (See Table SIV-4)	1.48	1.16	1.29
% Females in Labor Force, 1970 (See Table SIV-4)	41.4	48.7	42.0

FINDINGS AND SUGGESTED IMPLICATIONS

Both Mount Vernon and New Rochelle were *voluntary female-participatory* places. That is, both had a lower nonworker-to-worker ratio and a higher proportion of females in the labor force than the nation in 1970 (see Table SIV-4). Mount Vernon deviated more from the nation in both respects than did New Rochelle, as it had a 1.16 ratio compared to the nation's 1.48 and 7.3 percent more females in the labor force than the nation. Both communities had a larger proportion of older residents and a smaller proportion of younger residents (see Tables SIV-1 and SIV-2). The median age was approximately 6 years older than the national median. The cumulative fertility rate for married women 35 to 44 years old in both communities was considerably lower than the national, but Mount Vernon's increased less and New Rochelle increased more than the nation's. Both communities had a higher infant mortality than the nation's, with New Rochelle's (27.4) higher than Mount Vernon's (24.2) (see Table SIV-3). However, Mount Vernon's rate was increasing, while both New Rochelle and the nation's were decreasing. The family pattern in Mount Vernon showed deviations from that of New Rochelle and the nation in that there were more attenuated families (19.9 percent), more female-headed households (16.3 percent), and more children not living with both parents (26.2 percent) (see Table SIV-5). These family characteristics were increasing more in Mount Vernon than in either New Rochelle or the nation.

A greater difference existed between blacks and whites within each community in their sex-age profiles, family structures, and labor-force characteristics than between the two communities. The only exception was the ratio of nonworkers to workers in Mount Vernon, where the ratio was about the same for both races. It should be noted that black workers in Mount Vernon carried a much lesser burden (1.19) than those in the nation (1.79). In both communities the nonworker-to-worker ratio decreased slightly for whites and increased slightly for blacks during the decade. Black females participated significantly more in the labor force than did white females in both communities. In Mount Vernon, the median age of blacks was much lower (approximately 13 years) than that of the whites, as more than one third of the blacks were under 18 years of age compared to only one fourth of the whites (see Table SIV-2). Actually, the black population was getting younger while the white population was getting older. Not only were there 9.7 percent more black females of childbearing age than white females in Mount Vernon but their cumulative birth rate also was higher; the black birth rate was more than twice the white birth rate (see Table SIV-3). The highest infant mortality rates were found among the blacks of New Rochelle (42.9), followed by the blacks of Mount Vernon (31.5), the whites of New Rochelle (23.8), and the whites of Mount Vernon (16.5). Infant mortality remained relatively constant for both blacks and whites in Mount Vernon, whereas it had been cut in half for blacks and increased slightly for whites in New Rochelle. The black family patterns also differed substantially from those of the whites in both communities and the nation. The proportion of attenuated families was much greater among blacks than whites (20 percent higher) and comprised one third of all black families (see Table SIV-5). In fact, attenuated families increased among blacks and remained relatively constant among the whites during the decade. As a consequence, there were nearly three times as many female-headed households and nearly four times the proportion of children not living with both parents and living in female-headed households among the blacks than among the white. The most striking difference in life style between blacks and whites was that more than two fifths (42.7 percent) of all black children under 18 years of age did not live in the nuclear, two-parent family, in Mount Vernon, in New Rochelle, and in the nation. This was a significant increase for Mount Vernon and has important public policy consequences.

The predominant family life style in a community is related to the burden placed on its labor force. We offer the following speculations on the contributing factors and consequences of the more-burdened and less-burdened communities.

FIGURE SIV-3. SPECULATIONS ON THE CONTRIBUTING FACTORS
AND POSSIBLE CONSEQUENCES OF A MORE BURDENED
OR LESS BURDENED LABOR FORCE

Contributing Factors   *Consequences*

MORE BURDENED

Many children   High educational costs

Many aged   Special programs needed
                                       for youth
Few females in the
labor force   Special programs needed
                                       for the aged
Large proportion of
female-headed   Difficulty in increasing
households   local taxes

Tight labor market   High costs for public
                                       assistance and social
Norms against females   security
working

Large families

Job discrimination
against blacks, poor,
the young, and women

LESS BURDENED

High proportion of   Greater willingness to
middle-aged (16-65)   support community-oriented
                                       expenditures
Large number of
white-collar jobs   Support growth policies

Community is   Initiate and support
growing in both   governmental reform
size and economic
activity

Large proportion of
educated and
trained females

High proportion of
service activity

DISCUSSION

    1. What is your community's labor-force burden classification?

    2. What is the present condition of the following: the sex-age profile, vital statistics, and family structure of your community? To what extent have these factors changed during the past decade?

    3. To what do you attribute your level and kind of labor-force burden? (a) a high or low proportion of young and/or elderly persons, (b) a high or low level of unemployment, (c) a high or low level of public assistance and/or social security, (d) few or many opportunities for women to work, (e) norms for or against women working, (f) availability of day-care centers.

    4. Speculate on the way in which the burden on your labor force affects the following major areas of community life: (a) education, (b) housing, (c) crime, (d) health, (e) welfare, (f) economic opportunity, (g) cultural activities, (h) social tensions.

    5. Do you think it is important to change the burden of your labor force? If so, in what direction? What social, economic, and political strategies might be employed to bring about the desired change?

NOTES

    1. Conrad Taeuber, "Population: Trends and Characteristics," in *Indicators of Social Change* edited by Eleanor B. Sheldon and Wilbur E. Moore (Russell Sage Foundation, 1968), p. 49.

    2. Bernard Berelson and Gary A. Steiner (Eds.), *Human Behavior: An Inventory of Scientific Findings* (Harcourt, Brace and World, Inc., 1964), p. 594.

    3. Berelson, pp. 596-601.

    4. Iwao M. Moriyama, "Problems in the Measurement of Health Status," Eleanor B. Sheldon and Wilbur E. Moore, pp. 573-76.

    5. Ben J. Wattenberg and Richard M. Scammon, *This is U.S.A.* (Double-day and Co., 1965), pp. 182-85.

    6. Murray A. Straus, "Measuring Families," in *Handbook of Marriage and the Family* edited by Harold T. Christensen (Rand McNally and Co., 1964), p. 343.

    7. Johnson cited in Lee Rainwater and William L. Yancey, *The Moynihan Report and the Politics of Controversy* (The M.I.T. Press, 1967), p. 2.

    8.   Daniel Patrick Moynihan, *The Negro Family: The Case for National Action* (Office of Policy Planning and Research, U.S. Department of Labor, March, 1965), p. 5.

    9.   Moynihan, pp. 29-45.

    10.   *Ibid.*, p. 48.

    11.   Whitney Young, Jr. in Rainwater, p. 416. For a more complete discussion of the criticism of the Report see Rainwater.

    12.   Wattenburg and Scammon, pp. 27-28.

COMMUNITY DATA PROFILE SIV-A

(SIV-1) SEX AND AGE BY RACE, 1970

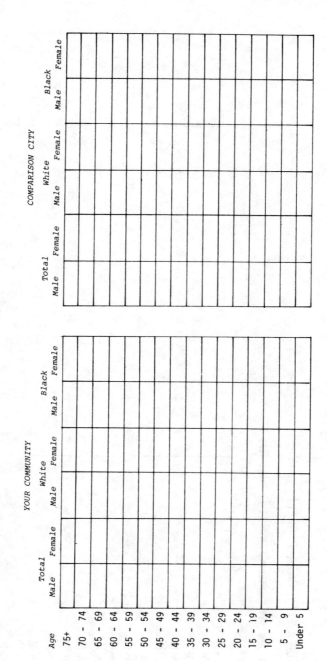

COMMUNITY DATA PROFILE   SIV-B

(FIGURE SIV-2) SEX-AGE PROFILE BY RACE, 1970

Age
75+
70-74
65-69
60-64
55-59
50-54
45-49
40-44
35-39
30-34
25-29
20-24
15-19
10-14
5-9
under 5

COMMUNITY DATA PROFILE SIV-C

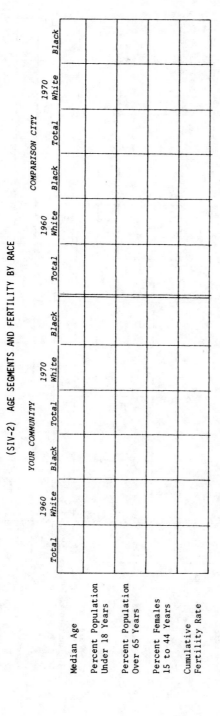

(SIV-2) AGE SEGMENTS AND FERTILITY BY RACE

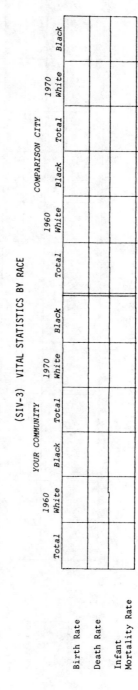

(SIV-3) VITAL STATISTICS BY RACE

COMMUNITY DATA PROFILE SIV-D

(SIV-4) LABOR FORCE STATUS BY SEX AND RACE

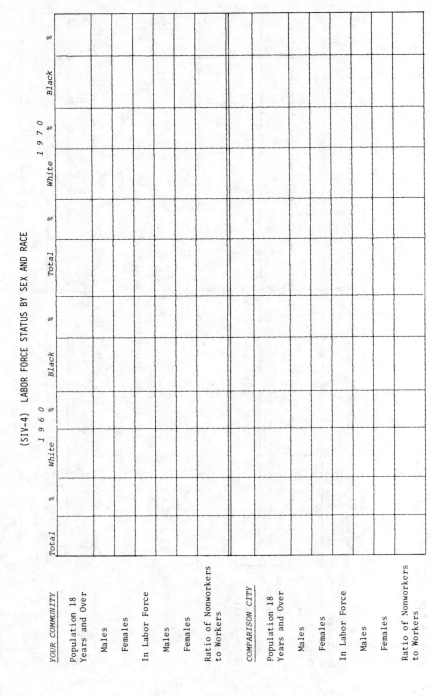

YOUR COMMUNITY	1960						1970					
---	Total	%	White	%	Black	%	Total	%	White	%	Black	%
Population 18 Years and Over												
Males												
Females												
In Labor Force												
Males												
Females												
Ratio of Nonworkers to Workers												
COMPARISON CITY												
Population 18 Years and Over												
Males												
Females												
In Labor Force												
Males												
Females												
Ratio of Nonworkers to Workers												

COMMUNITY DATA PROFILE SIV-E

(SIV-5) FAMILY STRUCTURE BY RACE

	1960 White Number	%	1960 Black Number	%	1970 White Number	%	1970 Black Number	%
YOUR COMMUNITY								
All Families								
Husband-Wife								
Attenuated								
Male Head								
Female Head								
Persons Under 18								
% Not Living with Both Parents								
% in Female Headed Households								
COMPARISON CITY								
All Families								
Husband-Wife								
Attenuated								
Male Head								
Female Head								
Persons Under 18								
% Not Living with Both Parents								
% in Female Headed Households								

CLASSIFICATION INDICATORS (SIV-4)

	YOUR COMMUNITY	COMPARISON CITY
Nonworker to Worker Ratio, 1970		
% Females in Labor Force, 1970		
CLASSIFICATION		

sv. SOCIOECONOMIC STATUS

WHAT SOCIAL STRATIFICATION PATTERNS OCCUR IN YOUR COMMUNITY?

CONCEPT

Some form of socioeconomic stratification or class scheme is the most frequently used way to characterize the social structure of communities. The concept of social stratification borrows heavily from the use of *class* as one aspect of the economic system and its emphasis on power at the societal or national level. At the community level ranked *status* is emphasized to characterize a social interactional, fact-to-face situation and is related more to prestige, respect, and deference given by one person to another. Class implies some degree of cohesion, consciousness, and even antagonism between the classes, whereas status refers more to differences in ways of life—manners, attitudes, beliefs, reputations, and so on. Bell and Newby caution against using these two terms interchangeably.[1] Dharendorf distinguishes between the clusters of class and the strata of stratification, "Class is always a category for the purposes of the analysis of the dynamics of social conflict and its structural roots, and, as such, it has to be separated strictly from *stratum* as a category for purposes of describing hierarchical systems at a given point of time."[2] Duncan has identified some of the mechanisms of stratification and the basis of social mobility as: (1) ascription (status conferred by birth), (2) inheritance, (3) genetics, (4) socialization, (5) access to opportunities, (6) environments, and (7) differential association.[3] He lists some scales of reward or bases of status: (1) wealth, assets, and property; (2) level of living and possessions; (3) prestige, honor, reputation, fame, and esteem; (4) education, knowledge, and skill; (5) style of life, status symbols, manners, and language; (6) power and authority; (7) legal status and freedom; and (8) welfare.[4]

Clark uses eight dimensions or ways of looking at the stratification of American communities:[5]

> 1. The unit to be ranked—families, individuals, culturally defined social behavior.

> 2. Vertical differentiation of the hierarchy—the height, number of levels, and the internal coherence of each stratum.

99

3. Classifying the shape of the hierarchy—pyramidal, diamond-shaped, rectangular trapezoidal, eliptical.

4. Horizontal differentiation of the hierarchy—the degree to which separate and distinct vertical hierarchies coexist within the system.

5. The values to be ranked—money and credit, control over jobs, organizations and interpretation of values, knowledge, and technical skills, popularity and commitment of followers, social prestige and access, and so on.

6. Interrelationships among hierarchies—the degree of autonomy, overlapping, and interactional patterns.

7. Autonomy of the system—the degree to which the stratification is linked as a whole or selectively to the larger societal system.

8. Social mobility—mapping paths of individuals moving vertically and/or horizontally.

The failure to take some of these factors into account led Polsby and others to attack the stratification theory of community power in its common assertions, namely that (1) the upper class rules in local community life, (2) political and civic leaders are subordinate to the upper class, (3) a single "power elite" rules in the community, (4) the upper class power elite rules in its own interests, and (5) social conflict takes place between the upper and the lower classes.[6]

Most stratification studies have used a variety of indicators as well as combining some of them into a single socioeconomic status index. Warner used occupation, source of income, house type, and dwelling area to formulate a six-"class" system.[7]

1. *Upper-upper*—the local social "aristocrats," members of families with long histories of wealth and social standing, who pretty much tended to stay within their own circles.

2. *Lower-upper*—in some individual cases, even wealthier than members of the upper-upper class, but lacking the properly distinguished backgrounds necessary for belonging to the higher group.

3. *Upper-middle*—mostly businessmen and professionals

4. *Lower-middle*—"white collar" clerks and small businessmen.

5. *Upper-lower*—workingmen and small tradesmen.

6. *Lower-lower*—those associated with lower incomes and poverty lifestyles, usually residing in the less desirable parts of town.

Vidich and Bensman, using the Keynesian notion about attitudes towards investment, hoarding, and consumption, formulated a fivefold social "status" system: (1) middle class—independent entrepreneurs, prosperous farmers, professionals, and skilled workers; (2) marginal middle class—aspiring investors, economic and social immobile ritualists, and psychological idiosyncratics; (3) traditional farmers; (4) old aristocrats; and (5) shack people.[8] It should be noted that social analysts use class and status interchangeably. Class generally refers to the economic system and the means of production while status pertains more to what people do with their money and their "style of life."[9]

With the use of census materials we propose the construction of several stratification profiles. One is based on family income, another on the occupation of those employed, and still another on the educational attainments of those 25 years or older. These three dimensions—income, occupation, and education—have been the most widely used measures of social status. There is generally a high correlation between them, i.e., those who have high occupational status generally have had considerably more education and receive high levels of income. Some analysts prefer to use one component such as income while others use a composite index of all three. The U.S. Census Bureau has developed a method to compile the socioeconomic status (SES) of residents of a community.[10] Unfortunately, in published census reports there are no data which combine education, occupation, and income for a single individual. Therefore, we have no combined index. We have chosen to examine each component separately and present four or five strata measured by nominal categories of greater or less statistical or analytical convenience. We have used national data to serve as a standard. (One might wish to use communities of comparable size or in the same region of the United States as a standard.) From this data, we can determine how each stratum of a community differs from that of the nation or some comparable place. That is, a community has a stratification profile that conforms generally with the national profile or it may have more or fewer high or low SES characteristics than the nation or some other comparable community.

The five strata of income have been grouped into categories roughly approximating the quintiles of the national distribution of family income from the lowest to the highest. We have changed the limits of the income categories from 1960 to 1970 because income generally increased (largely because of inflation); the cutoff point for the lowest quintile in 1960 was $2,999, whereas in 1970 it was $4,999. Median family income in the nation increased from $5,660 in 1960 to $9,590 in 1970. A comparative inspection of the income profile should reveal the deviation of a specific community from the national distribution pattern. Those who monitor income distribution over time show that the inequality of aggregate income received by each fifth of the population has remained relatively constant since the end of World War II (see Table SV-1). There has been, however, some improvement for those in the lowest quintile since the great depression of the 1930s.

TABLE SV-1

PERCENT OF AGGREGATE INCOME RECEIVED BY EACH FIFTH
OF THE NATION'S FAMILIES

Families	1950	1960	1970
Lowest quintile	4.5	4.8	5.4
Second quintile	11.9	12.2	12.2
Middle quintile	17.6	17.8	17.6
Fourth quintile	23.6	24.0	23.8
Highest quintile	42.7	41.3	40.9

Adapted from *U.S. Statistical Abstract,*
Table No. 619, p. 384.

More recently a simple index of *income concentration* has been used by the Bureau of the Census. The index ranges from 0.0 to 1.0; as it approaches the limit of 1.0, the inequality of the income distribution increases. For the nation the index is .364.

The occupational profile comprises two strata each of blue-collar and white-collar designations with each divided into upper and lower strata. Most analysts simply refer to the white-collar or the blue-collar nature of a community. The definition of each category has remained relatively constant for the two reporting periods 1960 and 1970; however, it should be noted that the Bureau of Census estimates that approximately 18 percent of those employed were incorrectly classified. As technology increases, the proportion of white-collar employees increases. By 1970 almost half the nation's workers were classified as white-collar. Of course, higher occupational status positions should mean higher earned incomes. Table SV-2 illustrates the national variations in median incomes between the higher and lower occupational strata. Those in the top stratum earn more than five times as much as those in the bottom categories. The table also shows the considerable difference between incomes earned by the females and males with comparable occupations. Males earn from two to three times more than their female counterparts.

TABLE SV-2

MEDIAN EARNINGS OF EXPERIENCED CIVILIAN LABOR FORCE,
BY SEX AND OCCUPATION—1969

Occupation	Male	Female
Total	$ 7,610	$3,649
Professional, technical, etc.	10,735	6,034
Managers, administrative, etc.	11,277	5,495
Sales workers	8,451	2,338
Clerical, etc.	7,265	4,232
Craftsmen, etc.	8,172	NA
Operatives, etc.	6,730	3,635
Transport equipment	6,903	2,574
Laborers, except farm	4,617	2,988
Farmers, farm managers	4,822	2,277
Farm laborers and foremen	2,570	1,087
Service workers	5,100	2,320
Private household	1,891	986

Adapted from *U.S. Statistical Abstract*, Table
No. 511, pp. 352-56.

The final profile is educational attainment as measured by the number
of years of schooling completed by those persons 25 years and older. Our
fivefold classification reflects educationally significant breaking-points.
The lowest category, less than a fifth-grade education, is generally referred
to as "functional illiterate." The next lowest category, fifth through
eighth grades, includes those who have completed grade school. The middle
category includes those who have attended high school but have not graduated,
while in the next category are the high school graduates. The highest group
includes all those who have attended college, those who have graduated from
college, and those who have engaged in postgraduate education. While the
categories themselves have remained constant between 1960 and 1970, there
has been a decided shift upward in the educational attainment at the national
level.

It is useful to show the connection between various levels of education
and income. Table SV-3 illustrates again that higher educational attainment
produces higher earned median income. Males with a graduate education earn
five times more than those with less than five years of schooling. The difference is even greater—six times—between females in the two extreme categories.

TABLE SV-3

MEDIAN INCOME OF PERSONS 18 YEARS AND OLDER,
BY YEARS OF SCHOOL COMPLETED AND SEX, 1969

Education	Males	Females
Total	$ 6,783	$2,480
Less than 5 years	2,605	1,231
5 to 7 years	4,206	1,491
8 years	5,340	1,705
Highschool, 1 to 3 years	6,433	2,247
Highschool, 4 years	7,502	3,126
College, 1 to 3 years	7,209	2,814
College, 4 years	11,192	4,936
College, 5 years or more	12,718	7,203

Adapted from U.S. Bureau of Census, *Detailed Characteristics, U.S. Summary*, Table 249, p. 860.

It should be apparent from the preceding discussion that there is a significant relationship among income, occupational, and educational status. However, it goes beyond the simple connection of high educational attainment preparing one for a higher occupational status position which yields higher income. Status differentials also are likely to be reflected in the kind of community or neighborhood a family selects to live in, the family's other preferences, and its ability and willingness to engage in different styles of life. These differentials also are likely to reflect different rates of political participation and preferred public policy alternatives. Virtually every study has shown a high correlation between high SES and high political participation. Verba and Nie not only find status a "powerful predictor of political activity" but also find that other social and psychological forces, such as affiliation with voluntary associations, political party membership, and political beliefs, stimulate upper-status persons to participate even more "through the development of a general set of 'civic' attitudes."[11] They note that blacks, with a growing group consciousness, have begun to narrow the participation gap.

Policy preference differs also by status sets in that upper-status citizens are more likely than lower-status persons to believe that the individual rather than the government is responsible for dealing with certain community problems such as poverty. Verba and Nie suggest that "If there is a skewing of the preferences of activists away from those found in the population as a whole—and, in particular, a skewing in the direction of

greater conservatism on welfare matters and lesser salience of serious welfare problems—the main source of this is the social composition of the
activist groups."[12] They also point out partisan differences, such as
". . . the tendency for those with conservative beliefs within the Republican
Party to be particularly active, while no such phenomena occurred among
Democrats or those with more liberal beliefs."[13]

     The national profiles of income, education, and/or occupation provide
arbitrary measures to illustrate the relative proportions of families,
employees, and individuals in each stratum of American society. With these
as a standard it is then possible to compare a local community's profiles
with those of the nation. It may in some instances be preferable to compare
a community with other places of similar size or those located in a specific
region of the country. In comparing the profiles, we note both status consistency and the degree of change in status during the past decade. That is,
in which strata does the local community deviate from the national profile?
A community may have a greater proportion of its residents in the upper stratum
and therefore fewer in the middle or lower strata. The community may deviate
more in the middle from the national profile and thereby also deviate in
the upper and lower strata. Similar comparisons can be made between profiles within a community. One can then state that a particular community
has a socioeconomic status consistency or that in some one profile—income,
occupation, and/or education—it deviates from the national profiles. The
analyst can also state whether any profile is changing more or less than that
of the nation as a whole.

     It is also possible to assess the character of each dimension by
illustrating the shape of its profile (see Figure SV-1). We develop eight social
stratification hierarchies. Clark believes that decision-making structures
generally correspond to social stratification structures.[14] One is the
horizontal rectangle that most closely represents an equalitarian system
where nearly all persons are in one stratum. Two is a vertical rectangle
that represents an equal distribution of persons among the various strata.
Three is a triangle representing a hierarchical pattern with few persons on
top and many on the bottom. Four is the inverted triangle illustrating the
opposite arrangement, with many on top and few on the bottom. Five is a
diamond shape, which best illustrates a community with bulging middle strata.
The sixth is the "hourglass," showing the converse of the diamond with a
bimodal distribution heavy on top and bottom with a small or absent middle
stratum. The seventh is a trapezoid shape, which has incrementally more on
the bottom than on the top, unlike the triangle, which has very few on the
top. Finally, there is an inverted trapezoid with incrementally more on the
top than on the bottom. It should be noted that one is not likely to find any
community fitting any one of these shapes exactly, but one may wish to indicate the tendency of a community's profiles to fit a pattern.

FIGURE SV-1

ALTERNATIVE HYPOTHETICAL SHAPES OF COMMUNITY STRATIFICATION

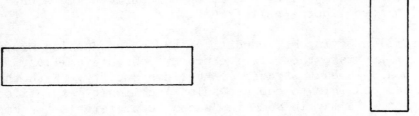

1. Horizontal rectangle

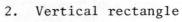

2. Vertical rectangle

3. Triangle

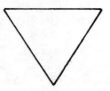

4. Inverted triangle

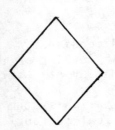

5. Diamond

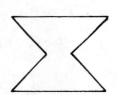

6. Hourglass

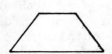

7. Trapezoid

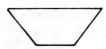

8. Inverted trapezoid

TYPOLOGY

We offer the following typology to classify the socioeconomic status of a community. One may use any one of the three stratification profiles based on the income, occupation, and education distributions of the residents (see Figure SV-2). A national profile is presented: The local deviations from the upper two strata make up one dimension of the typology. The other dimension is the relative degree of change in the same indicator of status, that is, the percent change (from 1960 to 1970) in median family income or median school years completed or the proportion of white-collar employees. An *increasing higher status* community not only has a greater proportion of its residents in the two upper strata than the nation but also a greater increase in the medians or percentages than that experienced by the nation. These communities are most likely to be economically developing, especially those with a scientifically and technologically based economy such as university towns with applied research development. Although the upper two strata of an *improving lower status* community are smaller than the national average, the community's indicators showed a greater increase during the decade than the nation. This is more likely to occur in a rapidly developing community located in an economically underdeveloped region of the country. A *slipping higher status* community is generally an older suburban place that is changing from a mainly residential economic base to an increasingly commercial, business, or industrial one. Upper-status residents tend to leave these communities for the sanctuary of "peace and quiet," further out in the suburbs. The older central cities of American are *declining lower status* places, that is, their upper-status persons are fewer and their status indicators are not increasing so much as the nation's. Their decline is associated with the in-migration a disproportionately larger share of poor and unskilled newcomers from rural and underdeveloped regions of the country.

FIGURE SV-2.   TYPOLOGY OF STRATIFICATION BASED ON INCOME
OR OCCUPATION OR EDUCATION

LOCAL DEVIATIONS FROM NATIONAL
PERCENTAGES OF UPPER TWO STRATA

	Above	*Below*
More	Increasing Higher Status	Improving Lower Status
Less	Slipping Higher Status	Declining Lower Status

PERCENT CHANGE IN
SES INDICATORS

SOURCES AND CAVEATS

   Data on income, occupation, and educational attainment can be
found in U.S. Bureau of the Census, *Census of Population: General
Social and Economic Characteristics,* Final Report Series PC(1)-C.
Similar data also can be found in Series PHC(1), *Census Tract Reports.*
It should be noted that a more detailed income breakdown appears in
state reports than in census tract reports.

   Be sure to be consistent in the income statistics used; that is,
always use "family income" if that is your interest; if your interest
is "family and unrelated individual income" use that same measure
throughout, whether it be in categories or in medians. Note that
comparability between 1960 and 1970 data on occupation is limited for
three reasons: (1) a new major group, "Transport equipment operatives,"
was added in 1970, which we have included in our category "lower blue
collar"; (2) the occupations "not reported" in 1960 have been allocated
in 1970 relative to 1960; and (3) persons 16 years of age or older
are defined as members of the labor force in 1970, whereas in 1960
those over the age of 14 were considered to be in the labor force.

PROFILE EXAMPLE

TABLE SV-4. FAMILY INCOME STRATA, MEDIANS, AND INDEX OF INCOME CONCENTRATION

	UNITED STATES 1960	1970	MOUNT VERNON 1960	Deviation From U.S.	1970	Deviation From U.S.	NEW ROCHELLE 1960	Deviation From U.S.	1970	Deviation From U.S.
Total Families	45,128,393	51,168,599	20,748	NA	19,309	NA	19,845	NA	19,804	NA
INCOME (%)										
Lowest Quintile	21.4	20.3	11.0	-10.4	14.2	-6.1	9.5	-11.9	11.4	-8.9
2nd Quintile	20.5	25.7	16.9	- 3.6	22.3	-3.4	13.0	- 7.5	17.5	-8.2
Middle Quintile	23.0	19.6	23.9	0.6	19.8	0.2	18.2	- 5.2	15.9	-3.7
4th Quintile	20.1	13.7	23.8	3.7	15.0	1.3	20.9	0.8	13.3	0.4
Highest Quintile	15.1	20.6	24.8	9.7	28.6	8.0	38.5	23.4	41.9	21.3
Deviation from US-Upper two Strata	NA	NA	NA	13.4	NA	9.3	NA	24.2	NA	21.7
Median Income	$5,660	$9,590	$6,873	$1,213	$10,973	$1,383	$8,131	$2,471	$13,183	$3,593
% Change in Median	NA	69.4	NA	NA	59.7	NA	NA	NA	62.1	NA
Index of income concentration	NA	.364	NA	NA	.476	.112	NA	NA	.545	.181

OPERATIONAL DEFINITIONS

Quintiles	1960	1970
Lowest	$2999 and under	$4999 and under
Second	$3000 to 4999	$5000 to 8999
Middle	$5000 to 6999	$9000 to 11,999
Fourth	$7000 to 9999	$12,000 to 14,999
Highest	$10,000 and above	$15,000 and above

$$\% \text{ in Quintile} = \frac{\text{All Families in Quintile}}{\text{Total of All Families}}$$

Deviation from U.S. = % in Community Quintile - % in U.S. Quintile

Deviation from U.S. Upper 2 Strata = [(% in Community Fourth Quintile + % in Community Highest Quintile)] - [(% in U.S. Fourth Quintile + % in U.S. Highest Quintile)]

$$\% \text{ Change in Median} = \frac{(\text{Median, 1970} - \text{Median, 1960})}{\text{Median, 1960}}$$

PROFILE EXAMPLE

TABLE SV-5. OCCUPATION STRATA

	UNITED STATES		MOUNT VERNON				NEW ROCHELLE			
	1960	1970	1960	Deviation From U.S.	1970	Deviation From U.S.	1960	Deviation From U.S.	1970	Deviation From U.S.
Total Employed*	64,639,247	76,553,599	33,073	NA	32,563	NA	31,743	NA	31,850	NA
OCCUPATION										
Lower Blue Collar	40.4	37.9	31.2	-9.2	37.0	-0.9	27.2	-12.8	26.3	-11.6
Upper Blue Collar	13.5	13.9	11.3	-2.2	11.5	-2.4	8.4	-5.1	9.0	-4.9
Lower White Collar	21.6	25.1	25.8	4.2	30.0	4.9	24.4	2.8	30.4	5.3
Upper White Collar	19.6	23.2	22.2	2.6	21.5	-1.7	31.2	11.6	34.4	11.2
Not Reported**	4.9	NA	9.6	4.7	NA	NA	8.8	3.9	NA	NA
Deviation From U.S. Upper Two Strata	NA	NA	NA	6.8	NA	3.2	NA	14.4	NA	16.5
% White Collar	41.2	48.3	48.0	6.8	51.5	3.2	55.6	14.4	64.8	16.5
% Change in White Collar	NA	6.1	NA		3.5		NA		9.2	

*Occupations were reported for those 14 years and older in 1960; in 1970 occupations were reported for those 16 years and older.
**In 1970 "occupations not reported" were allocated to occupational groups

OPERATIONAL DEFINITIONS

Lower Blue Collar = Operatives (all), Laborers, Farm Workers, Service Workers Private Household Workers

Upper Blue Collar = Craftsmen, Foremen and Kindred Workers

Lower White Collar = Salesworkers and Clerical and Kindred Workers

Upper White Collar = Professional, Technical and Kindred; Managers and Administrators, except Farm

% in Strata = $\dfrac{\text{All Persons in Strata}}{\text{Total Employed}}$

Deviation from U.S. = % in Community Quartile - % in U.S. Quartile

Deviation from U.S. Upper 2 Strata = (% in Community Lower White Collar + % in Community Upper White Collar) - (% in U.S. Lower White Collar + % in U.S. Upper White Collar)

% White Collar = $\dfrac{\text{Lower White Collar + Upper White Collar}}{\text{Total Employed}}$

% Change in White Collar = $\dfrac{\text{(% White Collar, 1970 - % White Collar, 1960)}}{\text{% White Collar, 1960}}$

PROFILE EXAMPLE

TABLE SV-6. EDUCATION STRATA AND MEDIANS

	UNITED STATES		MOUNT VERNON				NEW ROCHELLE			
	1960	1970	1960	Deviation From U.S.	1970	Deviation From U.S.	1960	Deviation From U.S.	1970	Deviation From U.S.
Persons 25 years old and over	99,438,084	109,899,359	48,396	-	44,996	-	47,126	-	45,692	-
EDUCATION (%)										
Less than 5th grade	8.4	5.5	6.7	-1.7	5.8	0.3	5.4	-3.0	4.2	-1.3
5th thru 8th grade	31.4	22.8	26.9	-5.5	23.7	0.9	21.2	-10.2	17.0	-5.8
Some Highschool	19.2	19.4	21.1	-1.9	19.8	0.4	17.3	-1.9	15.2	-4.2
Highschool Graduate	24.6	31.1	26.3	1.7	32.3	1.2	26.4	1.8	31.2	0.1
Some College or more	16.5	21.3	19.0	2.5	18.5	-2.8	29.7	13.2	32.4	11.1
Deviation from U.S. Upper 2 Strata	NA	NA	NA	4.2	NA	-1.6	NA	15.0	NA	11.2
Median Years Completed	10.6	12.1	11.3	0.7	12.0	-0.1	12.2	1.6	12.4	0.3
% Change in Median Years Completed	NA	14.2	NA		6.2	NA	NA		1.6	NA

OPERATIONAL DEFINITIONS

Less than 5th grade = No School Years + 1 to 4 Years Elementary School
5th thru 8th Grade = 5 to 7 Years + 8 Years
Some High School = 1 to 3 Years
High School Graduate = 4 Years High School
Some College or More = 1 to 3 Years College + 4 Years or More

$$\% \text{ in Strata} = \frac{\text{All Persons in Strata}}{\text{All Persons 25 Years and Older}}$$

Deviation from U.S. = % in Community Stratum - % in U.S. Stratum

Deviation from U.S. Upper 2 Strata = (% in Community High School Graduates = % Some College or More) - (% in U.S. High School Graduates + % Some College or More)

$$\% \text{ Change in Median Years Completed} = \frac{(\text{Median, 1970} - \text{Median, 1960})}{\text{Median, 1960}}$$

TABLE SV-7. STATUS AND CHANGE CONSISTENCY OF STRATIFICATION PROFILES RELATIVE TO NATION

	Income	Occupation	Education
MOUNT VERNON			
Status, 1970	Higher	Higher	Lower
Change, 1960 to 1970	Less	Less	Less
NEW ROCHELLE			
Status, 1970	Higher	Higher	Higher
Change, 1960 to 1970	Less	More	Less

PROFILE EXAMPLE

FIGURE SV-3. INCOME, OCCUPATION, AND EDUCATION PROFILES, 1970

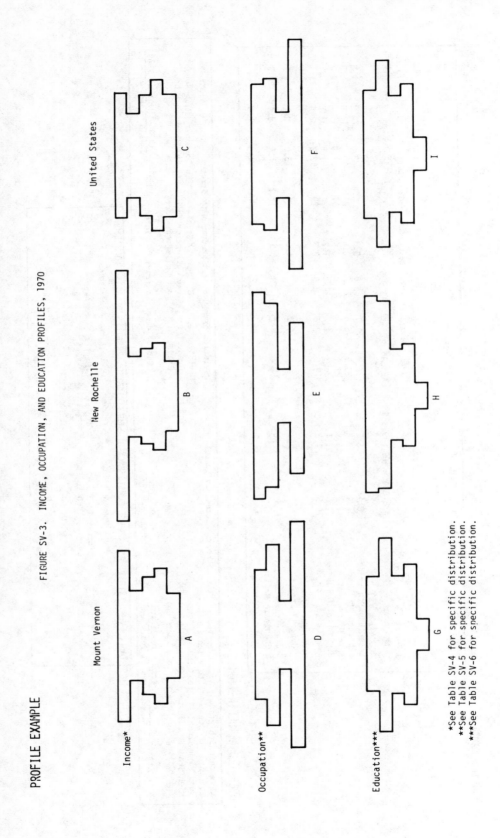

*See Table SV-4 for specific distribution.
**See Table SV-5 for specific distribution.
***See Table SV-6 for specific distribution.

CLASSIFICATION INDICATORS

	United States	Mount Vernon	New Rochelle
Deviation from U.S. **Upper Two Strata, 1970**			
Income	NA	9.3	21.7
Education	NA	-1.6	11.2
Occupation	NA	3.2	16.5
(See Tables SV-4, SV-6, SV-7)			
% Change, 1960 to 1970			
Median Income	69.4	59.6	62.1
Median Years of Education	14.2	6.2	1.6
Percentage of White-Collar Workers	6.1	3.5	9.2
(See Tables SV-4, SV-6, SV-7)			

FINDINGS AND SUGGESTED IMPLICATIONS

Mount Vernon in 1970 was a *slipping higher status* community in income and occupation and *declining lower status* in education. Its higher status was inconsistent in that its educational attainment was less than the nation's in the upper two strata while income and occupation were higher (see Table SV-7). Its SES indicators increased less than the nation's and thus it was consistently slipping. Although Mount Vernon's median income in 1970 was $10,973 or nearly $1,400 more than the nation's, its increase in median income from 1960 of 59.6 percent was less than the nation's increase, 69.4 percent (see Table SV-4). Similarly its percentage of white-collar workers, 51.5 percent, was greater than the nation's 48.3 percent, but Mount Vernon's increase in white-collar workers of 3.5 percent was less than the national increase, 7.1 percent (see Table SV-6). Median school years completed in 1970 was lower for Mount Vernon (12.0) than for the nation (12.1) and its change was less, .7 years compared to 1.5 years. An examination of the strata over time indicates that Mount Vernon's slipping status came about in part by its relative increase in the lower blue-collar categories, its relative increase in the lower two quintiles of income, and its lack of increase in the highest category of education. By 1970, Mount Vernon educationally had become a lower-status place. However, the city still had nearly 10 percent more families in the two upper income strata, its index of income concentration (.476) was

greater than the nation's (.364), and its proportion of white collar workers
was slightly higher than the nation's (see Table SV-5). The selective migration patterns of the 1960s posed a substantial challenge to Mount Vernon's
reputation as a part of the highly preferred suburbs of New York City. It
is not clear whether those who remained in town did not improve their lot as
much as the nation or whether the newcomers were of such low status that they
brought about Mount Vernon's slipping status. In any event the community
consistently lost ground to national socioeconomic status trends.

New Rochelle was a *slipping higher status* community on education and
income and an *increasing higher status* place occupationally. Its consistent
higher status was not paralleled by a consistent change in SES indicators.
Median income and median years of education did not increase as much as in the
nation, but the proportion of white-collar employees increased more so. The
fact that the increase in income and education did not keep pace with the
country was due in part to much higher medians at the beginning of the decade.
It appears that New Rochelle continued to attract higher-status newcomers
similar to the residents who already lived there.

Median income in New Rochelle was $13,183 in 1970, $3,600 more than
the nation's and $2,200 more than Mount Vernon's. However, its increase from
1960 to 1970 was 62.1 percent or 7.3 percent less than the national increase
but 2.5 percent more than Mount Vernon's. New Rochelle's index of income
concentration (.545) was higher than both Mount Vernon's and the nation's.
The proportion of white-collar workers in New Rochelle (64.8 percent) was
substantially greater than the nation's (48.3 percent) and Mount Vernon's
(51.5 percent). Its increase was also greater than the nation's and Mount
Vernon's (9.2 percent compared to 7.1 percent and 3.5 percent). Median school
years completed were 12.4 or .3 years more than the nation and .4 more than
Mount Vernon. However, the gain in New Rochelle's median was .3 years, whereas
the nation gained 1.5 years and Mount Vernon .7 years. New Rochelle's slipping status on income and education can be partially explained by an increase
in the highest categories that was less than the nation's. It should be noted
that New Rochelle began the decade with considerably higher proportions in
the upper categories, making a greater percentage increase difficult to attain.
Its increasing higher status in occupation can be explained by its significant
increase in the upper occupational strata.

When attempting to fit the various SES measures of community stratification to a pattern, we find that Mount Vernon's profiles are similar to
those of the nation on occupation and education (see Figures SV-3D, SV-3G,
SV-3F, SV-3I). They appear as a trapezoid for occupation and approaching a
diamond for education. Mount Vernon's income profile was an inverted trapezoid
differing from the nation's vertical rectangle (see Figures SV-3A, SV-3C).
New Rochelle's profiles, while similar in general shape to Mount Vernon's
on income and education, showed a larger proportion on the top (see Figures
SV-3B, SV-3H). Its occupational profile differed in that it was an inverted
trapezoid with a greater proportion of its employed persons in white-collar
jobs, whereas Mount Vernon's occupational profile was a trapezoid with more

of its employed on the bottom (see Figures SV-3E, SV-3D). The inverted
nature of all New Rochelle's profiles conformed to its consistent higher status. If the trend for New Rochelle continues, all of its profiles will grow
to be more like inverted triangles. The fact that Mount Vernon lost some of
its college educated will tend to change the shape of its educational profile
even more toward the diamond shape, which will be associated with a triangular
occupation profile and, for a period of time, a vertical rectangular income
profile, eventually becoming a triangle. In other words, New Rochelle will
become an increasing higher status community and Mount Vernon will continue
for a time as a slipping higher-status place gradually losing its high status.
This transition in Mount Vernon will more than likely bring about social,
political, and economic stress.

We offer the following speculations to delineate the factors that
generally have contributed to the dynamic quality of community status. That
is, what has happened to each type of community and what then are the likely
consequences of any one type of status for the community itself. Obviously
we are classifying these communities at a moment in time, and the consequences
may very likely cause a change in the future status profiles, depending on
the reactions and directions taken by leaders and citizens.

FIGURE SV-4. SPECULATIONS ON FACTORS AFFECTING
SOCIOECONOMIC STATUS AND THEIR CONSEQUENCES

Contributing Factors   *Possible Consequences*

INCREASING HIGHER STATUS

Increasing opportunities and rewards for   Community determined to maintain its
those with higher education.   character.

In-migration of young well-educated   Keeps out lower-status persons.
professionals.
                                                Exclusive social networks lead to increased
High commitment to excellence in   homogeneity.
public education
                                                Individualism limits scope of government.
Restrictive zoning and land use.
                                                High school tax place.

                                                Consensual leadership evolves.

SLIPPING HIGHER STATUS

Overemphasis on one type of status at   Out-migration of upper-status persons stimu-
the expense of the other two.   lates concern for community image.

Older community residents.   Growing heterogeneity contributes to break-
                                                down of consensus.
In-migration of persons attracted to
aging, less expensive housing.   Encourages economically oriented leaders
                                                to seek new means of increasing tax ratables.
Transformation from essentially residen-
tial to commerical and/or light industry.   Increased taxes in response to increasing
                                                demands for public services.

                                                Seek aggressive leadership.

IMPROVING LOWER STATUS

New economic opportunities tap under-   Community spirit of boosterism.
utilized potential.
                                                Use of market place model—as jobs are en-
In-migration of white-collar persons.   hanced people will improve their lives.

Stimulates growth.   No preferential treatment for disadvantaged.

Economic development program fostered.   Taxes increase.

                                                Competitive leadership patterns evolve.

DECLINING LOWER STATUS

Economic base is down-graded or major   Neither new economic firms nor upper-
firms leave.   status persons locate here.

Higher-status persons leave seeking   Population becomes more dependent on public
better opportunities.   services.

Older persons stay.   Tax base cannot keep pace with increasing
                                                needs for public services.
Lower-status persons attracted to lower-
priced housing.   Quality of life declines.

Increasing heterogeneity.   Growing dissatisfaction, apathy, and
                                                alienation.
City declines in population size and
matures.   Conservative consensual elite leadership
                                                patterns arise.

DISCUSSION

1. What are the stratification classifications of your community?
(a) income, (b) occupation, (c) education.

2. What are the median income, percent white-collar workers, and median years of education completed in your community? How have these factors changed during the decade?

3. To what do you attribute your community's income, occupation, and education stratification patterns? (a) proportion of dependent populations, on social security and/or public assistance; (b) kind of economic opportunities; (c) value placed on education; (d) type of selective in- and out-migration; (e) commitment of local government to provide public services; (f) image of the community—has many amenities, prideful, conflictful, friendly, professional, working-class.

4. Speculate on the ways in which the stratification patterns in your community affect the following major areas of community life: (a) education, (b) housing, (c) crime, (d) health, (e) welfare, (f) economic opportunity, (g) cultural activities, (h) social tensions.

5. Do you think it is important for your community to change its stratification patterns? If so, which ones? In what direction? What social, economic, and/or political strategies might be employed to bring about the desired change?

NOTES

1. Colin Bell and Howard Newby, *Community Studies* (Praeger Publishers, 1973), pp. 186-217.

2. Ralf Dahrendorf, *Class and Class Conflict in Industrial Society* (Stanford University Press, 1959), pp. 477-478.

3. Otis D. Duncan, "Social Stratification and Mobility," in *Indicators of Social Change* edited by Eleanor B. Sheldon and Wilber S. Moore (Russell Sage Foundation, 1966), pp. 683-86.

4. *Ibid.*, p. 687.

5. Terry N. Clark, *Community Structure and Decision-Making* (Chandler Publishing, 1968), pp. 25-32.

6. Nelson W. Polsby, *Community Power and Political Theory* (Yale University Press, 1963), pp. 8-11.

7. W. Floyd Warner, Marchia Mecheran, and Kenneth Eells, *Social Class in America* (Social Research Associates, 1949), pp. 34-44.

8.   Arthur J. Vidich and Joseph Bensman, *Small Town in Mass Society* (Princeton University Press, 1968), pp. 49-78.

9.   For a general discussion of the use of these terms and how social scientists have attempted to measure socioeconomic status see Bell and Newby, pp. 186-217, and Holger R. Stub, editor, *Status Communities in Modern Society* (Dryden Press, Inc., 1972).

10.   U.S. Bureau of the Census, *Methodology and Sources of Socio-economic Status,* Working Papers No. 15, 1963.

11.   Sidney Verba and Norman H. Nie, *Participation in American* (Harper and Row Publishers, 1972), p. 263.

12.   *Ibid.,* p. 298.

13.   *Ibid.,* p. 298.

14.   Clark, pp. 33-39.

COMMUNITY DATA PROFILE   SV-A

(SV-4) FAMILY INCOME STRATA

	YOUR COMMUNITY				COMPARISON CITY			
	1960	Deviation from U.S.	1970	Deviation from U.S.	1960	Deviation from U.S.	1970	Deviation from U.S.
Total Number of Families								
Lowest Quintile								
Second Quintile								
Middle Quintile								
Fourth Quintile								
Highest Quintile								
Deviation from US Upper Two Strata								
Median Income								
% Change in Median								
Index of Income Concentration								

(SV-5) OCCUPATION STRATA

	YOUR COMMUNITY				COMPARISON CITY			
	1960	Deviation from U.S.	1970	Deviation from U.S.	1960	Deviation from U.S.	1970	Deviation from U.S.
Total Employed								
Lower Blue Collar								
Upper Blue Collar								
Lower White Collar								
Upper White Collar								
Occupation Not Reported								
Deviation from US Upper Two Strata								
% White Collar								
% Change in White Collar								

COMMUNITY DATA PROFILE SV-B

(SV-6) EDUCATION STRATA

	YOUR COMMUNITY				COMPARISON CITY			
	1960	Deviation from U.S.	1970	Deviation from U.S.	1960	Deviation from U.S.	1970	Deviation from U.S.
Persons 25 Years and Over								
Less than 5th Grade								
5th thru 8th Grade								
Some High School								
High School Graduate								
Some College or More								
Deviation from US Upper Two Strata								
Median Years Completed								
% Change in Median								

CLASSIFICATION INDICATORS
(See Tables SV-4, 5, 6)

Deviation from US Upper Two Strata, 1970	Your Community	Comparison City
Income		
Education		
Occupation		
% Change in Medians		
Income		
Education		
% Change in White Collar Workers		

(SV-7) STATUS, CHANGE CONSISTENCY, CLASSIFICATION

Your Community	Income	Occupation	Education
Status			
Change			
CLASSIFICATION			
Comparison City			
Status			
Change			
CLASSIFICATION			

Part III
THE POLITICAL DIMENSION

PI. GOVERNMENTAL COMPLEXITY

WITHIN WHAT KIND OF METROPOLITAN GOVERNMENTAL COMPLEXITY IS YOUR COMMUNITY?

CONCEPT

All American cities are a part of the federal system of government with constitutionally prescribed authority. Although most citizens are familiar with the *vertical* relationships between the national and state governments and the local governments, they are less aware of the complex set of *horizontal* relationships between and among a variety of governmental units operating at the local level. These local governments include a number of metropolitan or regional councils, counties, municipalities, towns and townships, villages, special school districts (independent), and other single-function special districts. Each local unit, subject to state laws, has its own jurisdictional responsibility and functions to perform. Each is pursuing its own perceived self-interests, providing public services, and regulating some aspects of behavior of the constituents who reside in its locale. Occasionally these units duplicate functions or comprise a very unclear or complicated maze for the average citizen to traverse in order to determine who is responsible for what governmental action. Freeman has described the federal system in the following manner: "If it ever was a three-layer cake, it has to be, and has become a marble cake, with chocolate strands of governmental functions intertwined through it from top to bottom."[1] Gulick, emphasizing the metropolitan aspects of urban problems, proposes scrapping the "levels" of government in the federal system, as they imply a hierarchy of authority which does not exist or operate as such. He would substitute the concept "extension" for level, as he believes each governmental unit is partially autonomous and that services and controls "are intertwined *all at the same level*--the level where you and I work."[2]

For the most part there is no one government to formulate and administer public policy, collect taxes and allocate public revenues, or to coordinate and plan on a regional basis for the larger sense of community. Fragmented jurisdictions with overlapping and diffused authority are troublesome for practitioners and theorists. This condition led Greer to characterize the metropolis as the "schizoid polity," indicating the dichotomy of urban politics where there is a separation of numbers and wealth between the central city and the mosaic of suburban communities. "Thus, the power of city government is in the hands of the central-city electorate, while great investments affected by government are owned, managed, and manned by suburbanites."[3]

123

He perceives important consequences from this dichotomy as it relates to
resolving the governmental problems of providing public services, deciding
on the distribution of costs and benefits (the problem of equity), and the
long-term control and development of the future shape of the metropolis.
In an effort to provide metropolitan area-wide solutions there have been
three general approaches to governmental reform, with several specific
alternatives. The first is *consolidation* of two or more units of government, or the annexation of the rural-urban fringe into the central city.
The second is *cooperative* agreements between governmental units to deliver
and pay for public services. The third is *coordination* through planning
agencies, regional councils, or associations.[4]

   The disadvantages of traditional governmental arrangements are believed
to be that (1) there is no central authority or decision-making procedure,
(2) they foster undue competition and wasteful duplication, (3) there is
rarely an effective or efficient match of problems relating to need with the
resources to meet them, (4) those communities receiving benefits do not
coincide with taxing jurisdictions for the support of those benefits, and
(5) there are substantial differences in the quantity and quality of public
services provided by various local communities. Consolidation, cooperation,
and coordination have been adopted because they are considered the best way
to reduce waste and undue competition, to increase efficiency and effectiveness, and ultimately to fit organization capacity to expanding urban problems.
However, Bish and Ostrom suggest that one ought to look at "fragmentation of
authority and overlapping jurisdictions as creating opportunities to exploit
diverse economies of scale."[5] Although they recognize that the "spillover
effects" may generate competitive rivalries detrimental to any one local
community, they believe these can be resolved through cooperative arrangements
between overlapping governments. In fact, they believe, "a system of government composed of many different units will be more responsive to the interests
of citizens than a single government for any one urban region."[6] They cite
studies that have found little difference or no consistent relationships
between per capita expenditures and the number of governmental units in a
metropolitan area.[7] Hawkins, however, found that for some services "as fragmentation increases, spending decreases."[8]

   The combination of county and municipal governments and special districts can be seen as the *local* part of the American federal or vertical
system. Within the metropolis, however, these local units of government can
more appropriately be seen as horizontally related. Both the vertical and
horizontal relationships add to the decisional complexity of governance for
citizens and public officials. That is, if there are many units of local
government within a metropolitan area, they not only increase the fragmentation
of public authority, that is, if there are few or no coordinating mechanisms,
but also add to the complexity for citizens in their singling out which governmental unit is responsible for what service. For example, the citizens of
Fridley, Minnesota (pop. 15,173), are expected to exercise an informed control through the electoral franchise over eleven separate units of government
for whose support they are taxes: (1) city, (2) school, (3) sanitary sewers,
(4) sanctuary, (5) hospital, (6) soil conservation, (7) county, (8) airports,
(9) mosquito control, (10) state, and (11) United States.

In 1972 there were 243 SMSAs in the country. They cover 11.6 percent of the land area, and 70.5 percent of the population reside in them (see Table PI-1). Yet most of the 80,000 governmental units are outside the SMSAs, with only 29.5 percent of the country's municipalities located in SMSAs. The total governmental units include 18,517 municipalities, 16,991 townships, 15,781 independent school districts (there are 1,457 dependent city and township school districts), 3,044 counties and 23,885 special districts. There has been a significant reduction in the number of governments during the past decade, from 91,186 units in 1962. The Committee for Economic Development has recommended an even more drastic reduction to about 20,000 governmental units.[9]

TABLE PI-I

LOCAL GOVERNMENTS IN AND OUTSIDE THE STANDARD
METROPOLITAN STATISTICAL AREAS--1972

	Total	Inside SMSA	Outside SMSA
Population	203,235,298	143,268,853	59,966,445
Land Area	3,537,114	410,214	3,126,900
Local Governments			
All types	78,218	22,185	56,033
Counties	3,044	444	2,600
Municipalities	18,517	5,467	13,050
Townships	16,991	3,462	13,529
School districts	15,781	4,758	11,023
Special districts	23,885	8,054	15,831

One example of extensive consolidation has been in schools where the number of units has been reduced greatly. In 1932 there were 127,000 school districts; the number was reduced to 17,238 by 1972. School consolidation took place as professional educators searched for greater efficiency in the use of school finance and sought to bring more comprehensive educational programs to sparsely settled areas. In addition, educators have shown a preference for separating their speciality away from other functions of local government. To accomplish this objective they have formulated the fiscally independent school district with its own taxing authority and elected school board.

For public officials who perceive and wish to solve regional problems it is difficult to gain the cooperation and manage the coordination of public programs in this highly fragmented situation. Metropolitan councils and planning agencies have been created to facilitate a concerted approach to solve public problems. While some citizens, often unaware of the regional aspects of their community, prefer the small local units wherein they enjoy a close proximity to their own elected officials, those more active in solving the regional aspects of community problems find that magni-complexity makes it difficult to know which set of public officials is responsible for what. Civic leaders have created regional associations to develop a sense of public awareness to the metropolitan needs and resources.[10] Miller, in studying the development of civic activity and governmental growth in the megalopolis from Boston on the north to Washington, D.C. on the south, believes there is a widening community consciousness from localism to regionalism.

"Problems of urban civilization do not respect the traditional boundaries established for rural life. The result is that the efforts of government to plan and control are often blocked not only by the inadequate power of the city but also by jurisdictional battles between city, suburbs, and state. Nonetheless, the spread of civic participation and the innovation of new agencies are productive of bursts of civic activity."[11]

Although there have been few consolidations of governmental units in metropolitan areas, Rosenbaum and Kammerer have formulated a theory that encompasses three phases to explain successful attempts.[12] The first is a crisis climate or rapid changes with inappropriate governmental responses due to intransigence, conservatism, or impotence. The second is a power deflation with a growing lack of confidence in governmental personnel, authority, or resources, sometimes stimulated by the mass media's exposure. The third is the accelerator, which becomes the final critical event which is used to generate public support for change. ACIR suggests that such events include: (1) a major scandal involving public officials, (2) a major emergency demonstrating the inadequacy of existing organizations, (3) major criticism of local government by prestigious sources outside the community, and (4) a loss of important and symbolic leaders of the established regime.[13] ACIR has listed a number of factors which they believe influenced the electoral results on metropolitan reform proposals. Favorable factors are:[14]

1. A sympathetic and cooperative attitude on the part of state legislators from the area.

2. The use of local knowledgeable individuals as staff to conduct background research and to develop recommendations.

3. The conduct of extensive hearings by the responsible plan-preparing group.

4. Careful concern, in the design of the reorganization proposal for problems involving representation of various districts and population elements.

Unfavorable factors are:

1. Absence of a critical situation to be remedied—or of widespread popular recognition of such a situation.

2. Vagueness of specification as to some important aspects or implications of the reorganization proposal.

3. Active or covert opposition by some leading political figures in the area.

4. Discontinuity or lack of vigor in promotion of the reorganization proposal.

5. Popular suspicion of the substantial unanimity expressed for the proposal by metropolitan mass media (newspapers, TV, radio).

6. Inability of the proponents to allay popular fear of the effects of the proposed reorganization upon local taxes.

7. Failure by the plan proponents to communicate broadly, in a manner to reach relatively unsophisticated voters as well as others.

8. Failure by the proponents to anticipate and prepare for late-stage opposition efforts in the referendum campaign.

Although there has been little systematic evaluation of the impact of reducing governmental complexity, Erie, Kirlin, and Rabinovitz conclude propositions on what has been accomplished:

1. The increasing impact of professionals upon policy making has been a nearly universal effect of metropolitan reform.

2. In general, few scale economies have been associated with reform, except for the metropolitan special district.

3. In the short run, the access of minorities is guaranteed, but may in the long run be diluted.

4. The roles and norms of official decision makers do not guarantee any substantive conception of the areawide public interest. All that is guaranteed is a more minimal, procedural definition governing public policy making.

5. Performance levels tend to rise, but so do the fiscal burdens accompanying increased expenditures.

6. The functional emphasis upon tangible goods, rather than upon amelioration of social problems, remains unchanged.

7. There is no immediate, short-term impact upon the distribution of power and wealth.

8. By and large, restructuring is associated with reduced citizen participation in the local electoral process.

9. The character of citizen's understanding of and attitudes
toward the local and metropolitan political process remains largely
unchanged, being more a function of life style and experiences.[15]

TYPOLOGY

We offer the following typology on governmental complexity, to place
a community in its governmental context (see Figure PI-1). One dimension
is the measure of the number of persons per governmental unit in the SMSA.[16]
The other is the number of square miles of land per governmental unit. Both
are related to the metropolitan average found in the nation. In a *centralized*
context, both population and land per local government are above the national
average. That is, there are fewer governmental units in the area, allowing
for more centralization of authority. This kind of complexity is mainly found
in metropolitan areas that have consolidated city and county governments and
those which have annexed much of the suburbs. Those who advocate super-
agencies or administrative decentralization are generally in centralized
settings. Although they do not actually change the number of governmental
units, they attempt, each for a specific rationale, to alter the effects of
the centralized settings. As fewer governments deliver public services, it
is easier for citizens to know and attempt to influence their public officials.
In an *areal (land) complexity* context, the population is above and the amount
of land is below the national average. In this setting one usually finds large
cities and their suburbs, especially those in the highly urbanized SMSAs
with a wide proliferation of special districts to carry out specific public
functions.

FIGURE PI-1. TYPOLOGY OF GOVERNMENTAL COMPLEXITY IN THE METROPOLIS
(Relative to the Metropolitan Average)

POPULATION PER LOCAL GOVERNMENTAL UNIT

		Above	*Below*
		Centralized	Population Complexity
SQUARE MILES PER LOCAL GOVERNMENTAL UNIT	*Above*		
	Below		
		Areal (land) Complexity	Magni- Complexity

A *population complexity* setting exists where there is a below average
number of people but an above average amount of land per government. This
setting will be primarily found in the large geographic SMSAs that have smaller populations. Here the public official may experience fewer jurisdictional

disputes because there are fewer competing governmental units over a large area and fewer people with whom to contend. If in a very sparsely settled area there are fewer governmental units, citizens should know more easily which set of government officials are responsible for what service. However, if there are many governmental units for the few people, this may increase complexity for the citizenry.

The *magni-complexity* setting is found in the moderate-sized urbanized areas where there is a below-average population and a below average amount of land per governmental unit. That is, each governmental unit in these metropolitan areas competes with other units over relatively fewer people and less land area. Those who advocate community control as well as those who promote special districts would increase the magni-complexity of an SMSA.

SOURCES AND CAVEATS

The number of governmental units, the population, and the land area can be found in the U.S. Bureau of the Census, *Census of Governments, 1972, Vol. 5: Local Governments in Metropolitan Areas*. This exercise should be used only for those communities located within an SMSA.

PROFILE EXAMPLE

TABLE PI-2. LOCAL GOVERNMENT UNITS IN THE NEW YORK SMSA AND IN WESTCHESTER COUNTY

	SMSA		County		United States	
	1962	1972	1962	1972	1962	1972
Population	10,694,633	11,571,883	808,891	894,406	179,325,671	203,210,158
Square Mile	2,149	2,136	435	443	3,548,974	3,537,114
Total Governmental Units	555	538	125	121	91,186	78,218
Counties	4	4	1	1	3,043	3,044
Municipalities	132	137	28	28	18,000	18,517
Townships	36	36	18	18	17,142	16,991
School districts	198	185	48	45	34,678	15,781
Special districts	185	176	30	29	18,323	23,885
Fire districts	183	174	30	29		

OPERATIONAL DEFINITIONS

$$\text{Population per Government} = \frac{\text{Total Population}}{\text{Number Units of Government}}$$

$$\text{Land Area per Government} = \frac{\text{Land Area}}{\text{Number Units of Government}}$$

CLASSIFICATION INDICATORS

	New York[a] SMSA	United[b] States
Population per Local Governmental Unit	21,516	6,458
Square Miles per Local Governmental Unit	4.0	18.5

[a]See Table PI-2, [b]See Table PI-1

FINDINGS AND SUGGESTED IMPLICATIONS

Mount Vernon and New Rochelle, both in the same SMSA, are located in an *areal complexity* setting. In this highly urbanized area of the country there are significantly more persons (three to one) and less land (one-fourth) per governmental unit than in the metropolitan areas of the nation (see Table PI-2 and PI-1). The density of the New York SMSA results in many people being served by a few governmental units which have legal jurisdiction over a densely populated small land area. Both public officials and citizens have organized a number of metropolitan-wide agencies, councils, and associations to stimulate awareness and to cope with the governmental arrangements.

Mount Vernonites are mainly concerned with the three units of local government that have their own taxing power: the municipality, the school district, and the county. They elect representatives to all three. While the county officials participate in the Metropolitan Regional Council, municipal and school officials have been reluctant to become involved in regional programs as they tend to reflect their constituents' parochial interests in trying to remain autonomous or uninvolved in the metropolitan problems of the area. Of course, when specific local problems with regional implications develop, local officials appear before the metropolitan agencies to influence public policy that they believe is detrimental to their community.

Different types of governmental complexity present different concerns for public officials and citizens. We offer the following speculations on what some of these concerns might be.

FIGURE PI-2. SPECULATIONS ON CONCERNS OF PUBLIC OFFICIALS
AND CITIZENS IN DIFFERENT GOVERNMENTAL CONTEXTS

Public Officials	*Citizens*
CENTRALIZED	
More integration of authority	Able to hold a few public officials responsible
Diminishing returns as costs of public services increase	Remoteness of government
POPULATION COMPLEXITY	
Less competition from other local governments	More direct influence over public officials
Less efficient delivery of public services	More equitable distribution of public services
MAGNI-COMPLEXITY	
More autonomy	Persons with particular interests can apply selective pressure
More difficult to coordinate fragmented authority	Difficult to hold anyone accountable and apply pressure on area-wide problems
AREAL (LAND) COMPLEXITY	
Limited responsibility	Proximity to smaller units of government
More competition for resources and difficult to engage in cooperative actions	Difficult to protect local community against specialized government authorities

DISCUSSION

1. What is the governmental complexity classification of your community's SMSA?

2. To what do you attribute this complexity? (a) consolidation or annexation, (b) the establishment of special function districts, (c) the density of population, (d) the large land area covered?

3. Speculate on the effects of your type of governmental complexity on the following major areas of public life: (a) housing, (b) education, (c) health, (d) welfare, (e) economic opportunity, (f) cultural activities, (g) social tensions.

4. Do you think it important to change the governmental overlay of your community? If so, in what direction? What social, political and/or economic strategies could be employed to bring about the desired change?

NOTES

1. Orville L. Freeman, *The Mazes of Modern Government* (Center for the Study of Democratic Institutions, March, 1964), p. 8.

2. Luther Gulick, *The Metropolitan Problem and American Ideas* (Alfred A. Knopf, 1962), p. 30.

3. Scott Greer, *Governing the Metropolis* (John Wiley & Sons), p. 108.

4. For a further discussion on the differences, see Bert E. Swanson, *The Concern for Community in Urban America* (Odyssey Press, 1970), pp. 80-93.

5. Robert L. Bish and Vincent Ostrom, *Understanding Urban Government* (American Enterprise Institute for Public Policy Research, 1973), p. 72.

6. *Ibid.*, p. 73.

7. R. W. Bahl, *Metropolitan City Expenditures* (University of Kentucky Press, 1969), pp. 62-68.

8. Brett W. Hawkins, *Politics and Urban Policies* (Bobbs-Merrill, 1971), p. 94.

9. See recommendations of the Committee for Economic Development, *Reshaping Government in Metropolitan Areas,* 1970.

10. See for example, William A. Caldwell, *How To Save Urban America* (New American Library, 1973).

11. Delbert C. Miller, *Leadership and Power in the Bos-Wash Megalopolis* (John Wiley & Sons, 1975), p. 341.

12. Walter A. Rosenbaum and Gladys M. Kammerer, *Against Long Odds* (Sage Publishers, 1974), pp. 18-29.

13. See U.S. Advisory Commission on Intergovernmental Relations, *Factors Affecting Voter Reactions to Governmental Reorganizations in Metropolitan Areas* (Government Printing Office, 1965).

14. *Ibid.*, p. 16-23.

15. Steven P. Erie, John J. Kirlin, and Francine E. Rubinovitz, "Can Something Be Done? Propositions on the Performance of Metropolitan Institutions," in *Reform of Metropolitan Governments* edited by Lowdon Wingo (Resources for the Future, 1972), pp. 36-37.

16. Some have simply counted the number of governmental units in a county and/or related the number of public employees to the number of governmental units. See Byron E. Munson, *Changing Community Dimensions* (College of Administrative Sciences, Ohio State University, 1968), pp. 8 and 13.

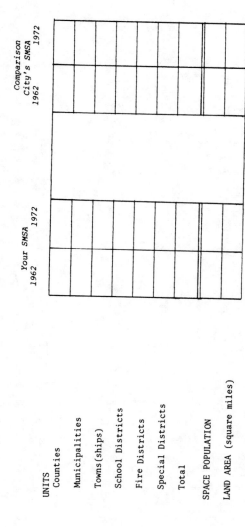

COMMUNITY DATA PROFILE PI-A

(PI-2) LOCAL GOVERNMENTAL UNITS IN THE SMSA

UNITS
  Counties
  Municipalities
  Towns(ships)
  School Districts
  Fire Districts
  Special Districts
  Total
SPACE POPULATION
LAND AREA (square miles)

Your SMSA
1962   1972

*Comparison
City's SMSA*
1962   1972

CLASSIFICATION INDICATORS (PI-2)

Your SMSA

*Comparison
City; SMSA*

Population per local government unit-1972

Square miles per local government unit-1972

CLASSIFICATION

PII. GOVERNMENTAL FORMS, REFORM, AND INFORMAL LEADERSHIP

WHAT GOVERNMENTAL FORM AND REFORMS HAVE YOUR COMMUNITY ADOPTED?

CONCEPT

In American communities the formation of public policy involves both formal government and informal leadership. Most communities use local government as the formal, legal basis to make collective decisions in behalf of all their citizens. Some communities are located in unincorporated areas and thereby may be governed by the county or township government which generally covers a much larger area than the immediate community. There are numerous other associations and community organizations that not only make many informal decisions involving their members but may attempt to persuade local public officials about those matters their members and leaders prefer. Since the broad legal authority of cities has been established by each state and administratively shared locally, there have come into being a number of different forms of city and town government.

While there are few cities with exactly the same form of government, four major types of local government have evolved: (1) mayor-council, (2) council-manager, (3) commission, and (4) town-meeting. (For the distribution of each, see Table PII-1.) (For the organization of the two most prevalent forms see Figure PII-1.)

TABLE PII-1
INCIDENCE OF REFORMISM IN AMERICAN CITIES

	Mayor-Council	Council-Manager	Commission	Town Meeting
Total Cities Reporting				
Number	825	886	111	53
Percent	44.0	47.3	5.9	2.8
Type of Election				
Partisan (%)	61.6	29.4	29.1	74.4
Nonpartisan (%)	34.6	65.6	65.8	20.9
Type of Constituency				
At Large (%)	56.5	75.6	89.2	73.3
Wards/Districts (%)	41.9	23.9	8.8	20.0

Adapted from *Municipal Year Book* (The International City Managers Association, 1972), pp. 16-25. Based on data from 1,882 cities.

FIGURE PII-1

TWO MAJOR MUNICIPAL FORMS OF GOVERNMENT

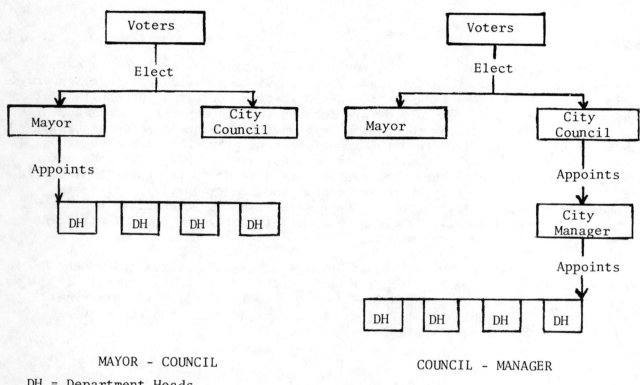

MAYOR - COUNCIL

COUNCIL - MANAGER

DH = Department Heads

    The mayor-council form follows most closely the tradition set in na-
tional government for the separation of powers between the executive (mayor)
and the legislative (city council) branches, a preference designed by the
founding fathers. While about half of the nation's cities use this form,
there is a tendency for some, the smaller cities of 5,000 to 10,000 people,
to use the "weak-mayor" type, while the large cities use the "strong-mayor"
type. The former, a product of Jacksonian democracy reflecting skepticism of
politicians and the fear of giving too much power to a single executive,
provides for the selection of department heads and the direct responsibility
for implementing policies to boards and commissions who, in turn, are chosen
sometimes by election or by the mayor with the consent of the city council.
Adrian and Press articulate the common criticism of the weak-mayor plan as
"clumsy, uncoordinated, and [having] for a long time, been declining in use
for all but the smallest cities."[1] The strong-mayor form provides for

administrative control under the mayor who has the authority to hire and fire department heads, to engage in the preparation and control of the budget for effective management in the delivery of public services, especially in the big systems, and permits the mayor to veto council decisions. This form leads citizens to expect the mayor to take charge and provide the necessary leadership.

Both the council-manager and the commission forms are part of the reform movements designed to bring about more efficient and effective local government by eliminating parties and politics from intruding into day-to-day operations. A city manager is appointed by and serves at the pleasure of the city council. The manager, in turn, hires and fires department heads, prepares the budget for council approval, and makes policy recommendations to the council, which is ultimately responsible to the public. The mayor essentially performs ceremonial functions but also presides over the city council meetings and votes in case of a tie. The council-manager form, which does not provide for the separation of powers, has been praised as bringing about professional management practices to local, often inefficient and sometimes corrupt, government. It has, however, been criticized for making public policy through a series of engineering, cost-benefit decisions that ignore human factors as well as overemphasizing the elusive distinction between politics and administration. The commission form provides a dual role for elected commissioners, who serve individually as the head of administrative departments while they serve collectively as the council or board on policy matters. It has lost favor because responsibility is not definitely fixed among the "amateurs" in the administration, because it is too small a board to provide representative points of view of the constituents, and because it lacks top-policy leadership.

Considerable attention by social scientists has been given to the study of community leadership. Heated debate has developed over the methodology used and the types of leadership patterns found in American communities. Three approaches have been used to determine community influence by identifying (1) those who control or exercise influence by virtue of their formal *position* in community institutions, (2) those who have a *reputation* for power and dominance in community affairs, and (3) those who *decide* by actually exercising their influence on specific policies and issues. Any one method, briefly described here may be sufficient to understand who the leaders are and how they get things done.

The positional approach identifies those who are elected and appointed to be leaders in community institutions and organizations.[2] It assumes that persons who hold formal positions can and do use the authority of their office to determine what is done in their own organizations as well as to affect community affairs. Such formal positions include those in local governmental agencies such as town councils and other special authorities. Other formal positions include owners and managers of local economic firms, the heads of voluntary community organizations such as volunteer fire associations, political parties, veteran groups, luncheon, garden, historical, and leisure time clubs, and leaders in local churches and fraternal organizations. An

inventory of those who hold such positions in town can easily be secured
first by obtaining a list of public, private, and voluntary organizations
and then by compiling a list of the officers or members of the board of
directors, trustees, and so on, of those organizations. If from the list
it emerges that some people hold two or more positions or hold overlapping
positions in two or more organizations, it is likely that an elite pattern
exists because, in actuality, only a few individuals control few key positions.
Conversely, if it is rare that one person holds two or more positions, then
it is more likely that a diffused or pluralistic pattern exists. Thus, if
the mayor is the head of the Chamber of Commerce and also the leading merchant in town, he may be the key leader of an elite system. However, if these
positions are held by three different persons, there would likely be more
competition or differences of opinion on selected policies resulting in a
pluralistic system. But, should different leaders be in essential agreement on
community issues, then the leadership pattern would be consensual elite.

The reputational approach first identifies a group of "knowledgeable"
persons who are most likely to know what is going on and who is influencing
community affairs.[3] These persons, often referred to by social scientists
as "key informants," may be the local newspaper publisher or editor, the
mayor or city manager, a banker, a realtor, an owner or manager of a key
economic firm, or some known critic of what is going on. Of these persons,
the questions generally asked are: (1) Who do you regard as the most influential persons in town? (2) If a project were before the community that required a decision by a group of leaders (leaders that nearly everyone would
accept) which people would you choose, regardless of whether you know them
or agree with them or not? or (3) Who would you go to for advice to get approval of a specific proposal and to see that it is implemented? The answers
to these questions should provide a list of reputed community leaders. Then,
they, in turn, should be interviewed for their perception of community problems and solutions as well as their sense of who else is involved. One could,
of course, stop with the half dozen or so interviews with knowledgeables.
In any case, those leaders receiving the most nominations are considered
the most influential. If there are only a few (2 or 3) persons with many
nominations, the leadership is more likely to be an elite; the more evenly
distributed the nominations, the more pluralistic the system is likely to
be. If these few influentials belong to the same organizations and clubs
and seem to agree on most community problems and programs, they may comprise
a consensual elite. The pluralistic system, on the other hand, should demonstrate more differences and even competition among the leaders.

The decisional approach is intended to correct the assumption that
a person who holds an important position, or who is perceived by others to
be influential, is *in fact* powerful and does control, dominate, or influence
what happens in the community. The decisional approach emphasizes instead
who does what on a specific community decision or issue.[4] One may begin by
identifying several recent decisions and identify who—individuals, groups,
or organizations—initiated the issues, what different set of solutions were
proposed, who supported or opposed them, what the bargaining process involved,
and who won or lost or what compromise was developed. One might conclude
that if there are just a few key persons initiating issues and establishing

proposals that prevail, the leadership is elite. But if more persons compete and require compromises, then the leadership pattern is pluralistic.

While most leadership studies of small towns have found the elite patterns of a few persons dominating community affairs, a number of studies using the decisional approach have found the pluralistic patterns of many different leaders competing against each other to determine who gets their way. This divergence among those who study community power has led to major quarrels among social scientists over their methods of study, their concepts of power, their identification process of community leaders, the places where decisions are made, and what kinds of community policies social scientists study. Perhaps no one approach should be relied on exclusively but rather one should be used to check out the results of the other.

Whichever method is used to determine community leaders, it is important to determine their social characteristics and their role in the community. The former includes social background, ethnicity, and political party membership. The latter pertains to whether they are generally influential and their specialized areas of influence.

Two major, quite opposite, patterns have been discerned by community analysts. One is most often referred to as *elite*, while the other is *pluralistic*. Other labels associated with the former are pyramidal, monolithic, concentrated, and so on. The latter is sometimes referred to as competitive, polylithic, diffused, and the like. Hunter discovered an elite pattern in Atlanta, Georgia while Dahl described New Haven, Connecticut as pluralistic. On the basis of his New Haven study Dahl formulated five leadership patterns.[5] The first is the "covert integration of economic notables" that corresponds with Hunter's findings in Atlanta. The second is an "executive-centered grand coalition of coalitions" where public officials coordinate the skills and resources of private individuals. The third is a "coalition of chieftans" where integration is a matter of negotiations among like-minded leaders who hold specialized influence by issue areas. The fourth is "independent sovereignties with spheres of influence" over a specific issue area and each leader goes about his tasks without much interaction with others. Where policies conflict, the fifth pattern comes into play, that of "rival sovereignties fighting it out." This type of leadership pattern generally involves appeals to the populace for support.

Two other influence patterns focus on the entire population rather than on leadership alone. Agger, Goldrich, and Swanson developed a fourfold classification of power based on the distribution of political power among citizens—broad or narrow—and the political leadership ideology—convergent or divergent. Their four types are: (1) consensual mass, (2) consensual elite, (3) competitive mass, and (4) competitive elite.[6] We also developed a fourfold classification of political regimes based on the probability of illegitimate sanctions blocking efforts to shift the scope of government —low and high—and the sense of electoral potency—high and low. The regimes were then classified as: (1) developed democracy, (2) guided democracy, (3) underdeveloped democracy, and (4) oligarchy.[7] Clark relates four community decision making systems: (1) polylithic, (2) monolithic, (3) pluralistic, and (4) mass participation to complex and simple hierarchial and egalitarian systems.[8]

A number of propositions have been formulated on what is associated with pluralistic leadership patterns:[9]

1. The larger the population size.

2. The older the city.

3. The more stagnant and declining the community.

4. The lower the socioeconomic status—education and occupation—of the residents.

5. The lower the management, officials, and proprietors (MOP) ratio.

6. The more socially heterogeneous the population—foreign stock and percentage of children attending private school.

7. The more industrialized the economic base.

8. The greater the degree of absentee owned manufacturing.

9. The stronger the labor unions.

10. The less "reformed"—partisan elections, mayor-council form of government.

11. The weaker the mayor's authority.

12. The less bureaucratized—the ratio of public employees to population.

13. The greater the vote for Democratic presidential candidates.

14. The more competitive electoral participation—options, preferences in general—and between and among leadership factions.

15. The more the leadership emphasizes widespread participation and political equality.

We look to elected officials, especially the mayor and the city council, to assume full responsibility for the conduct of local government. The number of elected officials per 10,000 population varies considerably. Small towns have a higher rate than do big cities. Similarly there is an enormous difference in this rate from high in the Plains states such as North Dakota, 251.2, to those in the East such as Maryland, 5.4 (see Table PII-2).

TABLE PII-2

RANK ORDER OF STATES BY THE NUMBER OF
POPULARLY ELECTED OFFICIALS PER 10,000 POPULATION, 1966

North Dakota	251.2	Indiana	22.9
South Dakota	239.1	Massachusetts	22.0
Vermont	178.9	Utah	22.0
Nebraska	132.4	Texas	21.4
New Hampshire	91.6	New Mexico	21.2
Kansas	81.5	Kentucky	20.6
Iowa	76.5	Mississippi	20.5
Minnesota	73.5	Tennessee	20.3
Wyoming	72.9	Ohio	20.2
Montana	72.4	West Virginia	19.8
Maine	69.7	Nevada	17.0
Idaho	55.5	Delaware	17.0
Arkansas	52.6	Georgia	16.2
Wisconsin	48.9	Rhode Island	14.3
Oregon	39.3	New Jersey	13.7
Oklahoma	38.5	Arizona	13.5
Missouri	38.2	New York	13.4
Connecticut	37.8	Louisiana	13.2
Alaska	35.7	South Carolina	11.9
Illinois	33.9	Alabama	11.5
Colorado	33.9	North Carolina	11.0
Pennsylvania	29.7	California	9.7
Michigan	27.9	Florida	8.5
Washington	26.7	Virginia	8.0
		Maryland	5.4
U.S.A.	26.7	Hawaii	2.6

Source: Census of Governments, *Popularly Elected Officials of State and Local Governments* (Vol. 6, No. 1).

Local officials generally create a number of special boards, commissions, and authorities to formulate policy and to implement day-to-day
program activities. These include planning commissions to review land use
practices, zoning commissions to examine variances, public housing authorities to provide shelter for low-income families, urban renewal agencies to
engage in redevelopment projects, and so on. In education, fiscally dependent school systems have been created that rely on the municipality to pro-
vice the funds and on a board of education, generally appointed by the mayor,
to set policy and to appoint in turn a superintendent of schools to operate
the system.

While concern over the form of government is generally expressed in
reference to policy making, another factor is control over the bureaucracy
or those who carry out the day-to-day activities (see Table PII-4). In
1970 for the nation nearly one-half (44.7 percent) of all local public
employees worked for school districts, one-third (30.9 percent) for municipalities, and one-sixth (17.6 percent) for county governments. In fact,
there are more than five teachers for every policeman employed by local government. Furthermore, during the past decade, school districts increased their
number of employees by 60.1 percent, compared to 50.8 percent for county
governments and 32.8 percent for municipalities.

One key aspect of control over the bureaucracy is the relative proportion of appointed public employees to elected officials. For comparison
purposes we have chosen to show the number of appointed employees engaged
in common municipal functions for every one elected public official. Small
towns will have a smaller ratio indicating a greater control of whatever the
bureaucracy by elected officials. On the other hand, big cities will have
a larger ratio indicating less control by the elected representatives of the
people. As the ratio grows larger there is a tendency to adopt managerial
systems in order to gain better supervision of the large number of public
employees. As the number of these appointed officials at the managerial
level grows and because their tenure is generally of a longer duration than
that of the elected representatives, there is a tendency for the bureaucracy
to become increasingly autonomous. This dynamic raises the questions of
who, in the last analysis, determines the level and quality of public services and how responsive the bureaucracy is in meeting the needs of the
people.

These employees not only involve problems of administrative supervision
and costs to taxpayers but can become a sizable voting bloc in local politics.
The nearly 7.4 million employees of local government have high stakes. As
Lineberry and Sharkansky point out, "they form interest groups that press for
group benefits, particularly wage and salary improvements; and they are themselves decision-makers who share the policies of municipalities, school districts, counties, and other local governments."[10]

Political parties have played a significant role in determining who
is elected to public office in local government. In fact, it is here that
the political machines of the past held sway. Greenstein describes the
machine as follows:[11]

1. There is a disciplined party hierarchy led by a single executive or board of directors.

2. The party exercises effective control over nominations to public office, and through this it controls the public officials
of the municipality.

3. The party leadership quite often is of lower-class social
origins—usually does not hold public office and sometimes does
not even hold formal party office. . . .

4. Rather, a core of loyal party officials and workers, as well
as a core of voters, is maintained by a mixture of material rewards and nonideological psychic rewards. . . .

Reformers attack partisan politics at the local level as leading to
excessive patronage, inefficiency, and corruption. They also believe that
local government has little or nothing to do with state and national politics,
which rely even more heavily on political parties. Much of the debate has
centered on "whether parties encouraged greater voter participation, greater
understanding by the electorate, more issue-oriented elections, more responsiveness by elected officials, greater cooperation among different levels
of government, more stable political systems, or greater efficiency and economy
in government."[12] Reformers have been successful in adopting the nonpartisan
ballot thereby removing the political party labels in almost two-thirds of
the cities over 5,000 population and moving local elections to "off years"
—a time other than when presidential and gubernatorial elections are scheduled. Adrian notes four patterns of nonpartisan elections:[13]

1. *Nominal*—as the political parties retain a dominant role in
nominating the candidates and providing resources in the campaign.

2. *Slates of candidates*—as political parties and other groups
put up slates of candidates who run together and are easily identifiable.

3. *Interest group slates of candidates*—as other groups play
the major role supplanting the political parties.

4. *Free-for-all*—as no political party or groups play an important role. The politics of acquaintance operates where the
candidates are known to the electorate and chosen on that basis.

Lineberry and Sharkansky believe the nonpartisan ballot has increased the
information cost to the voter, the financial cost of elections, and altered
participation to the effect of increasing "the representation of middle-class
interests in urban politics."[14]

Another focus of reformers has been the constituency of city councils.
Multi-member councils, ranging in size from three to fifty, can either be

elected at large (city-wide) or by ward or district. The party machines preferred wards, which were also the basis of their party precinct organizational structure. This allowed them to play a dominant role in the selection of, and campaign for, candidates as well as to receive benefits from their elected officials. Reformers, therefore, not only advocate nonpartisan elections but also at-large constituencies to further break the grip of political parties over local officials. Well over half the cities with more than 5,000 population use at-large constituencies, as do 70 percent of council-manager cities.

Since the turn of the century considerable effort has been made to reform the type of government (form), elections (partisanship), and constituency (geographic). Analysts have concentrated on discovering what social, economic, and political factors are most related to the development of reform and/or retention of traditional (unreformed) cities as well as determining what effect each type has on public policy. Banfield and Wilson have argued that the "middle class ethos" prefers "public regarding" virtues of reform rather than "private regarding" values of the ethnic political machines, seeking the good of the community as a whole rather than particular interests.[15] Wolfinger and Field conclude that "the ethos theory is irrelevant to the South . . . inapplicable to the West . . . fares badly in the Northeast . . . and, inconsistent and minimal in the Midwest."[16] Linebery and Fowler, while finding no marked difference on the level of expenditures between the reformed and the unreformed cities, found the former to have lower voter turnout. Duggar also observed that city-manager cities were slower to engage in urban renewal but that when they did, they demonstrated a slightly greater program achievement.[17]

The translation of social conflicts into public policy and the responsiveness of political systems to social class, racial, and religious cleavages differ markedly with the kind of political structure. Linebery and Fowler found that "Partisan electoral systems, when combined with ward representation, increase the access of two kinds of minority groups: those which are residentially segregated . . . and groups which constitute identifiable voting blocs. . . ."[18] Hawkins, more cautious, suggests that "many factors besides 'environmental conduciveness' in the form of ethnic, religious, class, and economic base differences can and do shape political institutions. These may include total disasters, scandals, and the special goals of elites (as opposed to broad population groupings)."[19]

TYPOLOGY

We offer the following typology, which distinguishes between the adoption of the council-manager from of government, on the one hand, and the introduction of some electoral reform such as nonpartisan election and at-large constituency on the other. A city that has adopted all three is *reformistic*. As Table PII-1 indicates, the vast majority of council-manager cities have also adopted the other reform measures. Such places are more ethnically and religiously homogeneous, moderate in population size, and mostly located in the West and the South. By contrast, the *traditional* community has adopted no electoral reform and continues to use the mayor-council form of government. Such cities are more often located in the Northeast, have a relatively stable heterogeneous population with high proportions of foreign-born, and tend to be manufacturing places. We have also distinguished between those communities that have adopted *professional reforms* (council manager forms) and those that have developed *electoral reform* (nonpartisan elections). A community has adapted electoral reform if it has instituted nonpartisan elections. At-large constituencies are not enough to classify a community as having electoral reform since many small cities and towns elect their officials on this basis. *Professional reform* has been adopted by communities experiencing population growth and mobility of people as well as by those where the economy is based on professional services, retail trade, and finance.

FIGURE PII-2. TYPOLOGY OF GOVERNMENTAL REFORM

	COUNCIL-MANAGER FORM OF GOVERNMENT	
	Yes	*No*
Yes	Reformistic	Electoral Reform
NONPARTISAN ELECTIONS		
No	Professional Reform	Traditional

Those with *professional reform* are mainly located in the West and especially in the South where, as Lineberry and Sharkansky point out, "the ethnic situation favors professional management. Because of sizable black communities in the cities, entrenched whites have regarded the professional manager as a device to isolate local government from the potential black vote."[20] Those communities relying more on *electoral reforms* are generally suburban and smaller places.

SOURCES AND CAVEATS

Data on the form of government, the mayor, the council, and other elected officials can be found for 1,908 cities in Alan Klevit, "City Councils and Their Functions in Local Government" in *The Municipal Year Book, 1972* (International City Management Association), pp. 28-54. Information on cities not included may be found in "Governmental Data for Cities Over 5,000 Population and Council-Manager Places Under 5,000" in *The Municipal Year Book, 1968,* pp. 52-131. If you cannot find your city in these publications, you may find the information at your city hall or at the local public library. Statistics on public employees appear in the U.S. Bureau of the Census, *The Census of Governments,* Vol. 3, *Public Employment,* No. 2, *Compendium of Public Employment,* for the years 1962 and 1972.

PROFILE EXAMPLE

TABLE PII-3   STRUCTURE OF LOCAL GOVERNMENT

	MOUNT VERNON	NEW ROCHELLE
Form of Government	Mayor-Council	Council-Manager
Form of Election	Partisan	Partisan
Mayor		
Selection	People elect	People elect
Term of Office	4 years	4 years
Right to Vote	Never	On all issues
Veto	Ordinances only	None
Council		
Number	5	4
At-Large	5	4
Ward or District	0	0
Overlapping Terms	No	No
Annual Pay	$7,000	$8,000
Fill Vacancy	by Council	by Council
Council Staff	Yes	No
Other Elected Officers	Comptroller 2 city judges	2 city judges
Planning		
Organization	Department	Department/Advisory Committee
Staff		
Professional	Yes	Yes
Size	1	1
Report to	Head of Dept.	Head of Dept.

TABLE PII-4   LOCAL PUBLIC OFFICIALS, GOVERNMENTAL BODIES, AND THEIR SELECTION

	MOUNT VERNON	NEW ROCHELLE
Officials		
Mayor	1 Elected by people	1 Elected by people
Council	5 " " "	4* " " "
Controller	1 " " "	1 Manager appointment
City Judge	2 " " "	2 Elected by people
Clerk	1 Council appointment	- - - -
Councils, Boards, and Commissions		
School Board	9 Elected by people	9 Mayor appointment
Planning Board	7 Mayor appointment	7 " "
Civil Service Comm.	3 " "	3 " "
Tax Assessment/Review	A department	3 " "
Zoning Board	6 " "	6 " "
Recreation Board	A department	7 " "
Human Rights Comm.	15 Mayor appointment	15 " "
Youth Board	14 " "	18 " "
Child Care	None	11 Manager appointment
Housing Authority	5 Mayor appointment	5 " "
Urban Redevelopment	5 Mayor-Council appt.	A department
Heads of Departments		
Law	Mayor appointment	Manager appointment
Public Works	" "	" "
Police	" "	" "
Fire	" "	" "
Health	" "	" "
Personnel	- -	" "
Tax Assessment	" "	" "
Building Department	" "	" "
Civil Defense	" "	" "
Vital Statistics	" "	" "
Veterans Service	" "	" "
Recreation	" "	" "

*Mayor sits on Council

PROFILE EXAMPLE

TABLE PII-5   EMPLOYEES OF LOCAL GOVERNMENTS - 1962-1972

| | MOUNT VERNON | | | | | NEW ROCHELLE | | | | |
| | 1962 | | 1972 | | | 1962 | | 1972 | | |
	#	Rate*	#	Rate*	% Change	#	Rate*	#	Rate*	% Change
Municipal Employees										
Full-time equivalents	755	99.3	854	117.0	17.8	850	110.4	940	125.3	13.5
Common municipal functions	700	92.1	716	98.1	6.5	789	102.5	767	102.3	-0.2
Highways	42	5.5	76	10.4	89.1	74	9.6	57	7.6	-20.8
Police protection	193	25.4	207	28.4	11.8	182	23.6	223	29.7	25.9
Fire protection	119	15.7	140	19.2	22.3	154	20.0	181	24.1	20.5
Sewerage	10	1.3	23	3.2	146.2	25	3.3	25	3.3	0.0
Sanitation	81	10.7	53	7.3	-31.8	129	16.8	120	16.0	-4.8
Park & recreation	41	5.4	56	7.7	31.5	42	5.5	54	7.2	30.9
Library	67	8.8	58	8.0	-9.1	43	5.6	43	5.7	0.0
Financial Adm.	17	2.2	20	2.7	22.7	17	2.2	17	2.3	0.0
General control	44	5.8	48	6.6	13.8	41	5.3	47	6.3	18.9
Water supply	24	3.2	35	4.8	50.0	NA	NA	NA	NA	NA
Other	63	8.3	NA	NA	NA	83	10.8	NA	NA	NA
Variable function	55	7.2	138	18.9	162.5	62	8.1	173	23.1	185.2
Elected officials	7	0.9	7	1.0		5	0.7	5	0.7	0.0
Ratio of appointed employees to elected officials	100		102		2.0	158		153		-3.2
Education										
Full-time equivalents	794	104.5	903	123.7	18.4	981	127.4	NA	NA	NA
Teachers	636	83.7	652	89.3	6.5	684	88.8	569	75.9	-14.4
Students per teacher	19		18		-5.3	18		20		11.1

OPERATIONAL DEFINITIONS

*Rate of Employees per 10,000 Population = $\dfrac{\text{Number of Employees}}{(\text{Total Population} \div 10,000)}$

% Change in Rate = $\dfrac{(1972\ \text{Rate} - 1962\ \text{Rate})}{1962\ \text{Rate}}$

Population per Employee = $\dfrac{\text{Total Population}}{\text{Number of Employees}}$

Students per Teacher = $\dfrac{\text{Total Students}}{\text{Number of Teachers}}$

Ratio of Appointed Employees to Elected Officials = $\dfrac{\text{Appointed Employees}}{\text{Elected Officials}}$

PROFILE EXAMPLE

TABLE PII-6   LEADERSHIP CHARACTERISTICS, 1967

	MOUNT VERNON Number	NEW ROCHELLE Number
1. Leaders interviewed	37	44
2. Leaders identified as generally influential	45	46
General influentials with 8 or more nominations	10	16
Second level leaders with 2 or more nominations	35	30
3. Leaders identified in specific areas		
Education quality	20	19
Parking/traffic	12	17
Mental health	7	9
School budget	20	15
Integrate schools	18	7
Hospital/medical facilities	10	12
Industrial development	18	16
City taxes	5	8
Intergroup relations	14	22
Welfare	16	10
Urban renewal	11	12
Recreation	15	12
Cultural	4	9
Crime and Juvenile delinquency	9	17
4. Proportion of the generally influential leadership considered influential in a number of specific areas		
Number of areas nominated in	%	%
5 or more	6	19
3 to 4	16	27
1 to 2	59	35
none	19	19
5. Mutual choices among the top generally influential	1	12
6. Functional areas of the generally influential		
Business	13	21
Labor	0	0
Education	7	2
Government	48	42
Independent professions	4	7
Religion	11	11
Society	2	0
Social welfare	15	9
7. Party affiliation of the generally influential		
Democratic	35	15
Republican	65	85
8. Racial background of the generally influential		
White	78	91
Black	22	8
9. Religious background of the generally influential		
Protestant	28	32
Catholic	41	36
Jewish	31	32

CLASSIFICATION INDICATORS

	Mount Vernon	New Rochelle
Form of Government[a]	Mayor-Council	Council-Manager
Type of Election[a]	Partisan	Partisan
Type of Constituencies[a] of City Council	At-large	At-large

[a]See Table PII-3.

FINDINGS AND SUGGESTED IMPLICATIONS

Mount Vernon has a *traditional* local political system with a mayor-council form of government and partisan elections. Its at-large constituency for the 5-member city council is more a function of its small geographic size (4 square miles) than a reform measure. The mayor, elected for a 4-year term, does not vote on council matters but can veto ordinances. An elected comptroller participates with the mayor and the president of the city council as the Board of Estimate (see Table PII-3).

New Rochelle is a city with *professional reform* as it has a city-manager and retains partisan elections. The mayor, elected for a 4-year term, votes on all matters before the city council but does not have the authority to veto council action. The city council has 4 members. The city comptroller is appointed by the city manager.

The mayor of New Rochelle appoints the 9-member school board which is fiscally independent and raises its own school revenues. In Mount Vernon the 9-member school board is directly elected by the citizens on a nonpartisan basis. In addition, the mayors of both communities appoint members to the following boards and commissions: Planning, Civil Service, Tax Assessment and Review, Zoning, Recreation, Youth, Poverty, and Human Rights (see Table PII-4). The members of the Housing Authority are appointed by the mayor in Mount Vernon and by the city manager in New Rochelle. The Urban Renewal Agency members are appointed jointly by the city council and the mayor in Mount Vernon while housing and redevelopment is a department under the supervision of the city manager in New Rochelle. Mount Vernon has a strong mayor form of government, in that all department heads are hired and fired by the mayor. In New Rochelle this is the prerogative of the city manager.

In 1972 both cities had a higher rate of municipal public employees than the nation; Mount Vernon had 117 per 10,000 and New Rochelle had 125, compared to 85 for the nation (see Table PII-5). The rate of municipal employees increased during the decade in both communities as it did for teachers. However, Mount Vernon's rate of teachers increased less than that of other public employees, and New Rochelle's rate for teachers actually declined. In 1972, Mount Vernon had 3.1 teachers for every policeman, and New Rochelle's ratio was 2.5:1. These ratios were lower than that of the nation which was more than 5 to 1. Priorities seemed to have shifted considerably in New Rochelle where the ratio in 1962 was 3.8 teachers for every policeman. In Mount Vernon this ratio remained relatively constant. The priorities of the two communities may be reflected in the relative proportions of public employees. Mount Vernon had more teachers, librarians, and highway personnel and New Rochelle had more policemen, firemen, and sanitation workers.

New Rochelle's ratio of appointed employees to elected officials was much greater than Mount Vernon's. This was to be expected because New Rochelle, a professionally reformed community with a city manager, has placed more reliance on managerial supervision whereas Mount Vernon, a traditional community, relies more on supervision by elected officials. The tenure of the city manager exceeds that of the mayors and the average city councilman which tends to provide autonomy for its bureaucracy.

A leadership study was conducted in both communities in 1967 using the reputational technique. It revealed that New Rochelle had a consensual elite leadership pattern whereas Mount Vernon's was pluralistic. In fact, there were 12 mutual selections in New Rochelle to only 1 in Mount Vernon. There were more leaders in Mount Vernon than in New Rochelle in the areas of education and welfare whereas there were more leaders in New Rochelle in the areas of intergroup relations, cultural affairs, and crime and juvenile delinquency. The general leaders in New Rochelle were also leaders in specific areas to a greater degree than in Mount Vernon. In both communities those in government positions—more elected officials in Mount Vernon, more appointed ones in New Rochelle—made up the largest proportion of the identified leaders. In New Rochelle businessmen played a more prominent role than their counterparts in Mount Vernon. The Republicans constituted an overwhelming majority of the leaders in New Rochelle (85 percent). Leadership was nearly evenly divided among the Protestants, Catholics, and Jews in New Rochelle. The Catholics, however, compromised the greatest proportion in Mount Vernon. Blacks in Mount Vernon, comprising approximately one-third of the population, received 12 percent of the leadership nominations.

The form and reform of local government and electoral systems of both communities were set years ago. Mount Vernon had considered a number of modifications to its form of government. These included the commission and city manager forms, the ward election of councilmen, a smaller city council, and even annexation to New York City. Only the reduction in city council size was adopted. We offer the following speculations on some of the factors associated with traditional and reformed governmental systems.

FIGURE PII-3. SPECULATIONS ON THE FACTORS ASSOCIATED
WITH TRADITIONAL AND REFORMED SYSTEMS

Traditional	*Reformed*
Larger cities, stable or declining	Smaller and growing cities
Large proportion of European ethnics	Middle- and upper-strata residents
Separation of powers	Without separation of powers
Patronage appointments	Civic service appointments
Shared responsibility by more elected officials	Few elected officials
Mass participation/grassroots contact	Lower participation
Competitive leadership patterns	Consensual elite leadership patterns
Special-interest groups	Holistic conception of community
Politicized problem approach	Professionalized problem approach
Bargaining/compromise	Rational/technical/planning
Belief in loyalty to party and personalities	Belief in structural reform

DISCUSSION

1. What is the classification of your community's governmental reform?

2. Which public authorities in your community are elected? What functions does your mayor perform? How many members make up your city council? How many public employees work for your local government? Which functions have the higher rates? Have the rates by function changed over time? If so, in what way?

3. To what do you attribute the kind of reform in your community? (a) the form of government, (b) the form of elections, (c) the type of constituency.

4. Speculate on the ways in which the kind of reform in your community affects the following major areas of community life: (a) housing, (b) education, (c) health, (d) welfare, (e) economic opportunity, (f) cultural activities, (g) social tensions.

5. Do you think it is important to change your form of government and/or degree of reform? If so, in what direction? What social, political, and/or economic strategies could be employed to bring about the desired change?

NOTES

1. Charles A. Adrian and Charles Press, *Governing Urban America* (McGraw-Hill Book Co., 1972), p. 212.

2. An example is Robert O. Schulze, "The Bifurcation of Power in a Satellite City," in *Community Political Systems* edited by Morris Janowitz (The Free Press of Glencoe, 1961), pp. 18-80.

3. An early example is Floyd Hunter, *Community Power Structure* (University of North Carolina Press, 1953).

4. For example, see Robert A. Dahl, *Who Governs?* (Yale University Press, 1961).

5. *Ibid.*, pp. 184-220.

6. Robert A. Agger, Daniel Goldrich and Bert E. Swanson, *The Rulers and the Ruled* (Duxberry Press, 1964), pp. 37-41.

7. *Ibid.*, pp. 43-45.

8. Terry N. Clark, *Community Structure and Decision-Making,* (Chandler Publishing Co., 1968), pp. 33-39.

9. Most of these propositions have been drawn from Michael Aiken, "The Distribution of Community Power" in *The Structure of Community Power*

edited by Michael Aiken and Paul E. Mott (Random House, 1970), pp. 487-525; others who have formulated similar propositions include: John Walton, "A Systematic Suvery of Community Power Research" In Aiken and Mott, *Ibid.*, pp. 443-464; C.W. Gilbert, *Community Power Structure* (University of Florida Press, 1972); Clark, pp. 96-126.

10.   Robert L. Lineberry and Ira Sharkansky, *Urban Politics and Public Policy* (Harper & Row, Publishers, 1971), p. 74-75.

11.   Fred I. Greenstein, "The Changing Pattern of Urban Party Politics," *The Annals of the American Academy of Political and Social Science,* 353 (May 1964), p. 3.

12.   Willis D. Hawley, *Nonpartisan Elections and the Case for Party Politics* (John Wiley & Sons, 1973), p. 1.

13.   Adrian and Press, pp. 153-154.

14.   Lineberry and Sharkensky, p. 86.

15.   Edward C. Banfield and James Q. Wilson, *City Politics* (Harvard University Press and M.I.T. Press, 1963), p. 41.

16.   Raymond Wolfinger and John Osgood Field, "Political Ethos and the Structure of City Government," *American Political Science Review,* 60 (June 1965), pp. 325-26.

17.   George S. Duggar, "The Relation of Local Government Structure to Urban Renewal," *Law and Contemporary Problems* (Winter 1961), pp. 57-62.

18.   Robert L. Lineberry and Edmund P. Fowler, "Reformism and Public Policies in American Cities," *American Political Science Review,* 61 (Sept. 1967), p. 812.

19.   Brett W. Hawkins, *Politics and Urban Policies* (Bobbs-Merrill Co.), 1971, p. 59.

20.   Lineberry and Sharkansky, p. 123.

COMMUNITY DATA PROFILE PII-A

(PII-3) STRUCTURE OF LOCAL GOVERNMENT

	Your Community	Comparison City
Form of Government		
Mayor		
Selection		
Term of Office		
Right to Vote		
Veto		
Council		
Number		
At-large		
Ward		
Annual Pay		
Who Fills Vacancy		
Council Staff		
Other Elected Officers		
Planning		
Organization		
Staff		
Professional		
Size		
Reports to		

COMMUNITY DATA PROFILE PII-B

(PII-4) LOCAL PUBLIC OFFICIALS, BODIES, AND THEIR SELECTION

	Method of Selection	
	Your Community	Comparison City
Officials		
Mayor		
Council		
Controller		
City Judge		
Clerk		
Councils, Boards, and Commissions		
School Board		
Planning Board		
Civil Service Commission		
Tax Assessment/Review		
Zoning Board		
Recreation Board		
Human Rights Commision		
Youth Board		
Child Care		
Housing Authority		
Urban Development		
Heads of Departments		
Law		
Public Works		
Police		
Fire		
Health		
Personnel		
Tax Assessment		
Building Department		
Civil Defense		
Vital Statistics		
Veterans Service		
Recreation		

COMMUNITY DATA PROFILE PII-C

(PII-5) EMPLOYEES OF THE LOCAL GOVERNMENT

Municipal Employees	Your Community 1962 #	Rate	1972 #	Rate	% Change	Comparison City 1962 #	Rate	1972 #	Rate	% Change
Full-Time Equivalents										
Common Municipal Functions										
Highways										
Police Protection										
Fire Protection										
Sewerage										
Sanitation										
Parks and Recreation										
Library										
Financial Administration										
General Control										
Water Supply										
Other										
Variable Function										
Elected Officials										
Ratio of Appointed Employees to Elected Officials										
Education										
Full-Time Equivalents										
Teachers										
Students per Teacher										

CLASSIFICATION INDICATORS

	Your Community	Comparison City
Form of Government		
Type of Election		
Type of Constituency		
CLASSIFICATION		

PIII. CITIZEN ELECTORAL PARTICIPATION

HOW MANY CITIZENS PARTICIPATE IN THE ELECTORAL PROCESS
IN YOUR COMMUNITY?

CONCEPT

One of the cardinal principles of American democratic thought is
the belief in pervasive political participation by the people. Participation takes many forms. Milbreath has arranged them in a hierarchy of
political acts from *spectator activities* such as exposing oneself to political stimuli, voting, discussions, and the like through *transitional
activities* such as contacting a public official, making a contribution,
and attending a political rally to *gladiatorial activities* such as campaigning for others, soliciting political funds, and holding public office.[1]
Although Berelson, Lazarsfeld, and McPhee[2] argue that political acts are
interchangeable, Verba and Nie believe "there are many types of activists
engaging in different acts, with different motives, and different consequences."[3] They report the following proportion of persons engaged in
various activities intended to influence governmental decisions:[4]

TABLE PIII-1

VARIOUS FORMS AND DEGREES OF CITIZEN PARTICIPATION

Percent	Activities
72	Vote regularly in Presidential elections
47	Always vote in local elections
32	Active in organization involved in community problems
30	Worked with others to solve community problems
28	Attempted to persuade others to vote as they do
26	Actively worked for party or candidates
20	Contacted a local government official about some issue
19	Attended political meeting or rally
18	Contacted state or national government officials about some issue
14	Formed group or organization to solve community problems
13	Gave money to party or candidates
8	Member of political club or organization

Watson contrasts some of the salient characteristics of the high and low participants as follows:[5]

FIGURE PIII-1

CONTRASTING HIGH AND LOW PARTICIPANTS

Characteristics	High	Low
Age	Middle-aged	Young (under 30)
		Older (over 60)
Sex	Men	Women
Race	Whites	Nonwhites
Class	College Graduates	Grade school only
	Professionals	Unskilled worker
	Affluent	Poor
Residence	Westerners	Southerners
	Suburbanites	Rural dwellers
	Long-time residents	Short-time residents
Party	Republican	Democrat
	Strong partisans	Independents

Campbell and his associates assert that the act of voting involves two decisions.[6] One is to choose between rival parties or candidates. The second is to decide whether to vote at all. Mitchell, discussing the second decision, firmly believes that it is worthwhile voting when one considers that (1) not to vote is itself voting; (2) the influence of a single vote is partially dependent on the size of the constituency; and (3) the consequence of a vote depends on the voter's own evaluation of the action.[7] When it comes to choosing a particular candidate, he suggests the voters assess the candidates on the basis of their (1) choice of issues, (2) positions on the issues, (3) past performances, (4) promises and promise of effectiveness, and (5) personal character.[8]

A number of schemes have been developed to identify various types of participating citizenry. Verba and Nie used survey data to identify six types of participants and their relative proportion in the American population: (1) inactives (22 percent); (2) voting specialists (21 percent); (3) parochial, who make particularized contact on matters that affect their personal lives (4 percent); (4) communalists, who combine willingness to be quite active in community affairs yet stay out of conflictful campaigns (20 percent); (5) campaigners (15 percent); and (6) complete activists (11 percent).[9] Almond perceives a four-level hierarchy with (1) the general public at the base, (2) an attentive public, (3) policy and opinion elites, and (4) the official policy leadership.[10] Rosenau, using a wide variety of data and aware of the difference between electoral behavior and that activity between elections, distinguishes between an attentive and a mobilizeable public. The former "communicate, with some regularity, ideas about public affairs to persons with whom they are closely associated,"[11] while the latter "within a reasonable period after they have been urged to do so by actors seeking to mobilize their support, act in a manner that corresponds with the request to establish first-hand contacts with some aspect of public affairs."[12]

Relying on readily available data such as voter registration and electoral returns, we have an eightfold classification of aggregate constituents: (1) *latent,* the number of persons 21 years or older eligible to vote (this has been reduced to 18 years or older for all elections from 1972 on); (2) *non-enfranchised,* those persons not eligible; (3) *manifest,* the number of persons registered and certified to vote; (4) *apolitical,* those eligible but not registered; (5) *active,* the percentage of the registered who vote;(6) *inactive,* those registered and not voting; (7) *mobilized,* the percentage of those eligible who vote; and (8) *inoperative,* those eligible but not voting (see Table PIII-2). Note that the number of "active" is the same as the number of the "mobilized" in that both groups are voters. The distinction is between the aggregate of which each is a part, that is, the "active" are the voters as a proportion of the "manifest" (registered) whereas the "mobilized" are the voters as a proportion of the "latent" (eligible).

The optimum level of citizen participation is unknown. Some argue that "too much" participation strains severely the effectiveness of the political system as high rates of citizen participation imply the activation of the less-educated, uninformed, and intolerant groups who are hostile towards each other and to democracy itself. Others argue in behalf of higher rates of citizen participation in order to secure adequate representation in policy-making processes. Lineberry and Sharkansky state that "Minimal local participation tends to shift policy-makers' search for information from the mass public to professional bureaucrats. Low participation also reduces the representation of those groups that participate least."[13]

Citizen participation is a function of stimuli, personal factors, social position, community and political setting. The following set of factors has been formulated by Lineberry and Sharkensky to explain *higher* rates of participation in community politics:[14]

1. Mayor-council or commission rather than city-manager forms of government.

2. Partisan rather than nonpartisan forms of election.

3. Ward rather than at-large types of constituencies.

4. Stronger rather than weaker political party systems.

5. Stable rather than unstable communities.

6. Higher intensity of conflict rather than lower.

7. Higher rather than lower social class.

8. Higher rather than lower stakes in policy outputs.

9. Ethnic rather than nonethnic population.

10. Higher rather than lower mobility of population.

Voter turnout for the presidency has declined significantly since the turn of the century from 73 percent in 1900 to 56 percent in 1972. Voter turnout of both *actives* and *mobilized* also varies significantly by level of election. That is, voting in local elections for the mayoralty, for instance, is much lower than for the presidency of the United States. Turnout for off-year congressional elections falls below 50 percent, seldom reaches 30 percent for municipal elections, and 5 to 10 percent for county, school, special districts, and local referenda elections. Banfield and Wilson, while finding some mayoralty elections as high as 50 percent, found the average turnout in large cities to be 15 to 20 percent less than in a presidential election.[15] Verba and Nie found voting turnout to be particularly high in isolated villages, rural areas, large suburbs, and core cities.[16]

Although it would be helpful to have survey research materials on a more comprehensive view of the various forms of participation, we will proceed to make the most of registration and voting decisions. These materials can be obtained through the official canvass of candidate votes for any particular election recorded generally at the Board of Elections in the county courthouse or city hall. An approximate indicator of the number of eligible voters can be obtained from the population census reports by finding the total number of people 18 years old or older (for data prior to 1971 one should use 21 years as the cut-off point in most states). Registration figures are also recorded by election officials of the county and of the school district. To vote one must be a citizen, a resident for varying periods of time up to one year in a community (now being challenged in the courts), and 18 years of age (prior to 1971, 21 years of age was the general rule), and not have been convicted of a felony or greater crime. Those eligible to vote must register at specified times prior to elections. Nimmo and McClesky found that the registration system itself affects voting participation.

> . . . a registration system is discriminatory to
> the extent that it filters out from the popula-
> tion of citizens eligible to vote in every other
> respect, those without the means and/or inclina-
> tion to achieve formal qualifications. It is at
> this point that such factors as age, sex, race-
> ethnicity, and occupation, and probably other social
> factors as well, exert their earliest and perhaps
> most decisive influence on voting participation.[17]

Phillips and Blackman discount the role of voter registration in the decline of turnout; instead, they believe it is more a function of "the growing malaise toward government and the existing political parties."[18] They state, "When the upturn in voting participation comes, political factors will almost certainly be responsible. Electoral reforms will be more corollary than cause."[19]

A concern for those screened out (the *apoliticals*) for whatever reasons, has led some to propose alternative means to increase citizen participation. The federal government has required various methods of securing citizen involvement in program areas such as poverty—by requiring "maximum feasible participation of the poor" through citizen advisory boards for urban reveual, model cities, and so on. In reviewing these developments Mogulof identified the following purposes served:

> (1) decentralizing governmental authority, (2) engineering the consent of the governed, (3) insuring equal protection to individuals and groups through a watchdog citizenry, (4) a form of therapy to cure alienation and other social diseases of our time, (5) employing residents so as to "humanize services," (6) creating cadres of anti-rioters, (7) building a constituency for the program, and (8) redistributing power and resources.[20]

TYPOLOGY

In order to classify the degree of citizen participation in American communities, we offer a typology that is based on the percentages of both the *manifest* (those registered to vote) and the *active* (those registered who actually vote). These indicators have been dichotomized, using the national proportions as the cutting points. For the U.S. as a whole, the *manifest* consitutued 68.2 percent and the *active* constituted 89.3 percent in the 1968 presidential election.

FIGURE PIII-2. TYPOLOGY OF ELECTORAL PARTICIPATION
(Relative to National Average)

		ACTIVE (Percentage Registered Actually Voting)	
		Above	*Below*
MANIFEST (Percentage Eligible Registered)	*Above*	Efficacious	Disenchanted
	Below	Civic Duty of the Select	Apathetic

This typology identifies four types of communities. The first type is the *efficacious* community in which the proportions of both the *manifest* and the *active* citizens is above the national average. The citizens in these communities feel free to register and believe that elections are important and that significant choices are offered.

In the second type, a sizeable proportion of eligible citizens are filtered out through the registration system, which is sufficiently discriminating to discourage some (by age, sex, race, ethnicity, or SES) from registering. Those *active* citizens who do vote represent the *civic duty of the select*. These voters are select not only in that they have met the criteria of registration but also because a higher proportion have a sense of civic duty. This selectivity may be engendered by a socialization to vote whenever there is an opportunity. These people probably believe they are the most capable citizens in the community and therefore have a greater obligation to participate, or they perceive the significance of the electoral issues and they vote to protect their own interests. Communities of this type may serve as ports of entry for foreigners and have an aggressive policy to discourage newcomers and disadvantaged persons from participating in the political process.

The third type is the *apathetic* community with many *inoperatives*, where not only do eligible citizens seem inhibited from registering but even those who are registered participate less than on the national average. Perhaps citizens under these circumstances are apathetic because they are unaware of the opportunity to vote or believe that voting is irrelevant to solving their problems. *Apathetic* communities are generally believed to have large proportions of lower-status persons and to prevail in the South.

The fourth is the *disenchanted* community, where the *manifest* are above the national average but the *actives* are below. Here the registered citizens appear "turned-off" by the election itself. Blank suggests this may be due to (1) lack of issue crystallization, (2) ambiguity of a multiplicity of issues, and (3) little real competition among political parties.[21] These communities may have a large proportion of the aged, who are registered but who choose not to vote.

SOURCES AND CAVEATS

For an estimate of those eligible to vote, see U.S. Bureau of the Census, *Current Population Reports* (1960 and 1970), series P-25, for your state. For registration (also legal requirements) and voting data, see the Board of Election for your county or city.

For voting data on the nation as a whole we have used two different years. The eligible or *latent* are based on population data by age as it appears in the census report of 1970. The *manifest* (percent eligible registered) and the *active* (percent registered voting) are for the presidential year of 1968 and can be found in the U.S. Bureau of the Census, *Statistical Abstract of the United States* (1970), Table 554, p. 368.

PROFILE EXAMPLE

TABLE PIII-2. TYPES OF CONSTITUENTS BASED ON THE PRESIDENTIAL ELECTION OF 1968 AND THE MAYORALTY ELECTION OF 1967

	UNITED STATES President 1968		MOUNT VERNON President 1968		Mayor 1967		NEW ROCHELLE President 1968		Mayor 1967	
	Number (in 1000's)	%	Number	%	Number	%	Number	%	Number	%
POPULATION	200,706		72,778				75,385			
Constituents										
Latent (eligible)	120,285	59.9	49,245	67.7	49,245	67.7	49,930	66.2	49,930	66.2
Non-enfranchised (non-eligible)	80,421	40.1	23,533	32.3	23,533	32.3	25,455	33.8	25,455	33.8
Manifest (registrants)	82,029	68.2	32,072	65.1	30,810	62.6	35,645	71.4	33,225	66.5
Apolitical (non-registered of eligible)	38,256	31.8	16,173	34.9	18,435	37.4	15,804	28.6	16,705	33.5
Active (Registrants voting)	73,212	89.3	29,493	95.7	27,099	88.0	33,533	94.1	28,328	79.5
Inactive (Registrants not voting)	8,817	10.7	1,317	4.3	3,711	12.0	2,112	5.9	7,317	20.5
Mobilized (eligible voting)	73,212	60.9	29,493	59.9	27,099	55.0	33,533	67.2	28,328	56.7
Inoperative (eligible not voting)	47,073	39.1	19,752	40.1	22,146	45.0	16,397	32.8	21,602	43.3

OPERATIONAL DEFINITIONS

$$\text{Latent} = \frac{\text{Population 21 Years or Older}}{\text{Total Population}}$$

$$\text{Non-enfranchised} = \frac{(\text{Total Population} - \text{Population 21 Years or Older})}{\text{Total Population}}$$

$$\text{Manifest} = \frac{\text{Registrants}}{\text{Population 21 Years or Older (Latent)}}$$

$$\text{Apolitical} = \frac{(\text{Population 21 Years or Older} - \text{Registrants})}{\text{Population 21 Years or Older (Latent)}}$$

$$\text{Active} = \frac{\text{Voters}}{\text{Registrants (Manifest)}}$$

$$\text{Inactive} = \frac{(\text{Registrants} - \text{Voters})}{(\text{Registrants (Manifest)})}$$

$$\text{Mobilized} = \frac{\text{Voters}}{\text{Population 21 Years or Older (Latent)}}$$

$$\text{Inoperatives} = \frac{(\text{Population 21 Years or Older} - \text{Voters})}{\text{Population 21 Years or Older (Latent)}}$$

PROFILE EXAMPLE

TABLE PIII-3. ELECTORAL PARTICIPATION FOR CHIEF EXECUTIVE AT THE NATIONAL, STATE, AND LOCAL LEVELS - 1960-1971

| | MOUNT VERNON | | | | | NEW ROCHELLE | | | | |
	Number Registered	Manifest	Number Voting	Active	Mobilized	Number Registered	Manifest	Number Voting	Active	Mobilized
PRESIDENT										
1960	36,861	70.9	33,199	90.1	63.9	36,993	73.0	35,488	95.9	70.0
1968	30,810	65.1	29,493	95.7	59.9	35,645	71.4	33,533	94.1	67.2
% Change	-16.4	-5.8	-11.2	5.6	-4.0	-3.6	-1.6	-5.5	-1.8	-2.8
GOVERNOR										
1962	31,530	60.6	27,251	86.4	52.4	32,453	64.0	28,006	86.3	55.2
1970	27,790	56.4	24,652	88.7	50.1	32,554	65.2	29,654	91.1	59.4
% Change	-11.9	-4.2	-9.5	2.3	-2.3	0.3	1.2	5.9	4.8	4.2
COUNTY EXECUTIVE										
1961	34,672	66.7	22,537	65.0	43.4	35,137	69.3	23,975	68.2	47.3
1969	29,770	60.5	19,187	64.5	39.0	33,593	67.3	21,841	65.0	43.7
% Change	-14.1	-6.2	-14.9	-0.5	-4.4	-4.4	-2.0	-8.9	-3.2	-3.6
MAYOR										
1959	31,766	61.1	26,971	84.9	51.9	30,766	60.7	26,694	86.8	52.7
1971	28,805	58.5	22,552	78.3	45.8	34,126	68.4	25,883	75.9	51.8
% Change	-9.3	-2.6	-16.4	-6.6	-6.1	5.2	7.7	-4.8	-10.9	-0.9
ELIGIBLE										
1960	51,983					50,680				
1970	49,245					49,930				
% Change	-5.3					-1.5				

OPERATIONAL DEFINITIONS

% Change (based on numbers) t_1 to t_2 = $\dfrac{(\text{Category } t_2 - \text{Category } t_1)}{\text{Category } t_1}$

% Change (based on %'s) t_1 to t_2 = (% t_2) - (% t_1)

CLASSIFICATION INDICATORS

	Mount Vernon	New Rochelle	United States
Manifest (% registered), 1968[a]	65.1	71.4	68.2
Active (% registered, voting), 1968[a]	95.7	94.1	89.3

[a]See Table PIII-2.

FINDINGS AND SUGGESTED IMPLICATIONS

Citizen participation in Mount Vernon is classified as *civic duty of the select*. That is, the *manifest* (proportion eligible registered, 65.1 percent) was below the national average, and the *active* (proportion registered actually voting, 95.7 percent) was substantially above the national average in the 1968 presidential election. The registration system filtered out some of those eligible, blacks for example; yet those who registered turned out to vote in overwhelming numbers. The *mobilized,* those eligible and voting, reflected the national average.

New Rochelle, by contrast, was an *efficacious* community, as the eligible citizens were both registered and voting to a greater degree than in the nation. There were 6.3 percent more *manifest* but 1.6 percent less *active* than in Mount Vernon. The higher proportion of *manifest* may have resulted from the higher SES of New Rochelle (see Exercise SV), which tended to limit filtering-out in the registration process.

Whereas in Mount Vernon there were smaller percentages of *actives* (7.7 percent) and *mobilized* (4.9 percent) for the mayoralty election in 1967 than for the presidential election in 1968 (see Table PIII-2), these figures were considerably above the usual turnout for local elections. The proportion of *actives* and *mobilized* in New Rochelle participating in their mayoralty race also was lower than for the presidential race. However, the proportion of *actives* in Mount Vernon for the mayoralty was approximately 10 percent higher than New Rochelle's. This may have been due to the amount of serious competition in the Mount Vernon mayoralty, with a black independent candidate running.

During the period 1959-71, there was a decline in the *manifests* for mayor in Mount Vernon (from 61.1 percent to 58.5 percent or a decline of 2.6 percent) compared to an increase in New Rochelle (from 60.7 percent to 68.4 percent or an increase of 7.7 percent) (see Table PIII-3). The *actives* and *mobilized* in both cities for chief executives were higher for the President than for the governor, for the governor than for the mayor, for the mayor than for the county executive. There was a decline in the *mobilized* in both communities, with the exception of those for governor in New Rochelle. Although here have been no systematic studies on electoral participation at all levels, lower turnout at state and local elections is often explained by the "off-year" elections phenomenon; i.e., elections on the local level are held on a year when there is no presidential election. Local elections, in both cities, in fact, have been deliberately scheduled to separate them from national presidential politics. Mount Vernon's nonpartisan school-board elections, conducted annually, are separated from other elections by being held in the spring. School-board turnout is much lower than that for the city council. The lower turnout for local elections may emphasize the lesser importance Americans place on local public officials. It also suggests that political parties put less effort—both manpower and financial—into mobilizing the electorate for local elections.

In sum, comparing the *mobilized* in different elections between cities and within the city, we can attempt to relate the propositions of Lineberry and Sharkansky, previously discussed:

1. No support. Mount Vernon with a mayor-council form of government had a lower turnout than New Rochelle with a city-manager form of government (see Exercise PII).

2. Support. Nonpartisan school-board elections in Mount Vernon had lower turnout than municipal partisan elections.

3. No support. New Rochelle's ward election for county legislators had a turnout equal to that for the city council's at-large election (see Exercise PVII).

4. No conclusions. Both cities had equally strong parties under a strong two-party system (see Exercise PIV).

5. Support. Mount Vernon, with its greater in- and out-migration was a less stable community and had less voter participation (see Exercise SII).

6. No support. Mount Vernon had more intense conflict (a civil disturbance in 1967) than New Rochelle but had a lower participation in the mayoralty election that followed (see Exercise PIII).

7. Support. Mount Vernon was a community lower in social status than New Rochelle and participated less (see Exercise SV).

8. Support. The stakes increased as Mount Vernon residents were faced with the desegregation of their schools and turnout for school-board elections increased substantially.

9. No support. Mount Vernon, which was and continues to be more ethnically diverse, participated less than New Rochelle (see Exercise SIII).

10. Support. Mount Vernon, with less social class (SES) mobility than New Rochelle, participated less (see Exercise SV).

It should, of course, be noted that none of these ten propositions
operates alone; rather, they occur simulatneously. It is difficult to sort
out which has greater effects. It is in this type of situation that a
regression analysis would be most helpful as it would explore the interrelationships of a number of variables.

A speculative explanation of declining electoral participation can be
found in the social, economic, and political controversies of the 60s—war
at the national level and civil disorders at the local level. It may be
that some believe government is neither able nor willing to resolve these
problems or that there is little difference between candidates—"Tweedle
Dee or Tweedle Dum." It may be that the complex problems facing public
officials require much more representative government than in the past
and that the legitimacy of present officials is in serious question, resulting in declining participation and confidence in the system. We offer
the following speculations to suggest some possible consequences of each
electoral participation pattern.

FIGURE PIII-3. SPECULATIONS ON SOME POSSIBLE CONSEQUENCES OF
              VARIOUS ELECTORAL PARTICIPATION PATTERNS

APATHETIC

>   Serious questions arise on the legitimacy of authorities.

>   Authorities do what they themselves want.

>   This leads to alienated behavior and the use of demon-
>   strations, civil disorders, and illegal acts.

DISENCHANTED

>   Authorities may try to meet the needs and demands of
>   constituents but are not able to overcome such con-
>   straints as insufficient public finance or lack of
>   widespread consensus.

>   Greater potential for opposition to be mobilized to sup-
>   port competitive elites.

>   Opportunity for charasmatic leader to win popular approval.

CIVIC DUTY OF THE SELECT

>   Mobilization of bias[22] favors the select as to who is
>   represented and on policy preferences.

>   As the nonselect become aware of the bias they may:
>   (a) mobilize a countermovement, (b) challenge the
>   operational norms of who shall govern, or (c) stimu-
>   late social tension.

>   The select who believe they should control tend to
>   resist change to the point where they may use coer-
>   cive practices.

EFFICACIOUS

>   A high sense of legitimacy of the authorities who may
>   be representative.

>   A willingness to play by the "rules of the game."

>   A large number of diverse demands for policy prefer-
>   ences are articulated; constituents expect that their
>   demands will be met.

>   Unresponsive authorities who choose not to or cannot
>   respond to demands are replaced, which may bring about
>   political instability.

>   If demands are too many and/or too competitive, the
>   system may develop policy paralysis.

DISCUSSION

1. What is the electoral participation classification of your community?

2. What are the proportions of (a) the latent, (b) the manifest, (c) the active, and (d) the mobilized in each of the following: (a) presidential elections, (b) gubernatorial elections, (c) county executive elections, and (d) mayorality elections? To what extent have these proportions changed over time?

3. To what do you attribute the levels of electoral participation in your community? (a) degree of difficulty in registering; (b) knowledge of time and place to register; (c) attitude toward registration; (d) implicit discouragement of some from registering; (e) level of SES in the community; (f) the sense among citizens that they can affect their own lives; (g) the degree to which voting is perceived as an important means to affect authorities and thereby public policy; (h) the degree to which choices among candidates are perceived to be meaningful; (i) the degree to which party, media, and campaign strategies stimulate an interest in voting; and (j) the degree to which voting or not voting will be perceived favorably or unfavorably.

4. Speculate on the ways in which the kind and degree of electoral participation affect the following major areas of community life: (a) housing, (b) education, (c) health, (d) welfare, (e) economic opportunity, (f) cultural activities, and (g) social tensions.

5. Do you think it important to change the electoral participation in your community? If so, in what direction? What social, political, and/or economic strategies could be employed to bring about the desired change?

NOTES

1. Lester W. Milbreath, *Political Participation* (Rand McNally & Co., 1965), p. 13; see also Robert E. Lane, *Political Life* (The Free Press, 1959).

2. Bernard Berelson, Paul E. Lazarsfeld, and William N. McPhee, *Voting* (University of Chicago, 1954), p. 24.

3. Sidney Verba and Norman H. Nie, *Participation in America* (Harper & Row Publishers, 1972), p. 45.

4. *Ibid.*, p. 31.

5. Richard A. Watson, *Promise and Performance of American Democracy* John Wiley & Sons, 1972), p. 306; President's Commission, *Report on Registration and Voting Participation* (U.S. Government Printing Office, 1963).

6. Angus Campbell, Phillip Converse, Warren Miller, and Donald Stokes, *The American Voter* (John Wiley & Sons, 1964), p. 49.

7. William C. Mitchell, *Why Vote?* (Markham Publishing Co., 1971), pp. 31-34.

8. *Ibid.*, p. 48.

9. Verba and Nie, pp. 79-80.

10. Gabriel A. Almond, *The American Public and Foreign Policy* (Frederick A. Praeger, 1960), p. 137; see also Donald J. Devine, *The Attentive Public* (Rand McNally & Co., 1970), and Roger W. Cobb and Charles D. Elder, *Participation in American Politics* (Allyn & Bacon, 1972).

11. James N. Rosenan, *Citizenship Between Elections* (The Free Press, 1974), p. 103; see also Robert E. Agger, Daniel Goldrich, and Bert E. Swanson, *The Rulers and the Ruled* (Duxbury Press, 1972).

12. *Ibid.*, p. 106.

13. Robert L. Lineberry and Ira Sharkansky, *Urban Politics and Public Policy* (Harper & Row Publishers, 1971), p. 63.

14. *Ibid.*, p. 54.

15. Edward C. Banfield and James W. Wilson, *City Politics* (Vintage Books, 1963), pp. 224-25.

16. Verba and Nie, p. 238.

17. Dan Nimmo and Clifton McClesky, "Voter Qualification and Participation in National, State and Municipal Elections," in *Community Politics* edited by C. M. Bonjean, T. N. Clark, and R. L. Lineberry (The Free Press, 1971), p. 113.

18. Kevin P. Phillips and Paul H. Blackman, *Electoral Reform and Voter Participation* (American Enterprise Institute for Public Policy Research, 1975), p. 73.

19. *Ibid.*, p. 75.

20. Melvin B. Mogulof, *Citizen Participation* (The Urban Institute, 1970, p. 9.

21. Blanch D. Blank, *American Government* (Aldine Publishing Co., 1973), pp. 153-54.

22. E. E. Schattschneider, *The Semi-Sovereign People* (Holt, Rinehart & Winston, 1960), pp. 20-46.

COMMUNITY DATA PROFILE PIII-A

(PIII-2) TYPES OF CONSTITUENCIES BASED ON A PRESIDENTIAL ELECTION

| POPULATION | Your Community | | | | Comparison City | | | |
| | President (19) | | Mayor (19) | | President (19) | | Mayor (19) | |
	Number	%	Number	%	Number	%	Number	%
Constituents								
Latent (eligible)								
Non-enfranchised (non-eligible)								
Manifest (registrants)								
Apolitical (non-registered)								
Active (registrants, voting)								
Inactive (registrants, not voting)								
Mobilized (eligible, voting)								
Inoperatives (eligible, not voting)								

COMMUNITY DATA PROFILE PIII-B

(PIII-3) ELECTORAL PARTICIPATION FOR CHIEF EXECUTIVES AT THE NATIONAL, STATE AND LOCAL LEVELS

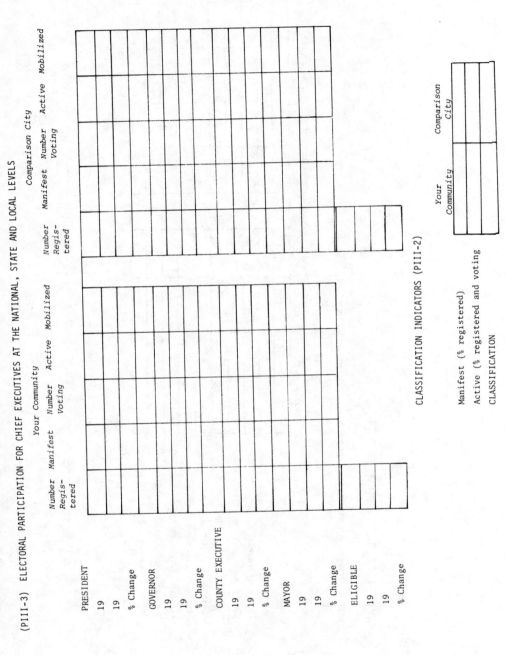

PIV. PARTY VIABILITY: POTENTIAL

WHAT IS THE POTENTIAL OF THE TWO MAJOR POLITICAL PARTIES
IN YOUR COMMUNITY?

CONCEPT

By the viability of an organization, one normally means that an organization is alive and "kicking." We use the notion to include both a
political party's potential and its effectiveness. Potential includes the
reservoir of popular good will, the party's organizational capability, and
its willingness to utilize its available resources in the electoral arena.
By effectiveness we mean the skill with which the party uses its potential
to affect electoral results and ultimately its impact on decision making
centers. Party effectiveness will be discussed in Exercise PVII and includes
such considerations as contests, coalitions, competition, victories (ma-
jority-plurality), and control.

In this exercise we discuss party potential in terms of the citizens'
party affiliation and the party organization. Most Americans are affiliated
or registered with one of the two major political parties—Democratic and
Republican. There are other minor parties that also attract voters' attention—liberal, conservative, socialist, and so on. Party identification of
constituents (see Exercise PIII) is kept on local registration roles for all
levels of primaries and elections. Although local reforms have eliminated
party use in the election of local public officials in many communities—
that is, there are nonpartisan local elections (see Exercise PII)—nonetheless parties are organized with the local community or county as the basic
building block of the state and national party system. Within each community a set of election precincts or districts with party personnel are
used to mobilize the voters in support of each party's candidates.

Despite the fact that most American registrants are affiliated with
a party, Nie, Verba, and Petrocik believe that the most dramatic political
change since the 1950s has been the decline in partisanship. They found:
"(1) Fewer citizens have steady and strong psychological identification
with a party. (2) Party affiliation is less of a guide to electoral choice.
(3) Parties are less frequently used as standards of evaluation. (4) Parties
are less frequently objects of positive feelings on the part of citizens.
(5) Partisanship is less likely to be transferred from generation to generation."[1]

There have been a number of major challenges to the political parties in American communities. One has been electoral reform which includes removal of the partisan label from local candidates and professionalization of the bureaucracy through eliminating political patronage (see Exercise PII). The second challenge has come from movements seeking alternatives to the two major parties. The movement may focus around a leading personality on an ad hoc basis or be centered around a policy position or an ideology that tends to persist for a longer period of time such as third parties (see Exercises PV and PVII). The third challenge stems from intraparty struggles over control of the party organization either by contesting at the precinct level or at the city-wide leadership level and primary battles between contenders for the right to carry the party banner (see Exercise PV). The fourth is the use of the media to by-pass the party apparatus.

Prior to World War I and the reform movement, many big cities were dominated by well-disciplined political machines which were generally ruled by a "boss" who exercised control over nominations for public office and distributed rewards to his followers. Today there are few if any political machines remaining. Lineberry and Sharkansky attribute their demise to (1) *affluence* and the decreased relative value of rewards from the machine such as jobs, (2) *the welfare state* that, through federally organized, financed, and supervised programs, provided more than the machines could, (3) *technology* that required skilled professionals and technicians who could not be recruited by the machine, and (4) *the impact of reform* that established city-manager forms of government and nonpartisan at-large elections involving larger constituencies than the machines' neighborhood-based organization.[2]

While the "boss" may have vanished from most of our big cities, the political party organization still survives.[3] It depends on the registered voter and is based on the precinct committee person who through caucuses and conventions selects partisan leaders and candidates for local, state, and national governmental office (see Exercise PV). Party functionaries participate in the campaign for their candidates as well as conduct door-to-door activities such as soliciting votes, raising money, registering voters, and poll-watching on election day. They are expected to have better access to public officials, at least those of their party, than the ordinary citizen. This access to public officials is considered especially important in communicating the interest of constituents as a two-way flow of information.

From time to time, factionalism within a party develops over issue positions, candidate preferences, and the acquisition of political favors. One form of battle takes place at the leadership level with efforts to persuade the existing party precinct workers to throw their support to one or the other of the contenders. When this approach fails, some reformers attempt to challenge the incumbent district leaders at the precinct level and establish a predominantly new party apparatus. The challenge within a party led Blank to characterize the struggle as one between the old time politicians and the reformers. She writes,

> The pols (that is, the professional politicians),
> whether they are Republicans, Democrats, Liberals,
> or Socialists, share a bond of brotherhood, a like-
> lihood of assessing the basic needs of the nation
> in the same way, and a deep appreciation of the fun
> and drama of political party life. To these people
> the central business of a polity is managing con-
> flict, and the best vehicle for doing so is a poli-
> tical party. Shifting coalitions, bargaining, com-
> promise are time-honored methods of managing conflict.
> To the reform-minded, however, all of these procedures
> smack of illegitimacy, the machine, competition, the
> lowest level of self-regarding opportunism. They
> have a naive faith in anything that promises them an
> escape from "politics." The name of the game is not
> compromise, but goal achievement.[4]

The most common reasons that Americans affiliate with the two major parties are: (1) tradition and social background (see Exercises SIII and SV), (2) the effectiveness of party organizations to recruit supporters, (3) the character and ability of party candidates (see Exercise PV), and (4) the parties' positions on public policies and prevailing issues. Campbell and his associates cite that "political socialization" typically begins "before the individual attains voting age and that this orientation strongly reflects his immediate social milieu, in particular his family."[5]

Flanigan suggests that the political parties develop specific strategies for different kinds of voters:

FIGURE PIV-1. POLITICAL PARTY STRATEGY TOWARDS SELECTED CONSTITUENTS

Voter Category	Party Strategy
Partisans and sympathizers of the party	Hold their votes and maximize turnout
Independents	Try to win their support
Partisans and sympathizers of the opposition	Try to win their support or appeal to them enough to reduce their turnout
Habitual nonvoters	Recruit few voters from potential supporters

Source: William H. Flanigan, *Political Behavior of the American Electorate* (Allyn and Bacon, 1972, 2nd Ed.), p. 41.

Democrats are generally considered to include lower-income urban groups, racial minorities, union workers, and the more liberally oriented professions. In contract, the upper-income group, big and small business-men, white Protestants, and the more conservative elements prefer the Republican party. Harris, reporting on peoples' perceptions of themselves, believes there is occurring a siginificant shift in the center of political gravity in the 1970s. He speculates on the following national changes in the electorate from 1968 to 1976:

TABLE PIV-1. EXPECTED POWER SHIFTS IN THE ELECTORATE

	1968 (%)	1976 (%)	Change (%)
Shrinking in power			
Under $5,000 income	25	19	- 6
Small-town voters	22	11	-11
Union members	23	15	- 8
Under 8th-grade education	19	11	- 8
Democrats	51	41	-10
$5,000-$9,999 income	43	23	-20
Increasing in power			
College-educated	29	40	+11
$15,000 and over income	12	25	+13
Independents	18	28	+10
Suburban residents	26	34	+ 8
Under-30 voters	18	27	+ 9
Professionals	9	20	+11

Source: Louis Harris, *Anguish of Change* (Norton, 1973), pp. 272-273

The kinds of candidates the political parties put forth is the most tangible evidence a voter has of the parties' position on who should govern. Barber, in his study of Presidents, suggests that people look for: (1) re-assurance that the President will take care of his people, (2) a sense of pro-gress and action, and (3) a sense of legitimacy in moral idealism.[6] Mitchell, recognizing that the party label in itself is an insufficient guide for a citizen to evaluate candidates, especially in a party primary where all candidates are of the same party, indicates that voters assess the candidates according to their likelihood of running a successful campaign and being effective in office.[7] For an incumbent in public office, general experience and achievement are important in assessing the candidate's records; and for the challenger, promises must be compared with the potential for fulfillment. In the last analysis, voters are looking for the best person to represent them.

In this connection two sets of considerations relating to candidacy are important. One is the social background, ethnicity (see Exercise SIII), religion, and socioeconomic status (see Exercise SV) of the candidates. That is, the political parties can select candidates to "fit," if somewhat loosely, the social characteristics of the constitutents. If Italian-Catholics are a large population segment, or if the Jewish community is politically relevant and has a large turnout, or blacks are an emerging bloc in the community, the political parties will "balance" their tickets to attract these population segments to support their party's candidates. The other factor is the policy positions the candidates take on the issues voters deem important to them, that is, with what campaign issues and public-policy questions the candidates and their party are associated. Do they favor urban renewal? Where do they propose to put public housing projects in the community? Are they big spenders (see Exercise EVI), and will their priorities benefit a particular neighborhood or interest or not? Do they have a program to reduce crime, to bring law and order to the community without costing too much in taxes and/or civil liberties?

As any politician knows, however, despite the fact that the party may have a long tradition, a viable party organization, sound candidates, and an articulated position on the current issues, if it does not get the votes, nothing matters. As Levy and Kramer point out:

> The difference between potential voters and actual
> voters in any given election can change the outcome.
> Voter rolls are like a giant inventory. . . . This
> flow of voters on and off the enrollment books can
> affect as much as 30 percent of the electorate in
> any given year.[8]

Thus, a real measure of party potential should be based not only on candidate selection and the relative proportion of registrants as a pool for the political party to draw upon but also on the degree to which those candidates can draw the *apoliticals* (see Exercise PIII) into the pool and actualize the party potential into votes.

TYPOLOGY

     The following typology indicates the relative potential of each major
party—Democrat and Republican. We refer to one party as the dominant party as
it has the largest share of the *manifest* (registrants). For example, the
Democratic Party is the dominant party nationally. That is, in 1968 based
on party affiliation of those states requiring registration, 54.1 percent of
the electorate was Democratic, 36.6 percent was Republican, and 8.1 percent
were registered with other parties or considered themselves independent.[9]
On the one hand, we measure the attractiveness of a political party to the
latent (eligible citizens) and the changes from 1960 to 1970 in the population of *manifest* (registered). On the other hand, we measure the organizational strength of each party compared to the other, that is, the proportion
of precinct committee positions filled, assuming that those who fill these
party positions will actually work to get out the vote. The party with the
largest voter registration will be referred to as the dominant party, and
each party will be classified in relation to the other.

     FIGURE PIV-2. TYPOLOGY OF TWO MAJOR POLITICAL PARTIES' POTENTIAL
                    (Relative to Each Other)

		PERCENTAGE INCREASE IN PARTY REGISTRATION	
		More	*Less*
	More	Strengthening with Organizational Edge	Slipping with Organizational Edge
PERCENTAGE OF ORGANIZATIONAL POSITIONS FILLED			
	Less	Aspiring with Organizational Slack	Weakening with Organizational Slack

     A political party that has increased its share of the *manifest* and has
a larger proportion of its organizational positions filled is characterized
as *strengthening with an organizational edge*. These political systems are
more likely to be found where a political machine dominates or continues to
be operational and receives no serious challenge. The party that has a larger
proportion of precinct positions filled but whose share of registrants is

increasing less than that of the other party is *slipping with an organizational edge*. Here the party is losing favor with the voters. The challenging party becomes more popular, perhaps because of a changing constituency, the presence of more attractive local candidates, or a greater hustle to register the *latent*. It may also result from the impact of state and national party affairs and the effect that candidates on those levels have on local politics. A party may gain in registration while having fewer precinct positions filled. In this case we refer to it as *aspiring with organizational slack*. Very often such a party challenges the dominant party by relying on such nonorganizational techniques as using the media to spotlight public policy issues, candidate personalities, or otherwise appeals directly to the voters. When a party increases its proportion of registration less than its competition and has fewer precinct committee positions filled, it is *weakening with organizational slack*. If this condition continues, the minority party will be less and less effective in challenging the dominant party.

SOURCES AND CAVEATS

For registration data sources, see "Sources and Caveats," Exercise PIII. Precinct committee positions filled can be found at the Board of Elections usually in the county courthouse or at the major political party headquarters. Other party information may be learned from party district-leader handbooks usually kept at party headquarters.

One should try to learn if there have been any factional attempts to take over or change the parties during the period of study. In addition, look for the growth and development of third parties and the use of coalitions by either party.

PROFILE EXAMPLE

TABLE PIV-2. POLITICAL PARTY REGISTRATION OF THE ELECTORATE, 1959-1972

| | MOUNT VERNON | | | NEW ROCHELLE | | |
Year	Registrants	% Republicans	% Democrats	Registrants	% Republicans	% Democrats
1959	31,766	54.7	31.1	30,766	51.4	29.8
1960	36,861	52.7	33.0	36,993	48.9	32.1
1961	34,672	52.6	33.0	35,137	48.2	32.8
1962	31,530	52.8	33.1	32,453	49.1	32.5
1963	31,343	51.6	33.7	32,443	48.8	33.1
1964	34,673	45.8	38.8	36,213	44.5	38.6
1965	32,725	45.1	39.5	34,266	44.4	36.9
1966	29,985	45.4	38.9	32,335	44.7	36.6
1967	30,810	44.0	39.7	33,225	44.3	36.9
1968	32,072	42.8	40.1	35,645	43.6	36.6
1969	29,770	44.5	41.8	33,593	43.6	36.6
1970	27,790	43.5	39.7	32,554	43.7	36.8
1971	28,805	41.3	41.3	34,126	41.9	38.7
1972	31,354	39.6	42.9	36,717	40.1	40.0
change (1959-72)	-412	-15.1	11.8	5,951	-11.3	10.2
% change (1959-72)	-1.3	-27.6	37.9	19.3	-22.2	34.2

OPERATIONAL DEFINITIONS

$$\text{\% Party Registrants} = \frac{\text{Registrants to Party}}{\text{Total All Registrants}}$$

Change (1959 to 1972) = Number Registrants, 1972 - Number Registrants, 1959

$$\text{\% Change (1959 to 1972)} = \frac{\text{Change (1959-1972)}}{\text{Total Registrants, 1959}}$$

TABLE PIV-3. POLITICAL PARTY PRECINCT POSITIONS FILLED, 1961-1969

| | MOUNT VERNON | | | | | NEW ROCHELLE | | | | |
| | Total | Republican | | Democrat | | Total | Republicans | | Democrat | |
Year	Positions	#	%	#	%	Positions	#	%	#	%
1961	102	102	100.0	90	88.2	102	102	100.0	101	99.0
1963	102	102	100.0	102	100.0	102	102	100.0	98	96.1
1965	102	101	100.0	102	100.0	102	102	100.0	98	96.1
1967	102	102	100.0	92	90.2	114	95	92.1	96	93.0
1969	104	100	96.1	92	88.5	114	110	96.5	100	87.7
TOTAL	512	507	99.0	478	93.4	534	511	95.7	493	92.3

OPERATIONAL DEFINITIONS

$$\text{\% Positions Filled} = \frac{\text{Number Positions Filled}}{\text{Total Positions}}$$

CLASSIFICATION INDICATORS

	MOUNT VERNON		NEW ROCHELLE	
	Republican	Democrat	Republican	Democrat
% Change party registration (1959-1972) (See Table PIV-2)	-27.6	37.9	-22.2	34.2
% Organizational positions filled (1961-1969) (See Table PIV-3)	99.0	93.4	95.7	92.3

FINDINGS AND SUGGESTED IMPLICATIONS

The Republican party in both cities was *slipping with an organizational edge,* while the Democratic party was *aspiring with organizational slack.* From 1959 to 1972 Republicans of Mount Vernon lost 27.6 percent of their registrants compared to an increase by 37.9 percent for the Democrats (see Table PIV-2). The Republicans dropped from the majority (54.7 percent) to the minority party (39.6 percent), while the Democrats changed their status to become the dominant party. The change was less dramatic in New Rochelle, where the Democrats gained 34.2 percent and the Republicans lost 22.2 percent. The Republicans, a majority in 1959, were even with the Democrats in 1972.

The Republican party in both communities had its precinct positions more completely filled than did the Democratic party (see Table PIV-3): 99.0 percent in Mount Vernon and 95.7 percent in New Rochelle. However, by 1969 they both had tapered off from their full complement at the beginning of the decade. The Democrats of Mount Vernon filled all their precinct positions during the middle of the decade, only to recede to 88 percent completion at the beginning of the next decade.

Challengers for precinct committee positions were numerous in New Rochelle in the period 1961 to 1969 and virtually nonexistent in Mount Vernon. Most of the contests in New Rochelle were within the Republican party. For example in 1963 when a factional dispute developed over who should be the Republican candidate for mayor, 41 of the 102 positions were contested by 122 individuals. The Republican contests reflected a factional struggle for power between the moderates and the conservatives (challengers) that persisted throughout the decade. The Democrats' contests were between moderates and progressives (challengers) who were supporting both the civil rights and the anti-Vietnam movements.

The factional contests at the precinct level in New Rochelle were repeated at the party leadership level. In Mount Vernon there were factional leadership struggles in both parties at various times during the decade although there were few contests at the precinct level. The struggle

within the Democratic party was initiated by an issue-oriented Reform Club.
The struggle within the Republican party was between the party regulars
and the civic leadership over who should be the party's candidate—the latter prevailed.

Few political parties remain stable over an extended period of
time, except perhaps in a one-party system (see Exercise PVII) or in a
stable community with little change in its social, political, and economic
character. In fact, most partisans see politics as a competitive game
well worth the effort to beat the opposition. We offer the following
speculations to suggest some contributing factors to the changing potentials of political parties' relative to each other and some possible
consequences of such changes.

FIGURE PIV-3. SPECULATIONS ON THE CONTRIBUTING FACTORS AND
LIKELY CONSEQUENCES OF CHANGING PARTY POTENTIAL

Contributing Factors	*Consequences*
STRENGTHENING WITH ORGANIZATIONAL EDGE	
Migration pattern that increases relative proportion of supporters	Increased party effectiveness
Preferable policy positions on key issues and decisions	Limited electoral options
	Frustrated minority party
Commitment to present party apparatus	Emphasized party doctrine
Inspiring party leaders	Responsiveness to selective elite
External party environment strengthened	Increased control over decision making process
	Party loyalists rewarded
SLIPPING WITH ORGANIZATIONAL EDGE	
Increased competition by opposing parties	Decreased party effectiveness
Nonresponsiveness to voter expectations	Attempt to expand electoral options
Unpopular policy positions	Develop alternative policy positions
Changing SES of voters to those less supportive	Increased opportunity for minority party development
Nonaggressive registration drive	Increased organizational rewards to party loyalists
Party corruption, scandal, and so on	Stimulates party reform
ASPIRING WITH ORGANIZATIONAL SLACK	
Influx of potential/actual party supporters	Increased inter- and intra-party competition
Taste of victory locally/externally	Stimulates greater variety of electoral options
Changing policy trends	Stimulates efforts to strengthen party organization and to control it
Effective mass media approach	
Strong registration drive	Increases bargaining and coalition formation among party factions
Visible party representatives (attractive candidates and elected officials)	Enhances party's chances to win elections and influence decision making process
Party reform	Stimulates opposition party to increase its efforts
	Some economic interests support party for long-range rewards
WEAKENING WITH ORGANIZATIONAL SLACK	
Overwhelmed by opposition party	Demoralized by defeats; difficult to attract candidates
Insufficient organizational activity	
Party corruption, scandal, and so on	Disaffected supporters attracted to third parties or become "turned off"
Fewer rewards for party loyalists	
	Propensity for ideologues to attempt to take over party
	Search for new leadership

DISCUSSION

1. What are the classifications of the two major political parties' potential in your community?

2. To what do you attribute each party's potential: (a) change in population characteristics, (b) relative positions taken on key issues by each party, (c) differences in party activities, (d) growth of third parties, or (e) types of candidates put forth?

3. Speculate on the ways in which the major parties' potential affects the following areas of public life: (a) housing, (b) education, (c) health, (d) welfare, (e) economic opportunity, (f) cultural activity, and (g) social tensions.

4. Do you think it important to change the parties' potential? If so, in what way? What social, political, and/or economic strategies might be employed to bring about the desired change?

NOTES

1. Norman M. Adler and Blanche D. Blank, *Political Clubs in New York* (Praeger Publishers, 1975)

2. Norman Nie, Sidney Verba and John R. Petrocik, *The Changing American Voter* (Harvard University Press, 1976), p. 48.

3. Robert Lineberry and Ira Sharkansky, *Urban Politics and Public Policy* (Harper & Row, Publishers, 1971), pp. 81-82.

4. Blanche Blank, *American Government and Politics* (Aldine Publishing Co., 1973), p. 161.

5. Angus Campbell, Philip Converse, Warren E. Miller, and Donald E. Stokes, *The American Voter* (John Wiley & Sons, Inc., 1967), p. 86.

6. James D. Barber, *The Presidential Character* (Prentice Hall, Inc., 1972), pp. 8-9.

7. William C. Mitchell, *Public Choice in America* (Markham Publishing Co., 1971), pp. 172-176.

8. Mark R. Levy and Michael S. Kramer, *The Ethnic Factor* (Simon & Schuster, 1972), p. 13.

9. About two thirds of the states require party affiliation. For a breakdown of party registration by state, see Michael Barone, Grant Ujifusa, and Douglas Mathews, *The Almanac of American Politics* (Gambit, 1972).

COMMUNITY DATA PROFILE PIV

(PIV-2) POLITICAL PARTY REGISTRATION OF THE ELECTORATE

	Your Community			Comparison City		
	Number Registered	% Republican	% Democrat	Number Registered	% Republican	% Democrat
1959						
1960						
1961						
1962						
1963						
1964						
1965						
1966						
1967						
1968						
1969						
1970						
1971						
Change 1959-1971						
% Change						

(PIV-3) POLITICAL PARTY PRECINCT POSITIONS FILLED

		Your Community					Comparison City			
Year	Total Positions	Republican Number Filled	%	Democrat Number Filled	%	Total Positions	Republican Number Filled	%	Democrat Number Filled	%

CLASSIFICATION INDICATORS

	Your Community		Comparison City	
	Republican	Democrat	Republican	Democrat
Percent Change Party Registration				
Percent Organizational Positions Filled				
CLASSIFICATION				

PV. ELECTORAL OPTIONS

WHAT ARE THE VARIOUS ELECTORAL OPTIONS PRESENTED TO THE
VOTERS OF YOUR COMMUNITY?

CONCEPT

The electoral options available to the voters can be found on the
ballot. Most of the options involve choosing who shall be selected to
hold public office and govern. Other options are available on the approval of budgets and bond proposals as well as those concerning public policies such as the adoption of a city manager, the fluoridation of the water
supply, or the reapportionment of representative seats. The development
of options is in large measure determined by public authorities, the political parties, some organized groups, and individual self-starters. The
election laws of the state and local government specify not only how many
positions are to be filled through election, but also when these elections are to be held and other "rules of the game" of politics. Some of
the rules are believed to significantly affect how the "game of politics"
is most likely to be played, who "plays," and who is more likely to govern
the political system.

One key rule is how many and which public officials should be elected.
This involves not only the size or number of members to be on the city
council, the school board, or the county commissions but also whether certain positions such as the sheriff, police commissioner, comptroller, or
tax assessor should be elected by the people rather than appointed (see
Exercise PII). For example, in 1967 there were some 521,758 elected officials in the United States, an average of 8 elected for municipalities
and 4.9 for school districts. Advocates of the long ballot—many elected
offices on the ballot—believe the electorate should have many electoral
options. Reformers prefer the short ballot to fix political responsibility
on just a few elected officials. Another rule pertains to when elections
are held. Most local elections are held in an "off year" (not when the
President is elected), and even in an "off-off year" (different from gubernatorial elections). This timing is expected to reduce the "coat-tail
effect" of local candidates riding into office upon the popularity of
state and national political party candidates. Other rules designate not
only whether elections are partisan or nonpartisan but whether candidates
run from single- or multi-member districts or from wards or at-large constituencies, as discussed in Exercise PII.

Another important set of rules indicates who shall select the candidates to be placed on the ballot. Normally the political party leadership

selects its own slates or tickets in partisan elections. In nonpartisan communities citizen committees are formed to carry out the same function. Individual candidates or a faction within the party may file their candidacy with the appropriate election officials, thereby challenging the party leadership. In partisan elections primaries are conducted to allow voters registered to a particular party to directly select who are to be their party's candidates in the general election (see Table PV-4). The primary is especially important in traditionally one-party political systems such as in the South where intra-party factionalism has developed to determine who shall govern.

Ranney observes that in primary elections (1) there are fewer contestants when incumbents run, (2) there are more contestants when the party's chances of winning are good, and (3) voter turnout, except for the South, is lower in primaries than in general elections.[1] An important aspect of options is, in fact, to have competitive alternatives on the ballot (see Table PV-2). Electoral options require contests offered by the competing parties, groups, and individuals. Contests may be between factions within a political party, between the political parties, or between representatives of various interests. Of course, the more contests, the more political competition. However, very often it is difficult to discern much difference between contestants who project a similar style or personality unless positions on issues are articulated that distinguish between candidates.

The construction of a winning ticket is a major task that involves a number of factors. Of course, some candidates prefer to run alone or even against established tickets. If a party or faction is to win an election, it must seek candidates that both attract the voters and stimulate the members of the organization to work for them (see Table PV-1). Ticket-makers consider the characteristics of each potential candidate as well as the composition of the entire ticket. To assess the winning potential of individual candidates requires taking into account such factors as reputation and popularity, experience and record of achievements, connections in the community and their representation of various important voting blocs, loyalty and past services. Not to be ignored is where the candidates stand on the important campaign issues that need to be articulated or are likely to develop during the campaign.

Ticket-makers give serious consideration to the entire slate in order to maximize its appeal to the major population segments. Ethnicity is generally the most significant criterion (see Table PV-5). Putting together a balanced ticket in a heterogeneous community is, as a former Tammany Hall leader of New York City, put it, ". . . of tremendous importance in preserving the fabric of democratic government, in preserving the confidence of all elements in the community, in sustaining the willingness of minority groups to accept the status of minority *participants* in government, and in stimulating the confidence of minorities that they are in fact *part* of the community and *part* of a great majority."[2]

Party reformers in New York City, however, attacked the practice as placing a large proportion of unqualified candidates on the ticket and thereby into public office. Reformers prefer instead, as Wilson suggests, to "democratize" the party apparatus, to improve the caliber of candidates and emphasize programs and principles whereby "Blue-ribbon candidates would be selected, not only for the important highly visible posts at the top of the ticket, but also for the less visible posts at the bottom. . . . Voters would be offered candidates who run on an elaborate, meaningful platform to which (in the eyes of reformers) they would be explicitly committed."[3] Costikyan defends the balanced ticket as the price we pay "to create one community instead of fifteen or twenty separate and antagonistic ones."[4] He notes that "balancing a ticket doesn't mean more votes for the ticket. But consistent unbalancing means trouble. Whatever the theoretical rights or wrong, in the end good politicians will instinctively seek balance in tickets. They may articulate no theories to justify balance, they will be willing to forego it from time to time, but deep feeling tells them good government and good politics call for representation of all significant ethnic and religious groups on the ticket, in the party, and in the government."[5]

Another more complicated, if not more dangerous, strategy is to form a coalition with others. (Machiavelli cautioned against a minority joining with a much larger group, suggesting that it would be absorbed into the majority and lose its identity.) It should be noted that the two major parties are themselves coalitions, with many diverse interests affiliating and expecting their party to fulfill their expectations. Beyond this, however, third parties or factions sometimes are developed by those who either cannot win within a party, those who believe they can gain more leverage outside the party, or as part of a countermovement. In the American two-party system, third-party candidates have generally been doomed to failure on the national level, but on all levels—national, state, and local—they have demonstrated their effectiveness in influencing the major parties, as when from time to time their votes spell the difference between victory or defeat (see Table PV-3). In 1965, for example, John Lindsay, a Republican congressman, became mayor of Democratic-dominated New York City with the third-party Liberal line. In 1969, defeated in his own Republican primary, he won reelection as a Liberal and hastily formed an Urban Party line.

Coalitions also are formed in nonpartisan elections by various groups that have at least some interests in common. Blacks may join with liberal whites. Taxpayer associations may link up with fiscal conservatives. Those being dislocated by urban renewal may seek the support of reactionaries who oppose governmental interference with private property. Greeley, aware of how bargaining permeates the political process, states, "Coalition formation, and the bargaining that is part of convening, maintaining, or extending coalitions is the very lifeblood of the American political and social process. One may not like it, but he will be hard-pressed to change it."[6]

It is difficult to measure how representative any ticket is of the electorate, and yet some effort should be made to ascertain some indication of this as minorities—blacks, women, and young people—complain about the nonrepresentative nature of those who govern them and society as a whole (see Table PV-5). Their charge is generally true, as most communities are governed by white, middle-aged men. As the underrepresented segments of our communities have become more aware of these discrepancies, they have entered the contest to become more a part of the political process. Consult the social-profile materials (see Table PV-5) to determine what proportions of your community are (1) male and female, (2) white and black, and (3) of various national origins and religions. From a list of candidate characteristics obtained from campaign materials or newspaper biographical sketches, compare the social profiles with a composite profile of the parties' candidates for office to determine how representative the candidates are.

Incumbency is another important aspect to observe about the electoral options presented to the voters (see Table PV-1). Very often incumbents choose to run for reelection and are considered to have an enormous edge over their challengers because they are viewed as having greater familiarity with community problems and have had greater visibility throughout the community. However, they are also vulnerable since, in office, the incumbent may have offended the voters or failed to achieve what was expected, thus giving the challenger an edge.

In some communities there is only one choice as an incumbent runs uncontested or receives the endorsement of both major political parties. This is more likely to occur in communities with one-party political systems (see Exercise PVII) or in those with nonpartisan systems. Of course, competition among candidates may not in itself provide really viable options, that is, a real difference in ideologies, solutions to problems, commitments to action, and so on. However, in some communities there is considerable competition, with many challengers presenting the voters with electoral opportunities. Not only can candidates challenge each other in general, primary, and run-off elections, but they also sometimes resort to using a number of different labels to attract those voters disaffected from the two major parties, Republican and Democratic (see Table PV-3). New York City, for example, has witnessed the inclusion of more than fifty independent parties or bodies on their voting machines since 1920. Some are "splinter" groups, some are personal instruments of an individual, some are adjuncts of the major parties, and some, as Sayre and Kaufman suggest, "explode into temporary prominence and upset many political calculations in individual elections. . . . By itself, perhaps, this possibility would probably not cause any deep concern to the leaders of the Democratic party, but added to all the other uncertainties they face, it builds up the forebodings with which they approach Election Day."[7]

TYPOLOGY

We offer the following typology to help classify the electoral opportunities available to the *manifest*. It pertains to both partisan and nonpartisan systems. We focus on both the number of positions or legislature seats open for constituency choice and on the number of candidates seeking these positions in general or run-off elections..

FIGURE PV-1.   TYPOLOGY OF ELECTORAL OPPORTUNITY
(Relative to the Nation)

NUMBER OF VOTES PER CONSTITUENT
FOR CITY COUNCIL

		Above	*Below*
INDEX OF CANDIDATE OPTIONS	*Above*	Optimal	Restricted but Competitive
	Below	Underutilized	Limited

On one side of the typology is indicated the number of votes the constituents have for the city council (see Table PV-2).   That is, if there are 5 city council positions, all elected at large, then each constituent has 5 votes.   If the 5 council members are elected by wards or districts, then each voter has only 1 member for whom he can cast a vote, that representing his district.   If some council positions are at-large and some are by district, then each constituent has 1 vote for each position at-large and one for the district where he lives.   In New York City, for example, of the 37 members of the city council, 10 are elected at-large and 27 by districts, thereby providing each constituent with 11 votes.   This is in sharp contrast to Chicago, which has a 50-member city council, all elected by district, where each voter has but 1 vote.

On the other side of the typology is the index of candidate options presented to the voters.   The index simply counts the number of candidates who offer themselves in general and run-off elections until a victor is declared.   We also count in this total the number of party labels any candidate may use to attract voters who are disaffected from the major party labels.   Thus, a 5-way contest for 1 seat in an election that requires a run-off election between 2 top vote-getters yields an index of 7 candidate options.   In a partisan general election of 1 Republican and 1 Democrat who also has a third-party label, the index is 3 candidate options.   Both the number of votes per constituent and the index of candidate options are relative to the average number in the nation.   The average number of councilmanic votes per constituent was 4.9, for the 1908 cities surveyed by the International City Management Association in 1971.[8]   We calculated that the average number of candidates running for the U.S. House of Representatives was 2.3, as of the 1970 election.   We used as our criterion the number of elections necessary to replace or reelect all members of the decision-making body.

Because all members of the House stand for reelection every two years, the average for one year was sufficient.[9] At the local level, the custom is to have staggered terms for city council members, which means that one portion of the council stands for election in one year and another in a succeeding election. We therefore have averaged the candidate options for the election periods that represent a complete chance for the voters to elect or turn over city council members (2 elections or 4 years).

A community with *optimal* electoral opportunities has not only an above-average number of voters per constituent but also an above-average index of candidate options for constituents. Here the electoral arrangements provide more councilmanic positions to vote for, and the political activists make full use of these options through competition among candidates. These kinds of opportunities are found in electoral reform cities which provide more votes for constituents and at the same time experience more competition among candidates. Such places are those with heterogeneous populations and considerable issue controversy. A community with *restricted but competitive* opportunities has a small-sized council and/or a ward system yet an openly competitive set of candidates maximizing whatever electoral opportunities there are. This could occur in a very competitive inter-political party system or in a nonpartisan place that because of issues attracts many candidates.

Underutilized opportunities occur when candidate options are lower and votes per constituent are higher than the national average. This is more likely to prevail in an electoral system where the at-large constituency has been adopted (see Exercise PII) and yet civic elites exercise sufficient control to regulate who shall run for office. This type of electoral opportunity may result from either a ritualistic approach to democracy where an above-average number of city councilmen gives constituents more opportunities to vote but the selection of candidates is manipulated and many are inhibited from contesting political positions. These could also be communities where constituents are satisfied with their candidates, thus discouraging many from contesting. The community with *limited* opportunities provides both fewer positions and fewer candidates for whom constituents can vote. This situation is most often found in one-party places or in elite-dominated systems where a few hand-pick those who shall run, thus severely limiting opposition.

SOURCES AND CAVEATS

Candidates for various offices and their party affiliations are listed in the canvas books kept at the Board of Elections. Other candidate characteristics must be obtained from campaign literature, newspaper articles, or reports put out by local civic organizations such as the League of Women Voters' "Know Your Candidates." At any rate, most university or local libraries possess or have access to past newspapers on microfilm (through interlibrary loans). Knowledge-able, long-time party leaders are another source of information about candidate characteristics.

PROFILE EXAMPLE

TABLE PV-1. CANDIDATES FOR MAYOR AND CITY COUNCIL, 1959-72

MOUNT VERNON

MAYOR

1959 - R. Sirignano (R), lawyer, Italian-Catholic
       H. Aronson (D-L), lawyer, Jewish

1963 - J. Vaccarella (D-L), former mayor, Italian-Catholic
       P. Sirignano (R), lawyer, Italian-Catholic
       H. Krause (C), Protestant

1967 - J. Vaccarella (D-L), incumbent, Italian-Catholic
       A. Petrillo (R-C), contractor, former school board member, Italian-Catholic
       S. Austin (New Voice), clergyman, Black, Protestant

1971 - A. Petrillo (R), incumbent, contractor, Italian-Catholic
       L. DeVito (D), contractor, former Republican city councilman who switched to Democratic party, Italian-Catholic
       A. Traeger (C), lawyer, urban renewal director, switched from Democratic party to Conservative, Jewish

CITY COUNCIL

1960 - (1 position)
       J. Garthe (R), printer, Protestant
       A. DeEsso (D-L), building supervisor, Italian-Catholic

NOTES: D - Democrat
       R - Republican
       L - Liberal
       C - Conservative

NEW ROCHELLE

MAYOR

1959 - G. Vegara (Reform), incumbent, Italian-Catholic
       T. Greene (R), merchant, Jewish
       S. Church (D-L), former mayor, Protestant

1963 - A. Ruskin (R), councilman, lawyer, Jewish
       R. Calgi (D), architect, Italian-Catholic

1967 - A. Ruskin (R), incumbent, Jewish
       J. Eagan (D), educator, Irish-Catholic

1970 - F. Garito (R), contractor, Italian-Catholic
       M. Potroff (D-L), Director of Human Relations Commission, Jewish

1971 - F. Garito (R), incumbent, Italian-Catholic
       D. Molinoff (D), lawyer, Jewish

CITY COUNCIL

1961 - (2 positions)
       D. Weir (R), incumbent, Protestant
       G. Vergari (R), former mayor, Italian-Catholic

MOUNT VERNON

CITY COUNCIL, Cont.

1961 - (3 positions)
R. Ragette (R), incumbent, real estate, Italian-Catholic
L. DeVito (R), incumbent, contractor, Italian-Catholic
G. Bantz (R), incumbent, silversmith, Protestant
H. Wiggs (D-L), printer, Black, Baptist
F. Ueblacker (D-L), insurance, Protestant
A. DeEsso (D-L), building supervisor, Italian-Catholic

1963 - (2 positions)
I. Kendall (R), incumbent
J. Garthe (R), incumbent, printer, Protestant
H. Zimmerman (D-L), lawyer, Protestant
Dr. W. Randolph (D-L), physician, Black, Protestant
F. Goffi (C)
L. Aitken (C)

1965 - (3 positions)
G. Bantz (R-C), incumbent, silversmith, Protestant
L. DeVito (R-C), incumbent, contractor, Italian-Catholic
R. Ross (R-C), lawyer, county legislator, Jewish
R. Cerchiara (D-L), county legislator, lawyer, Italian-Catholic
Alterman (D-L), Jewish
R. Channon (D), sales manager, Irish-Catholic
S. Needleman (L), Jewish

1967 - (2 positions)
J. Ragno (R-C), lawyer, county legislator, Italian-Catholic
H. Wood (R-C), lawyer, county legislator, Black, Protestant
W. Randolph (D-L), incumbent, physician, Black, Protestant
B. Herman (D-L), lawyer, city corp. council, Jewish

1969 - (4 positions)
L. DeVito (R-C), incumbent, contractor, Italian-Catholic

NEW ROCHELLE

1961 - (2 positions)
N. D'Onofiro (D), Italian-Catholic
F. Glassbery (D), Jewish
D. Days (I), Black, Protestant
L. Yagoda (L), Jewish

1963 - (2 positions)
T. Green (R), former councilman, Jewish
J. Pisani (R), incumbent, Italian-Catholic
H. Doyle (D), insurance, Irish-Catholic
C. Seidenstein (D), Jewish
S. Aronson (L), Jewish
H. Henry (L), Protestant

1965 - (2 positions)
T. Green (R), former councilman, Jewish
R. McGrath (R), Irish-Catholic
C. Seidenstein (D), Jewish
A. Pully (D), Black, Protestant
N. Stanton (L-Reform), Protestant
F. Moroze (L-Reform), Italian-Catholic
A. Petro (C), Italian-Catholic
F. Ippolito (C), Italian-Catholic
G. Vergari (I), incumbent, Italian-Catholic

1966 - (1 position)
J. Evans (R-L), incumbent, Black, Protestant
N. D'Onofino (D), Italian-Catholic
R. Cole (C), Protestant

CITY COUNCIL, Cont.

MOUNT VERNON

R. Ross (R-C), incumbent, lawyer, county legislator, Jewish
R. Blackwood (R-C), salesman, county legislator, Black, Protestant
L. Grippo (R-C), lawyer, county legislator, Italian-Catholic
U. Bullock (D-L), social worker, Black, Protestant
P. Scarpino (D-L), city attorney, Italian-Catholic
R. Cerchiara (D-L), incumbent, lawyer, Italian-Catholic

B. Brown (D-L), retired, Jewish
J. Bornstein (P), retail merchant, Jewish

NEW ROCHELLE

1967 - (2 positions)
J. Evans (R-L), incumbent, Black, Protestant
J. Belserene (R), Italian-Catholic
H. Doyle (D-C), incumbent, Irish-Catholic
J. Jackson (D), Black, Protestant
R. Gorman (C), Jewish

1969 - (2 positions)
T. Greene (R-C), incumbent, Jewish
J. O'Brien (R-C), Irish-Catholic
D. Streger (D-L), Jewish
R. Syracuse (D-L), contractor, Italian-Catholic

PROFILE EXAMPLE

TABLE PV-2. CITY COUNCIL POSITIONS AND CANDIDATE OPTIONS, 1969 and 1971

	MOUNT VERNON			NEW ROCHELLE			UNITED STATES*		
	Posi-tions open	Candi-dates running	Party lines	Posi-tions open	Candi-dates running	Party lines	Posi-tions open	Candi-dates running	Party lines
1969	4	9	17	2	4	8			
1971	2	7	9	2	7	9			
Total	6	16	26	4	11	17	435	961	1003
Average		2.7			2.8			2.2	
Index of Candidate Options			4.3			4.3			2.3

*For U.S. House of Representatives 1970

OPERATIONAL DEFINITIONS

Lines = Number of Designations on Ballot

$$\text{Index of Candidate Options} = \frac{\text{Number of Lines}}{\text{Number of Positions}}$$

TABLE PV-3. THE USE OF THIRD PARTY LABELS BY TWO MAJOR PARTIES (1959-1971)

	REPUBLICAN			DEMOCRAT		
	Only Own	Used Third Party		Only Own	Used Third Party	
	#	#	%	#	#	%
Mount Vernon						
Mayor[a]	3	1	25.0	1	3	75.0
City Council[b]	6	9	60.0	1	14	80.0
Total	9	10	52.6	2	17	89.5
New Rochelle						
Mayor[a]	5	0	0.0	3	2	40.0
City Council[b]	7	4	36.4	8	3	27.3
Total	12	4	25.0	11	5	31.3

[a] 1959-71

[b] 1961-69

OPERATIONAL DEFINITIONS

$$\% \text{ 3rd Party} = \frac{\text{Use 3rd Party}}{(\text{Only Own + Use 3rd Party})}$$

TABLE PV-4. PRIMARIES FOR TWO MAJOR PARTIES, 1961-1971

	MOUNT VERNON		NEW ROCHELLE	
Year	Republican	Democratic	Republican	Democratic
1961		City Council		
1963		Mayor	Mayor City Council	
1965		City Council		City Council
1966		City Council		City Council
1967			County Supervisor	
1969			City Council	
1970			Mayor	
1971		Mayor	City Council	City Council
Total Primaries	0	5	6	3

PROFILE EXAMPLE

CHARACTER	Community %	All #	Total Candidates %	Republican #	%	Democrat #	%	Independent #	%
MOUNT VERNON									
Sex									
Male	46.5	45	100.0	19	100.0	19	100.0	7	100.0
Female	53.5	0	0.0	0	0.0	0	0.0	0	0.0
Race									
White	72.4	38	84.4	17	90.0	15	78.9	6	85.7
Black	27.6	7	15.6	2	10.5	4	21.1	1	14.3
Religion/National Origin*									
Protestant- White	8.0	8	17.8	4	21.1	2	31.6	2	28.6
Black	35.0	7	15.7	2	10.5	4	21.1	1	14.3
Catholic Italian	40.0	20	44.4	10	52.6	9	47.4	1	14.3
Irish	5.0	1	2.2	0	0.0	1	5.3	0	0.0
Jewish	12.0	9	20.0	3	15.8	3	15.8	3	42.9
NEW ROCHELLE									
Sex									
Male	46.4	43	97.7	16	100.0	15	93.8	12	100.0
Female	53.6	1	2.3	0	0.0	1	6.3	0	0.0
Race									
White	86.1	39	88.6	14	87.5	14	87.5	11	91.7
Black	13.9	5	11.4	2	12.5	2	12.5	1	8.3
Religion/National Origin*									
Protestant White	10.0	5	11.4	1	6.3	1	6.3	3	25.0
Black	14.0	5	11.4	2	12.5	2	12.5	1	8.3
Catholic Italian	32.0	14	31.8	5	31.3	4	25.0	5	41.7
Irish	7.0	5	11.4	2	12.5	3	18.8	0	0.0
Jewish	37.0	15	34.1	6	37.5	6	37.5	3	25.0

TABLE PV-5. REPRESENTATIVES OF CANDIDATES FOR ALL MUNICIPAL OFFICES (1959-1971)

*
 Estimate

OPERATIONAL DEFINITIONS

% Party Candidates from Group = $\dfrac{\text{(Number Candidates from Group, 1961-1969)}}{\text{Total Party Candidates}}$

PROFILE EXAMPLE

TABLE PV-6. ETHNICALLY "BALANCED TICKETS" FOR LOCAL OFFICES, 1961-1969

	R E P U B L I C A N					D E M O C R A T S				
Year MOUNT VERNON	Italian Catholic	Jewish	Protestants	Black	Irish	Italian Catholic	Jewish	Protestants	Black	Irish
1961	4	1	2	1	2	4	1	3	2	0
1963	3	2	2	1	1	3	0	2	2	2
1965	4	2	2	1	0	3	3	0	1	2
1967	4	3	0	2	0	3	3	1	2	0
1969	3	2	0	1	0	3	2	0	1	0
Total	18	10	6	6	3	16	9	6	8	4
% of Total (1961-1969)	41.9	23.3	13.9	13.9	7.0	37.2	20.9	13.9	18.6	9.3
NEW ROCHELLE										
1961	2	0	4	0	0	3	2	0	0	1
1963	2	2	1	0	2	2	3	1	0	1
1965	1	2	1	0	3	3	2	0	1	1
1967	2	1	1	1	2	2	2	0	1	2
1969	2	1	0	0	2	4	1	0	0	0
Total	9	6	7	3	9	14	10	1	2	5
% of Total (1961-1969)	28.1	18.8	21.8	3.1	28.1	43.8	31.3	3.1	6.3	15.6

OPERATIONAL DEFINITIONS

$$\% \text{ of Total (1961-1969)} = \frac{\text{All Candidates, One Ethnic Group}}{\text{All Candidates}}$$

CLASSIFICATION INDICATORS

	Mount Vernon	*New Rochelle*	*United States*
Number of seats for which constituents vote (see Table PII-2)	5.0	4.0	4.9
Index of candidate options (see Table PV-2)	4.3	4.3	2.3

FINDINGS AND SUGGESTED IMPLICATIONS

The electoral opportunities in Mount Vernon were *optimal*. Its 5-member city council elected at-large was above the average in the number of positions for which constituents can vote compared to the nation's cities. On the average there were also more candidate options offered for these seats than the average in the nation (see Table PV-2). Candidates of the two major parties frequently resorted to third-party labels (see Table PV-3), and independent candidates ran, increasing the number of candidate options among which constituents could choose. The Democrats freely used third-party labels (89.5 percent of the time) during the decade for the city council in contrast to the Republicans (52.6 percent). It was not until the Democrats won several seats in the city council and county legislature with the Liberal party label that the Republicans began reluctantly to use the Conservative party label. Prior to this decision the Conservatives had put forth their own candidates to bring about their defeat or produce very narrow victories. The Republicans were most reluctant to join with the third parties in mayoralty elections. In 1967, when they did use the Conservative line, they were challenging the incumbent Democratic mayor who was also threatened by the loss of the customary black vote by an independent black candidate who in fact drew away many votes.

New Rochelle's voters, by contrast, had *restricted but competitive* electoral opportunities as its city council had fewer members but there were more candidate options than the average for the nation. Here both the Republican and Democratic parties used third-party labels, however, much less frequently (Democrats, 25 percent, and the Republicans, 31 percent) than in Mount Vernon. The Republican candidates for the mayoralty did not use third-party labels at all.

During the decade, New Rochelle experienced 9 primaries compared to 5 in Mount Vernon (see Table PV-4). Most of the primaries (6) were held by the Republican party and carried all offices at one time or another. The Democrats held primaries for city council candidates only. In Mount Vernon all the primaries occurred inside the Democratic party, 2 for mayoralty candidates and 3 for city council candidates. Two types of Republican primary challengers took place in New Rochelle. One was by an independent

reform ex-mayor attempting to come back into power through the Republican
party by challenging its candidate for mayor (the independent was defeated).
The second was a factional fight between moderate and conservative Republicans for the city council candidacy. The Democratic primaries in New
Rochelle were issue oriented. They were challenged by a group, the Independent Democrats, that preferred candidates who took a pro-civil rights and
an anti-Vietnam War position.

The Mount Vernon primary challengers within the Democratic party
reflected a minor anti-crime effort by one individual and a major struggle
for control of the Democratic party at the leadership level. Some reformers attempted to formulate through issues an alternative to the ethnically
based strategies of the regular party organization and lost.

The ethnics were well represented among the candidates in both communities (see Table PV-5). Italian-Catholics comprised by far the largest
proportion of candidates offered by both Mount Vernon's political parties.
In New Rochelle, Catholics constituted the largest proportion of candidates
with the Republican party selecting equal numbers of Italian-Catholics and
Irish-Catholics. The Democratic party relied most heavily on Italian-Catholics,
followed by Jewish candidates. Black candidates were much more numerous in
Mount Vernon—reflecting its growing black population—than in New Rochelle.
The Democrats in Mount Vernon selected blacks slightly more often than did
the Republicans. Mayoralty candidates in Mount Vernon were exclusively
Italian-Catholic as both parties sought to be attractive to the major voting
bloc in town. It appears that an Italian connection was more important
than political party affiliation.

Both parties in both communities ethnically balanced their tickets
(see Table PV-6). It is difficult to infer, however, in retrospect what
the strategic considerations were in putting these party tickets together.
Did each party calculate the relative proportions of each population segment in the constituency? Did the parties' leadership believe certain kinds
of candidates would attract some voters to cross over from their traditional
party preferences? Did they consider the candidates' social and cultural
class status in the community, their skill in campaigning, and/or their
position on some of the key community issues? Did they simply weigh the
selective popularity and attractiveness of their candidate against that of
the opposition?

When candidates are considered as a whole the males are vastly overrepresented in both communities although women compromise more than half the
population (53 percent). In New Rochelle the candidates reflected the community's racial and religious composition more equitably than did those in
Mount Vernon. That is, Italian-Catholics, Jews, Protestants, and blacks had
their fair share of candidates; only the Irish-Catholics were overrepresented.
In Mount Vernon, on the other hand, while the Italian-Catholics had their fair
share, the Protestants and Jews were overrepresented two to one; the blacks
were underrepresented by one-half.

While representativeness is an important element in electoral options,
there are other social, political, and economic characteristics that should
be considered. We offer the following speculations on some of the characteristics most often associated with maximized and minimized electoral opportunities.

FIGURE PV-2. SPECULATIONS ON MAXIMIZED
AND MINIMIZED ELECTORAL OPPORTUNITIES

Characteristic	Maximized	Minimized
STRUCTURE	Large representative assembly elected at-large	Small representative assembly elected by wards
PARTISAN	Competitive two-party systems with third parties and coalitions	Strong party, "boss"-dominated and one-party systems, use of party caucus
NONPARTISAN	Issue-oriented and personalized politics	Caucus by screening committees
GOVERNMENTAL FORM	Mayor-council	City manager
CITIZEN PARTICIPATION	Higher	Civic duty of the select
SOCIAL DISPARITIES	Pluralistic approaching party	Social cleavages
ETHNICITY	Cohesive group identity pluralistically balanced following period of confrontation	One dominant ethnic group exclusionary and coercive
MEDIA	When not part of establishment, and exposing corruption, inefficiency and ineffectiveness	When part of establishment, support authorities and their "rules of the game"
ECONOMIC ELITE	When adversely regulated, and seeking reform	When key influentials in the system
LABOR	Strong labor unions with hostile economic elites	Weak, coopted unions

DISCUSSION

1. What is the electoral options classification of your community?

2. To what extent are the candidates in your community representative of (a) the proportions of national-origin segments, (b) the proportions of males and females, (c) the racial proportions, and (d) the religious proportions? Has the representativeness of the candidates changed over time? If so, in what directions?

3. To what do you attribute the electoral opportunities in your community? (a) the size of the council, (b) the degree of controversy in the community, (c) special groups who put up their own candidates, (d) party control of the candidates, (e) the use of third-party labels, (f) at-large elections, and (g) elections by ward or district?

4. Speculate on the ways in which the kind and degree of electoral opportunities affect the following major areas of community life: (a) housing, (b) education, (c) health, (d) welfare, (e) economic opportunities, (f) cultural activities, and (g) social tensions.

5. Do you think it important to change the electoral opportunities in your community? If so, in what direction? What social, political, and/or economic strategies could be employed to bring about the desired change?

NOTES

1. Austin Ranney, "Parties in State Politics," in *Politics in the American States* edited by Herbert Jacobs and Kenneth W. Vines (Little, Brown, 1965), p. 74.

2. Edward N. Costikyan, *Behind Closed Doors* (Harcourt, Brace & World, Inc., 1966), p. 180.

3. James Q. Wilson, *The Amateur Democrat* (University of Chicago Press, 1962), p. 128.

4. Costikyan, p. 180.

5. *Ibid.*, pp. 181-182.

6. Andrew Greeley, *Building Coalitions* (New Viewpoints, 1974), p. 134.

7. Wallace S. Sayre and Herbert Kaufman, *Governing New York City* (W. W. Norton & Co., 1965), pp. 194-195.

8. See Table 3-20, Alan Klenit, "City Councils and Their Functions in Local Government," in *The Municipal Year Book, 1972* (International City Management Association, 1972), pp. 28-54.

9. Richard M. Scammon, *American Votes*, Vol. 9 (Congressional Quarterly, 1972).

COMMUNITY DATA PROFILE PV-A

(PV-1) CANDIDATES FOR MAYOR AND CITY COUNCIL

OFFICE _____   *Y O U R   C O M M U N I T Y*

Year	Name	Party	Identification Profession/Position	Ethnicity/ Religion

*This is a sample worksheet. More of these will need to be drawn or copied to list the candidates for offices for both Your Community and Comparison City.

COMMUNITY DATA PROFILE PV-B

(PV-2) CITY COUNCIL POSITIONS AND CANDIDATE OPTIONS

	Your Community			Comparison City		
Year	Positions	Candidates	Lines	Positions	Candidates	Lines
19__						
19__						
Total Average						

(PV-3) THE USE OF THIRD PARTY LABELS BY TWO MAJOR PARTIES

	Republican			Democrat		
	Only Own	Use 3rd	% 3rd	Only Own	Use 3rd	% 3rd
Your Community						
Mayor						
City Council						
Total						
Comparison City						
Mayor						
City Council						
Total						

(PV-4) PRIMARIES FOR TWO MAJOR PARTIES

	Your Community		Comparison City	
Year	Republican	Democratic	Republican	Democratic
19__				
19__				
19__				
19__				
19__				
19__				
19__				
19__				
19__				
19__				
Total				

COMMUNITY DATA PROFILE   PV-C

(PV-5) SELECTIVE REPRESENTATIVENESS OF LOCAL CANDIDATES

CHARACTER	Community %	Total All Candidates #	%	Republican #	%	Democrat #	%	Independent #	%
YOUR COMMUNITY									
Sex									
Male									
Female									
Race									
White									
Black									
Religion/ National Origin*									
Protestant- White									
Black									
Catholic- Italian									
Irish									
Jewish									
COMPARISON CITY									
Sex									
Male									
Female									
Race									
White									
Black									
Religion/ National Origin*									
Protestant- White									
Black									
Catholic- Italian									
Irish									
Jewish									

*Substitute other national origin groups if appropriate

COMMUNITY DATA PROFILE PV-D

(PV-6) ETHNICALLY "BALANCED TICKETS"

| | *REPUBLICAN* | | | | | *DEMOCRAT* | | | |
	I.	II.	III.	IV.		I.	II.	III.	IV.
Your Community									
19__									
19__									
19__									
19__									
19__									
Total									
%									
Comparison City									
19__									
19__									
19__									
19__									
19__									
Total									
%									

CLASSIFICATION INDICATORS (PV-2)

	Your Community	Comparison City
Number of Votes per Constituent (19__)		
Index of Candidate Options (19__)		
CLASSIFICATION		

PVI. ELECTORAL PATTERNS AND OUTCOMES

WHAT PATTERNS OF ELECTORAL PREFERENCES AND COMPETITION PREVAIL IN YOUR COMMUNITY?

CONCEPT

Psephology is the study of elections. The term is based on the ancient Greek custom of citizens casting their votes by dropping colored pebbles into the ballot box to signify their preferences. Election returns stimulate the curiosity of politicians and political analysts alike. They look not only for winners and losers but for cues that indicate trends and meanings of electoral responses to the options presented. The search for voting patterns, as Phillips suggests, involves "a kaleidoscope of sociology, history, geography and economics. Of course, the trends are very tangled and complex, but they can be pulled apart. . . . Voting patterns can be structured and analyzed in such a way as to show an extraordinary amount of social and economic behaviorism at work."[1] It is therefore important to go beyond the counting of votes to consider why the electorate voted the way it did and to ask what one election foretells about the next one. Perhaps more important is the need to develop relevant theory on the formation and expression of political attitudes.

The analysis of elections as citizens choose who shall govern can provide a number of insights into the political system. It should be remembered that by citizens here we refer to those actually voting. (see Exercise PIII). From voting trends attempts are made to examine the stability of the system; that is, the longer a particular political party or faction is preferred by the voter, the more stable the polity. Another focus might be on the vertical components of the electoral system—national, state, and local elections. Voter turnout varies sharply by levels with greater turnout at the national than at the local level. One might expect that higher turnout at the national level enhances a mass-based political party such as the Democrats are believed to be, while lower turnout at the local level enhances the more elite-based Republican party.

Electoral preferences may change as they have in the South, where the solid Democratic tradition has begun to break down, with more and more voters preferring Republican presidential, senatorial, and congressional candidates. Yet Southerners retain their traditional Democratic preference for local candidates. Another concern is the horizontal consistency of voter preferences among executive and legislative candidates at all levels—national, state, and local. There has been increasingly more

211

"ticket-splitting" as voters elect an executive from one party while choosing legislators from the other. This may be a result of a changing constituency, the diversity of the electorate, the declining importance of political parties, or of the voters exercising constraint against the monopoly of power by one party.

Another important aspect for study is election trends. Scammon and Wattenberg suggest that "the first requisite is to acknowledge that there are not only tides, but waves and ripples also, and that there are times when only ripples and perhaps a few waves are visible on the horizon."[2] They believe we are in for a tidal political era of change. Harris notes both the instability in the vote for President—veering from 61 percent Democratic in 1964 to 61 percent Republican in 1972—and the concurrent remarkable stability in the vote for Congress. He agrees with Scammon and Wattenberg on the fact that there is a demography of change, but diasgrees on the kind of demographic changes and more importantly on what political impact they will have. For Harris, the electorate grows younger, better educated, more suburban, affluent, and independent. This new electorate has become the center of voting power, which promises not only to wreck havoc with existing political parties, but also to emerge as a majority *for change*.[3] Whereas Scammon and Wattenberg see the great majority as "unyoung, unpoor, and unblack; they are. middle-aged, middle-class, middle-minded,"[4] they believe the voters who constitute the center are "fed-up" with the social issues of crime, integration, drugs, civil disorder, pornography, dissent, and so on. All of these of course spell out great change and are frightening. Golembiewaski, Welsh, and Crothy suggest that the socialization process shapes political attitudes.[5] They take into account not only the candidates and their campaign effort but also the social background, conditions, and attitudinal sets of the voter as well as the feedback of the implications that flow from past elections.

Campbell and his associates, in explaining the electoral changes of recent years which indicate surges and declines, use such basic concepts as (1) political stimulation, (2) political interests, (3) party indentification, (4) core and peripheral voters, and (5) high- and low-stimulus elections.[6]

American voters have turned more and more since the end of World War II toward divided loyalties. That is, after electing a candidate of one party or faction, they soon reverse themselves or choose another candidate representing a different party or policy perspective. Voters are behaving as though they are undergoing "cross-pressure." By this is meant that socioeconomic status may predispose a person to vote in one direction, but his ethnic background or ideological persuasion may stimulate that same person to want to vote in the opposite or another direction.[7] Thus, an affluent and liberal Jewish voter may feel conflicting pressures when prefering a fiscally conservative candidate while actually voting for a candidate who promises to alleviate the problems of the poor. Flanigan offers the following predictions of voting behavior when consistent or cross-pressure is experienced:

FIGURE PVI-1. PREDICTING VOTER BEHAVIOR

	Consistent Pressure	Cross Pressure
Ticket voting	Straight	Split
Decision on vote	Early	Late
Interest in politics	High	Low
Levels of information	High	Low
Attitudes	Consistent	Conflicting

The election returns are then the voice of the people determining who our governors shall be and indirectly what shall be our public policy. V. O. Key points out, however, that "the voice of the people is but an echo. . . . as candidates and parties clamor for attention and vie for popular support, the people's verdict can be no more than a selective reflection from among the alternatives and outlooks presented to them."[9]

The aggregate of the people's voices are amply recorded at the polls. The distribution of the election results reflects the consensual or competitive nature of the electorate. Most analyses of the distribution of votes have focused on interparty competition. Five types of measures have been used.[10] One is the pendulum effect or the unexpected gains and losses of a party's votes. Second is the percentage of elections won or lost. Third is the proportion of legislative seats held by a party. Fourth is the alternation in office by parties. The final one is the percentage of the vote received by the winners and the losers. We have chosen the last for its simplicity and its applicability to both partisan and nonpartisan elections. We can therefore measure the margin of difference between winners and losers, whether it be a matter of incumbency, partisanship, or other factors (see Tables PVI-2, PVI-3, and PVI-4).

From 1960 through 1972 those winning presidential elections averaged 53.8 percent of the vote, whereas the losers (the candidate receiving the next largest number of votes) averaged 42.0 percent of the vote, providing the winners with an average margin of 11.8 percent. Two elections, those in 1960 and 1968, were determined by less than 1 percent of the vote (see Table PVI-1).

In municipal elections Gilbert and Calgue found in their study of cities with populations of one-half million or more that the margin of winning was not dependent upon whether the locality held partisan or nonpartisan elections.[11] Instead, they found the margin closer for mayors than for councilmanic positions and in multi-member at-large electoral systems rather than single-member districts or ward systems.

Competition between those with different ideological positions and between those of different ethnicity (see Table PVI-6) can also be measured, but only if the positions and/or ethnicity of those vying for office can be clearly differentiated. If two Italians run against each other, the effect of ethnicity on competition cannot be measured.

TABLE PVI-1. ELECTORAL COMPETITION FOR PRESIDENT AND CONGRESSMAN

Year	President[a]			Congressman[b]		
	Winner	Loser	Margin	Winner	Loser	Margin
1960	49.7(D)	49.5(R)	0.4	52.6(R)	47.4(D)	5.2
1962	NA	NA		60.9(R)	39.1(D)	21.8
1964	61.1(D)	38.5(R)	22.6	54.9(R)	38.5(D)	12.4
1966	NA	NA		69.3(R)	25.4(D)	43.9
1968	43.4(R)	42.7	0.7	61.9(R)	23.1(D)	38.8
1970	NA	NA		66.4(R)	18.0(C)	48.4
1972	60.7(R)	35.7(D)	23.2			
Average	53.8	42.0	11.8	61.0	31.9	29.1

[a]Adapted from U.S. Bureau of the Census, *Statistical Abstract of the United States* (1974), Table 680, p. 422.

[b]Data are for the Congressman from the 26th Congressional District encompassing Mount Vernon and New Rochelle. Adapted from Richard M. Scammon, *American Votes* (Governmental Affaris Institute), published every two years.

Eulau and Prewitt believe that the importance of electoral competition, "rests on the assumption that the status of political officeholders is probationary. It is not competition as such but the transitory tenure of officeholding resulting from competition that protects a measure of democracy."[12] We have constructed a flow chart (Figure PVI-3) which illustrates the succession of elected public officials. From this chart one can discern whether a person in public office has been reelected or "turned over"—replaced or evicted. By replacement we mean the incumbent did not rerun for any one of a variety of reasons. By evicted we mean that the incumbent has been defeated by a challenger. As Eulau and Prewitt suggest, incumbent eviction indicates the difficult problem of leadership succession, relates to the stress of political opposition, and undergirds the notion of periodic review of public policy.[13]

TYPOLOGY

We propose the following typology to classify the level of electoral competition. In order to make this exercise useful for both partisan and nonpartisan elections, we focus on competition as the common basis of analysis. Without party labels, we are limited to measuring the degree of competition by calculating the margin of difference between the winning and the losing candidates. Here we intend to classify the relative degree of competition shown for the mayor and the President, and/or for city council and congressional candidates. All votes the candidate receives are counted (see Tables PVI-2 and PVI-3), not only their major party vote. That is, to measure the executive pattern, on the one side, we measure the average margin of difference between the winning and losing presidential candidates in the community relative to the average margin of difference in the nation for President. On the other side, we indicate the average margin of difference between the winning and losing mayoralty candidates relative to the community's margin of difference between presidential candidates. To measure the legislative pattern separately, we contrast by the same method the average margin of difference between winners and losers for the congressional positions and for city council positions (see Table PVI-3).

FIGURE PVI-2. TYPOLOGY OF THE PATTERNS OF ELECTORAL
COMPETITION FOR EXECUTIVE AND/OR LEGISLATIVE OFFICE

		AVERAGE MARGIN OF VICTORY FOR NATIONAL OFFICES[a]	
		More	*Less*
AVERAGE MARGIN OF VICTORY FOR LOCAL OFFICE COMPARED TO NATIONAL OFFICE[b]	*More*	Consensual	Nationally Competitive
	Less	Locally Competitive	Generally Competitive

[a]Community margin for President relative to national margin for President. To use for legislative classification, the community margin for the congressional candidate is compared to the congressional district margin for the congressional candidate.

[b]Community margin for mayor compared to community margin for President. For legislative classification, the community margin for the city councilmen is compared to the community margin for its congressman.

A *generally competitive* electoral pattern indicates greater competition in the community for national office than the average in the nation and greater competition for local offices than for national offices. That is, there is more competition for the office of President than there is on the average in the nation and more competition over the mayoralty than over presidential candidates within the community. There is more competition for the congressional seat than the district average and more for councilmanic seats than for the congressional position. This pattern is more likely to occur in viable two-party systems and in rapidly changing communities.

A *locally competitive* place demonstrates greater voter competition for local elected officials than for national officials, both for executive and legislative positions. There is, however, less competition among presidential candidates locally than the average in the nation and less for congressional candidates than the average in the congressional district. This may occur where there are coalitional developments on the local level but not for national candidates. The city-manager form of government may stimulate greater competition for councilmanic positions, although for the mayoralty it seems to reduce the amount of competition, and more certainly the electoral turnout. Another possible factor to explain greater local competition for the mayoralty is the development of more sharply distinctive ideological presidential candidates, such as Goldwater in 1964 and McGovern in 1968. These candidates reduced the level of competition for national offices.

A *nationally competitive* place produces votes more evenly divided between the presidential candidates and between congressional candidates than between their counterparts in local government. Nonpartisan local elections may bring this about by reducing the contrast between candidates compared to the sharper party divisions among national candidates.

The *consensual* electoral pattern indicates that the local constituency is in more agreement than the nation on presidential and congressional candidates, and in more agreement on local candidates than on national ones. This is more likely to occur where the prevailing dominant party consistently secures its majorities in local, state, and national elections with its tightest control on the local level.

SOURCES AND CAVEATS

See Exercise PIII for local election data sources. Congressional voting data can be found in local canvass books or in Richard M. Scammon, *American Votes* (Governmental Affairs Institute). Be sure when calculating winners and losers to use all party labels or all lines on the ballot for any candidate.

Note that in order to facilitate an analysis of turnover, we have constructed a flow chart (see Figure PVI-3), which illustrates the succession of officeholders for the decade. From this chart, incumbents who have been reelected can be identified as well as those who have evicted or replaced authorities.

PROFILE EXAMPLE

TABLE PVI-2. ELECTORAL COMPETITION* FOR EXECUTIVE OFFICES

	MOUNT VERNON			NEW ROCHELLE		
	Winner %	Loser %	Winner Margin %	Winner %	Loser %	Winner Margin %
President						
1960	50.6(R)	49.2(D-L)	1.4	50.0(D-L)	49.7(R)	0.3
1964	68.8(D-L)	31.1(R)	37.7	69.7(D-L)	30.2(R)	32.5
1968	52.9(D-L)	40.8(R)	12.1	53.3(D-L)	41.5(R)	11.8
1972	53.3(R-C)	46.3(D-L)	7.0	54.8(R-C)	44.8(D-L)	10.0
Average			14.6			13.7
Governor						
1962	59.7(R)	37.5(D-L)	22.2	61.4(R)	35.8(D-L)	25.6
1966	51.4(R)	31.8(D)	19.6	54.7(R)	29.1(D)	25.6
1970	53.9(R)	40.3(D-L)	13.6	55.2(R)	39.3(D-L)	15.9
Average			18.5			22.4
County Executive						
1961	58.0(R)	48.0(D-L)	10.0	52.7(R)	47.3(D-L)	5.4
1965	51.3(R)	46.6(D-L)	4.7	49.6(D-L)	46.9(R)	2.7
1969	49.6(R)	43.6(D-L)	6.0	50.4(D-L)	44.3(R)	6.1
Average			6.9			4.7
Mayor						
1959	56.9(R)	43.2(D-L)	13.7	41.7(D-L)	37.3(R)	4.4
1963	45.3(D-L)	41.8(R)	3.5	51.8(R)	43.0(D)	8.8
1967	52.3(R-C)	32.9(D-L)	19.4	76.4(R)	17.7(D)	58.7
1970	NA	NA	NA	45.0(R)	39.1(D-L)	5.9
1971	54.5(R)	37.7(D)	16.8	58.8(R)	31.5(D)	27.3
Average			10.7			21.0

*Percentages will not add up to 100 if there were more than 2 candidates.

OPERATIONAL DEFINITIONS

$$\% \text{ Winner's Vote} = \frac{\text{Votes for Winner, All Lines}}{\text{Total Vote Cast for Office}}$$

$$\% \text{ Loser's Vote} = \frac{\text{Votes for Runner-Up, All Lines}}{\text{Total Vote Cast for Office}}$$

Winner Margin = Winner's % of Vote - Loser's % of Vote

$$\text{Average Winner Margin} = \frac{\Sigma(\text{Winner's Margins})}{\text{Number of Contests}}$$

PROFILE EXAMPLE

TABLE PVI-3. ELECTORAL COMPETITION FOR LEGISLATIVE OFFICE

	MOUNT VERNON			*NEW ROCHELLE*		
Congress	*Winner*	*Loser*	*Winner Margin*	*Winner*	*Loser*	*Winner Margin*
1960	50.1(R)	49.9(D-L)	0.2	55.3(D-L)	44.7(R)	10.6
1962	55.8(R)	44.2(D-L)	11.6	52.9(R)	47.1(D-L)	5.8
1964	47.4(R)	45.6(D)	1.8	47.0(R)	44.8(D)	2.2
1966	66.7(R)	29.1(D)	37.6	66.9(R)	28.3(D)	38.6
1968	61.1(R-L)	30.1(D)	31.1	66.7(R-L)	25.6(D)	41.1
1970	64.8(R-L)	21.4(D)	43.4	69.6(R-L)	15.0(D)	54.6
Average			21.0			25.5
City Council						
1960	51.3(R)	48.7(D-L)	2.6			
1961a	56.6(R)	43.4(D-L)	13.2	49.1(R)	42.2(D)	6.9
b	56.5(R)	43.5(D-L)	13.0	48.5(R)	39.5(D)	9.0
c	55.6(R)	44.4(D-L)	11.2			
1963a	56.0(R)	43.0(D-L)	13.0	54.9(R)	40.7(D)	14.2
b	51.5(D-L)	48.5(R)	3.0	47.0(D)	46.8(R)	0.2
1965a	50.6(R-C)	47.3(D-L)	3.3	38.2(R)	34.5(D)	3.7
b	53.2(R-C)	41.4(D)	11.8	35.9(R)	30.0(D)	5.9
c	53.2(D-L)	47.4(R-C)	5.8			
1966a				48.7(R-L)	45.6(D)	3.1
1967a	56.3(R-C)	49.2(D-L)	7.1	61.6(R-L)	27.1(D)	34.5
b	55.4(R-C)	41.1(D-L)	14.3	55.1(D-C)	48.3(R)	6.8
1969a	59.0(R-C)	41.0(D-L)	18.0	54.1(R-C)	48.4(D-L)	5.7
b	56.3(R-C)	49.2(D-L)	7.1	52.4(R-C)	44.5(D-L)	7.9
c	55.4(R-C)	41.1(D-L)	14.3			
d	50.0(R-C)	38.0(D-L)	12.0			
Average			10.0			8.9

a, b, and c indicate individual seats.

PROFILE EXAMPLE

TABLE PVI-4. ELECTORAL COMPETITION BETWEEN INCUMBENTS AND CHALLENGERS

| | MOUNT VERNON | | | NEW ROCHELLE | | |
Mayor	Incumbent	Challenger	Incumbent Margin	Incumbent	Challenger	Incumbent Margin
1959	NA	NA		21.1(I)	41.7(D)	-20.6
1963	41.8(R)	45.3(D)	- 3.5			
1967	32.9(D)	52.3(R)	-19.4	76.4(R)	17.7(D)	58.7
1971	54.5(R)	37.7(D)	16.8	58.8(R)	31.5(D)	27.3
Average			- 2.0			21.8
City Council						
1961a	56.6(R)	43.4(D)	13.2	49.1(R)	42.4(D)	6.9
b	56.5(R)	43.5(D)	13.0			
c	55.6(R)	44.4(D)	11.2			
1963a	56.0(R)	43.0(D)	13.0	46.8(R)	47.0(D)	- 0.2
b	48.5(R)	51.5(D)	-3.0			
1965a	47.4(R)	53.2(D)	- 5.8			
b	53.2(R)	41.4(D)	11.8			
1967a	41.1(D)	55.4(R)	-14.3	61.6(R)	27.1	34.5
b				55.1(D)	48.3(R)	6.8
1969a	59.0(R)	41.0(D)	18.0	54.1(R)	48.4(D)	5.7
b	56.3(R)	41.1(D)	15.2			
c	49.2(D)	56.3(R)	- 7.1			
Average			5.9			10.7

OPERATIONAL DEFINITIONS

$$\% \text{ Vote Candidate} = \frac{\text{Vote Received by Candidate}}{\text{Total Vote Cast for Office}}$$

Margin of Incumbent = % Vote for Incumbent - % Vote for Runner-Up

$$\text{Average Margin} = \frac{\Sigma (\text{Margins of Incumbents})}{\text{Number of Contests}}$$

PROFILE EXAMPLE

TABLE PVI-5. INCUMBENT TURNOVER FOR EXECUTIVE AND LEGISLATIVE OFFICE - 1959-1972

	MOUNT VERNON					NEW ROCHELLE					UNITED STATES				
	Seats Open	Re-Elected	Re-Placed	Evicted	Turn-Over	Seats Open	Re-Elected	Re-Placed	Evicted	Turn-Over	Seats Open	Re-Elected	Re-Placed	Evicted	Turn-Over
Executive															
Total	3	1	0	2	2	4	2	2	0	2	4	2	2	0	2
%		33.3	0.0	66.7	66.7		50.0	50.0	0.0	50.0		50.0	50.0	0.0	50.0
Legislative															
Total	17	9	4	4	8	15	6	7	2	9	2610	2224	146	240	386
%		52.9	23.5	23.5	47.1		40.0	46.7	13.3	60.0		85.2	5.6	9.2	14.8

OPERATIONAL DEFINITIONS

Turnover = Replaced + Evicted

% Each Outcome = $\dfrac{\text{Number Each Category}}{\text{Total All Seats}}$

TABLE PVI-6. REPRESENTATIVENESS OF WINNERS FOR MAYOR AND CITY COUNCIL, 1959-1971

	MOUNT VERNON							NEW ROCHELLE						
	Community %	Total No.	Total %	Republican No.	Republican %	Democrat No.	Democrat %	Community %	Total No.	Total %	Republican No.	Republican %	Democrat No.	Democrat %
Characteristic														
Sex														
Male	46.5	20	100.0	17	100.0	3	100.0	46.4	16	100.0	13	100.0	3	100.0
Female	53.5	0	0.0	0	0.0	0	0.0	53.6	0	0.0	0	0.0	0	0.0
Race														
White	72.4	17	85.0	15	88.2	2	66.7	86.1	14	87.5	11	84.6	3	100.0
Black	27.6	3	15.0	2	11.8	1	33.3	13.9	2	12.5	2	15.4	0	0.0
Religion/ National Origin														
Protestant-														
White	8.0	2	10.0	2	11.8	0	0.0	10.0	2	12.5	1	7.6	1	33.3
Black	35.0	3	15.0	2	11.8	1	33.3	14.0	2	12.5	2	15.4	0	0.0
Catholic-														
Italian	40.0	12	60.0	10	58.8	2	66.7	32.0	4	25.0	4	30.8	0	0.0
Irish	5.0	0	0.0	2	0.0	0	0.0	7.0	4	25.0	2	15.4	2	66.7
Jewish	12.0	3	15.0	3	17.7	0	0.0	37.0	4	25.0	4	30.8	0	0.0

OPERATIONAL DEFINITIONS

% Winners from Specific Group = $\dfrac{\text{Number of Group Winners}}{\text{Total Candidates}}$

PROFILE EXAMPLE

FIGURE PVI-3. FLOW CHART OF MAYOR AND CITY COUNCILMEN, 1959-1971

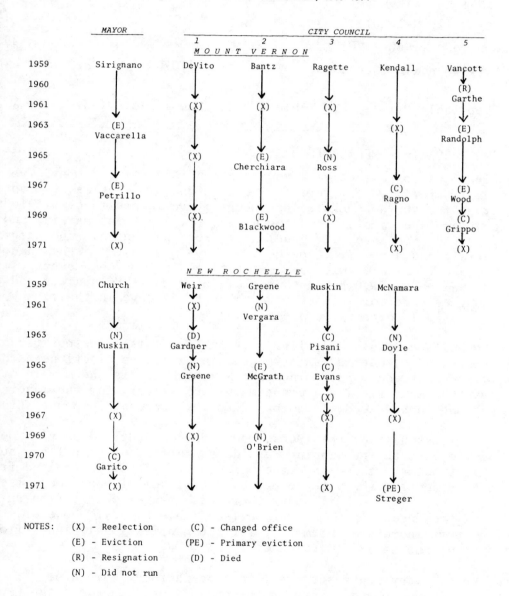

NOTES: (X) - Reelection   (C) - Changed office
         (E) - Eviction   (PE) - Primary eviction
         (R) - Resignation   (D) - Died
         (N) - Did not run

CLASSIFICATION INDICATORS

Average Percentage Margin Between Winner and Loser	Mount Vernon	New Rochelle	United States
President (1960-1972)	14.6[b]	13.7[b]	11.8[a]
Mayor (1959-1970)	10.7[b]	21.0[b]	NA
Congress (1960-1970)	21.0[c]	25.5[c]	29.1[a]
City Council (1960-1969)	10.0[c]	8.9[c]	NA

[a]See Table PVI-1, [b]See Table PVI-2, [c]See Table PVI-3.

FINDINGS AND SUGGESTED IMPLICATIONS

In elections for executives, Mount Vernon is *locally competitive* but *generally competitive* for legislative candidates. That is, the voters on the average for the decade are less competitive in presidential elections (14.6 percent average margin) than the nation (11.8 percent margin) and are more evenly divided on mayoralty candidates (10.7 percent average margin) than on presidential candidates (14.6 percent average margin). At the same time, councilmanic elections are twice as competitive (10.0 percent average margin) as congressional ones (21.0 percent margin) among Mount Vernonites and candidates for Congress are more competitive than the average in their congressional district (29.1 percent average margin).

New Rochelle displays a similar pattern for legislative positions, *generally competitive,* but it is *consensual* in executive elections. The major difference between Mount Vernon and New Rochelle is the margin of victory given the mayors. The average margin of victory for the mayoralty was 21.0 percent in New Rochelle compared to 10.7 percent in Mount Vernon.

For the first half of the 1960s, Mount Vernon provided varying percentages of the vote to its winning candidates for executive office, but during the last half of the decade the winners consistently received from 49.6 to 54.5 percent of the vote no matter what level of government (see Table PVI-2). For city council seats there was greater competition during the middle of the decade in Mount Vernon (see Table PVI-3). However, the margin of victory increased enormously for the congressional winner from the beginning of the decade to the end.

New Rochelle, by contrast, experienced a narrower margin of difference between winners and losers at the end of the decade for the President and the governor and at the beginning of the decade for the mayor. For city council the competition was greater during the middle of the decade, whereas the congressional winner increased his margin fivefold from the beginning to the end of the decade.

Incumbency was an advantage for both mayors in New Rochelle who chose to rerun; between them they averaged 43 percentage points more than their challengers (see Table PVI-4). Incumbency, however, did not help the mayors of Mount Vernon as only 1 out of 3 won reelection. In 1963 a former mayor not only evicted the incumbent but also stimulated turnover of councilmanic and county legislative positions. One black councilman was elected with the mayor, only to be defeated four years later by a black opponent when the mayor was evicted. Only one city councilman in Mount Vernon remained in office throughout the decade (see Figure PVI-3). He attempted to run for mayor unsuccessfully. It helped to be an incumbent when running for the city council in both communities; 9 out of 17 incumbents won in Mount Vernon and 6 out of 15 in New Rochelle. The turnover of municipal officers in Mount Vernon was primarily the result of evictions (6 out of 10 turnovers), whereas in New Rochelle replacements were the main cause of turnover (9 out of 11 turnovers).

Of those who won elective office in Mount Vernon during the decade, all were male; the vast majority (85.0 percent) were white (see Table PVI-6). Italian-Catholics dominated the politics of Mount Vernon as they won 60.0 percent of the local elections. All mayors and more than one-half of the city councilmen were Italian. The Jewish and black candidates were next most successful. It is clear that male, white, and Jewish constituents were overrepresented, while women and blacks were underrepresented among those winning public office in Mount Vernon.

Similarly in New Rochelle 100.0 percent of the winning candidates were white males. The ethnic politics of New Rochelle were much more balanced, as the Irish-Catholic candidates, the Italian-Catholic, and the Jewish candidates each won 25.0 percent of the races, the white Protestants 12.5 percent, and the blacks 12.5 percent. The blacks won fewer elections in New Rochelle, but they also comprised a smaller constituency than they did in Mount Vernon. Despite the ethnic balance, the male, white, Irish, and Jewish population components were overrepresented, whereas women and blacks were underrepresented in New Rochelle.

Whether competition is greater for local candidates than for national ones is dependent upon a number of factors. We suggest the following speculations on some than might contribute to greater competition for mayor than for President and for city councilmen than for congressmen.

FIGURE PVI-4. SPECULATIONS ON FACTORS ASSOCIATED WITH
HIGHER LEVELS OF COMPETITION FOR LOCAL THAN FOR
NATIONAL EXECUTIVE AND LEGISLATIVE OFFICES

	More Competitive for Mayor than for President	*More Competitive for City Councilmen than for Congressman*
HETEROGENEITY	Candidates for mayor have closer fit to local diversity	Closer fit to local neighborhood diversity
SOCIAL DISPARITY	Relatively balanced strata in community	Interneighborhood balance
GOVERNMENTAL FORM	Less reformed at municipal level (partisan)	More reformed (at-large elections)
PARTICIPATION	Higher participation at municipal level	Lower participation at congressional district level
ELECTORAL OPTIONS	Coalitional for municipal candidates	More positions per constitutents
CANDIDATES	Mayoralty candidates less charismatic	More balanced loyalty
PARTY TACTIC	Minority party forms coalition on municipal level	Balanced tickets
INFORMATION	High media coverage of city hall and mayor	Personalized public appearance in neighborhoods
RHETORIC	Mayoralty slogans less extreme	More concrete and specific
IDEOLOGY	Balanced public-private regardingness at municipal level, status oriented	Interneighborhood balance of public-private regardingness, welfare oriented.

DISCUSSION

1. What are the electoral competition classifications of your community for (a) the executive and (b) the legislators?

2. What are the margins of victory for executives on the following levels: (a) national, (b) state, (c) county, and (d) local? To what extent have these margins changed over time?

3. What are the margins of victory for legislative candidates on the following levels: (a) local and (b) national? To what extent have these margins changed over time?

4. What has been the effect of the following factors on the outcomes of elections: (a) incumbency, (b) ethnicity, (c) race, (d) the sex of the candidate, and (e) political party?

5. To what do you attribute the competition pattern in your community for executives and legislators: (a) composition of the population, (b) options being offered, (c) party effectiveness, or (d) community issues?

6. Speculate on the ways in which the level of competition for executive and legislative offices in your community affect the following major areas of community life: (a) housing, (b) education, (c) health, (d) welfare, (e) economic opportunities, (f) cultural activities, and (g) social tensions.

7. Do you think it important to change the electoral pattern and outcomes in your community? If so, in what direction? What social, political, and economic strategies could be employed to bring about the desired change?

NOTES

1. Kevin P. Phillips, *The Emerging Republican Majority* (Doubleday & Co., 1970), p. 39.

2. Richard M. Scammon and Ben J. Wattenberg, *The Real Majority* (Coward-McCann, 1970), p. 29.

3. Louis Harris, *The Anguish of Change* (W. W. Norton, 1973), pp. 248-275.

4. Scammon and Wattenberg, p. 21.

5. Robert T. Golembiewski, William A. Welsh, and William J. Crotty, *A Methodological Primer for Political Scientists* (Rand McNally & Co., 1969), pp. 389-419.

6. Angus Campbell, Philip Converse, Warren Miller, and Donald Stokes, *Elections and the Political Order* (John Wiley & Sons, 1967), pp. 40-62.

7. See Bernard Berelson, Paul Lazarsfeld, and William McPhee, *Voting* (University of Chicago Press, 1954), and Angus Campbell, Phillip E. Converse, Warren E. Miller, and Donald Stokes, *The American Voter* (John Wiley & Sons, Inc., 1960), pp. 77-88.

8. William H. Flanigan, *Political Behavior of the American Electorate* (Allyn and Bacon, Inc., 1972, 2nd ed.), p. 37.

9, V. O. Key, Jr., *The Responsible Electoral* (Vintage Books, 1966), p. 2.

10. David G. Pfeiffer, "The Measurement of Inter-Party Competition and Systemic Stability," *American Political Science Review,* Vol. 61, No. 2, (June, 1967), p. 457.

11. Charles E. Gilbert and Christopher Clague, "Electoral Competition and Electoral Systems in Large Cities," in *Urban Political Analysis* edited by David R. Morgan and Samuel A. Kirkpatrick (The Free Press, 1972), p. 172-189.

12. Heinz Eulau and Kenneth Prewitt, *Labyrinths of Democracy* (Bobbs-Merrill Co., Inc., 1973), p. 253.

13. *Ibid.,* p. 252.

COMMUNITY DATA PROFILE PVI-A

(PVI-2) ELECTORAL COMPETITION FOR EXECUTIVE OFFICES

Year	YOUR COMMUNITY Winner	Loser	Winner Margin	COMPARISON CITY Winner	Loser	Winner Margin
President						
19__						
19__						
19__						
19__						
Average						
Governor						
19__						
19__						
19__						
19__						
Average						
County Ex.						
19__						
19__						
19__						
19__						
Average						
Mayor						
19__						
19__						
19__						
19__						
19__						
Average						

COMMUNITY DATA PROFILE   PVI-B

(PVI-3) ELECTORAL COMPETITION FOR LEGISLATIVE OFFICE

	YOUR COMMUNITY			COMPARISON CITY		
Year	Winner	Loser	Winning Margin	Winner	Loser	Winning Margin
Congress						
19___						
19___						
19___						
19___						
19___						
19___						
Average						
City Council						
19___						
a						
b						
c						
19___						
a						
b						
19___						
a						
b						
c						
19___						
a						
b						
19___						
a						
b						
c						
Average						

COMMUNITY DATA PROFILE   PVI-C

(PVI-4) ELECTORAL COMPETITION BETWEEN INCUMBENTS AND CHALLENGERS

	YOUR COMMUNITY			COMPARISON CITY		
	Incumbent	Challenger	Incumbent Margin	Incumbent	Challenger	Incumbent Margin
Mayor						
19__						
19__						
19__						
19__						
19__						
Average						
City Council						
19__						
a						
b						
c						
19__						
a						
b						
c						
19__						
a						
b						
c						
19__						
a						
b						
c						
19__						
a						
b						
c						
19__						
a						
b						
c						
Average						

COMMUNITY DATA PROFILE PVI-D

(PVI-5) INCUMBENT TURNOVER

	YOUR COMMUNITY					COMPARISON CITY				
Year	Seats Open	Re-Elected	Re-Placed	Evicted	Turn Over	Seats Open	Re-Elected	Re-Placed	Evicted	Turn Over
Executive										
Total										
%										
Legislative										
Total										
%										

(PVI-6) REPRESENTATIVENESS OF WINNERS

Characteristic	YOUR COMMUNITY Community %	Total #	%	Republican #	%	Democrat #	%	COMPARISON CITY Community %	Total #	%	Republican #	%	Democrat #	%
Sex															
Male															
Female															
Race															
White															
Black															

Religion/
National
Origin*

Protestant															
White															
Black															
Catholic															
Italian															
Irish															
Jewish															

*Substitute other national origin groups if appropriate

CLASSIFICATION INDICATORS

	YOUR COMMUNITY	COMPARISON CITY
President		
Mayor		
Congress		
City Council		
CLASSIFICATION		
Executive		
Legislative		

PVII. PARTY VIABILITY: EFFECTIVENESS

HOW EFFECTIVE ARE THE POLITICAL PARTIES IN YOUR COMMUNITY?

CONCEPT

Party effectiveness is the readiness, willingness, and ability of a party not only to contest with other parties, but also to demonstrate a reasonable probability of winning some elections and of controlling, dominating, or at least constituting a majority from time to time in local decision-making centers. Of course, effectiveness must relate to the party potential, the concept developed in Exercise PIV. Electoral options and outcomes are also related to party effectiveness, but here we concentrate on their political party dimensions. A political party analysis should include some of the following considerations: (1) party *context* of the state in which the community is located, (2) *contesting* candidates, (3) *coalition* formation, (4) *proficiency* in securing the party's share of the vote, (5) proportion of party *victories*, (6) the degree of interparty *competition*, (7) the party's *representative* share of elective positions, and (8) the extent of party *control* of local decision-making centers.

Most democratic theorists attempt to classify the political party *context*. They assume that a two-party system is preferable to a one-party system. They believe party competition is necessary for effective democratic control of government. Fenton explains that:

> two-party competition almost invariably leads to
> appeals for the support of lower income voters
> because they are so numerous, while other politi-
> cal systems tend to be more oligarchical and less
> responsive to the needs and desires of the poor.
> Consequently, it is believed, two-party competi-
> tion is more likely to lead to subsequent govern-
> ment actions addressed to these needs.[1]

Local political parties should be viewed as part of a larger context, the most significant of which is the state organization. Thus, the local party's potential will to some degree be shaped by the state candidates, issues, and campaigns. It is useful therefore to use classifications of state party systems. Pfeiffer has classified each state on the basis of the percentage of the popular vote received by the parties for all state-wide general elections for the period from 1940 to 1964. His sevenfold

classification is: (1) one-party Democratic (8 states); (2) modified
one-party Democratic (3 states); (3) weak two-party leaning towards the
Democrats (5 states); (4) two-party (28 states); (5) weak two-party leaning
towards the Republicans (5 states); (6) modified one-party Republican
(1 state); and (7) one-party Republican (no states)[2] (see Table PVII-1).

TABLE PVII-1.   THE STATES CLASSIFIED BY DEGREE OF INTER-PARTY COMPETITION

One-Party Democratic

Alabama (79.03%)
Arkansas (82.34%)
Florida (73.62%)
Georgia (90.50%)
Louisiana (84.46%)
Mississippi (88.06%)
South Carolina (87.30%)
Texas (80.03%)

*Modified One-Party
Democratic*

North Carolina (66.44%)
Tennessee (64.60)
Virginia (66.65%)

*Weak Two-Party Leaning
Toward the Democrats*

Alaska (58.89%)
Arizona (56.28%)
Hawaii (59.94%)
Oklahoma (56.67%)
Rhode Island (58.67%)

Two-Party

California (53.35%R)
Colorado (50.36%R)
Connecticut (50.21%D)
Delaware (49.99%R)*
Idaho (51.84%R)
Illinois (50.01%R)
Indiana (51.50%R)
Iowa (53.46%R)
Kentucky (54.48%D)
Maryland (53.91%D)
Massachusetts (51.56%D)
Michigan (50.00%R)*
Minnesota (50.48%R)
Missouri (54.98%D)
Montana (52.93%D)
Nevada (55.03%D)
New Hampshire (54.88%R)
New Jersey (51.39%R)
New Mexico (54.68%D)
New York (49.55%R)*
Ohio (51.26%R)
Oregon (55.29%R)
Pennsylvania (50.56%R)
Utah (49.97%D)
Washington (51.25%D)
West Virginia (54.84%D)
Wisconsin (51.08%R)
Wyoming (52.05%R)

*Weak Two-Party
Leaning Toward the
Republicans*

Kansas (56.25%)
Maine (57.05%)
Nebraska (59.43%)
North Dakota (56.38%)
South Dakota (58.10%)

*Modified One-Party
Republican*

Vermont (62.12%)

One-Party Republican

(none)

*In Delaware, New York, and Utah the split was so close to 50.00% that the
third party vote produced the following: Delaware, 49.79% Democratic,
44.99% Republican, 0.22% Other; New York, 46.87% Democratic, 49.55% Republican,
3.57% Other; and Utah, 49.97% Democratic, 48.46% Republican, 1.57% Other. In
Michigan the following held: 49.55% Democratic, 50.00% Republican, 0.45% Other.

Source: David G. Pfeiffer, "The Measurement of Inter-Party Competition and
Systemic Stability," *American Political Science Review,* Vol. 61, No. 2 (June,
1967), p. 464.

Ranney found that interparty competition is related to "differences in certain social and economic traits and historical experiences and traditions."[3] Concerned with policy implications, Dye finds there are no significant relationships between party competition and tax and revenue decisions, and he suggests instead that "economic development produces both interparty competition and higher tax and revenue levels."[4] Dawson, whose theory holds that the party is an articulator of demands and operates as a conversion mechanism, found instead that "High levels of party competition and liberal state policies both seem to be related independently to highly developed socioeconomic conditions."[5]

Although America is a two-party political system, there are important regional deviations such as in the one-party states of the Democratic South and Republican New England. In addition, the big cities have historically been controlled by the Democratic party. However, as Eulau points out, the urban environment is theoretically conducive to a competitive party system:

> the city, in contrast to the open country, is char-
> acterized by a greater range of individual variations,
> a more pervasive segmentatization of human relation-
> ship making for membership in widely divergent groups
> as well as for divided allegiances, a more compli-
> cated class structure and heightened social and
> physical mobility, a greater division of labor and
> more intense economic rivalry, a wider range of ideas
> and more secular attitudes.[6]

Perhaps all this diversity has not yet effected the political parties or they have responded to it by working out these differences within, say, the Democratic party, with party primaries resolving important differences inside the party. As the political machine has declined the parties have been "nationalized" as Schattschneider suggests, which has shifted the locus from sectional party cleavages to a national alignment which "tends strongly to draw all political organizations, i.e., the pressure groups, Congress, and so on, into the vortex of party conflict."[7]

A viable party, if it is to be more than a paper organization, must enter electoral *contests* with its list of preferred candidates. The number of contests can be determined by referring to the chronology of elections in Table PVII-2. The actual list of candidates can be seen in Table PV-1. Here we are interested only in interparty contests, as intraparty contests (primaries) are discussed in Exercise PIV. A two-party system experiences prolific contests up and down the ballot. Interparty contests are less frequent, if they occur at all, in a one-party system. Intraparty contests are more likely to occur where individuals, minorities, or reform groups with limited resources attempt to challenge party regulars.

Some parties attempt to enhance their effectiveness through *coalition* formations, especially with minority third parties. The use of coalitions can be found by examining the party labels of candidates (see Table PV-1), and their value can be seen in election outcomes (see Table PVII-3). Coalitions, of course, are used to attract those voters who prefer not to cast their votes for one of the major parties but will vote for the major party candidate if he also uses a label more to their liking. The dominant party (with largest proportion of registrants) often hesitates to use third-party associations but will do so reluctantly when the challenging party succeeds in winning elections through the use of a coalition. It should be noted that the two major political parties are themselves coalitions representative of a number of interests.

A party's *proficiency* is the demonstrated ability of the party to get out the vote for its candidates. Our index of proficiency is measured by the relationship between the share of the vote for the party's candidates and its proportion of total registrants (see Table PVII-5). Of course, not all party members vote for their party's ticket, as they may be attracted to the personality, policy position, and/or campaign activities of the other party. Proficiency is in part dependent upon the candidate, on the campaign, and on the party's organizational strength. A minority party can win if it is able to get out its members' votes and to attract the vote of at least some proportion of those registered either to the dominant party, third parties, or those considered to be independents.

Obviously, the major purpose of political parties is to win elections in order to place their candidates into positions of public authority. Party *victories* can be determined easily by counting up the number of times a party's candidates win (see Table PVII-4). It is important to note whether a party wins by a majority (more than 50 percent of the vote) or a plurality (a vote greater than that received by the runner-up), and whether it wins on its own or by using third-party coalitions (see Table PVII-3). Often the "rules of the game" specify that the winning candidate must obtain an absolute majority of the vote. This requirement sometimes results in intraparty primaries and "run-off" elections. It may also be a reason for using multiple party labels. If the rules do not specifically require a clear majority, a simple plurality will suffice to win an election.

To identify the degree of interparty *competition,* we measure the margin of difference in the votes received by the victor over those of the runner-up (see Table PVII-5). The smaller the difference, the greater the competition. Flannigan suggests that a "highly competitive" race has the winner receiving less than 52 percent of the vote, in a "marginal" race the victor receives less than 55 percent of the vote, and in a "safe" or "one-sided" race the winner receives more than 55 percent.[8] For national office he points out that half of the congressional districts are considered safe.

To ascertain a party's *representative* share of the positions in the decision-making centers involves calculating the proportion of executive and legislative positions occupied by those of a designated party relative to that party's proportion of votes received. Thus, if the Democrats received 60 percent of the vote, then ideally they should occupy 60 percent of the seats in the legislative body and/or executive positions. The closer the fit, the more representative is the political system, at least as it measures the political party's share.

The explicit intent of party organizations is to *control* the decision-
making centers. To determine who controls, simply record which party holds
a majority of positions in the legislative chamber and executive branch
(see Table PVII-6). It is important to note how stable the control is
by recording the duration of a party's hold on the majority of positions
over time. One party may control both the executive offices (mayor, comptroller, assessor, district attorney) as well as the legislative positions (city council). In some communities one party may control one
center but the opposition control the other. Although a party may control
a majority of the city council, that in itself does not necessarily
mean the party controls the council, as there may be coalitions based
on ideology and ethnicity within the council that transcend party considerations.

A number of these considerations on the relative fortunes of the
political parties can be analyzed by examining election trends. That
is, are party loyalties unchanging or are they undergoing short or long
term shifts. Analysts have classified elections and characterized periods
of change and stability. Pomper, for example, has identified five significant changes in electoral behavior and four periods of stability throughout American history. The electoral changes occured at the time of
(1) Van Buren, 1836; (2) Lincoln's reelection, 1864; (3) populist-McKinley
and Bryan period; 1892-96, (4) just before and during the New Deal with
the 1928 election being critical; and (5) the victories of Kennedy and
Johnson, 1960 and 1964. The stable periods include (1) 1844-60, Van
Buren to the Civil War; (2) 1876-88, the time between the Reconstruction
and the upheavals of the populists; (3) 1900-20, era of the Republican
Party supremacy; and (4) 1932-48, the heyday of the New Deal.[9]

Figure PVII-1 illustrates 4 hypothetical electoral trends.[10] The
first is *maintaining* where the dominant party continues to win. This type
of trend is generally found in one party systems. The second is *short-
term variations* where both parties win some of the time. This type is
generally found in a highly competitive two-party system where short term
forces tend to favor one party for a time and then the other. The third
is *gradual realignment* where the minority party incrementally gains favor
with the electorate to the point where it becomes the winning party and
stays in the dominant position for a substantial period of time. This
generally takes place where there is a significant change in the composition of the electorate, in the issues, or in the party image. The fourth
is *critical realignment* where the minority party becomes the majority
party suddenly and maintains its dominance for a number of succeeding
elections. This type of realignment generally results from a crisis for
which the two parties offer clearly contrasting solutions. Campbell
describes this type of shift at the national level:

> The fear of the vote was not a temporary reaction
> to a heroic figure or a passing embarassment of
> the party in power; it reflected a reorientation
> of basic party attachments brought about during
> critical periods of the nation's history.[11]

FIGURE PVII-1
HYPOTHETICAL ELECTORAL TRENDS

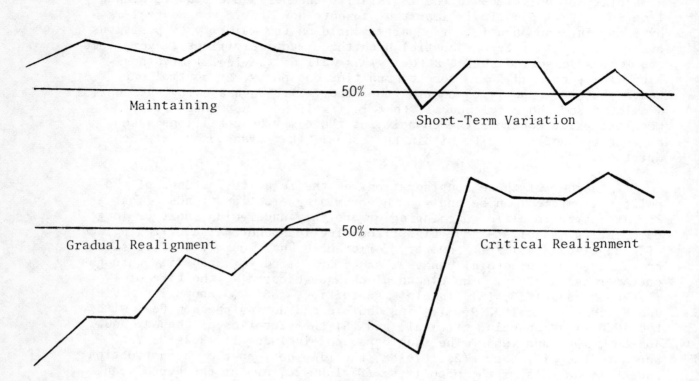

Maintaining

Short-Term Variation

50%

Gradual Realignment

Critical Realignment

50%

Most analysts have been interested in electoral change and have attempted to identify "critical" elections. Burnham reviews electoral trends, interpreting them as indicating a tendency toward

> the progressive dissolution of the parties as
> action intermediaries in electoral choice and
> other political relevant acts. It may also be
> indicative of the production of a mass base for
> independent political movements of ideological
> tone and considerable long-term staying power.[12]

He believes the policy consequences of party decomposition will be profound:

> Political parties, with all their well-known
> human and structural shortcomings, are the only
> devices thus far invented by the wit of Western
> man which with some effectiveness can generate
> countervailing collective power on behalf of the
> many individuals powerless against the relatively
> few who are individually—or organizationally—
> powerful.[13]

Nie, Verba and Petrocik, in studying political attitudes and voting behavior, demonstrate a number of political changes occurring during the 1960s:

1) Partisanship has decreased.

2) Electorate has more coherent set of issue positions.

3) Party organizations have grown weaker.

4) Candidates are more independent of parties.

5) Less social difference between two major parties in the country except in the South.

6) Increased intraparty cleavages.

    a. Actives more conservative than rank and file Republicans.

    b. Actives more liberal than rank and file Democrats.

7) Voters are more dissatisfied with political process.

8) Elections turn on more short-term forces.

9) Elections are less predictable.

They explain these developments by changes in the issues—the Vietnam War, racial conflict, and Watergate—and the entrance of new age groups that are not only more independent but more likely to be non-voters. The authors are dubious that a new party system will emerge. Instead, the "politics of individuation" with ad hoc electoral organizations mediated by television will continue with candidate-based political coalitions and issue-based factions. This post-partisan era may provide more "effectiveness of decisions, responsiveness to the public, and continuity of an open political process."[14]

Nowhere nearly so pronounced is the decomposition of the political parties, as in the election of local public officials on a nonpartisan basis in cities whose electoral reform has taken place (see Exercise PII). Whether these reforms dissolved the political parties or shifted their relative importance and role in American politics has been examined by Hawley, who believes that

> nonpartisan elections tend to decrease the influ-
> ence of Democrats in urban political systems.
> Furthermore, this partisan Republican bias of non-
> partisan city elections fosters public policies that
> are relatively conservative and unresponsive to
> demands for social change and for aggressive use of
> governmental power to remedy social problems.[15]

TYPOLOGY

        We offer the following typology on party effectiveness. On the one
hand, the party's proficiency in receiving its average share of the vote
over a given time period is calculated by dividing the number of registered party members into the number of votes received by the party's candidate. The party's average proficiency for city council candidates is
added to the average proficiency for mayor and then divided by 2. On the
other hand, the party's representation over a given time period is calculated by dividing the proportion of elected positions held by the party by
the percentage voting for the party's candidates. Again the average representation for city council candidates is added to the average representation for mayor and then divided by 2. Both measures are computed for each
of the two major parties and compared to determine the relative effectiveness of each.

FIGURE PVII-2. TYPOLOGY OF POLITICAL PARTY EFFECTIVENESS
(One Party Relative to the Other)

		AVERAGE PROFICIENCY (% VOTES COMPARED TO % REGISTERED)	
		More	*Less*
AVERAGE REPRESENTATION (% ELECTED SEATS COMPARED TO % VOTE)	*More*	Prevailing	Effective but Inefficient
	Less	Efficient but Ineffective	Low Viability

        The *prevailing* political party receives both more than its share of
the votes and elective seats. This is most likely to occur in a two-party
political context where there are independents and third-party options.
A *prevailing* party has demonstrated organizational strength by campaigning
vigorously for its candidates with a more than likely full complement of
precinct workers. Such a party also attempts to maximize the electoral
options through coalitions and selection of the most representative or
balanced ticket to attract voters. A *prevailing* party may also operate
within a community where party attachment among the constituents is cohesive and durable. The party with *low viability* not receiving its share
of either votes or seats is generally the minority party in a one-party
political context. Such a party in a two-party context, however, has
demonstrated little organizational strength, whether in its campaign

activity or the behavior of its precinct cadres. It is unable to select sufficiently attractive candidates or to form effective coalitions. It may also reflect a long history of ineffectiveness that has created a sense of defeat in the organization and reduced the willingness to compete against great odds. Perhaps the most depressing experience for the membership of parties with *low viability* is to witness each new effort to compete responded to by the increased effort and strength of the prevailing party. Democrats have experienced this in upper-status suburbs and Republicans in the South.

A party may be *effective but inefficient* in that it receives more than its share of seats but less than its share of votes. This obviously is the case of the dominant party in a one-party political context. It operates with the secure sense that its opposition cannot win, so it generally has a slack organization and low level of campaign activity. It offers pro forma electoral options that have worked in the past and sees no need to form coalitions. Its candidates are aimed at satisfying the party regulars rather than the broad array of constituents.

An *efficient but ineffective* party through its striving is able from time to time to attract more than its share of votes for its candidates but not enough to win a comparable share of elected seats. This party has the reputation of the subordinate or minority party in either a one-party or a two-party political context. Although it has considerable organizational strength and generally attempts to maximize its electoral options through coalitions and balanced tickets, it is unable to overcome its reputation. It is nonetheless an aspiring party with the eternal hope that it can and will change its subordinate status. One stimulus to its aspiration is the success or even dominance of the party at other levels of government.

SOURCES AND CAVEATS

See Exercise PIII, "Sources and Caveats," for election data sources. Be sure that you have covered all the elections for local offices which may be held on "off" or "off-off" years. Find out the schedule of when positions are open and check for special elections that occur to replace a public official who resigns or dies.

PROFILE EXAMPLE

TABLE PVII-2. THE CHRONOLOGY OF ELECTORAL PREFERENCES IN PERCENTAGES FOR REPUBLICAN
DEMOCRATIC CANDIDATES: 1959-1971

| | MOUNT VERNON | | | NEW ROCHELLE | | |
1959	Total	Republican	Democrat	Total	Republican	Democrat
Registered	31,766	54.7	31.1	30,766	51.4	29.8
Mayor	26,971	56.9*	36.9	26,694	37.3	35.0
1960						
Registered	36,861	52.7	33.0	36,993	48.9	32.1
President	33,199	50.6	43.3*	35,488	49.7	43.5*
U.S. Congress 26th	33,805	50.1*	44.0	33,944	44.7*	48.6
State Senate 30th	31,961	50.6*	43.9	34,092	48.5*	46.5
State Assembly 3rd	32,274	53.1*	40.8	14,460	51.9*	42.9
State Assembly 4th				19,526	46.6*	44.5
City Council	33,986	51.3*	43.2			
1961						
Registered	34,672	52.6	33.0	35,137	48.2	32.8
County Executive	22,537	58.0*	38.4	23,975	52.7*	40.8
County Supervisor	22,169	58.0	38.6	24,694	49.7	34.7
a		57.6*	40.8	4,585	53.0*	42.3
b		59.2*	36.3	4,829	57.7*	35.0
c		59.4*	36.5	11,481	40.7	49.0*
d		58.2*	38.8	3,839	47.1	47.4*
e		55.5*	40.3			
City Council	22,739	56.2	38.7	24,745	48.8	40.8
a		56.4*	36.8		48.5*	42.2
b		55.6*	41.3		49.1*	39.5
c		56.6*	38.0			
1962						
Registered	31,530	52.8	33.1	32,453	49.1	32.5
U. S. Senate	26,742	65.3*	30.0	27,402	69.9*	27.9
U. S. Congress 26th	26,154	55.8*	40.6	27,381	52.9*	42.9
Governor	27,251	59.7*	34.4	28,006	61.4*	32.1
State Senate 30th	24,104	56.3*	40.0	26,267	53.6*	42.2
State Assembly 3rd	24,865	55.0*	41.1	5,894	58.6*	38.6
State Assembly 4th				15,777	48.6*	44.3
1963						
Registered	31,343	51.6	33.7	32,443	48.8	33.1
County Supevisor	23,386	45.0	41.5	26,683	48.9	45.7
A		45.3*	39.2	4,682	55.0*	41.3
B		43.2	43.8*	5,191	57.9*	38.3
C		46.7*	38.3	13,098	47.0	44.3*
D		44.7	46.0*	3,712	36.0	59.9*
E		44.7	40.4*			
Mayor	26,189	41.8	40.5*	27,200	51.8*	43.0
City Council	24,728	46.2	39.7	26,564	50.8	43.8
A		48.5*	39.7		46.8	47.0*
B		44.0	39.7*		54.9*	40.7
1964						
Registered	34,673	45.8	38.8	36,213	44.5	38.6
President	32,845	31.1	61.8*	34,420	30.2	62.6*
U. S. Senate	32,809	42.6	47.8*	34,385	45.8	44.5*
U. S. Congress 26th	31,358	47.4*	45.6	33,497	47.0*	44.8
State Senate 30th	28,682	40.5	52.3*	32,211	41.8	49.7*
State Assembly 3rd	29,523	45.3*	48.1	7,171	46.9*	46.7
State Assembly 4th				18,859	39.6*	50.6

*winner

PROFILE EXAMPLE

TABLE PVII-2 Cont.

		MOUNT VERNON			NEW ROCHELLE	
1965	Total	Republican	Democrat	Total	Republican	Democrat
Registered	32,725	45.1	39.5	34,266	44.4	36.9
State Senate 39th	23,729	50.5*	45.1	22,925	47.1*	45.2
State Assembly 99th	24,433	55.0*	41.0	3,907	56.6*	38.1
State Assembly 100th				21,235	48.8*	43.2
County Executive	23,642	51.3*	42.7	24,534	46.9*	42.4
County Supervisor	28,966	39.1	36.3	25,078	42.6	47.9
A		42.4*	38.7*	4,561	48.5*	40.0
B		39.9*	37.7	4,948	47.9*	40.3
C		38.4*	37.1	12,377	37.7	47.8*
D		37.8*	35.8	3,192	36.6	63.4*
E		37.1	32.3			
City Council	23,979	48.5	44.0	25,726	37.1	32.3
A		50.6*	48.4*		38.2*	34.5
B		50.3*	42.8		35.9*	30.0
C		44.7	40.9			
1966						
Registered	29,985	45.4	38.9	32,350	44.7	36.6
U. S. Congress 26th	23,979	66.7*	29.1	26,008	66.9*	28.3
Governor	26,007	51.4*	31.8	28,168	54.7*	29.1
State Senator 35th	20,851	58.4*	35.6	32,428	56.2*	37.5
State Assembly 88th	23,889	61.4*	33.3	14,706	47.4*	42.9
State Assembly 90th				11,195	59.8*	30.7
City Council				27,029	40.7*	45.6
1967						
Registered	30,810	44.0	39.7	33,225	44.3	36.9
County Supervisor	28,092	40.8	33.3	27,291	53.0	37.8
A		42.4*	36.6	6,892	56.1*	35.4
B		41.2*	35.4	5,886	62.0*	26.7
C		40.8*	32.4	8,191	52.1*	41.7
D		40.7*	31.1	6,322	44.7	47.5*
E		39.2*	31.0			
Mayor	27,099	47.7*	30.7	28,328	76.4*	17.7
City Council	24,042	49.3	39.3	26,513	52.8	37.7
A		52.4*	36.9		58.1*	47.5*
B		46.3*	41.8		48.3	27.1
1968						
Registered	30,810	44.5	40.1	35,645	43.6	36.6
President	29,493	40.8*	46.6	33,533	41.5	46.2*
U. S. Senate	28,557	40.0*	31.7	32,840	44.4*	27.8
U. S. Congress 26th	26,749	53.6*	30.0	31,442	57.9*	25.5
State Senate 35th	22,988	56.1*	34.4	27,176	54.7*	33.6
State Assembly 88th	26,585	54.6*	35.6			
State Assembly 90th				15,543	45.2*	41.3
State Assembly 91st				13,274	57.5*	30.7
County Supervisor				7,186	26.7	21.2
1969						
Registered	29,770	43.2	39.8	33,593	43.5	36.9
County Executive	19,187	49.6*	39.0	21,841	44.3*	45.0
County Supervisor		44.4	43.5	21,000	48.0	42.5
A	14,168	46.5*	40.7	4,427	49.5*	39.2
B	4,819	43.2*	46.9	6,109	48.3*	46.6
C				10,464	46.1*	41.8
City Council	19,092	48.0	42.8	21,678	46.4	41.2
A		49.2*	44.3		47.2*	42.9
B		48.3*	37.0		45.7*	39.6
C		43.1*	33.8			
D		51.5*	36.0			

PROFILE EXAMPLE

TABLE PVII-2 Cont.

		MOUNT VERNON			NEW ROCHELLE	
1970	Total	Republican	Democrat	Total	Republican	Democrat
Registered	27,790	43.5	39.7	32,554	43.7	36.8
U. S. Senate[1]	24,170	17.5	40.1	29,269	17.5	37.3
U. S. Congress 26th	22,460	55.6*	21.4	27,983	57.6*	15.0
Governor	24,652	52.5*	34.7	29,654	54.3*	32.8
State Senate 35th	19,267	48.9*	33.3	23,894	51.1*	30.9
State Assembly 88th	22,065	48.8*	33.7			
State Assembly 90th				15,391	49.2*	35.7
State Assembly 91st				11,565	63.9*	24.1
Mayor				29,267	45.0*	31.7
1971						
Registered	28,805	41.3	41.3	34,126	41.9	38.7
Mayor	22,552	54.5*	37.7	25,883	58.8*	31.5
1972						
Registered	31,354	39.6	42.9	36,717	40.1	40.0
President	28,869	47.6*	42.9	33,761	49.3*	41.4

[1]James Buckley, Conservative, received 35.9% in Mount Vernon, 38.2% in New Rochelle.

OPERATIONAL DEFINITIONS

$$\% \text{ Voting for Party Candidates} = \frac{\text{Number Voting Party Candidate on Major Party Line}}{\text{Number Total Votes Cast}}$$

PROFILE EXAMPLE

TABLE PVII-3. ELECTORAL OUTCOMES AND BASIS OF VICTORY

| | | | | 3rd Party | 3rd Party | Own Party Victory By | Own Party Victory By |
	Positions	Contests	Victors	Used	Needed	Majority	Plurality
REPUBLICANS							
Mount Vernon							
Mayor[a]	4	4	3	1	-	2	1
City Council[b]	15	15	13	9	5	8	-
Total	19	19	16	10	5	10	1
Percent		100.0	84.2	52.6	31.3	62.5	6.3
New Rochelle							
Mayor[a]	5	5	4	-	-	3	1
City Council[b]	11	11	9	4	3	2	4
Total	16	16	13	4	3	5	5
Percent		100.0	81.3	25.0	23.1	38.5	38.5
DEMOCRATS							
Mount Vernon							
Mayor[a]		4	1	3	1	-	-
City Council[b]		15	2	14	2	-	-
Total		19	3	17	3	-	-
Percent		100.0	15.8	89.5	100.0		
New Rochelle							
Mayor[a]		5	1	2	1	-	-
City Council[b]		11	2	3	-	1	1
Total		16	3	5	1	1	1
Percent		100.0	18.8	31.3	33.3	33.3	33.3

[a] 1959-71
[b] 1961-69

OPERATIONAL DEFINITIONS

% Contests = $\dfrac{\text{Total Contests}}{\text{Total Position}}$

% Victors = $\dfrac{\text{Total Victors}}{\text{Total Contests}}$

% Used Third Parties = $\dfrac{\text{Total Used Third Parties}}{\text{Total Contests}}$

% Needed Third Parties = $\dfrac{\text{Total Needed Third Parties}}{\text{Total Victors}}$

% Own Party Victory by Majority (Plurality) = $\dfrac{\text{Won by Majority (Plurality)}}{\text{Total Victors}} = \dfrac{\text{Victories Without Need of Third Party}}{}$

PROFILE EXAMPLE

TABLE PVII-4. ELECTORAL PARTY PREFERENCES FOR PRESIDENTIAL AND MAYORALTY CANDIDATES
IN PERCENTAGES, 1926-1972

| | MOUNT VERNON | | | NEW ROCHELLE | | |
President	Republi-can	Demo-crat	Republican Margin	Republi-can	Demo-crat	Republican Margin
1920	71.3	18.6	52.7	73.9	20.2	53.7
1924	65.3	18.2	47.1	65.3	20.9	44.4
1928	59.9	37.6	22.3	53.0	44.9	8.1
1932	50.2	44.6	5.6	48.4	46.2	2.2
1936	48.3	47.1	1.2	48.7	48.0	0.7
1940	60.8	34.6	26.2	61.4	34.8	26.6
1944	32.4	58.7	-26.3	34.7	57.9	-23.2
1948	57.4	33.3	24.1	58.4	32.3	26.1
1952	60.8	33.0	27.8	62.9	31.5	31.4
1956	64.6	31.4	33.2	65.6	30.2	35.4
1960	50.6	43.3	7.3	49.7	43.5	6.2
1964	31.1	61.8	-30.7	30.2	62.6	-32.4
1968[a]	40.8	46.6	- 5.8	41.5	46.2	- 4.7
1972	47.6	42.9	4.7	49.3	41.4	7.9
Mayor						
1921	46.4	49.0*	- 2.6	56.9*	40.2	16.7
1923	54.0*	42.7	11.3	62.5*	34.4	28.1
1925	NA	NA	NA	52.1*	35.7	16.4
1927	53.6*	44.2	9.4	58.4*	41.6	16.8
1929	NA	NA	NA	40.2	59.8	-19.6
1931	38.7	58.2*	-19.5	49.2	50.8*	- 1.6
1935	58.8*	39.2	19.6	53.3	44.5	8.8
1939	51.3*	40.3	11.0	42.0	55.8*	-13.8
1943	70.6*	25.5	45.1	38.5	50.7*	-12.2
1947	61.8*	36.1	25.7	30.2	69.8*	-39.6
1951	30.8	34.7*	- 3.9	36.7	52.6*	-15.9[b]
1955	42.6	52.3*	- 9.7	31.1	27.9	3.2
1959	56.9*	36.9	20.0	37.3	35.2*	2.1
1963	41.8	40.5*	1.3	51.8*	43.0	8.8
1967	47.7*	30.7	17.0	76.4*	17.7	58.7
1970	NA	NA	NA	45.0*	31.7	13.3
1971	54.5*	37.7	16.8	58.8*	31.5	27.3

*Winner

[a]Wallace, A.I.P., received 12.6% in Mount Vernon and 12.6% in New Rochelle.

[b]Vergara, Independent, won, receiving 36.9%.

OPERATIONAL DEFINITIONS

Republican Margin = % of Vote Won by Republican Candidate on Republican Line -
                    % of Vote Won by Democratic Candidate on Democratic Line.

TABLE PVII-5. PARTY COMPETITION FOR EXECUTIVE AND LEGISLATIVE OFFICES, AVERAGE FOR THE
DECADE, 1959-1972

| | MOUNT VERNON | | | NEW ROCHELLE | | |
	Republi-can %	Demo-crat %	Republican Margin	Republi-can %	Demo-crat %	Republican Margin
Executive						
President	42.5	48.7	- 6.2	42.7	48.4	- 5.7
Governor	54.5	33.6	20.9	56.8	31.3	25.5
County Executive	53.0	40.0	13.0	48.0	42.7	5.3
Mayor	50.2	36.5	13.7	53.9	31.8	22.1
Legislative						
U.S. Senate	43.9	37.5	6.4	44.4	34.4	10.0
U.S. Congress	54.9	35.1	19.8	54.5	34.1	20.4
State Senate	51.6	40.7	10.9	50.4	40.8	9.6
State Assembly	53.3	39.1	14.2	48.7	42.9	5.8
County Supervisor	45.5	38.6	6.9	48.4	41.7	6.7
City Council	49.9	41.3	8.6	45.3	41.0	4.3

OPERATIONAL DEFINITIONS

See Table PVII-2 for percentages received by party candidates for each office for each
election. Add percentages for decade and divide by the number of elections.

Dominant Party Margin = % of Vote Received by Dominant Party in Decade - % Vote Received
                        by Minority Party in the Decade

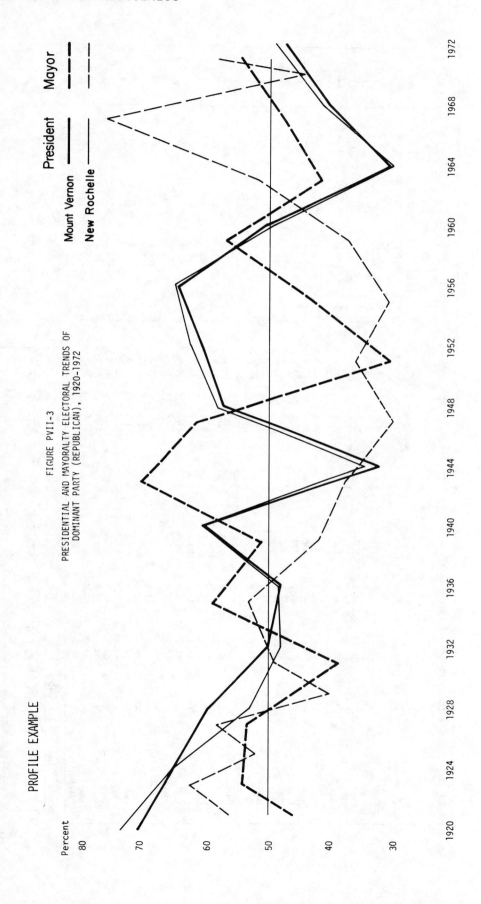

PROFILE EXAMPLE

FIGURE PVII-3

PRESIDENTIAL AND MAYORALTY ELECTORAL TRENDS OF
DOMINANT PARTY (REPUBLICAN), 1920-1972

PROFILE EXAMPLE

TABLE PVII-6. PROFICIENCY, REPRESENTATION, AND COMPETITION IN PERCENTAGES OF THE TWO MAJOR POLITICAL PARTIES, 1959-1971

	Positions #	REPUBLICAN Regis-tered	Vote	Profic-iency	Seats #	Represen-tation	DEMOCRAT Regis-tered	Vote	Profic-iency	Seats #	Represen-tation	Competition
Mount Vernon												
Mayor												
1959	1	54.7	56.9	104.0	1	175.8	31.1	36.9	118.7	0	0.0	20.0
1963	1	51.6	41.8	81.0	0	0.0	33.7	40.5	120.2	1	296.7	1.3
1967	1	44.0	47.7	108.4	1	227.3	39.7	30.7	77.3	0	0.0	17.0
1971	1	41.3	54.5	132.0	1	242.1	41.3	37.7	91.3	0	0.0	16.8
Average		47.9	50.2	104.8		158.2	36.5	36.5	100.0		74.2	13.7
City Council												
1960	5	52.7	51.3	97.3	5	194.9	33.0	43.2	130.9	0	0.0	8.1
1961	5	52.6	56.2	106.8	5	177.9	33.0	38.7	117.3	0	0.0	17.5
1963	5	51.6	46.2	89.5	4	173.2	33.7	39.7	117.8	1	50.4	6.5
1965	5	45.1	48.5	107.5	3	123.7	39.5	44.0	89.8	2	90.9	4.5
1967	5	44.0	49.3	112.0	4	162.3	39.7	39.3	99.0	1	50.9	10.0
1969	5	43.2	48.0	111.1	5	208.3	39.8	42.8	107.5	0	0.0	5.2
Average		48.2	49.9	103.5		173.8	36.5	41.3	113.2		32.2	8.6
New Rochelle												
Mayor												
1959	1	51.4	37.3	72.6	0	0.0	29.8	35.0	117.5	1	284.1	2.3
1963	1	48.8	51.8	106.2	1	193.1	33.1	43.0	129.9	0	0.0	8.8
1967	1	44.3	76.4	172.5	1	130.9	36.9	17.7	48.0	0	0.0	58.7
1970	1	43.7	45.0	103.0	1	222.2	36.8	31.7	86.1	0	0.0	13.3
1971	1	41.9	58.8	140.3	1	170.1	38.7	31.5	81.4	0	0.0	27.3
Average		46.0	53.9	117.2		147.3	35.1	31.8	90.6		62.8	22.1
City Council												
1961	4	48.2	48.8	101.3	4	204.9	32.8	40.8	124.4	0	0.0	8.0
1963	4	48.8	50.8	104.1	3	147.6	33.1	43.8	132.3	1	57.1	7.0
1964	4	44.5	40.7	91.5	3	184.3	38.6	45.6	118.1	1	54.8	- 4.9
1965	4	44.4	37.0	83.3	3	202.7	36.9	32.2	87.5	1	77.6	- 4.8
1966	4	44.7	40.7	91.1	3	184.3	36.6	45.6	124.6	1	54.8	- 4.9
1967	4	44.2	52.8	119.5	3	142.1	36.9	37.7	102.2	1	66.3	15.1
1969	4	43.5	46.4	106.7	3	161.6	36.9	41.2	111.7	1	60.7	5.2
Average		45.5	45.3	99.6		173.5	36.0	41.0	113.9		52.2	4.3

OPERATIONAL DEFINITIONS

Proficiency = $\dfrac{\text{% Vote Received on Party Line}}{\text{% Registered to Party}}$ Representation = $\dfrac{\text{% Positions Held by Party}}{\text{% Vote Received by Party}}$

Competition = % Vote Received by Dominant Party - % Vote Received by Minority Party

PROFILE EXAMPLE

TABLE PVII-7. POLITICAL PARTY CONTROL OF EXECUTIVE AND LEGISLATIVE POSITIONS BY LEVEL OF POLICY-MAKING, 1960-1970

Year	NATIONAL			STATE (New York)			COUNTY (Westchester)		Mount Vernon		LOCAL New Rochelle	
	Executive	U.S. Senate	U.S. Congress	Executive	State Senate	State Assembly	Executive	Board of Legislators	Executive	City Council	Executive	City Council
1960	R	D	D	R	R	R	R	R	R	R	D	R
1961	D	D	D	R	R	R	R	R	R	R	D	R
1962	D	D	D	R	R	R	R	R	R	R	D	R
1963	D	D	D	R	R	R	R	R	R	R	D	R
1964	D	D	D	R	R	R	R	R	D	R	R	R
1965	D	D	D	R	D	D	R	R	D	R	R	R
1966	D	D	D	R	R	D	R	R	D	R	R	R
1967	D	D	D	R	R	D	R	R	D	R	R	R
1968	D	D	D	R	R	D	R	R	R	R	R	R
1969	R	D	D	R	R	R	R	R	R	R	R	R
1970	R	D	D	R	R	R	R	R	R	R	R	R
% Control												
Republican	27.3	0.0	0.0	100.0	90.9	63.6	100.0	100.0	63.6	100.0	63.6	100.0
Democrat	72.7	100.0	100.0	0.0	9.1	36.4	0.0	0.0	36.4	0.0	36.4	0.0

R = Republican
D = Democrat

OPERATIONAL DEFINITIONS

Control = Majority of Seats in Legislative Body or Holding Executive Position

$$\% \ Control = \frac{Number \ of \ Years \ in \ Control}{Total \ Years \ in \ Period}$$

CLASSIFICATION INDICATORS

	MOUNT VERNON		NEW ROCHELLE	
	Republican	Democrat	Republican	Democrat
Proficiency				
Executive	104.8	100.0	117.2	90.6
Legislative	103.5	113.2	99.6	113.9
Average	104.2	106.6	108.4	102.3
Representation				
Executive	158.2	74.2	147.3	62.9
Legislative	173.8	32.2	173.5	52.2
Average	166.0	53.2	160.4	57.6

See Table PVII-6.

FINDINGS AND SUGGESTED IMPLICATIONS

The Republican party in Mount Vernon was *effective but inefficient*. That is, the proficiency of the Republican party was lower than the Democratic party's but its representation was higher. For these same reasons, the Democratic party was *efficient but ineffective*. New Rochelle's Republican party, on the other hand, was *prevailing* and its Democratic party of *low viability*. That is, the Republican party had both greater proficiency and representation than the Democratic party.

The proficiency of Mount Vernon Democrats was impressive as they received their share of the votes for mayors and more than their share for city council positions. They were, however, underrepresented for the mayoralty and even more so in the city council.

Both communities, located in New York State, were operating within a two-party system (see Table PVII-1). While both parties contested and entered candidates for local office upon every opportunity, the Republican party won most of the time in both communities (see Table PVII-3). The Republicans won 84 percent of the elections for mayor and city council in Mount Vernon and 81 percent in New Rochelle.

Interparty competition was much closer for the city councilmen than the winning and losing margins suggest (see Table PVI-3). The Republican margin of difference in votes was closer for councilmen than for mayoralty elections in both communities (see Table PVII-5). The Republican margin was closest for the city council in New Rochelle, and averaged 4.3 percent during the decade compared to 8.6 percent in Mount Vernon. Electoral competition for the mayoralty was lowest in New Rochelle, with the Republicans obtaining a comfortable average margin of 22.1 percent compared to 13.7 percent in Mount Vernon. On the two occasions when the Democratic candidate won the mayoralty, once in each community, the Republican candidates obtained a favorable margin over the Democrats but, because of third-party contests, lost the election. In Mount Vernon, the Republicans outpolled the Democrats by 1.3 percent in 1963, yet lost to the Democratic-Liberal candidate, a former mayor, who won by a plurality of 45.3 percent. In this case no candidate won a majority, as a conservative Citizen Independent candidate drew off sufficient votes to deny the winner a majority. Similarly, in New Rochelle a former Democratic mayor won by a plurality with the help of the Liberal label (35.0 percent) in 1959 even though the Republican candidate outpolled him as a Democrat by 2.3 percent. The incumbent Citizen Reform candidate attracted 21.1 percent of the vote, precluding the winner from receiving a majority of the vote. Of the 16 Republican victories in Mount Vernon, 62.5 percent were by an outright majority, whereas of the 13 Republican victories in New Rochelle 38.5 percent were by a majority and 38.5 percent were by a plurality.

As the dominant party, Republicans used third-party coalitions less than the Democrats, who relied heavily on this means to compete with their opponents (see Table PVI-3). However, Republicans were more likely to use third-party labels in city council races than for the mayoralty. Mount Vernon Republicans were twice as prone to do so as their counterparts in New Rochelle, but even then they used coalitions much less often than did the Democrats. The Republicans of Mount Vernon used the Conservative party label only once in four mayoralty elections, whereas the Democrats used the Liberal party label in three of the four races. In the fourth race the Liberals did not endorse the Democratic candidate because he was a long-term Republican city councilman who had switched his party affiliation to contest the election of the incumbent Republican mayor. The Republicans of New Rochelle did not use third-party labels for the mayoralty because the Democrats in that city were also less inclined to do so. In fact, the Liberals and the Conservatives switched their traditional alliance; one Democratic councilman successfully used the Conservative label and the Liberals successfully joined a (black) Republican's bid for the city council.

As the dominant party in both communities, the Republicans carried all executive contests on their own without needing their third-party votes, whereas Democrats absolutely needed the third-party label to win the mayoralty. However, the Republican victors in Mount Vernon for city council needed third-party labels in one-third of their victories. On the one hand, the Democratic councilmanic candidates never won without a third-party line. In New Rochelle the Republican victors in city council races needed the third-party line one-fourth of the time, whereas the Democrats needed such labels one-third of the time.

Interparty competition for executive and legislative offices from national to local officials varied considerably in the two communities during the decade (see Table PVII-5). On the one hand, Democratic Presidential candidates won by an average margin of 6 percent while Republican gubernatorial candidates won by more than a 20 percent margin. The range in Republican margins was less for legislative offices in both communities. The Republican margin ranged from a comfortable 20 percent for the congressman to less than 10 percent for the U.S. Senator, county supervisors, and city councilmen.

Neither Mount Vernon nor New Rochelle experienced the *critical realignment* of the New Deal that the nation did for the Presidency (see Figure PVII-3). Rather, their electoral trends displayed *short-term variations* in Presidential elections, giving the Democratic candidates a majority in 1944 and 1964 and a plurality in 1968. However, the critical election in the nation in 1928 brought the Democratic percentages of the vote in both cities up from about 20 percent to a point where they were competitive.

Presidential politics seemed to have little effect on the mayoralty outcomes in either Mount Vernon or New Rochelle. The election trend for mayor in Mount Vernon could be classified as one of *short-term variations* (see Figure PVII-4), with the Republicans in dominance from 1923 to 1931, 1935 to 1951, 1959 to 1963, and from 1967 through the 70s. The Democrats, on the other hand, were in control of the mayoralty for 16 out of the 51 year trend.

In New Rochelle there was a *gradual realignment* from 1921 to 1939 from Republican to Democratic dominance of the mayoralty. The Democrats continued to hold the mayor's office from 1939 until 1963 with a one-term interruption (1955-59) by an Independent candidate. In 1963, a *critical realignment* took place that reestablished Republican control of the mayoralty on into the 1970s.

Despite the vigor of the two-party system, a complete contesting, the free use of coalitions, near parity of proficiency, and closeness in the margins of electoral competition, the bottom line for partisans was that Republicans controlled most of the decision-making centers in both communities. From 1960 through 1970 the Republicans controlled the mayoralty 63.6 percent of the time and the city councils 100.0 percent of the time. The Democrats never controlled (constituted a majority of) the city council, while there were periods when Republicans comprised 100 percent of the council. In fact, it is at the federal level only that the Democrats were able to feel any sense of control from 1961 through 1968. The other three years the White House was controlled by a Republican (see Table PVII-4). At the state level, the Republicans controlled the governorship and only briefly did the Democrats control the legislature (1965-66). The county government during the 1960s was controlled by the Republican party.

In sum, extrapolating from our type of data we will attempt to compare the partisan behavior for local offices of Mount Vernon and New Rochelle with the national trends found through interviewing by Nie, Verba, and Petrocik.

1) No data. There has been only a slight increase in independent registration.

2) Support in Mount Vernon with racial change stimulating reformulation of public issues. No support in New Rochelle with electoral outcomes dependent primarily upon party labels or personalities.

3) No support. Party organizations maintained a nearly full compliment of party workers (see Exercise PIV) maintaining relatively unchanged organizational strength. Parties continue to offer candidates at every opportunity. Both parties in both communities were drawing their share of registered voters in general elections. However, with the exception of the Republican party in Mount Vernon, the party organizations had some difficulty in designating their candidates without intraparty primaries. The two parties were somewhat weakened by the growing role of third parties—Liberal and Conservative.

4) Support. Both communities had independent candidates running for both mayoralty and city council positions. The candidates of the two major parties sought third party support but less so in New Rochelle than in Mount Vernon. The most difficult problem for the parties perhaps was the switch over of candidates from one party to another. This happened twice in Mount Vernon during the decade.

5) Support. At the end of the decade, both parties in both communities had registrants who were rich and poor, black and white, Italian, Jewish, and Anglo-Saxon Protestant.

6) Using as our measure of "actions" the prevailing faction of each party, we examine their candidate selection strategy.

   a. No support. In Mount Vernon, the prevailing faction of the Republican party moved from its conservative posture to a more moderate one providing a "closer fit" with its rank and file. In New Rochelle the prevailing faction moved from a conservative position to a more moderate one to match the shift of its rank and file in that direction.

   b. No support. The prevailing faction in the Democratic party of Mount Vernon moved from a position of more liberal than its rank and file to one of a "closer fit" to match the shift of the electorate toward the right. In New Rochelle the prevailing faction of the Democratic party remained in the center attempting to balance off the preferences of a conservative Southside constituency and a progressive Northside one.

7) Support. The percentages of the actives (registered voting) decreased in both communities during the decade.

8) Support for Mount Vernon; no support for New Rochelle. The electoral trends for the mayoralty in Mount Vernon display short-term variations with Republican control interrupted by the Democrats three times during a 50 year period for a total of 16 years. In New Rochelle, on the other hand, there was a gradual realignment from Republican to Democratic from 1921 to 1939 followed by Democratic control of the mayoralty for

nearly 24 years and a critical realignment in 1963 bringing
control back to the Republicans.

9) Support for Mount Vernon, no support for New Rochelle. If the
percentage of registrants to the parties is used as a predictor,
then Mount Vernon's mayoralty elections were unpredictable.
When the Republicans had a substantial edge in registration over
the Democrats, a Democrat was elected mayor three times. When
a shift in registration brought the Democrats and Republicans
even in their percentages registrants, a Republican was elected
mayor. Challenges by independent candidates and the use of third
parties brought about unexpected election outcomes. In New
Rochelle, however, election outcomes became more predictable in
the 60s with the dominant Republican party's candidates winning
all the mayoralty elections. Prior to the 60s, a Democrat had
been mayor for 16 years and finally was defeated by an independent.

Despite evidence that there was some weakening of the two major
parties as controlling political institutions, they remain viable instruments in the selection of who shall govern the local community. In a
competitive party system it is important to assess the factors which contribute to the relative position of one party to another and the likely
consequences. We offer the following speculations on four types of party
viability.

FIGURE PVII-4. SPECULATIONS ON FACTORS CONTRIBUTING TO
AND POSSIBLE CONSEQUENCES OF VARIOUS KINDS OF
POLITICAL PARTY EFFECTIVENESS

Contributing Factors	*Possible Consequences*
PREVAILING	
Reflects majority of *actives'* values and ideologies.	One party controls decision-making centers and dominates policy outputs.
Candidate options are more representative of body politic.	Party regulars are rewarded.
Aggressive party organization.	Encourages intraparty cliques.
	Demoralizes minority opposition.
LOW VIABILITY	
Party values and ideologies do not reflect the constituency.	Ideologues or "extremists" may attempt to take over party.
Candidate options are not popular.	It becomes difficult to attract good candidates.
Low-energy party organization exists and is unskilled in converting limited political resources.	Intraparty factionalism develops.
	Party registrants seek other alternatives.
Lack of state support or context is unfavorable to party.	
EFFECTIVE BUT INEFFICIENT	
Overconfidence develops.	Intraparty reform factions may attempt to take over party.
Slack in organization grows.	Party favors and promotes popular incumbents.
Opposition candidates have broader appeal than partisan.	Party begins to replace marginal incumbents, anticipating possible defeat.
Aspiring and competitive minority party grows in strength.	Dominant party tends to emulate those strategies of minority party that are perceived as successful.
INEFFECTIVE BUT EFFICIENT	
Aggressive party organization works against great odds with insufficient constituent support.	Encourages intraparty recriminations.
Popular candidates are put forth that transcend partisanship.	Careful scrutiny is given to third-party issues, "ticket-balancing," and ultimately coalitions.
Party selects centrist candidates that attract independent and third-party registrants.	Dominant party begins to see aspiring party as a threat.
Unskillful use of party resources hinders overcoming dominant party strength.	

DISCUSSION

1. What are the political parties' effectiveness classifications for your community?

2. How would you characterize: (a) the state party context, (b) candidate contests, (c) coalition formations, (d) proportion of victories, (e) margin of competition, (f) the control of local decision-making centers? To what extent have these factors changed in the decade under consideration?

3. To what do you attribute each party's effectiveness: (a) social characteristics of the population, (b) resources of the party organizations, (c) kind of electoral options offered, (d) the campaigns being waged, (e) the party context, and (f) the scheduling of elections?

4. Speculate on the ways in which the relative effectiveness of the political parties in your community affects the following major areas of community life: (a) housing, (b) education, (c) health, (d) welfare, (e) economic opportunities, (f) cultural activities, and (g) social tensions.

5. Do you think it important to change the effectiveness of any or all the parties in your community? If so, which one(s) and in what direction? What social, political, and/or economic strategies could be employed to bring about the desired change?

NOTES

1. John H. Fenton, *People and Parties in Politics* (Scott, Foresman & Co., 1966), p. 32.

2. David G. Pfeiffer, "The Measurement of Inter-Party Competition and Systemic Stability," *American Political Science Review,* Vol. 61, No. 2 (June, 1967), p. 464.

3. Austin Ranney, "Parties in State Politics" in *Politics in the American States* edited by Herbert Jacob and Kenneth N. Vines (Little Brown, 1965), p. 70.

4. Thomas R. Dye, *Politics, Economics, and the Public* (Rand McNally & Co., 1966), p. 206.

5. Richard E. Dawson, "Social Development, Party Competition, and Policy," in *The American Party Systems* edited by William N. Chambers and Walter D. Burnham (Oxford University Press, 1967), p. 237.

6. Heinz Eulau, *Micro-Macro Political Analysis* (Aldine Publishing Co., 1969), p. 250.

7. E. E. Schattschneider, *The Semi-Sovereign People* (Holt, Rinehart & Winston, 1960), p. 95.

8.   William H. Flanigan, *Political Behavior of the American Electorate* (2nd ed., Allyn and Bacon, 1972), pp. 34-35.

9.   Gerald M. Pomper, *Elections in America* (Dodd, Mead & Co., 1970), p. 103.

10.   These trends have been adapted from Pomper, *ibid.,* p. 103.

11.   Angus Campbell, "A Classification of the Presidential Elections," in *Elections and the Political Order,* Angus Campbell, Philip Converse, Warren Miller, and Donald Stokes, (John Wiley & Sons, 1966), p. 76.

12.   Walter D. Burnham, *Critical Elections and the Mainsprings of American Politics* (W. W. Norton, Inc., 1970), pp. 130-131.

13.   *Ibid.,* p. 133.

14.   Norman H. Nie, Sidney Verba, and John R. Petrocik, *The Changing American Voter* (Harvard University Press, 1976), pp. 345-352.

15.   Willis D. Hawley, *Nonpartisan Elections and the Case for Party Politics* (John Wiley & Sons, 1973), p. 5.

COMMUNITY DATA PROFILE   PVII-A

(PVII-2) THE CHRONOLOGY OF ELECTORAL PREFERENCES

| | *YOUR COMMUNITY* | | | *COMPARISON CITY* | | |
	Total	*Republican*	*Democrat*	*Total*	*Republican*	*Democrat*
19__ Registered Elections*						
19__ Registered						
19__ Registered						
19__ Registered						

*Enter all appropriate elections for each year.

Repeat worksheet for number of years necessary.

COMMUNITY DATA PROFILE PVII-B

(PVII-3) ELECTORAL OUTCOMES AND BASIS OF VICTORY

			R E P U B L I C A N S				*D E M O C R A T S*			
				3rd Party	Carried By				3rd Party	Carried By
				Used Needed	Major- Plural-				Used Needed	Major- Plural-
	Positions	Contests	Victors		ity ity	Contests	Victors		ity ity
Your Community										
Mayor										
City Council										
Total										
Comparison City										
Mayor										
City Council										
Total										

COMMUNITY DATA PROFILE PVII-C

(PVII-4) ELECTORAL PARTY PREFERENCES FOR PRESIDENTIAL
AND MAYORALTY CANDIDATES IN PERCENTAGES, 19__ to 19__

President	*YOUR COMMUNITY*			*COMPARISON CITY*		
	Republi-can	*Demo-crat*	*Margin*	*Republi-can*	*Demo-crat*	*Margin*
19__						
19__						
19__						
19__						
19__						
.19__						
19__						
19__						
19__						
19__						
19__						
19__						
19__						
19__						
Mayor						
19__						
19__						
19__						
19__						
19__						
19__						
19__						
19__						
19__						
19__						
19__						
19__						
19__						
19__						
19__						

(PVII-5) PARTY COMPETITION FOR EXECUTIVE AND LEGISLATIVE OFFICES,
AVERAGE FOR THE DECADE 19__ to 19__

	YOUR COMMUNITY			*COMPARISON CITY*		
Executive	*Republican*	*Democrat*	*Margin*	*Republican*	*Democrat*	*Margin*
President						
Governor						
County Executive						
Mayor						
Legislative						
U.S. Senate						
U.S. Congress						
State Senate						
State Assembly						
County Supervisor						
City Council						

COMMUNITY DATA PROFILE PVII-D

(PVII-6) PROFICIENCY, REPRESENTATION, AND COMPETITION IN PERCENTAGES OF THE TWO MAJOR POLITICAL PARTIES, 19___ to 19___

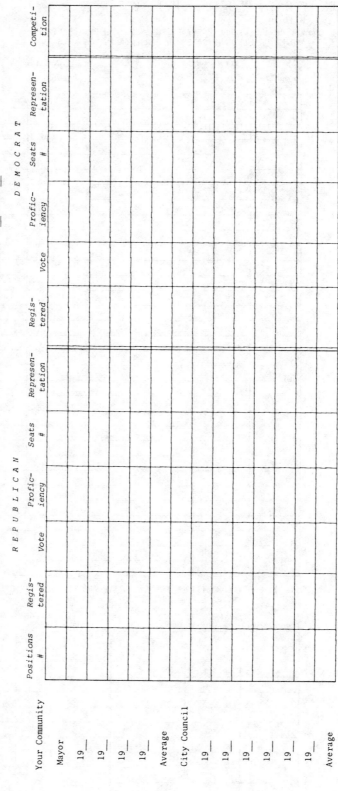

*Copy worksheet for comparison city.

COMMUNITY DATA PROFILE PVII-E

(PVII-7) POLITICAL PARTY CONTROL OF EXECUTIVE AND LEGISLATIVE POSITIONS BY LEVEL OF POLICY-MAKING

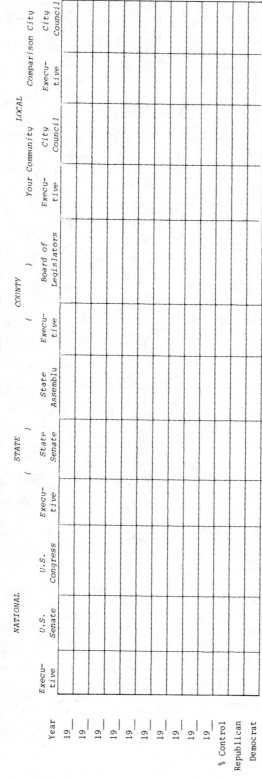

Part IV
THE ECONOMIC DIMENSION

E1. ECONOMIC FUNCTION

WHAT ARE THE MAJOR ECONOMIC FUNCTIONS OF YOUR CITY?

CONCEPT

One does not have to be an economic determinist to realize the importance of the local economy. It provides the jobs, the earned income, and the prime motive for most Americans to move into town. As Reisman states:

> The economic character of the city is almost as
> evident as its size. . . . The architecture of the
> city's economic activity is apparent in its factories,
> banks, office buildings, ball parks, restaurants, and
> retail stores. . . . the city, especially the metro,
> is a specialized economic environment distinctly con-
> centrated in the secondary and tertiary industries of
> manufacturing and service.[1]

These economic activities affect the city not only as to employment and land use patterns, but also as to the kinds of people who choose to live there, their support for certain levels of public expenditures, and often their influence in community affairs.

One of the earliest systematic ways to classify cities was by economic function. That is, cities were classified according to their greatest economic activity. The functional types developed were industrial, commercial, resort, and so on. It was, however, through the work of Harris in the 1940s, using 1930 census data, that clear criteria were first established.[2] Harris based his classification on employment figures from each industrial and trading establishment within each city and supplemented these figures with occupation figures for the residents. He recognized that most cities were multifunctional but chose to focus on the main activity. Harris and those who followed him classified cities on the basis of simple percentages arrived at by dividing those employed in each of four categories, i.e., manufacturing, retail trade, wholesale trade, and specialized service, by the total of all those employed in the four categories. This total was called aggregate employment.

We use a system developed by Jones, Forstall, and Colliver which first appeared in 1963 and was modified in 1967.[3] They classify cities also on census data of employment in manufacturing, retailing, wholesaling,

and selected service establishments on a *place-of-work basis* (see Table
EI-3). The five main types of cities include: (1) *Manufacturing (Mm)*,
where 50 percent or more of aggregate employment is in manufacturing and
less than 30 percent is in retail trade; (2) *Industrial (M)*, where 50
percent or more of aggregate employment is in manufacturing and over 30
percent is in retail trade; (3) *Diversified-Manufacturing (Mr)*, where
employment in manufacturing is greater than in retail but less than 50
percent of aggregate employment; (4) *Diversified-Retailing (Rm)*, where
employment is greater in retailing than in manufacturing but the latter
is at least 20 percent of aggregate employment; and (5) *Retailing (Rr)*,
where retail employment is greater than manufacturing or any other component of aggregate employment and manufacturing is less than 20 percent of
aggregate employment. Jones and his colleagues found that these five
types comprised over 85 percent (1,557 our of 1,679 cities classified)
of the American communities with populations of 10,000 or more. The
remaining 122 cities reported by Jones et al. as specialized cities "are
those in which some unusual economic activity forms the principal support
of the city." The specialized functional categories include the following:
*Wholesaling (W), Mining (Mg), Transportation (T), Resort (X), Government (G),
Armed Forces (AF), Professional (PR), Hospital (H), Education (Ed), and
Service (S)*. Of these, those which specialize in wholesaling and service
were classified on the basis of aggregate employment data; the others were
classified on the basis of labor-force data (see Table EI-2).

A study of functional classification by region, city size, and metropolitan status reported interesting patterns of distribution. Changes over
time from 1958 to 1967 displayed shifts in the classification of individual
cities as well as changes in the percentages of all cities in certain classifications. It should be noted, however, that the classifications of some
cities changed because there were new categories or redefinitions of old
categories and not because their functions actually changed.[4]

Jones and his colleagues also developed a Employment/Residence (E/R)
ratio, which is the ratio of aggregate employment to the corresponding
categories of the resident labor force. The ratio, they state, is a rough
measure of net commuting for the economic activities involved. They
classified cities with different E/R ratios: (1) employing (E)——116 or
more; (2) balanced (B)——85 to 115; and (3) dormitory (D)——84 or less.
These ratios are only approximations because of methodological problems
noted by the authors. (In 1967 an additional economic classifiction was
added based on the E/R ratio: that of the dormitory community (D). The
D cities are generally suburban communities in which aggregate employment
is less than 67 percent of the estimated total of resident workers engaged
in the same activities and in which commuting is the most significant
activity.) Changes in E/R ratios can be accounted for by an (a) increase
in local employment more rapid than the increase in population, (b) a
decentralization of population more rapid than that of employment,
(c) annexation of residential areas, and (d) rapid population growth
that exceeds local gains in employment.

Whereas the Jones approach is based on employment patterns, Rand
McNally has classified cities by their dollar volume of sales and manufacturing. They provide several measures. One is the Ranally City

Ratings system, which places each city in a hierarchy of commercial importance in the United States.[5]   Another classifies cities in terms of their business scope so that 27 National Business Centers, 163 Regional Business Centers, and 561 Significant Local Business Centers have been identified.[6] In addition, there is the Ranally sales index, which measures a city's proportion of the total U.S. sales, with all U.S. sales equal to one million units (see Table EI-4).   Similarly the Ranally manufacturing index measures a city's proportion of all U.S. manufacturing, again using one million units for the national total.   Finally the sales/manufacturing index is the relationship between the sales index and the manufacturing index—the higher the index the greater the concentration on retail sales.

It should be noted that the classification of cities by various economic activities is not without its critics.   Reisman, for instance, states that they do not measure up well sociologically, as the system of classification is too arbitrary and after all is said and done not much has been learned about the city.   Reisman raises such questions as: "(1) Are there differences, say, in social cohesion between a manufacturing city and a wholesale trade center?   (2) What are the differences of social organization of a university town as compared with a resort center?   (3) Does the temporary residence of a large proportion of the population in both types make them alike or are there other factors— for example, money spent—that account for significant differences?"[7]

Others have attempted to relate the economic system to the social and political systems.   Beshers, for example, indicates that the specific relationship between the economic system and the social structure of a particular city is not simple, except "When a single, locally owned industrial concern dominates the economy of a small city, then the patriarchal, not to say the feudal, effects upon the social structure will be quite clear."[8]   More specifically, he states that social structure must reflect economic variations of place as well as economic variations of time if there are any economic effects at all.   In terms of the relationship between economic function and political structure Scoble and Alford found that the council-manager form of government appears less frequently in industrial/manufacturing cities than in retail and diversified ones.[9]   They also found that dormitory cities are more likely than employing or balanced cities to have city-manager types of government.

One ought to note a broader economic context wherein the community is located.   Although there have been a number of ways to distinguish the economic dimensions of a state, we have chosen to use Hofferbert's industrialization factor score.   This factor includes a number of variables, with value added by manufacturing and the percentage employed in manufacturing loading the most heavily.   In Table EI-1 the states were rank ordered from the most industrialized (New Jersey) to the least (Wyoming).

TABLE EI-1. INDUSTRIALIZATION FACTOR SCORES
FOR THE STATES: 1960*

State	Industrialization Factor Score	State	Industrialization Factor Score
New Jersey	2.1	Maine	-0.2
Illinois	2.0	South Carolina	-0.2
Connecticut	1.9	Texas	-0.2
New York	1.9	West Virginia	-0.2
Massachusetts	1.6	Oregon	-0.3
Delaware	1.2	Alabama	-0.4
Pennsylvania	1.2	Florida	-0.4
Rhode Island	1.2	Kentucky	-0.4
Ohio	1.1	Vermont	-0.4
California	1.0	Colorado	-0.5
Michigan	0.9	Kansas	-0.5
Indiana	0.8	Utah	-0.6
Maryland	0.8	Nebraska	-0.7
Wisconsin	0.5	Arkansas	-0.8
Missouri	0.4	Mississippi	-0.8
New Hampshire	0.3	Oklahoma	-0.8
Washington	0.0	Arizona	-1.0
Minnesota	-0.1	Idaho	-1.2
North Carolina	-0.1	Nevada	-1.2
Tennessee	-0.1	New Mexico	-1.3
Virginia	-0.1	Montana	-1.3
Georgia	-0.1	South Dakota	-1.4
Iowa	-0.2	North Dakota	-1.5
Louisiana	-0.2	Wyoming	-1.5

*Alaska and Hawaii are excluded from this [ranking] because they were granted statehood late in the period covered by much of the state policy research.

Source: Richard I. Hofferbert, *The Study of Public Policy* (Bobbs-Merrill, 1974), p. 157. The following variables in order of their loadings were positively associated with industrialization: value added by manufacture per capita, percentage employed in manufacturing, value per acre of farmland and buildings, population per square mile, percent foreign, total population, percent urban, telephones per 1,000 population, average number of employees per manufacturing establishment, personal income per capita, percent failures business plus commerical establishments, estimated value real property per capita, percent black, percent illiterate. The variables negatively associated with industrialization include: percent increase in population, median school years completed, percent farms operated by tenants, percent housing owner occupied, divorce rate, acreage per farm, motor vehicle registration per 1,000 population.

You may classify your community by finding it in one of the afore-mentioned listings or attempt to do so yourself using, as we have, the method of Jones et al.

FIGURE EI-1. TAXONOMY OF ECONOMIC FUNCTION

Functional Classification	EMPLOYMENT-RESIDENCE RATIO		
	116 or more	85 to 115	84 or less
> 50% in manufacturing < 30% in retail trade	(Mm)E	(Mm)B	(Mm)D
> 50% in manufacturing > 30% in retail trade	(M)E	(M)B	(M)D
Manufacturing > retail Manufacturing < 30%	(Mr)E	(Mr)B	(Mr)D
Retail trade > manufacturing Manufacturing > 20%	(Rm)E	(Rm)B	(Rm)D
Retail trade > manufacturing and other components Manufacturing < 20%	(Rr)E	(Rr)B	(Rr)D

OPERATIONAL DEFINITIONS

Functional classification (Jones et al. method): percentage of those employed in manufacturing compared to percentage of those employed in retail trade.

$$\% \text{ Employed in Manufacturing} = \frac{\text{Number Employed in Manufacturing}}{\text{Aggregate Employment (Place-of-Work)}}$$

$$\% \text{ Employed in Retail Trade} = \frac{\text{Number Employees and Proprietors, Retail Trade}}{\text{Aggregate Employment (Place-of-Work)}}$$

$$\text{Employment/Residence Ratio} = \frac{\text{Aggregate Employment (Place-of-Work)}}{\text{Aggregate Employment (Place-of-Residence)}} \times 100$$

SOURCES AND CAVEATS

Aggregate employment data by *place-of-work* can be found in U.S. Bureau of the Census, *Census of Manufacturers,* Vol. III, *Area Statistics,* for the years 1958 and 1967; U.S. Bureau of the Census, *Census of Business,* Vol. II, *Retail Trade—Area Statistics,* for the years 1958 and 1967; U.S. Bureau of the Census, *Census of Business,* Vol. IV, *Wholesale Trade Area Statistics,* for the years 1968 and 1967; U.S. Bureau of the Census, *Census of Business,* Vol. V, *Selected Services—Area Statistics,* for the years 1958 and 1967. Aggregate employment data by place-of-residence can be found in U.S. Bureau of the Census, *Census of Population, General Social and Economic Characteristics,* for the years 1960 and 1970, Tables 73 and 75, for each state.

For a fuller discussion on the limitations of the employment-residence ratio see Jones et al.

PROFILE EXAMPLE

TABLE EI-2. LABOR FORCE, EMPLOYMENT BY INDUSTRY (PLACE-OF-RESIDENCE), 1960 and 1970

| | MOUNT VERNON | | | | NEW ROCHELLE | | | |
	1960 Number	%	1970 Number	%	1960 Number	%	1970 Number	%
Total Employed	33,073		32,563		31,743		31,850	
Mining	41	.1	NA	NA	30	.1	NA	NA
Construction	1,935	5.9	1,721	5.3	1,498	4.7	1,370	4.3
Manufacturing*	7,666	23.2	6,850	21.0	5,812	18.3	5,768	18.1
Transportation	1,151	3.5	1,085	3.3	917	2.9	1,026	3.2
Communication, Utility & Sanitary Services	1,105	3.3	1,390	4.3	932	2.9	1,171	3.7
Wholesale Trade*	1,802	5.4	1,649	5.1	1,934	6.1	1,982	6.2
Retail Trade*	4,628	14.0	4,923	15.1	4,298	13.5	5,081	16.0
Business & Repairs*	1,311	4.0	1,425	4.4	1,236	3.9	1,323	4.2
Private Household	1,586	4.8	1,387	4.3	2,342	7.4	1,195	3.8
Other Personal Service*	1,213	3.7	1,296	4.0	967	3.0	25	.7
Hospitals	680	2.1	1,997	6.1	726	2.3	2,095	6.6
Educational Services	1,485	4.5	2,095	6.4	1,916	6.0	3,005	9.4
Other Professional & Related	2,081	6.3	2,330	7.2	2,299	7.2	2,072	6.5
Public Administration	1,361	4.1	1,820	5.6	1,353	4.3	1,352	4.2
Other Industries (not reported)	5,028	15.2	756	2.3	5,483	17.3	900	2.8
Aggregate Employment	16,620	-	16,143	-	14,247	-	14,179	-

*Components of Aggregate Employment

OPERATIONAL DEFINITIONS

Aggregate Employment (Place-of-Residence) = Number Engaged in Manufacturing + Number Engaged in Wholesale Trade + Number Engaged in Retail Trade + Number Engaged in Selected Services (Business and Repair Services, other Personal Services)

TABLE EI-3. EMPLOYMENT BY INDUSTRY (PLACE-OF-WORK), 1960 and 1970

| | MOUNT VERNON | | | | NEW ROCHELLE | | | |
	1958 Number	%	1967 Number	%	1958 Number	%	1967 Number	%
Manufacturing	9,333	51.0	10,900	52.0	3,463	33.3	4,900	37.1
Retail Trade	4,193	22.9	3,514	16.8	4,703	45.2	4,571	34.6
Wholesale Trade	2,483	13.7	3,385	16.2	672	6.5	1,456	11.0
Selected Services	2,302	12.6	3,147	15.0	1,576	15.1	2,283	17.1
Aggregate Employment	18,311	-	20,946	-	10,414	-	13,210	-

OPERATIONAL DEFINITIONS

Aggregate Employment (Place-of-Work) = Number Employed in Manufacturing + Number Employed (Employees and Proprietors) in Retail Trade + Number Employed (Employees and Proprietors) in Wholesale Trade + Number Employed (Employees and Proprietors) in Selected Services.

TABLE EI-4. RANALLY SALES/MANUFACTURING INDEX, 1967

Index	MOUNT VERNON	NEW ROCHELLE
Sales	340	515
Manufacturing	491	219
Sales/Manufacturing	69	237

OPERATIONAL DEFINITIONS

$$\text{Sales/Manufacturing Index} = \frac{\text{Sales Index}}{\text{Manufacturing Index}} \times 100$$

CLASSIFICATION INDICATORS

	MOUNT VERNON	NEW ROCHELLE
Functional Classification, 1967		
% employed in manufacturing	52.0	37.1
% employed in retail trade	16.8	34.6
Employment-residence ratio, 1967/1970 (see Tables EI-2 and EI-3.)	129(E)	93(B)

FINDINGS AND SUGGESTED IMPLICATIONS

According to 1967 data Mount Vernon was a *manufacturing (Mm)* city. The Ranally sales/manufacturing index provides further evidence of this (see Table EI-4). In 1970 it was also an *employing* city, meaning that the aggregate employment in local establishments was greater than that of the resident labor force. This was a change from the E/R ratio in 1960 which had placed Mount Vernon in the category of a *balanced* city in that it employed in the major functions as many people locally as there were residents in these occupations. New Rochelle, on the other hand, was a *diversified-manufacturing (Mr)* city in 1967. It shifted from *diversified-retailing (Rm)* in 1958 to *diversified-manufacturing* in 1967. Nonetheless the Ranally sales/manufacturing index remained high. In 1970, New Rochelle was also a *balanced* city, employing nearly as many people as there were residents in the significant categories.

One implication of Mount Vernon's change to an employing city was the erosion of its suburban character, which may have encouraged those who desired that style of life to leave the community. As the character of the community changes industrialization is even more likely to occur. Although this change may create more jobs and a greater tax yield, depending on the industry type industrialization may actually increase the demand for public service. Industrialization brings with it more blue-collar residents who traditionally have voted less than white-collar workers. This factor could have contributed to Mount Vernon's decreased voter participation. Moreover, since manufacturing workers tend to be registered Democrats, further inroads into the Republican majority may occur.

If new industries are attracted to the community, the planned location for them is on the south side, an area which houses mostly black residents. Such an encroachment undoubtedly would anger the blacks and increase racial tension as it has in the past. The political leadership of the community, representing divergent economic and social interests, may find itself in a struggle over the direction of future economic growth and development. We offer the following speculations on factors associated with employing and dormitory communities.

FIGURE EI-2.   SPECULATIONS ON FACTORS ASSOCIATED WITH EMPLOYING AND
DORMITORY COMMUNITIES

EMPLOYING (Central Cities)

SOCIAL

Increases size and density during the day.

Increases amount of social interaction and exchange.

Invaders have limited concern, around the job.

Residents resentful of outside competitors.

Possible differences in and clashes of life styles.

Difficult to differentiate invaders from residents.

POLITICAL

Provide public service needs to hold on to employing firms.

Invaders have no citizen rights, duties, or responsibilities.

Increases motivation to extend boundaries to incorporate outlying residential
areas.

Economic firms and labor unions gain political power relative to numbers they
control despite the fact that the employees are not local voters.

If the suburbanites engage in reform in the central city, they tend to impose
their priority of economic development rather than human resource development.

Invaders vote the interests of their home communities which are generally anti-
thetical to the central city where they work. They vote for state and national
legislators who represent an area rather than an economic interest.

ECONOMIC

Difficult to assess cost/benefit ratio of the invaders.

Fiscal policy must include ways to get invaders and those who employ them to share
costs of their influx.

Fiscal policy includes ways to attract economic firms who employ outsiders anti-
cipating multiplier effect on the economy generally and on assessibles specifically.

Cost of supporting those who are attracted to an industrial area but do not find
jobs drives many upper class and middle class residents into the suburbs, leaving
those in the central city who are least able to support its service costs.

Substantial proportion of earned income leaves the city and is spent in invaders
home base.

DORMITORY (Suburbs)

SOCIAL

Left with daytime population dominated by women and children.

Status based on residence type and location rather than occupation.

Social organizations serve individual interests of residents rather than
economic or community interests.

Exclusionary.

POLITICAL

Commuters show little interest in local politics allowing "localites" to dominate
decision-making.

Political interests are parochial.

Minimal scope of government centered around the school system.

Regulate against in-migration and encroachment upon autonomy.

ECONOMIC

Very narrow economic base.

Public finance primarily dependent upon residential property.

Beginning to attract economic firms.

Economic dominants of central cities reside here with loyalties divided among
their economic firms, their social networks, and their resident community.

Affluent commuters with great capacity (wealth and income) live in these areas
with low public service needs depriving the central city with greater service
needs of a substantial tax base.

DISCUSSION

1. What are the economic function and E/R ratio classifications of your community? To what extent have they changed?

2. What are the following indices of your community: (a) sales, (b) manufacturing, and (c) sales/manufacturing? Are they changing?

3. To what would you attribute your economic function and E/R ratio? (a) location, (b) tax policy, (c) master plan, (d) political ideologies, (e) national or regional economic trends, (f) changing population types, or (g) decisions of selective types of economic firms to leave or enter the community?

4. Speculate on the ways in which your economic function and E/R ratio type affect the following major types of community life: (a) housing, (b) education, (c) crime, (d) health, (e) welfare, (f) economic opportunity, (g) cultural activities, and (h) social tensions.

5. Do you think it is important to change your community's economic function or E/R ratio? If so, in what direction would you change them? What social, political, and economic strategies might be employed?

NOTES

1. Leonard Reisman, *The Urban Process* (The Free Press, 1964), p. 78.

2. Chauncey D. Harris, "A Functional Classification of Cities in the United States," *The Geographical Review,* 33 (1943), pp. 86-89.

3. Victor Jones, Richard L. Forstall, and Andrew Collver, "Economic and Social Characteristics of Urban Places," *Municipal Yearbook, 1967* (International City Managers Association), pp. 30-65.

4. Richard L. Forstall, "A New Social and Economic Group of Cities," *Municipal Yearbook* (1971), pp. 102-159.

5. *Rand McNally City Rating Guide* (Rand McNally, 1971).

6. Ranally City Ratings in *Rand McNally Commercial Atlas and Marketing Guide* (Rand McNally, 1971).

7. Leonard Reisman, pp. 80-81.

8. James M. Beshers, *Urban Social Structure* (The Free Press of Glencoe, Inc., 1962), pp. 52-53.

9. Robert R. Alford and Harry M. G. Scoble, "Political and Socio-Economic Characteristics of American Cities," *The Municipal Yearbook, 1965* (International City Managers Association), pp. 86-87.

COMMUNITY DATA PROFILE EI-A

(EI-2) LABOR FORCE, EMPLOYMENT, (PLACE-OF-RESIDENCE)

| | YOUR COMMUNITY | | | | COMPARISON CITY | | | |
	1960 Number	%	1970 Number	%	1960 Number	%	1970 Number	%
Total Employed								
Mining								
Construction								
Manufacturing								
Transportation								
Communication, Utility & Sanitary Services								
Wholesale Trade								
Retail Trade								
Business and Repairs								
Private Household								
Other Personal Service								
Hospitals								
Educational Services								
Other Professional & Related								
Public Administration								
Other Industries (not reported)								
Aggregate Employment								

(EI-3) EMPLOYMENT (PLACE-OF-WORK)

| | YOUR COMMUNITY | | | | COMPARISON CITY | | | |
	1958 Number	%	1967 Number	%	1958 Number	%	1967 Number	%
Manufacturing								
Retail Trade								
Wholesale Trade								
Selected Services								
Aggregate Employment								

(EI-4) RANALLY SALES/MANUFACTURING INDEX, 1967

	YOUR COMMUNITY	COMPARISON CITY
Sales		
Manufacturing		
Sales/Manufacturing		

CLASSIFICATION INDICATORS (Tables EI-2 and EI-3)

	YOUR COMMUNITY	COMPARISON CITY
Functional Classification, 1967		
% Employed in Manufacturing		
% Employed in Retail Trade		
Employment Residence Ratio		
CLASSIFICATION		
FUNCTIONAL		
E/R		

EII. COMMUNITY WEALTH AND INCOME

HOW MUCH WEALTH AND INCOME IS THERE IN YOUR COMMUNITY?

CONCEPT

There are three realms of economic activity: (1) the market economy where the value of the goods and services are measured by the exchange of money, (2) the domestic household where the products are not exchanged in the market (the farm, housewife's services), and (3) the public household wherein governmental revenues and expenditures are managed for the satisfaction of public needs and wants. Bell suggests

> We have no integrated theory of economics and politics of public finance, no sociology of the structured conflicts between classes and social groups on the decisive question of taxation, no political philosophy (with the recent exception of John Rawls, but nothing from socialist writers) which attempts a theory of distributive justice based on the centrality of the public household in the society."[1]

The economic base of a community essentially describes the character of the private economic sector. The American economy severely restricts the development of public enterprises. Therefore local government must tap privately owned resources for public purposes. These resources are in the form of either wealth or income. Wealth is the accumulation of assets over time and income is the net addition from one period to another of a person's command over resources.

Both wealth and income reflect to a large degree what people believe and accept as the worth of certain natural resources, man-made material as well as human talents and services. Not everything of value is priced.

Gross includes as natural wealth the air, light, water, soil, minerals, flora, and fauna and also the following man-made assets: (1) the physical infrastructure composed of roads, bridges, dams, harbors, buildings, and houses; (2) farms (with or without livestock), timberland, and fisheries; (3) energy-producing facilities that can supplement the muscle-power of people and animals; (4) machinery and tools that use such energy in agriculture, mining, manufacturing, construction, transportation, communication and other activities; and (5) the stock of consumers' and producers' goods

held for future use.[2]   Income, on the other hand, as spending power includes
receipts in money, fringe benefits, interest, profits, and capital appreciation. As Gross points out

> in a monetized society money income is such a powerful
> symbol of status and power, as well as of the things
> that can be bought with money, that it comes to serve
> as a direct indicator of interest satisfaction. In-
> creases bring gratification, decreases deprivation.
> In both cases, the absolute figures may be less mean-
> ingful than those bearing on "relative deprivation" or
> "relative gratification."[3]

The distribution of wealth and income in America reveals a high degree
of inequality. Lundberg found in 1962 that 45 percent of the nation's households were in debt, had no assets, or held no more than $5,000 whereas 2 per-
cent of the households held $100,000 or more. In addition, he states

> the lower wealth-holders mostly own inert assets such
> as automobiles, small amounts of cash and some residen-
> tial equity, while the upper wealth-holders mostly own
> corporate equities in an aggregate amount sufficient
> to show that they are in full control of the production
> side of the economic system."[4]

Similarly, there is considerable inequality in the distribution of
family income. Table SV-1 indicates that the lowest 20 percent of American
families earn about 5 percent of the income while the top 20 percent earn
about 41 percent of the income. This pattern has remained relatively stable
for the past 25 years.

A recent study of income distribution within New York City showed its
distribution to parallel the national pattern closely: "the highest fifth
is *more than fifteen times* richer than the lowest fifth."[5] Income inequalities are in part believed to be related to inequalities in the distribution
of wealth, educational attainment, occupational status, and available opportunities and the motivation to seek them.

There is great variation in the range of per capita income among the
states. Table EII-1, a rank ordering of the states by per capita income in
1970, illustrates this range with Connecticut on top ($3,885) and Mississippi
on the bottom ($1,925). Not all communities within a state reflect these
per capita incomes, nor does the per capita income necessarily reflect the
quality of public services. They do, however, provide an indication of the
financial capacity within a state to support public services should it choose
to do so.

TABLE EII-1.   RANK ORDER OF STATES BY PER CAPITA INCOME, 1969

Connecticut (3,885)	Colorado (3,106)	Utah (2,697)
Alaska (3,725)	Indiana (3,070)	Oklahoma (2,694)
New Jersey (3,674)	Pennsylvania (3,006)	Idaho (2,644)
California (3,614)	Florida (3,058)	Georgia (2,640)
New York (3,608)	Minnesota (3,038)	Maine (2,548)
Nevada (3,554)	Wisconsin (3,032)	North Carolina (2,474)
Maryland (3,512)	Virginia (2,996)	North Dakota (2,469)
Illinois (3,495)	New Hampshire (2,985)	Tennessee (2,464)
Massachusetts (3,408)	Missouri (2,952)	New Mexico (2,437)
Hawaii (3,373)	Arizona (2,937)	Kentucky (2,425)
Michigan (3,357)	Kansas (2,929)	South Dakota (2,387)
Washington (3,265)	Iowa (2,884)	West Virginia (2,333)
Delaware (3,265)	Wyoming (2,854)	Louisiana (2,330)
Ohio (3,199)	Nebraska (2,792)	Alabama (2,317)
Oregon (3,148)	Texas (2,792)	South Carolina (2,303)
Rhode Island (3,121)	Vermont (2,772)	Arkansas (2,104)
UNITED STATES (3,119)	Montana (2,696)	Mississippi (1,925)

Source: U.S. Bureau of the Census, *County and City Data Book* (1972).

It is important to identify and measure the wide range of items of wealth that is currently located within the community and held by individual citizens and economic firms. Attempts have been made in recent years to provide an economic accounting system at the national and community level. Individual wealth can and has become a reservoir upon which public authorities base their taxation policies. Three dimensions of wealth are generally used: (1) physical assets in land and improvements put upon that land, (2) financial assets such as bank deposits and securities, and (3) claims against these assets including debts and equity. The basis for real property taxes then is calculated on the assessed value for local purposes or on the full value (fair value or market value) for county and state purposes and for any other comparative purposes. To arrive at full value we use the assessment-sales price ratio as published in the Census of Governments. This ratio indicates the percentage that the assessed value of property is of the actual sales price of the property. Therefore, a property assessed at $240,000 and sold for $480,000 yields an assessment-sales price ratio of 50.0. The assessment-sales price ratio makes it possible to compare one community's full value of property with another's by dividing the assessed value of each by its appropriate ratio (see Table EII-2). In 1971 the country's per capita assessed value of real property for local purposes was $2,723, and the per capita full value was $8,327. Thus assessments on the average comprise about one-third the market or full value.

It would be useful if one could determine the distribution of property wealth within a community. That is, who—individuals, groups, organizations, and institutions—own or control what proportion of the community's wealth. The ownership in the contemporary American Community is believed to be quite diverse in that there are different industrial, commercial, and residential ownership patterns. If possible one should determine the relative proportions of these types of properties (see Table EIV-5). In 1971 the gross assessed value of real property for twenty-eight large assessing jurisdictions was 10.7 percent industrial, 26.1 percent commercial, and 58.4 percent residential.

The most readily available information on income is the reports for families and unrelated individuals found in the U.S. Census (see Table EII-3). These are expressed in terms of per capita figures, means, and medians. In 1970 for the nation, the per capita income was $3,119, the mean family income $11,106, and the median family income $9,586.

Another important source of community income is derived from local business activity. Such activities include trade through retail, wholesale, and service-connected activities, as well as value added by manufacturing. In a sense this is a considerable part of the Gross National Product (GNP), which in 1970 was nearly a trillion dollars.

Both wealth (especially property) and income are used by public officials to determine the level of taxation that should be levied upon private individuals and economic firms for public purposes. We have chosen (a) property value, (b) per capita income, and (c) business activity as the most readily available indicators of community wealth and income. These all are potential sources for taxation. Each community, subject to state constitutional and legislative constraints, selects its own combination of taxes to levy upon these sources.

TYPOLOGY

The following typology provides one way to classify a community's financial resources, by wealth and income. An *affluent* community has both per capita income and per capita property at full value above the national level. These communities are generally found in suburbia and in the northeast. *Deprived* communities, on the other hand, are below the national average in both per capita property at full value and per capita income. Typically they are found in economically depressed or declining regions.

The remaining two types of communities, while advantaged, are distinguished by their predominance of either property or income. The *property prosperous* communities are those which are living with a residual of high property values while their residents have changed—high-income people have left for the suburbs while lower-income ones remain and are attracted into

the community. Many of the older central cities fall into this classification. The communities which are *money prosperous,* i.e., high relative to
the nation in per capita income but low in per capita property at full value,
are the new and developing cities and middle-class bedroom communities where
the residents have relatively high incomes but capital investment has not yet
developed or has been kept at a minimum.

FIGURE EII-1. TYPOLOGY OF WEALTH AND INCOME
(Relative to the Nation)

PER CAPITA REAL PROPERTY
AT FULL VALUE

	Above	*Below*
	Affluent	Money Prosperous
PER CAPITA INCOME *Above*		
Below	Property Prosperous	Deprived

SOURCES AND CAVEATS

Assessed value and the assessment-sales price ratio for real property can be found in the U.S. Bureau of the Census, *Census of Governments,* Vol. 2, Part 1, *Taxable Property Values,* for the years 1962 and
1971. If data for your community do not appear in the *Census of Governments,* you may obtain such data from your state's financial reports or
from local financial reports. Per capita and median income can be
found in the U.S. Bureau of the Census, *County and City Data Book,* for
the years 1962 and 1972. Business activity data appears in U.S. Bureau
of the Census, *Census of Manufacturers,* Vol. 3, *Area Statistics,* for
the years 1958 and 1967; U.S. Bureau of the Census, *Census of Business,*
Vol. 2, *Retail Trade-Area Statistics,* for the years 1958 and 1967; U.S.
Bureau of the Census, *Census of Business,* Vol. 4, *Wholesale Trade-Area
Statistics,* for the years 1958 and 1967; and U.S. Bureau of the Census,
Census of Business, Vol. 5, *Selected Services-Areas Statistics,* for the
years 1958 and 1967.

The classification indicators of per capita full value are based
on taxable assessed value and the assessment-sales price ratio as they
appear in the *Census of Governments.* (In 1971, the average assessment-
sales price ratio for the United States was 32.7, assessed value subject to taxes for local purposes $552.7 million, and the population,
203 million.) This data is the most appropriate for interstate comparative purposes. However, it should be noted that the assessment data for
some communities are not included, and even when they are there are

there are often variations between them and what are reported by state and local financial reports. In addition, the assessment-sales price ratio from census reports, although based on sample sales, varies considerably from state or local equalization rates. For example, the assessment-sales price ratio in 1971 for Mount Vernon was 31.6, while the state equalization rate was 48.0. It should also be noted that the *Census of Governments* reports data for different years (1967, 1971) than are reported in the *Census of Population*.

An important consideration for any comparisons of dollar amounts over time should, of course, take into account the effects of inflation or the change in the value of the dollar. For a realistic evaluation of changes in property value, income, business activities, the purchasing power of taxes, and expenditures, dollar amounts should be deflated by the appropriate measure. The following table shows the implicit price deflators for component parts of the Gross National Product; it uses 1958 as equal to 100.[6]

IMPLICIT PRICE DEFLATORS

To Be Applied To	Deflator (Index, 1958=100)	1959	1960	1967	1969	1970
Property value (true and assessed)	Total gross private domestic investment	102.6	103.4	115.9	126.4	132.4
Income	Personal consumption expenditures	101.3	102.9	114.4	123.5	129.2
Value added, retail and wholesale trade, service receipts	Gross national product by sector—private	101.4	102.8	114.8	124.3	130.1
Revenues and expenditures	Government purchases of goods and services— state and local	102.6	105.9	136.4	153.9	165.1

PROFILE EXAMPLE

TABLE EII-2. INTERSTATE MEASURES OF REAL PROPERTY VALUE, 1971

	MOUNT VERNON	NEW ROCHELLE	UNITED STATES
Assessed Value (1000's)	$197,123	$376,113	$552,700,000
Median Assessment-Sales Price Ratio	31.6	26.1	32.7
Full Value (1000's)	623,807	1,441,046	1,690,214,000
Per Capita Full Value	8,569	19,116	8,318

TABLE EII-3. REAL PROPERTY VALUE, INCOME FACTORS*, AND BUSINESS ACTIVITY**

Real Property (Intrastate)	MOUNT VERNON 1960	1970	% Change	NEW ROCHELLE 1960	1970	% Change
Assessed Value (1000's)	$187,872	$200,903	6.9	$326,138	$384,931	18.0
Equalization Rate	64	48	-	84	68	-
Full Value (1000's)	293,550	418,548	42.6	388,260	566,075	45.8
Income Factors						
Aggregate Income (1000's)	$196,000	$280,293	43.3	$257,000	$379,111	47.5
Per Capita Income	2,579	3,860	49.7	3,333	5,029	50.9
Median Income (family)	6,873	10,966	59.6	8,131	13,183	62.1
Business Activity (1000's)						
Value Added (mfg.)	$77,108	$132,500	71.8	$31,972	$57,200	78.9
Wholesale Trade	202,419	368,434	82.0	59,267	155,645	162.6
Retail Sales	100,430	117,034	16.5	110,579	148,766	32.7
Service Receipts	17,980	34,907	94.1	14,495	22,869	57.8
Total	397,937	641,875	61.0	216,413	384,480	77.7

*Income data are for the years 1959 and 1969
**Business activity data are for the years 1958 and 1967

OPERATIONAL DEFINITIONS

$$\text{Interstate Full Value} = \frac{\text{Assessed Value of Real Property Taxable for Local Purposes}}{\text{Assessment-Sales Price Ratio}}$$

$$\text{Per Capita Full Value} = \frac{\text{Full Value}}{\text{Total Population}}$$

$$\text{Intrastate Full Value} = \frac{\text{Assessed Value Taxable for Local Purposes}}{\text{Equalization Rate}}$$

Aggregate Income - Per Capita Income x Total Population

Total Business Activity = Value Added by Mfg. + Wholesale Trade + Retail Trade + Service Receipts

$$\text{Percent Change} = \frac{\text{Category, } t_2 - \text{Category, } t_1}{\text{Category } t_1}$$

TABLE EII-4. DEFLATED SELECTED WEALTH AND INCOME ITEMS

	MOUNT VERNON 1960	1970	% Change	NEW ROCHELLE 1960	1970	% Change
Full Value (1000's)	$293,898	$316,124	11.4	$375,493	$427,549	13.9
Per Capita Income*	2,546	3,126	22.8	3,290	4,072	23.8
Median Family Income*	6,785	8,879	30.9	8,027	10,674	33.0
Total Business Activities (1000's)	397,937	568,706	42.9	216,413	334,913	54.8

*Income figures are for 1959 and 1969
**Business activity figures are for 1958 (the base year which need not be deflated) and 1967

OPERATIONAL DEFINITIONS

$$\text{Deflated Real Property Value (1960)} = \frac{\text{Real Property Value (1960)}}{103.4}$$

$$\text{Deflated Real Property Value (1970)} = \frac{\text{Real Property Value (1970)}}{132.4}$$

$$\text{Deflated Income (1959)} = \frac{\text{Income (1959)}}{103.3} \qquad \text{Deflated Income (1969)} = \frac{\text{Income (1969)}}{123.5}$$

$$\text{Deflated Business Activity (1967)} = \frac{\text{Business Activity (1967)}}{114.8}$$

CLASSIFICATION INDICATORS

	Mount Vernon	New Rochelle	United States
Per capita full value, real property, 1971	$8,569	$19,116	$8,318
Per capita income, 1969 (see Tables EII-2 and EII-3)	3,860	5,029	3,119

FINDINGS AND SUGGESTED IMPLICATIONS

Both Mount Vernon and New Rochelle are affluent communities with per capita full property value and income above the national figures. However, New Rochelle is considerably more affluent than both Mount Vernon and the national average.

The assessment-sales price ratio indicates that the assessed value of New Rochelle property sold in 1971 was on the average 26.1 percent of its market price while that of Mount Vernon was 31.6 percent of its market price (see Table EII-2). This is in sharp contrast to New York state's ratio of assessment to full value (equalization rate), which indicated that New Rochelle property was assessed at 68 percent of full value and Mount Vernon at 48 percent of full value (see Table EII-3). In dollar amounts New Rochelle's taxable property was valued by the city at $385 million, by the county and state at $566 million, and using the Census of Governments' ratio at $1,441 million. The national estimate of full value was nearly 4 times the city's assessed value and 2.5 times the county/state value. Mount Vernon assessed its property at $201 million, while the federal assessment-sales price ratio indicated a value of $624 million, and the county/state $419 million. By national figures Mount Vernon's full value was 3 times as great as the city's assessed value and 1.5 times as great as the county/state value.

Consequently, based on the assessment-sales price ratio, both communities understated their real property value. This had significant implications for public finance since, for example, for tax purposes Mount Vernon's real property value is only one-third of what it might be and New Rochelle's only one-fourth; therefore tax rates must compensate for underassessments (see Exercise EIV for a discussion of assessment practices). In addition, Mount Vernon's assessed value reduced its tax limit by approximately two-thirds, and New Rochelle's limit was reduced by nearly three-fourths.

Although we have used the Census of Governments' assessment-sales price ratio to determine per capita full property value for classification purposes, we turn now to discuss the property wealth of the two communities, based on local assessments and county/state equalization formulae because they are the only data available for the two time periods and are the basis of tax rates, limits, and margins.

Mount Vernon's wealth in 1960 (in real property at full value) was
$294 million, according to New York state evaluation, providing much less
potential for property taxes than New Rochelle's, $388 million. In Mount
Vernon, 41 percent of assessed property value was in residential property,
19 percent in apartments, 14 percent in commercial, and 9 percent in industrial. More of New Rochelle's assessed value was in residential property
at 56 percent; a similar amount was in apartments, and commercial property
was at 13 percent, but there was less in industrial property, 4 percent,
than in Mount Vernon (see Table EIV-5).

Similarly, the aggregate income of those living in Mount Vernon was
less than that of New Rochelle by $61 million. This was reflected in a
per capita income $754 less than that of New Rochelle. Mount Vernon's
business activity of $400 million, on the other hand, generated nearly twice
as much dollar value as New Rochelle's. Half of this business activity
was in wholesale trade.

By 1970 Mount Vernon's real property at full value increased (42.6
percent) to $419 million (according to the Census, full value in 1971 was
$624 million); that of New Rochelle's increased slightly more (45.8 percent)
to $566 million (the Census reports $1,441 million for New Rochelle). The
mix of assessed value generally followed the 1960 distribution with a slight
decrease in the proportion of residential property in both communities and
a 4 percent increase in industrial property for Mount Vernon. Aggregate
income increased by more than two-fifths in both communities to $281 mil-
lion in Mount Vernon and $379 million in New Rochelle. By 1967, although
business activity continued to generate greater dollar value in Mount Vernon, the increase was greater in New Rochelle, at 78 percent compared to
61 percent for Mount Vernon. For Mount Vernon the greatest gain was in
service receipts, followed by wholesale trade, both of which nearly doubled.
By contrast, starting with a lower base, New Rochelle had its greatest
gain in wholesale trade, which increased 162 percent. Both communities
increased their manufacturing activity by three-fourths, but Mount Vernon's
dollar volume was twice as much in this component.

During the decade, despite inflation, Mount Vernon's wealth and income
increased somewhat but less than that of New Rochelle (see Table EII-4).
When property values were deflated, Mount Vernon's full value increased by
11.4 percent whereas New Rochelle's increased by 13.9 percent. Aggregate
income increased more than property wealth in both Mount Vernon and New
Rochelle. Overall business activity in Mount Vernon increased by 43 percent,
whereas that in New Rochelle increased more (55 percent). Significantly,
Mount Vernon's retail trade was stagnant, showing no growth during the decade
when controlled for inflation.

The fact that Mount Vernon's property values did not increase as much
as New Rochelle's may be associated with its greater density (little open
space for new buildings) and rapid racial change. Therefore Mount Vernon's
affluence may be more a function of its suburban past than a prospect for
its future. The lesser appreciation of real property stimulated some Mount
Vernon public officials and civic leaders to seek alternative land uses,
i.e., additional commercial firms and light industry. This would modify the

1970 relative proportions of property——residential, 58 percent (38 percent in one- to three-family houses and 20 percent in apartments); commercial, 13 percent, and industrial, 13 percent. Although the distribution of
property types followed the national pattern, it is not typical of suburbia,
which generally has less industrial and commercial property. In fact, Mount
Vernon leaders see its advantageous location with access to good transportation as a means to attract industry. They have succeeded to the extent that
the employment/residence ratio has changed from that of a dormitory city to
an employing city (see Exercise EI).

   Given the fiscal crisis faced by American communities in the 1960s
and 1970s, with rising demands and costs for public services outpacing the
increase in property values, or at least in the assessed value, public
officials search for additional ways to increase their revenues. On one
hand, they seek new economic units, increased state and federal aid; on the
other, they explore new forms of taxation related to income——sales taxes
and income taxes. The lower the income, the less likely it is that increased
taxes——property, sales, and income——will be advanced by leaders and approved
by voters. It should be understood that changes in the ways of tapping the
wealth and income of a community may lead to changes in the social, political,
and/or economic character of the community.

   We offer the following speculations on the considerations of increasing
assessibles from the viewpoints of potential entrepreneurs and the community.

FIGURE EII-2. SPECULATIONS ON THE CONSIDERATIONS OF INCREASING
ASSESSIBLES FROM THE VIEWPOINTS OF THE POTENTIAL
ENTREPRENEUR AND THE COMMUNITY

Entrepreneur	*Community*
INDUSTRIAL	
Space and buildings	Jobs provided
Proximity to material	New assessibles
Labor pool	Economic spinoffs
Proximity to markets	Drain on existing public
Transportation access	services and demands for new ones
Tax rates	Pollution and congestion
Political climate	Change in character of
Amenities of life for executives	the community
	Neighborhood objections
COMMERCIAL	
Character of market	Jobs provided
Established and potential competition	Convenience and amenities
	New assessibles
Traffic flow and parking	Potential civic leadership
Transportation	pool
Sales tax	Drain on existing services
Property tax	and demand for new services
Community support	Increase in traffic congestion
Community stability and growth	
NEW RESIDENTIAL PROPERTY	
Land availability and cost	Introduction of young residents
Market for housing	Increase in local consumer
Zoning restrictions	spending
Availability of utilities	New assessibles
Access to transportation	Drain on existing public
Level of public services	services and demand for new services
Property taxes	Limits on open space
Reputation of community	Code enforcement
Community stability and growth	
Political climate	
URBAN REDEVELOPMENT	
Difficulty in assembling land parcels	Elements of project maximize objectives
Securing the capital	Introduction of master plan
Finding the contractor	Neighborhood tension over
Supportive and competent public authorities	change in land use
	Political and civic opposition
Demolition costs	Responsibility of complying
Relocating problems	with federal and state guidelines
Zoning variances	Increase in assessibles
Tax abatement	Drain on existing services
Federal, state, local red tape	and demand for new services
Potential market	Kind of persons attracted to project

DISCUSSION

1. What is the wealth and income classification of your community?

2. What are the (a) aggregate income, (b) median income, and (c) business activity in your community? What is the distribution of the property assessment role in your community? In what way have these factors changed over time? What has the effect of inflation been on the components of wealth and income?

3. To what do you attribute the level of wealth and income in your community? (a) the desirability of locating industry, commerce, and residences in your community, (b) the opportunity for your residents to earn money, (c) the attractiveness of your community to certain occupational types, or (d) the location utility of your community for industrial production and distribution, wholesale trade, retail trade, and service activity?

4. Speculate on the ways in which the level of community wealth and income affect the following major areas of community life: (a) education, (b) housing, (c) crime, (d) health, (e) welfare, (f) economic opportunity, (g) cultural activity, and (h) social tensions.

5. Do you think it important to change the level of wealth and income in your community? If so, in what direction? What social, political, and/or economic strategies might be employed to bring about the desired change?

NOTES

1. Daniel Bell, *The Cultural Contradictions of Capitalism* (Basic Books, Inc., Publishers, 1976), p. 221.

2. Bertram M. Gross, *The State of the Nation* (Tavistock Publications, 1966), pp. 52-53.

3. *Ibid.*, p. 95.

4. Ferdinand Lundberg, *The Rich and the Super-Rich* (Bantam Books, 1969), p. 16.

5. William A. Caldwell, *How to Save Urban America* (New American Library, 1973), p. 145.

6. *Economic Report of the President*, February 1971, pp. 200-201.

COMMUNITY DATA PROFILE EII-A

(EII-2) INTERSTATE MEASURES OF REAL PROPERTY VALUES

	YOUR COMMUNITY			COMPARISON CITY		
	1960	1970	% Change	1960	1970	% Change
Assessed Value (1000's)						
Mean Assessment-Sales Price Ratio						
Full Value						
Per Capita Full Value						

(EII-3) INTRASTATE MEASURES OF REAL PROPERTY VALUE, INCOME FACTORS, AND BUSINESS ACTIVITY

Real Property	YOUR COMMUNITY			COMPARISON CITY		
	1960	1970	% Change	1960	1970	% Change
Assessed Value (1000's)						
Equalization Rate						
Full Value (1000's)						
Income Factors						
Aggregate Income (100's)						
Per Capita Income						
Median Income (family)						
Business Activity (1000's)						
Value Added (Mfg.)						
Wholesale Trade						
Retail Sales						
Service Receipts						
Total All Business Activities						

(EII-4) DEFLATED SELECTED WEALTH AND INCOME ITEMS

	YOUR COMMUNITY			COMPARISON CITY		
	1960	1970	% Change	1960	1970	% Change
Full Value						
Per Capita Income						
Median Income (family)						
Total All Business Activities						

CLASSIFICATION INDICATORS (Table EII-3)

	YOUR COMMUNITY	COMPARISON CITY
Per Capita Full Value Real Property, 1971		
Per Capita Income, 1969		
CLASSIFICATION		

EIII. PUBLIC FINANCE: MUNICIPAL REVENUES

WHAT ARE THE REVENUE PATTERNS OF YOUR COMMUNITY?

CONCEPT

In a highly decentralized federal system, the budgets of local governments reflect the priorities and values of a community. The budget represents many decisions accumulated over time. It reflects the decisional preferences of constituents for certain kinds of public goods and services, as well as those they have elected to govern, and those who have been appointed to operate the machinery of local government. It also reflects the character of the support base, whether it be the economic base or the authority granted by the state constitution or the cash transfers of state and federal aid. Lee and Johnson state that in the last analysis the

> Series of intricate processes that link both political
> and economic values are integral to budgetary systems.
> Making budget choices about ends and means specifically
> involves making political decisions that allocate scarce
> economic resources between the private and public sectors
> of society and decisions that allocate these resources
> within the public sector among alternative uses.[1]

Yet little is generally known about local public finance except by a few who have become the "experts." Among them there is a variety of concerns. Some, macroeconomists, focus on the countercyclical nature of local government finance as affecting the economy as a whole. General welfare economists give their attention to

> the distributive vs. the service function of state and
> local finance; the use of municipal-enterprise pricing
> policies for welfare purposes; methods of policy decision-
> making as between the majority and minorities; the eco-
> nomic problems of the central city at the metropolitan
> core; the role of state and federal aid in economically
> depressed local governments and in school finance within
> federally-impacted areas.[2]

Political scientists, more concerned with who controls the purse strings, examine such forces as the alignment of various community groups the legal framework of government to make fiscal decisions, the bureaucracy of financial administration, and intergovernmental relationships. Finance

291

administrators are interested in the problems of

> tax incidence; the effects of particular taxes upon indi-
> vidual industries or businesses; the use by municipalities
> of certain nonproperty tax revenues; grant-in-aid programs;
> the problems presented by state-collected, locally shared
> taxes; the tax-exempt feature of state and municipal securi-
> ties; other state-local and federal-state fiscal relationships;
> and questions of equity as to specific proposals in the tax
> structure.[3]

The taxpayers have their own self-interest, as suggested by the attention ladder in Figure EIII-1.

FIGURE EIII-1. HYPOTHETICAL CITIZEN ATTENTION LADDER ON PUBLIC FINANCE

1.   The individual tax bill.

2.   The established tax rate.

3.   Property assessment.

4.   The overall budget made salient by budget elections.

5.   The amount of debt made salient by bond elections.

6.   Expenditure allocations among governmental functions.

7.   The established tax limit and margin.

8.   The established debt limit and margin.

9.   The relative flow of intergovernmental transfers.

10.   The amount of interest on the outstanding debt.

11.   The "full" value of property and equalization rate.

Each of these elements of public finance is difficult to comprehend for the
average citizen, except his tax bill, and as Netzer states, "The financing
of governmental activities is among the most dismal aspects of the 'dismal
science' for the solutions are bound to make many unhappy with the outcome."[4] On the other hand, Meltsner suggests that with "withheld tax at the
federal level, property taxes prorated as part of a monthly mortgage payment, and the use of indirect taxation by state and local authorities, our
tax system has been designed to reduce the public's tax consciousness."[5]

We intend to shed some light on the subject by discussing some of
these items and other concerns of local public finance in the following four

exercises. The first topic is *general revenues,* the various sources of monies made available for public spending discussed in this exercise. The second, *local property taxation,* receives special attention because it is generally the major source of local revenues (see Exercise EIV). The third is the allocation of *local expenditures* for specific governmental functions (see Exercise EV). The fourth is the *debt* incurred for capital outlays and their long-term and short-term commitments (see Exercise EVI).

Thus, the decisions facing the mayor, city council, and others involved in preparing, approving, implementing, and living with the consequences of the community's annual budget must be made with a consideration for each component. That is, to decide whether to hire more policemen, teachers, or garbage collectors, or increase their salaries, elected and appointed officials need to know how much money will be available. This depends not only on what amount of local taxes is collected from various sources but often awaits the decisions of the state legislature as to what kinds of financial aid it is willing to provide the locality as well as what mandates it will impose upon it. Decisions on local property taxes must be seen not only in the context of total revenues but also in the context of the ability and willingness of taxpayers to accept present levels or proposed increases.

Expenditure decisions should be seen as the result of competing demands by those who prefer better education, cleaner streets, or slum clearance. Very often the money available is insufficient to meet current public preferences especially for capital projects such as building a new fire station or school house. For long-term projects the city often enters the bond market to borrow money which will be paid back at some date in the future. Incurring debt spreads the cost of the projects over a longer period of time and is paid for by users during that time. The problems of budget-making often leave public officials scrambling for the most acceptable ways to raise additional money, as their constituents generally want to consume more public services than current revenues can support. They, as Pettengill and Uppal suggest, do their bit by "finding new taxpayers, adopting the least painful new taxes, raising old tax rates, borrowing, or getting outside aid."[6]

Overall, a good revenue system, according to Moax and Hillhouse, requires that it

1. Should not be unduly sensitive to cyclical economic fluctuations.

2. Should stir tax consciousness among the voters so they can be more responsible in regard to the purpose and method of spending.

3. Should have as little adverse affect as possible on economic growth.

4. Should avoid very high taxes that can create economic distortions and weaken revenue sources.

5. Should be easy to provide fair and efficient adiminstration.

6. Should be equitable in three respects:

(a) progressive in the sense of the ability to pay, (b) sensitive
to the relationship between tax costs and public service benefits
received, and (c) appreciative of the accumulative effects of the
taxation pyramid of federal, state, and local governments.[2]

The budgetary process has been characterized as both an art and a science.
The final product evolves through many steps, from estimating revenues and
costs to securing political support. Once adopted it is an operational instru-
ment that has the force of law with obligations imposed both on taxpayers to
pay their taxes and on public officials to spend within their budgeted amounts.

The budgets of local government are expected to be balanced and without
deficits by the end of the fiscal year. Several forces operate to provide
fiscal integrity. One is the widespread public belief that the city should
not spend beyond its means; an unbalanced budget therefore amounts to fiscal
immorality. A second force is the investment market that makes loans to local
government and which frowns on deficits and tends to charge higher interest
rates to compensate for its greater risks. The third is the supervisory role
of state government, which wishes to protect the good reputation of its cities
in the bond market. Nonetheless, some cities under financial stress do experience fiscal deficits. However, they often resort to financial "gimmicks" to
show a balanced budget as required by the state. New York City, for example,
has used several methods to cover up its deficits. One is to overestimate
revenues and/or underestimate expenditures. Another is to shove one year's
expenses into another year's budget and/or bring one year's revenues into
another. They have also put current expense budget items into their capital
budget and depleted reserve funds set aside for other purposes. In the case
of New York City it is estimated that nearly 10 percent of the city's long-
term debt or $700 million can be attributed to these "gimmicks." In addition,
combined interest costs in 1976 of $210 million could be traced to unsound
fiscal practices. This amount of interest is more than the city spends on
park maintenance, consumer affairs, public health services, street repair,
housing code enforcement, rent control, and relocation costs combined.

There are many ways to put a budget together. Crecine has outlined a
rational budget-making process.[8] Less systematic but perhaps more realistic,
public officials, the mayor or city council and their administrative staff,
proceed through a number of calculations. One is revenue estimates that indicate whether the city will receive more, the same, or less money, and in what
way this varies by source. Revenue estimating tends to follow the principle
of "conservatism" to avoid deficits. Burkhead identified two estimating techniques long used in American governmental budgeting: the rule of the pen-ulti-
mate year (the last year's revenue is the next year's estimate) and the method
of averages (a rate of change over time for each revenue source).[9] Meltzner found
in Oakland that estimators paid more attention to large dollar revenue sources,
general fund revenues, and unexpended balances.[10] Two is a review of probable
added costs, for example salary increases that were budgeted for city
employees or commitments were made to add policemen. Three, if there is a
revenue surplus, the officials may reduce taxes or choose to spend more by
bolstering existing programs or by implementing new projects which have been
delayed because of a shortage of funds. Four, if there is a revenue gap
(costs exceed estimated income), the officials then must decide either to

increase present taxes, search for new sources of revenue, reduce present or projected expenditures, or borrow funds.

Crecine suggests that most local public officials attempt to have their budget (a) be balanced, (b) maintain existing service levels, (c) provide for increases in city employees' wages, and (d) avoid tax increases.[11] To achieve this they should identify all proposed public service needs, cost them out on a per unit basis, draw up the expense budget, and establish the necessary tax rates to proceed.

The general pattern has been both to increase local taxes and to seek external aid from the state and federal governments. Revenues for the cities in the nation have risen sharply from $15 billion to $31 billion during the 1960-1970 decade. This increase is similar to that experienced by the federal government. In 1970 two-thirds (68.3 percent) of the general revenue for local governments was derived from local sources, and the remainder was raised from state and federal governments. Of local revenue three-quarters were derived from various taxes and one-quarter was collected from charges and miscellaneous fees.

Property taxes constitute two-thirds of all local taxes. Other forms of taxation are sales taxes, which 3,409 cities in 19 states had adopted by 1972, and income taxes, which were used by 53 cities as well as by 328 localities in Ohio and 3,400 in Pennsylvania (a wage tax). The wide variety of taxes used by municipalities can be illustrated by those levied in New York City where the residents are subjected to 22 different municipal taxes, probably the greatest variety of taxes levied by any American city. While property taxes pay for about 24 percent of the budget, sales taxes pay for about 6 percent, and personal income taxes about 4 percent. The remaining revenues are derived from a range of taxes on cigarette, tar and nicotine content, coin-operated amusement boxes, commercial motor vehicles, commercial rent or occupancy, commuter earnings, financial corporations, general corporations, horse-race admissions, hotel-room occupancy, occupancy for vending machines, real-property transfers, transportation, corporations, unincorporated business, utilities, vaults under the sidewalk, auto use, leaded gasoline, and offtrack betting.[12]

Some communities operate utilities systems that return nearly one-fifth of their total revenues. These include utilities such as water, gas, and electric distribution systems, as well as transit systems and liquor stores. Over the years these have been established to meet certain specific problems. Municipal water systems, the most widely used of these utilities, were developed primarily to insure a safe drinking supply free of contagious diseases. Electric utilities often were established to provide a cheaper energy supply and thereby a device to attract new industries. Although almost all municipal utilities are nonprofit ventures and pay no taxes, they do—especially electric utilities—make payments to the cities "in lieu of taxes." These payments are generally smaller than what a private utility would be required to pay, but in some communities they are substantial. In Gainesville, Florida, for example, the Regional Utility Board provides approximately one-fourth of the annual operating budget of the city.

As mentioned earlier, general revenues for municipalities doubled from 1960 to 1970 or increased by 105 percent. Much of this increase can be attributed to inflation. In fact, the implicit price deflator for local governmental revenues and expenditures was 165.1 in 1970 (see Exercise EII, Sources and Caveats). In other words, a 1970 dollar collected or spent by local government was worth approximately 60 cents in 1958 dollars.

Perhaps the most dramatic shift bearing on local revenues is the growing reliance on intergovernmental aid from state and federal governments. During the decade 1960 to 1970 intergovernmental aid increased from $2.3 to $9.7 billion, comprising an increase from 19.9 to 31.7 percent of the revenues of the nation's cities. In 1970 the states provided three-fourths of all such aid, and the federal government contributed nearly one-fifth. The level of state aid to localities varies considerably from state to state, with California providing nearly ten times as much aid to its cities as does New Hampshire.[13] In addition, states have varied their priorities and assumed greater responsibilities for some functions such as education, welfare, health, roads, and urban redevelopment than for others. For example, New York state provides one-half the revenues for education, health, and hospitals, one-third for highways, and one-fourth for public welfare[14] (see Table EIII-1).

The formula for allocating state aid also varies. Rebates on state gas taxes, for instance, are often determined by the number of registered motor vehicles in the locality. Educational monies often are awarded to insure a basic foundation or minimal program support and then on the basis of the average daily attendance of students. Generally, state funds are received as a matter of right rather than requiring applications and/or matching funds. State-aid formulae depend on the decisions of state legislatures, which encourage some local officials to lobby not only for more support but also for the type of support they believe will best help their city. The larger cities appear to benefit most, with more than one-third (36.3 percent) of the local budget of cities over one million in population coming from their states, compared to less than two-fifths for smaller cities.

Federal aid has been much more modest but is changing in its form and level of support to local government. While the federal government provided $1.9 billion in direct aid in 1970, it also provided another $6 billion that was "passed through" the states. Categorical grant-in-aid programs have been the most widely used means of supporting local government financially. Grants are given for specific purposes, with the local government agreeing to make partial contributions and to administer the program according to certain prescribed requirements. For example, if the federal government develops a priority to solve the problems of slum housing, poverty, or health, local governments are then expected to follow its lead by making application for funds to alleviate these conditions locally. In 1970, the largest amounts of federal funds were spent on public welfare, highways, medical assistance, education, and urban renewal.

By 1972 general revenue-sharing was adopted, which shifted the method of federal support by abolishing the "strings" and providing money to localities as a matter of right. Some $30 billion has been authorized for state and local governments during the five-year period 1972 to 1977. About two-thirds of

TABLE EIII-1
PERCENTAGE OF LOCALLY FINANCED EXPENDITURES
BY SELECTED FUNCTIONS BY STATE

State or Other Jurisdiction	Local Schools 1972-73 Local Funds	Highways 1970-71 Local Funds	Public Welfare 1970-71 Local Funds	Health & Hospitals 1970-71 Local Funds
United States	51.2	18.8	11.7	46.7
Alabama	18.9	11.3	0.2	57.9
Alaska	11.7	11.0	-	14.7
Arizona	54.3	9.1	1.3	56.8
Arkansas	36.7	5.0	8.5	45.1
California	56.5	18.2	15.6	62.5
Colorado	64.3	15.1	10.3	42.2
Connecticut	73.8	19.7	1.7	10.1
Delaware	23.9	18.4	-	0.9
Florida	35.3	17.0	1.0	62.8
Georgia	34.5	23.2	2.9	63.6
Hawaii	3.0	30.1	0.2	3.1
Idaho	48.0	12.2	10.5	57.8
Illinois	55.2	11.0	3.3	36.4
Indiana	63.8	4.7	29.9	34.2
Iowa	63.6	21.5	11.6	69.5
Kansas	64.6	32.8	21.7	41.6
Kentucky	29.1	5.9	2.1	38.0
Louisiana	29.7	19.9	-	26.2
Maine	56.2	24.8	3.8	14.5
Maryland	45.3	4.6	5.6	24.1
Massachusetts	70.7	30.1	-	32.9
Michigan	48.6	13.7	6.2	42.7
Minnesota	40.5	31.6	25.1	53.7
Mississippi	24.2	17.5	0.2	65.5
Missouri	56.8	18.5	0.2	43.1
Montana	66.3	15.9	25.0	32.3
Nebraska	75.8	32.1	10.8	53.0
Nevada	52.1	10.8	24.4	79.9
New Hampshire	89.8	27.4	13.6	17.2
New Jersey	68.7	25.8	13.9	55.1
New Mexico	18.9	4.8	0.5	57.7
New York	52.6	34.4	25.7	51.7
North Carolina	20.8	9.2	13.6	27.7
North Dakota	59.1	24.2	7.3	7.6
Ohio	61.2	15.5	5.0	53.7
Oklahoma	42.2	8.2	-	41.0
Oregon	75.6	8.9	0.4	37.9
Pennsylvania	46.2	12.4	2.2	11.7
Rhode Island	53.8	29.6	-	1.6
South Carolina	27.9	4.8	2.6	44.1
South Dakota	72.3	27.2	4.5	36.5
Tennessee	41.9	11.7	4.1	62.6
Texas	43.0	30.6	0.8	51.8
Utah	37.9	10.7	0.9	33.9
Vermont	60.9	14.2	0.2	2.6
Virginia	50.0	11.5	8.5	10.0
Washington	44.0	14.3	-	43.0
West Virginia	31.7	2.6	2.3	42.4
Wisconsin	64.5	43.3	25.5	40.0
Wyoming	61.3	3.2	15.1	66.1
Dist. of Columbia	87.2	42.9	50.7	95.2

*Local here means municipal, county, and school districts, and other local special districts.

Source: The Council of State Government, *The Book of the States, 1970-1971*, pp. 272-73.

this is for local governments and is allocated on the basis of population size, effort shown in taxing local resources, and the incidence of poverty. Local government authorities may spend their general revenue-sharing funds pretty much as they wish, subject only to the following restrictions:[15]

1. Allotments are to be made within certain priority areas: public safety, environmental protection, transportation, health, recreation, libraries, social services for the poor and aged, financial administration, and capital expenditures.

2. Funds are not to be used as matching funds for other grant programs.

3. There is to be no discrimination based on race, color, national origin, or sex.

4. Construction wages must meet the prevailing local rates.

5. Authorities must publish their plans and publicly account for the use of funds.

In addition to categorical grants and general revenue-sharing, the federal government provides other types of aid to local communities and their citizens.[16] The federal government provides loans, loan guarantees, tax credits, and exemptions and makes major contributions to the cost of facilities and services such as airports, highways, hospitals, parks, and university research. In addition, it participates in a number of direct benefits to individuals such as social security payments to the aged, benefits to those in the armed forces who are retired, and aid to the disabled and to dependent children. The total amount of federal contribution to the locality and its residents can be examined for each agency of the executive branch of the federal government and the amounts each provides cities with populations of 25,000 or more, as well as for states and counties (see Table EIII-7). For example, New York state with 8.8 percent of the nation's population received 11.6 percent of the federal outlays in 1974.

Intergovernmental transfers are intended to assist hard-pressed urban governments, but there are those who argue that they also should have a *stimulating effect* on local revenues, for example, state aid for schools should encourage the locality to spend more of its own money on education. Sacks and Harris found in 1960 that public welfare stimulation amounted to 20 cents per dollar of state aid compared to 52 cents for education, 67 cents for highways, and $2.50 for health and hospitals.[17] Some believe that external aid, in fact, has had a *substitutive effect,* that is, the funds have been used to reduce local spending and consequently taxes.

It is important to note the revenue context within which your community is located. Table EIII-2 shows the ranking of states by their level of per capita state and local resources. They range from Alaska with $1,562 to Arkansas with $488. The level of resources provides an indication of the propensity of these governments to raise monies for public services.

TABLE EIII-2. RANK ORDER BY STATES OF PER CAPITA STATE AND
               LOCAL REVENUES, 1970-1971

Alaska ($1,562)	Maryland ($730)	West Virginia ($612)
Hawaii ($965)	Oregon ($729)	Oklahoma ($602)
Wyoming ($961)	Connecticut ($723)	Indiana ($596)
New York ($953)	South Dakota ($722)	Mississippi ($593)
Nevada ($935)	Illinois ($721)	Kentucky ($584)
California ($917)	Arizona ($713)	Georgia ($583)
Vermont ($800)		Virginia ($578)
Delaware ($788)	UNITED STATES ($703)	Florida ($578)
Washington ($785)		New Hampshire ($564)
North Dakota ($774)	New Jersey ($964)	Texas ($562)
Minnesota ($771)	Utah ($674)	Missouri ($560)
New Mexico ($768)	Nebraska ($680)	Ohio ($557)
Massachusetts ($764)	Rhode Island ($674)	Alabama ($550)
Montana ($743)	Louisiana ($652)	Tennessee ($534)
Wisconsin ($742)	Idaho ($649)	North Carolina ($534)
Michigan ($735)	Kansas ($648)	South Carolina ($491)
Colorado ($730)	Pennsylvania ($635)	Arkansas ($488)
	Maine ($618)	

Source: U.S. Bureau of the Census, *Statistical Abstract of the United States* (1973), table no. 672.

It becomes apparent also when observing differing communities that the level of revenues available for public purposes varies considerably. The following set of socioeconomic and governmental factors has been formulated by Lineberry and Sharkansky to explain *higher* community levels of revenue and expenditures:[18]

FIGURE EIII-2. FACTORS AFFECTING HIGHER COMMUNITY LEVEL OF REVENUE AND EXPENDITURES

Socioeconomic

1. Higher rather than lower income.
2. Manufacturing economic base rather than other types.
3. Lower percentage of owner-occupied housing rather than higher.
4. Greater rather than lesser ethnicity.
5. Central city rather than suburbs.

Governmental

6. Greater local rather than state responsibility.
7. Higher intergovernmental aid rather than lower.
8. Unrestrictive rather than restrictive state tax and debt limits.
9. Higher rather than lower previous budgets.

The authors examined a number of other factors and found present knowledge to be incomplete or to present a mixed set of findings making it premature to conclude at this point. These other factors include density or growth rate, the degree of governmental reformism, electoral participation, and political party competition.

Other socioeconomic factors not examined but suggested as affecting levels of spending are the incidence of poverty, the type of industrial activity, general age of the buildings, and climate. Lineberry and Sharkansky carefully note that their findings are only tendencies, which may "mask" deviant cases. They suggest other political factors affecting levels of spending such as:

> the attitudes of community residents, the nature of the local power structure, and the risk-taking propensities of the local officials called upon to propose budget and tax increases. A community dominated by public-regarding people may spend more than one dominated by private-regarding people. A monolithic power structure, ruling in the interest of the upper class, may be less supportive of tax and expenditure increases than would a pluralistic structure.[19]

Several additional structural-functional considerations may also have a significant effect on the level of revenues collected and used for public purposes. One is population size. That is, the greater the number of people the greater will be the costs to service them, as it takes more teachers to instruct more students, more policemen to protect more residents, and more sanitation workers to collect the garbage from more homes. Wood found that population size accounted for the overwhelming proportion of variation in available local revenues in the New York metropolitan area.[20] Some argue that the larger the city, the lower the per-unit cost of the operation. However, some analysts of municipal and school governments suggest that such efficiencies are realized from increased size only up to a point, after which costs tend to increase.

Hirsch, for example, specifies that "in terms of economies of scale, governments serving from 50,000 to 100,000 urbanites might be most efficient."[21] (To control for population size, revenues and expenditures should be measured in per capita amounts.)

A second consideration is whether the community includes a dependent or independent school system. The latter, prevailing for about 80 percent of the nation's school districts, has a separate board of education created to decide school policies and generally granted separate taxing power to support its schools. Dependent school districts, on the other hand, are part of and rely on municipal governments for their budgets, and generally the members of the board of education are chosen by the mayor. Under these circumstances educational funds, often one-half or more of all costs of local governments, are included in municipal budgets. It should be apparent that any general comparison between the two kinds of communities—those with dependent schools and those with independent schools—would be most misleading. The type of school system not only affects the total level of revenues and expenditures but also the level of intergovernmental transfers, the amount of property taxes collected, the accumulated debt, and the interest on that debt.

The third consideration is whether or not municipalities carry on county functions in addition to their municipal ones. There are some sixty cities that are essentially urban counties and that carry on all, most, or many county functions such as administering the public assistance programs of their states, providing health services and hospital facilities, and carrying on some law enforcement and highway activities.

While most analysts of public revenues and expenditures use the data provided by the *Census of Government* as given, pointing out from time to time certain cautions in their explanations, we have disaggregated the cities with populations of 50,000 and over into (1) six population-size groups, (2) two groups according to type of school district—dependent or independent, and (3) those cities which carry out municipal functions only and those carrying out both municipal and county functions (see Figure EIII-3). This provides a more realistic basis upon which to compare communities. That is, comparisons should be made among cities with dependent school districts and among cities carrying out county functions. This, of course, does not preclude examining the variations among all municipalities.

FIGURE EIII-3. MUNICIPALITIES WITH POPULATIONS OF
50,000 OR OVER BY SIZE WITH COUNTY FUNCTIONS
AND/OR DEPENDENT SCHOOL DISTRICTS*

1,000,000 or more

New York, N.Y.(cd)   Philadelphia, Pa.(c)

500,000 to 999,999

Baltimore, Md.(cd)   Jacksonville, Fla.(c)
Boston, Mass.(cd)   Memphis, Tenn.(d)
Denver, Colo.(c)   New Orleans, La.(c)
Honolulu, Haw.(c)   San Francisco, Calif.(c)
Indianapolis, Ind.(c)   Washington, D.C.(cd)

300,000 to 499,999

Buffalo, N.Y.(d)   Newark, N.J.(d)
Cincinnati, Ohio(d)   Norwalk, Va.(cd)
Nashville, Tenn.(cd)

200,000 to 299,999

Baton Rouge, La.(c)   Rochester, N.Y.(d)
Jersey City, N.J.(d)   Yonkers, N.Y.(d)
Richmond, Va.(cd)

100,000 to 199,999

Albany, N.Y.(d)   New Haven, Conn.(cd)
Alexandria, Va.(cd)   Newport News, Va.(cd)
Bridgeport, Conn.(d)   Patterson, N.J.(d)
Cambridge, Mass.(d)   Portsmouth, Va.(cd)
Chattanooga, Tenn.(d)   Providence, R.I. (cd)
Columbus, Ga.(c)   Stamford, Conn.(d)
Elizabeth, N.J.(d)   Syracuse, N.Y.(d)
Hampton, Va.(cd)   Trenton, N.J.(d)
Hartford, Conn.(cd)   Virginia Beach, Va.(cd)
Knoxville, Tenn.(d)   Waterbury, Conn.(d)
Madison, Wisc.(d)   Worchester, Mass.(d)
New Bedford, Mass.(d)

50,000 to 99,999

Appleton, Wisc.(d)   Manchester, N.H.(d)
Arlington, Mass.(d)   Medford, Mass.(d)
Bayonne, N.J.(d)   Meridan, Conn.(d)
Bloomfield, N.J.(d)   Milford, Conn.(d)
Bristol, Conn.(cd)   Nashua, N.H.(d)
Brockton, Mass.(d)   New Britain, Conn.(d)
Chesapeake, Va.(d)   Newton, Mass.(d)
Chicopee, Mass.(d)   Norwalk, Conn.(d)
Clifton, N.J.(d)   Oshkosh, Wisc.(d)
Cranston, R.I.(d)   Passaic, N.J.(d)
Danbury, Conn.(d)   Pawtucket, R.I.(d)
East Hartford, Conn.(d)   Pittsfield, Mass.(d)
East Orange, N.J.(d)   Portland, Me.(d)
Edison, t.p., N.J.(d)   Quincy, Mass.(d)
Fairfield, Conn.(cd)   Roanoke, Va.(cd)
Fall River, Mass.(d)   Somerville, Mass.(d)
Framington, t., Mass.(d)   Union City, N.J.(d)
Greenwich, Conn.(d)   Waltham, Mass.(d)
Holyoke, Mass.(d)   Warwick, R.I.(d)
Irvington, N.J.(d)   Wauwatosa, Wisc.(d)
LaCross, Wisc.(d)   West Allis, Wisc.(d)
Lawrence, Mass.(d)   West Hartford, Conn.(d)
Lowell, Mass.(d)   West Haven, Conn.(d)
Lynchburg, Va.(cd)   Weymouth, t., Mass.(d)
Lynn, Mass.(d)   Wilmington, Del.(d)
Malden, Mass.(d)

*Those cities in each size group not listed carry out only municipal functions.
t or tp refers to towns or townships which carry out functions similar to
municipalities.
c = county functions   d = dependent school districts
cd = county functions and dependent school districts

If, however, there is interest in comparing the public finance of two communities carrying out different functions, this may be accomplished by several different approaches. One is to look at a single function such as comparing per capita expenditures for police in one city with per capita expenditures for police in another. The second is to determine the per capita amounts spent on municipal functions that are carried out in common. These include: highways, police and fire protection, sewerage, sanitation, parks and recreation, and libraries. Thus expenditures for education, public assistance, health and hospitals, and housing and urban renewal are not included in the comparative expenditures. The third approach is to include along with the common functions any noncommon functions that two or more places may engage in. For example, include education if the comparison is among cities with dependent school districts but do not include public assistance if some of these communities carry out county functions but the others do not. The fourth is to combine all revenues expressed in per capita terms raised by various local governments and special districts that cover the array of municipal, school, and county functions.

TYPOLOGY

We offer the following typology of general revenues. On one side is the per capita general revenues and on the other side is the percentage of revenue that is derived from intergovernmental transfers relative to the national average of cities of comparable size and type. Cities with above-average general revenues and intergovernmental aid are the *advantaged and supported*. These places are more likely to be located in states with higher levels of support, granting aid mainly on a per capita basis. In addition, these communities are generally the bigger cities with an aggressive policy of securing state and federal aid.

FIGURE EIII-4. TYPOLOGY OF GENERAL REVENUES AND
INTERGOVERNMENTAL AID FOR CITIES BY TYPE AND SIZE
(Relative to the Average for Their Group)

PER CAPITA GENERAL REVENUES

		Above	*Below*
PERCENT INTER-GOVERNMENTAL TRANSFERS OF GENERAL REVENUES	*Above*	Advantaged and Supported	Disadvantaged Despite Aid
	Below	Independently Advantaged	Underfinanced

Independently advantaged cities have higher per capita revenues but do not receive as much external aid. They provide higher levels of public services but choose to do so from their own resources. If a city has below the national average of revenues but received an above average amount of external aid, it is *disadvantaged despite aid*. This type of city is most likely to have a lower fiscal capacity or willingness to spend but is either located in a state with higher levels of support or receives a considerable proportion of its funds from the federal government. Should a city be below the average in both general revenue and intergovernmental aid, it is *underfinanced*. These communities are either unable or unwilling to generate much local revenue and do not receive much state and federal aid. They are probably small towns or communities with low levels of representation in state legislatures and Congress and a lack of interest or ability to seek out and secure grants for special programs and projects.

SOURCES AND CAVEATS

Revenue data for cities with populations of 50,000 or more can be found in U.S. Bureau of the Census, *The Compendium of City Government Finances,* published annually. This report also includes per capita revenue figures. Revenue data for municipalities and townships having 10,000 or more inhabitants can be found in the U.S. Bureau of the Census, *Census of Governments,* Vol. 4, *Government Finances,* no. 4: *Finances of Municipalities and Township Governments,* published every five years, that is 1962, 1967, 1972. Data on federal outlays is published in the U.S. Department of Commerce, National Technical Information Service, *Federal Outlay in . . .* (by state). Data is reported for every county and for each city where the population exceeds 24,000. These reports have been published annually since 1968. We have provided a listed breakdown by size, type of school district, and whether county functions are assumed for cities of 50,000 or more population (see Figure EIII-3). For smaller municipalities and townships the type of functions should be checked out in the 1962 and 1972 *Census of Governments,* Vol. 1: *Governmental Organization.*

Note that selected revenue items have been controlled for inflation (see Table EIII-3). The implicit deflators used appear in Exercise EII.

PROFILE EXAMPLE

TABLE EIII-3. MUNICIPAL REVENUES (1,000's), 1960 and 1970

| | MOUNT VERNON | | | NEW ROCHELLE | | |
	1960	1970	% Change	1960	1970	% Change
General Revenue	$6931	$14,846	114.2	$7733	$18,071	113.7
Intergovernmental Revenue	738	4,291	481.4	733	3,188	312.4
From State Government	735	2,990	306.8	754	2,740	263.4
From Federal Government	NA	1,278	NA	NA	315	NA
From Local Governments	NA	23	NA	NA	133	NA
General Revenue Own Sources	6193	10,555	70.4	6960	14,883	113.8
Taxes	5501	8,675	58.7	6016	11,993	99.4
Property	5280	8,383	58.8	5745	11,656	102.9
Gen. Sales & Gross Rec'ts						
Select. Sales & Gross Rec'ts	98	115	17.3	101	148	46.5
Other	123	117	43.9	170	189	11.2
Current Charges	525	924	76.0	615	1,506	144.9
Miscellaneous	167	956	472.5	329	1,385	321.0
Water Supply Revenue	610	983	61.1			
Water Supply Expenditures	502	945	88.2			
Other Utility Revenue						
Other Utility Expenditures						

TABLE EIII-4. SELECTED MUNICIPAL REVENUE ITEMS DEFLATED (1,000's), 1960 and 1970

| | MOUNT VERNON | | | NEW ROCHELLE | | |
	1960	1970	% Change	1960	1970	% Change
General Revenue	$6,545	$9,921	33.8	$7,302	$10,946	49.9
Intergovernmental Revenue	697	2,599	272.9	730	1,931	164.5
Taxes	5,195	5,254	1.1	5,581	7,264	27.9
Property	4,986	5,078	1.8	5,425	7,059	30.1
Current Charges	496	560	12.9	581	912	57.0
Miscellaneous	158	579	266.5	311	839	169.8

OPERATIONAL DEFINITIONS

$$\% \text{ Change in Revenue Item} = \frac{(\text{Amount, 1970} - \text{Amount, 1960})}{\text{Amount, 1960}}$$

$$\text{Revenue Item Deflated, 1960} = \frac{\text{Amount, 1960}}{105.9} \qquad \text{Revenue Item Deflated, 1970} = \frac{\text{Amount, 1970}}{165.1}$$

TABLE EIII-5. PER CAPTIA AMOUNTS OF SELECTED MUNICIPAL REVENUES, 1960 and 1970

| | MOUNT VERNON | | | NEW ROCHELLE | | |
	1960	1970	% Change	1960	1970	% Change
General Revenue	$91.18	$203.99	123.7	$100.67	$239.72	138.1
Intergovernmental Revenue	9.71	58.96	502.7	10.06	42.29	320.4
Taxes	72.37	119.20	64.7	78.32	159.09	104.4
Property	69.46	115.19	65.6	74.79	154.62	106.7
Other	2.91	2.43	-16.5	3.53	2.51	-28.9
Charges and Misc.	9.10	24.73	171.8	12.29	38.35	212.0

OPERATIONAL DEFINITIONS

$$\text{Per Capita Amounts} = \frac{\text{Revenue Item}}{\text{Total Population}}$$

PROFILE EXAMPLE

TABLE EIII-6. SELECTED MUNICIPAL REVENUES AS A PERCENTAGE OF TOTAL GENERAL REVENUE, 1960 and 1970						
	MOUNT VERNON			NEW ROCHELLE		
	1960	1970	% Change	1960	1970	% Change
General Revenue	100.0	100.0	-	100.0	100.0	-
Intergovernmental Revenue	10.7	28.9	18.2	10.0	17.6	7.6
Taxes	79.4	58.4	-21.0	77.8	66.4	-11.4
Property	76.2	56.5	-19.7	74.3	64.5	-9.8
Other	1.8	1.2	-0.6	2.2	1.1	-1.1
Charges and Misc.	10.0	12.7	2.7	12.2	16.0	3.8

OPERATIONAL DEFINITIONS

$$\text{Revenue Item as \% of Total Revenue} = \frac{\text{Revenue Item}}{\text{Total General Revenue}}$$

Simple Percent Change = %, 1970 - %, 1960

TABLE EIII-7.   FEDERAL OUTLAYS FOR MOUNT VERNON AND NEW ROCHELLE, 1972-1974 (in 1,000's)

AGENCY	MOUNT VERNON		NEW ROCHELLE	
	1972	1974	1972	1974
Agriculture				
School Lunch	-	259	-	95
Total	266	289	269	110
Defense				
Prime Supply Contract	3,994	3,752	1,726	1,878
Retired Pay	128	115	440	527
Reserve/Guard	134	-	449	543
Total	4,938	4,905	3,125	3,529
Health, Education & Welfare				
Disability Insurance	1,422	2,231	1,182	2,015
Retirement Insurance	15,198	16,150	17,772	19,040
Survivors Insurance	-	4,626	-	5,618
Basic Grants	-	-	-	730
Mental Health	-	-	-	354
Total	16,833	23,137	20,218	28,963
Housing & Urban Development				
Urban Renewal	499	310	-	-
Basic Water/Sewer	718	-	-	-
Total	1,217	310	-	-
Justice				
Law Enforcement Assistance	3	-	13	30
Total	3	-	13	30
Labor				
Manpower Development & Training	194	187	30	29
Unemployment Insurance	320	246	291	216
Total	1,636	1,234	995	288
Transportation				
Coast Guard	11	35	77	91
Total	11	35	77	91
Treasury				
Revenue Sharing	NA	619	-	512
Interest on Federal Debt	-	40,375	-	41,448
Total	-	41,182	-	42,312
Office of Economic Opportunity				
Community Action	9	-	129	91
Total	9	-	129	91
Small Business Administration				
Economic Opportunity Loans	-	-	-	20
Total	-	-	-	47
TOTAL	58,829	98,765	59,337	86,025
Per Capita	808	1,357	787	1,141

CLASSIFICATION INDICATORS

Municipalities in 1970-71 with	1,000,000 or more	500,000 to 999,999	300,000 to 499,999	200,000 to 299,999	100,000 to 199,999	50,000 to 99,999
Dependent school districts and county functions	N=1*	N=3	N=2	N=1*	N=8	N=4
Per capita revenues	$954.90	$802.08	$400.79	$540.00	$432.62	$387.60
% intergovernmental transfers	47.5	41.6	39.9	35.6	36.7	27.0
Dependent school districts	N=0	N=1*	N=3	N=3	N=15	N=47
Per capita revenues	0	$360.58	$422.28	$446.78	$403.11	$372.66
% intergovernmental transfers	0	55.6	33.1	38.2	34.2	24.1
Independent school districts and county functions	N=1*	N=7	N=0	N=1*	N=1*	N=0
Per capita revenues	$361.72	$335.23	0	$158.00	$162.34	0
% intergovernmental transfers	31.5	26.92	0	9.3	8.0	0
Municipal functions only	N=4	N=10	N=16	N=12	N=64	N=178
Per capita revenues	$221.24	$183.47	$172.81	$180.68	$155.97	$126.02
% intergovernmental transfers	23.7	22.7	20.7	24.0	20.7	22.1

POPULATION SIZE

Mount Vernon
Per capita revenues $203.99
% intergovernmental transfers of all revenues   28.9

New Rochelle
Per capita revenues $239.72
% intergovernmental transfers of all revenues   17.6

Note: See Figure EIII-3 for city size and type and Tables EIII-3 and 4 for classification data.

*There are six cities which are unique for their size; that is, no other city in their size group carries out similar functions. These are New York, N.Y. and Philadelphia, Pa. (1,000,000 or more); Memphis, Tenn. (500,000 to 999,999); Richmond, Va. and Baton Rouge, La. (200,000 to 299,999); and Columbus, Ga. (100,000 to 199,999). These cities are virtually incomparable. However, if you are studying these cities, you may wish to get some idea of their standing by comparing them to cities in the next size group either one size smaller or one size larger.

FINDINGS AND SUGGESTED IMPLICATIONS

The revenue pattern of Mount Vernon, a city with an independent school district carrying out only municipal functions, indicated that it was an *advantaged and supported* community. Both Mount Vernon's per capita general revenue and proportion of intergovernmental aid were well above the average for cities of its size and type. Its $204 per capita revenue exceeded the $126 figure for other comparable cities. Its general revenues doubled from nearly $7 million in 1960 to nearly $15 million in 1970 (see Table EIII-3). Its intergovernmental transfers were also significantly above that of other municipalities of its type and size. Such external support constituted 28.9 percent of revenues for 1970 and, in fact, increased nearly six-fold during the decade (see Table EIII-6). Most of this increase came from the state government, yet federal aid made up nearly one-fourth of all external aid. More significant is that nearly one-half of the increase in general revenues, which doubled during the decade, came from external sources. Nevertheless property taxes comprised the single largest proportion of general revenues from over three-fourths (76.2 percent) in 1960 to slightly over half (56.5 percent) in 1970, a dramatic decrease. At the end of the decade other components of local revenue (nonproperty) comprised only 14 percent of all revenues.

New Rochelle, on the other hand, was an *independently advantaged* community that was dramatically above the average in its per capita general revenue ($240) for places of its size and type but received proportionately less intergovernmental aid (17.6 percent). Its general revenues increased from $7.7 million in 1960 to $18 million in 1970, which gave it $3.2 million more in revenue to meet its needs than Mount Vernon had despite $1 million less in external aid. New Rochelle's public officials chose to provide this additional revenue through higher levels of property taxation despite the fact that its external aid increased threefold. Perhaps New Rochelle's greater financial ability, as measured by the full value of real property and median family income (see Exercise EII) made it easier for the authorities to raise taxes and make the most use of external aid.

It appears that intergovernmental transfers were stimulative in both communities but more so in New Rochelle than in Mount Vernon; that is, $2.4 million in additional external aid, essentially from the state, in New Rochelle was accompanied by a $7 million increase in revenues from local sources. An even larger increase in external aid ($3.5 million) to Mount Vernon provided a smaller increase ($4.3 million) in revenues from local sources. As both cities received a similar amount from the state, it is apparent that New York state provides aid on a straight per captia basis for municipal purposes rather than attempting to respond to differential needs.

It is important to note that despite an enormous increase in general revenue (more than doubling) during the decade, when taking inflation into account, purchasing power for public goods and services increased only one-third in Mount Vernon and by one-half in New Rochelle (see Table EIII-4). In fact, per capita taxes in Mount Vernon, which increased by two-thirds, actually provided deflated revenues equal in purchasing power to those of a decade ago. In New Rochelle per capita property taxes doubled but when deflated yielded only a 30 percent increase in purchasing power. It would appear that had intergovernmental transfers not tripled (in deflated dollars) in Mount Vernon, the municipality would have remained at its 1960 level of consumption for goods and services. It is useful to repeat that external aid has been much more stimulative in its effect for New Rochelle and per-mitted it to increase taxes beyond the level of keeping up with inflation. Mount Vernon, on the other hand, was with the help of external aid only able to keep pace with inflationary increases.

While Mount Vernon received $1.3 million in federal aid to its muni-cipal government in 1970, federal outlays to individuals and economic firms in the city involved over $28 million in 1974 (see Table EIII-7). The vast proportion ($23 million) of this went to those receiving social security and other retirement and disability payments. Federal outlays comprised about 6 percent of the total aggregate income for both communities by the end of the decade. The Department of Defense spends nearly $5 million in Mount Vernon, most of it in military supplies. The city receives $619 thousand in federal general revenue-sharing funds annually. The startling fact is that $500 per capita is allocated for interest on the federal debt. This is nearly two and one-half times the general revenues available for municipal purposes.

In sum, considering the level of revenues of Mount Vernon and New Rochelle, we have attempted to relate the propositions of Lineberry and Sharkansky (see Figure EIII-2).

1. Support. New Rochelle with greater income (see Table EII-3) had higher levels of revenue than Mount Vernon.

2. No support. Mount Vernon with a greater manufacturing ratio (see Table EI-4) raised less revenue.

3. No support. New Rochelle with greater owner occupancy raised higher revenues.

4. No support. Mount Vernon with heavier ethnicity (see Table SIII-3) raised less revenue than New Rochelle.

5. No conclusion. Both cities are suburban places.

6. No conclusion. Both cities are in the same state.

7. No support. Mount Vernon with more intergovernmental aid (see Table EIII-3) raised less revenue than New Rochelle.

8. No conclusion. Both cities are subjected to the same state restrictions.

9. Support. New Rochelle with higher previous budgets (see Table EIII-3) continued to raise more revenue than Mount Vernon.

Most local public officials face increasing demands for expanding the scope of government. At the same time, the cost of public services has increased considerably. To fulfill these demands, even selectively, and balance the budget requires a corresponding increase in revenues. Added revenues may be secured from local or external sources or a combination of the two. We offer the following speculations on the advantages and disadvantages of increasing revenues from internal sources and external sources.

FIGURE EIII-4. SPECULATIONS ON THE COSTS AND BENEFITS
OF INCREASING REVENUES FROM INTERNAL OR EXTERNAL SOURCES

Internal	*External*
BENEFITS	
Retain autonomy	Reduces local financial burden
Set own priorities	Receive return from taxes paid to external governments
Not subject to changing external policies	Demonstrates political effectiveness of local officials
Discourages tax-conscious people from moving in	Helps focus on target populations with special needs
	Categorical grants reduce competition for funds
COSTS	
Increases local financial burden	Generally unperceived increases in external taxes
Taxpayer resistance grows	Need to meet specific guideline requirements
Increased competition over allocations	Increased community competition at federal and state levels
Stimulates out-migration of tax-conscious residents	Benefits go to selective groups in the community
Increases turnover of local authorities	Local priorities are distorted, which may jeopardize community viability
Disadvantaged residents get slighted	Separates tax-paying responsibility from the benefits of public services

DISCUSSION

1. What is your community's general revenue classification?

2. For what general purposes does your community raise monies?
(a) municipal only, (b) municipal plus dependent school system, (c) municipal and county, (d) municipal, dependent school, and county?

3. What are your community's per capita (a) intergovernmental revenue,
(b) taxes, and (c) charges and miscellaneous revenue? To what extent did
these change from 1960 to 1970?

4. What proportion of your general revenues come from (a) intergovernmental revenue, (b) property taxes, (c) other taxes, and (d) charges
and miscellaneous revenues? To what extent did these proportions change
from 1960 to 1970?

5. What is the extent of your community's federal outlays? What
are the major areas receiving federal monies?

6. To what would you attribute your amount of per capita general
revenue and/or your proportion of intergovernmental transfers: (a)
your city type, (b) its economic base, (c) its wealth and income, (d)
its attitude toward public services, (e) public authorities' success in
gaining external aid, or (f) your state's formula for distributing aid?

7. Speculate on the ways in which your level and composition of
general revenues affects the following major areas of community life:
(a) education, (b) housing, (c) crime, (d) health, (e) welfare, (f)
economic opportunities, (g) cultural activity, and (h) social tensions.

8. Do you think it important to change your level of general revenues
and/or its composition? If so, in what way? What social, political, and/or
economic strategies could be employed to bring about the desired change?

NOTES

1. Robert D. Lee and Ronald W. Johnson, *Public Budgeting Systems*
(University Park Press, 1973), p. 1.

2. Lennox L. Moax and Albert M. Hillhouse, *Concepts and Practices
in Local Government Finance* (Municipal Finance Officers Association, 1975),
p. 19.

3. *Ibid.*, p. 19.

4. Dick Netzer, *Economics and Urban Problems* (Basic Books, Inc.,
Publishers, 1970), p. 167.

5. Arnold J. Meltsner, *The Politics of City Revenue* (University of
California Press, 1971), p. 261.

6.   Robert B. Pettengill and Jogindar S. Uppal, *Can Cities Survive?* (St. Martins Press, 1974), p. 35.

7.   Moax and Hillhouse, pp. 35-54.

8.   John P. Crecine, *Governmental Problem-Solving* (Rand McNally, 1969), p. 192.

9.   Jesse Burkhead, *Government Budgeting* (John Wiley & Sons, 1956), p. 378.

10.   Meltsner, pp. 121-124.

11.   Crecine, pp. 32-34.

12.   *New York Times,* May 18, 1975.

13.   Pettengill and Uppal, p. 55.

14.   The Council of State Government, *The Book of the States 1970-1971,* pp. 272-73.

15.   *The Budget of the United States Government, Fiscal Year 1974* (Government Printing Office, 1973), p. 163.

16.   Office of Economic Opportunity, *Federal Outlays in New York* (1974).

17.   Seymour Sacks and Robert Harris, "The Determinants of State and Local Government and Intergovernmental Expenditures of Low Funds," *National Tax Journal,* Vol. 17, No. 1 (March 1964), p. 83.

18.   Robert Lineberry and Ira Sharkansky, *Urban Politics and Public Policy* (Harper & Row, 1971), pp. 218-27.

19.   *Ibid.,* p. 208.

20.   Robert C. Wood, *1400 Governments* (Doubleday Anchor, 1964), pp. 39-40.

21.   Werner Z. Hirsch, *About the Supply of Urban Public Services* (Institute of Government and Public Affairs, University of California, Los Angeles, 1967), p. 48.

COMMUNITY DATA PROFILE EIII-A

(EIII-3) MUNICIPAL REVENUES (1000's)

| | YOUR COMMUNITY | | | COMPARISON CITY | | |
	1960	1970	% Change	1960	1970	% Change
General Revenue						
Intergovernmental Revenue						
From State						
From Federal						
From Other Local						
General Revenue Own Sources						
Taxes						
Property						
General Sales & Gross Rec'ts.						
Selected Sales & Gross Rec'ts.						
Other						
Current Charges						
Miscellaneous						
Water Supply Revenue						
Water Supply Expenditures						
Other Utility Revenue						
Other Utility Expenditures						

(EIII-4) SELECTED MUNICIPAL REVENUE ITEMS DEFLATED (1000's)

| | YOUR COMMUNITY | | | COMPARISON CITY | | |
	1960	1970	% Change	1960	1970	% Change
General Revenue						
Intergovernmental Revenue						
Taxes						
Property						
Current Charges						
Miscellaneous						

(EIII-5) PER CAPTIA AMOUNTS OF SELECTED MUNICIPAL REVENUES

| | YOUR COMMUNITY | | | COMPARISON CITY | | |
	1960	1970	% Change	1960	1970	% Change
General Revenue						
Intergovernmental Revenue						
Taxes						
Property						
Other						
Charges & Miscellaneous						

(EIII-6) SELECTED MUNICIPAL REVENUES AS A PERCENTAGE OF TOTAL GENERAL REVENUE

| | YOUR COMMUNITY | | | COMPARISON CITY | | |
	1960	1970	% Change	1960	1970	% Change
General Revenue						
Intergovernmental Revenue						
Taxes						
Property						
Other						
Charges & Miscellaneous						

COMMUNITY DATA PROFILE EIII-B

(EIII-7) FEDERAL OUTLAYS (in 1000's)

AGENCY	YOUR COMMUNITY 1972	1974	COMPARISON CITY 1972	1974
Agriculture				
School Lunch				
Total				
Defense				
Prime Supply Contract				
Retired Pay				
Reserve/Guard				
Total				
Health, Education and Welfare				
Disability Insurance				
Retirement Insurance				
Survivor's Insurance				
Basic Grants				
Mental Health				
Total				
Housing and Urban Development				
Urban Revewal				
Basic Water/Sewer				
Total				
Justice				
Law Enforcement Assistance Act				
Total				
Labor				
Manpower Development and Training				
Unemployment Insurance				
Total				
Transportation				
Coast Guard				
Total				
Treasury				
Revenue Sharing				
Interest in Federal Debt				
Total				
Office of Economic Opportunity				
Community Action				
Total				
Small Business Administration				
Economic Opportunity Loans				
Total				
TOTAL				
PER CAPITA				

CLASSIFICATION INDICATORS (Tables EIII-3 and EIII-4)

	YOUR COMMUNITY	COMPARISON CITY
Per Capita General Revenue, 1970		
Percent Intergovernmental Transfers of General Revenue, 1970		
CLASSIFICATION		

EIV. PROPERTY TAXATION

HOW IS PROPERTY IN YOUR COMMUNITY TAXED FOR MUNICIPAL PURPOSES?

CONCEPT

Property taxes, the largest single source of revenue for local governments, have long been the major way for local officials to tap the reservoir of private wealth and income (see Exercise EII) and convert part of it each year to public purposes. Lynn points out that "property taxation has developed out of an essentially agrarian background and, despite the efforts of many over a rather extended period, is not yet well adjusted to an essentially urban society."[1] Nonetheless, "the salient fact is that the real property tax is *the* essential component of local government finance and that it is intended to reflect a crude cost-benefit relationship between the property (and its owner) and the services provided to the property by the municipality."[2]

Property taxes in 1970 made up the single largest source of local revenue (48.1 percent) and of local taxes (66.5 percent) for American cities. Municipalities raised $76.07 per capita in property taxes in 1970, an increase of 68.8 percent from the $44.80 per capita in 1960. However, reliance on property taxes has declined considerably since 1960, when they comprised 73.1 percent of local taxes. The decline has been made up by other forms of taxes and charges. The reliance on property taxes as a source of revenue varies by the type of local government. That is, in 1971-72 townships were the most dependent, 62.3 percent; followed by school districts, 47.5 percent; counties, 33.6 percent; municipalities, 31.5 percent; and special districts, 18.3 percent.

There are two separate and distinct functions in administering the property tax—assessment and taxation. The former is the judgmental process by which a local assessor determines the value of real property for tax purposes. The latter is the charge placed upon the value of the real property which the owner is obligated to pay.

The property to be assessed varies by type, location in the community, and the value it is expected to receive in the marketplace (see Table EIV-5). Some properties, i.e., those used for governmental, religious, educational, and other nonprofit purposes, are tax exempt and therefore no taxes are levied upon them. The value placed on the type of local property varies according to whether it is undeveloped (vacant), residential, commercial, or industrial. Phares suggests,

> that a community is better off (vis-à-vis its tax
> base) the higher is the proportion of industrial pro-
> perty within its taxing jurisdiction. . . . There
> are of course, additional demands exerted upon the
> local fisc by property of a commercial or industrial
> nature, e.g., higher levels of fire and police pro-
> tection, additional sewerage and water facilities and
> increased usage of street and highways.[3]

The basis of all property taxation is the assessed value of real property. The cardinal principal in assessment is that property of similar
value be assessed uniformly and fairly. In most states the law specifies
that the assessed value be the current market value or true or full value
(see Exercise EII). However, few cities follow this rule as they practice
static fractional assessment, that is, they list property on the tax rolls
at only a fraction of its actual value and seldom update the value to con-
form to changing market conditions.

Ecker-Racz depicts fractional assessment as "one of the villains in the
property tax piece."[4] Shannon lists four rationalizations that proponents
have used for this traditional static fractional approach. First is the
uniformity argument that any fractional value is acceptable as long as it is
uniformly applied. The weaknesses of this rationale are that the lower the
assessment level the more able assessors are to hide their mistakes and favoritism and to constrict the fiscal policy of local governments where tax and
debt limits are applied. Second, the *normal-value* argument states that inflat-
ed market prices do not reflect the intrinsic value of property. This argument has been thoroughly discredited, because there has been a constant increase in the value of real property since World War II. Shannon believes
assessors accept this approach "to obscure their unwillingness to accept the
political consequences inherent in any decision to comply with the constitutional market-value mandate."[5] Third, the *aggravation* argument indicates that
any blanket increase in assessments will tend to increase the inequities in
the original assessments. The fallacy of this argument is that increases
would be proportional and inequities therefore no greater. In addition some
argue that the administration of assessment is defective in that locally elected
assessors, untrained, ill-equipped, and poorly paid tend to accept without
question the owner's valuation or what was already on the tax roll. Some propose that appointed assessors with technical assistance can bring about some
improvement in assessment practices—but these reforms are generally insufficient when there is great disparity between the legal requirement and actual
practice.

Shannon proceeds to identify four political barriers to securing full-
value assessment. The first is the misdirection of political responsibility,
that is, assessors fear that they will be blamed for higher levels of taxation
if they gear assessments to rising price levels and city officials fail to
reduce tax rates commensurate with the increase in the tax base. They believe
there is less political risk in raising tax rates than in raising assessments.
In the competition for scarce tax dollars, those governing municipal affairs
prefer static fractional assessment, which tends to force school officials

to raise their rates for additional revenues, eventually to the point where they must run the risk of referring their budgets to the voters for approval. "This strategy can then given those who control local assessment policy far-reaching control over local school budgets."[6] Similarly, state officials find it politically risky to press for full value because they would be held responsible for a rise in local property taxes.

Second, the tradition of local assessment autonomy has left state assessment officials without sufficient support to effectively control the local assessment process. Instead, some form of state equalization is used to secure state-wide uniformity. Third is the existence of extralegal classification of property, whereby various types of property are assessed at different fractions of full value. Oldman and Aaron found in Boston, for example, that the average assessment-sales price ratio was 34 percent in the case of single-family residences, 42 percent for two-family houses, 52 percent for three- to five-family houses, 58 percent for housing for six or more families, and 79 percent for commercial property. They also found considerable difference in the assessment of residential property between neighborhoods. In a well-to-do white neighborhood single family homes were assessed at 31 percent of their sales value whereas in a decaying black neighborhood homes were assessed at 54 percent of their sales value.[7] This selective inequity in assessments stimulated Brandon, Rowe, and Stanton to state that the

> blatant discrimination is much more likely the result
> of . . . assessors failing to keep assessments up-to-
> date; property values in poor neighborhoods rising very
> slowly, even falling while jumping quickly in wealthier
> neighborhoods; assessors taking the path of least resis-
> tance--wearing kid gloves when dealing with individuals
> or groups who are likely to complain and have clout;
> renters not seeing their assessments directly and not
> giving the assessor a hard time since the tax they pay
> is buried in their rent.[8]

Any attempt to bring all assessments to full value would cause a radical redistribution of the tax load. For instance, single-family homeowners would experience a sharp increase in taxes as they reached parity with owners of commercial property. State officials generally fear political repercussions from redistribution.

Finally, there are ideological limitations on state and local tax and debt powers. Bringing undervalued assessment levels to full value weakens the power of conservatives within the community to restrain local spenders, both municipal and school. Because constitutional tax and debt limits are often based on some multiple of assessed value, the lower the assessments, the lower the limits. If, for example, property is assessed at 25 percent of its current market value, then the tax and debt raising capacity of local government will be constricted to 25 percent of its legal entitlement. "In short, deep underassessment permits those persons controlling local assessment policy both to intensify the tax and debt restrictions imposed by the state and to force local legislation bodies thereby to seek the approval of the electorate for tax-rate increases."[9]

Even if local assessors chose to reassess all property up to full value, the task would be complex in that the market price is what is paid for a specific property at a specific moment in time whereas value may vary depending on economic conditions and motivations of both buyers and sellers. The difficulty would be compounded because most properties have not been priced or placed on the market for many years. In addition, two pieces of property are seldom the same in character, so that the market price of one does not necessarily reflect the value of the other. Yet most states have attempted to use a formula to provide full value based on the market price or sales price of similar pieces of property.

The practice of fractional assessments forces counties or states that rely to some degree on the property tax and local assessments to adjust for the differentials in assessed values among communities so that the taxes they impose are equitable. In order to equalize assessments between communities many, but not all, counties and states use an equalization rate. The equalization rate is used to determine both the rate for county and state property taxes and the constitutional tax and debt limits for each city in the state of New York (see Table EIV-4). Without some form of equalization, the state and county would be taxing the residents of communities quite unequally and there would be no basis upon which to compare community taxes. Equalization rates are constantly being reviewed and need to be checked for each year being studied.

The state context in which local assessments take place shows variations in legal standards and differences in sales-assessment ratios, as well as considerable lack of uniformity (see Table EIV-1). Kentucky, for example, shows the most equitable situation; it requires assessment of 100 percent, has a sales-assessment ratio of 83.8, and has the least inequity among properties. Idaho is the converse; using a fractional system it shows the most inequality.

The assessment process provides only one part of the taxation process; it establishes the tax base. The next step is to determine the amount of total property taxes that needs to be levied. This levy generally gills the gap that exists between projected expenditures and estimated revenues from sources other than property taxes. Distributing the tax burden is the next step in the process and requires arriving at a charge for a certain assessed dollar amount of property, in other words, arriving at the tax rate. The rate is the quotient of the determined total tax levy divided by the total taxable assessed value of real property and is generally expressed in mills per dollar, dollars per hundred dollars, or dollars per thousand dollars of assessed value.

Most states have placed a limit on the amount of property taxes local governments may levy. Their restrictions fall into three general categories. One is an overall property tax limit established by putting a ceiling on the aggregate rates for all local governmental units—Michigan, Nevada, Ohio, Oklahoma, and Washington are limited in this way by their constitutions—and Indiana, New Mexico, Rhode Island, and West Virginia have statutory limits of this type. Two is a limit on rates of certain kinds (or capacity) of a governmental unit or limits on the rate levied by a particular type of local

TABLE EIV-1

LEGAL ASSESSMENT STANDARDS, ACTUAL RESIDENTIAL
PROPERTY ASSESSMENTS, AND ASSESSMENT UNIFORMITY BY STATE, 1971

State	Legal Assessment Standard	Ratio of Assessed Value to Sales Price	Assessment Uniformity
FULL VALUE			
Oregon	100	87.1	16.5
Kentucky	100	83.8	12.5
Alaska	100	75.1	21.5
New Hampshire	100	65.1	15.0
Florida	100	63.2	18.1
Maine	100	52.9	18.5
Massachusetts	100	49.3	18.2
Maryland	100	47.8	19.6
District of Columbia	100	47.5	Not Applicable
Wisconsin	100	46.7	Not Computed
Delaware	100	36.5	30.0
West Virginia	100	36.2	25.7
Virginia	100	34.8	17.0
New Mexico	100	27.5	22.8
Pennsylvania	100	26.6	30.0
New York	100	25.8	26.8
Missouri	100	23.1	26.5
Texas	100	18.0	25.7
Mississippi	100	14.7	25.6
South Carolina	100	4.0	27.9
FRACTIONAL VALUE			
Tennessee	35	32.6	21.4
Georgia	40	35.7	32.6
Iowa	27	23.3	22.9
Michigan	50	41.5	14.6
California	25	20.0	15.7
Nebraska	35	27.5	18.9
FRACTIONAL VALUE, Cont.			
Nevada	35	27.1	13.4
Hawaii	70	54.0	17.2
Illinois	50	37.8	23.0
Ohio	up to 50	36.9	19.5
Washington	50	36.1	23.9
Kansas	30	21.8	22.5
Indiana	33 1/3	23.5	23.1
Colorado	30	20.7	16.9
Alabama	30	19.7	28.1
Arkansas	20	12.5	30.2
South Dakota	60	36.5	22.3
Arizona	18	10.7	24.7
Idaho	20	10.6	31.6
Oklahoma	35	18.2	26.1
Utah	30	14.9	24.1
North Dakota	50	15.1	15.7
Minnesota	30	8.5	22.2
Montana	30	7.7	23.3
VARYING VALUATION—DETERMINED LOCALLY			
Connecticut	up to 100	47.8	16.0
Louisiana	Not Below 25	13.1	25.1
New Jersey	20-100	58.3	16.9
North Carolina	1	44.6	22.5
Rhode Island		50.5	24.1
Vermont	Up to 100	33.3	21.2
VALUE DETERMINED BY STATE TAX COMMISSION			
Wyoming	2	16.6	25.8

1 Uniform percentage, determined locally.
2 At a fair value in conformity with values and procedures prescribed by the state tax commission.

Source: Adapted from Robert M. Brandon, Jonathan Rowe, and Thomas H. Stanton, *Tax Politics* (Pantheon Books, 1976), Figures 50 and 51, pp. 188-189.

government—Alabama, Arizona, Arkansas, Florida, Illinois, Kentucky, Louisiana, Missouri, New York, Texas, and Wyoming are limited in this way by constitutional provisions, whereas Georgia, Idaho, Iowa, Kansas, Minnesota, Mississippi, Montana, Nebraska, North Carolina, North Dakota, Pennsylvania, South Carolina, Utah, and Wisconsin are limited by statutes. Three is the limit on rates which would increase levies above a certain percentage of the previous year's increase, unless approved by local election—Colorado and Oregon have this type of limit.[10]

The difference between the tax limit and the taxes levied is the tax margin. Where limits are set in relation to the local community's assessed or true value, the margin is computed by subtracting the dollar amount of the taxes levied from the dollar amount of taxes permitted. Where the limit is expressed as a "maximum rate of taxation" or a "tax cap," the margin is computed by subtracting the tax rate in effect from the top rate permitted and multiplying the assessed value by the difference.

Although there is growing criticism of state-imposed limits, there are those who still support them. Proponents of state restrictions suggest that they (a) tend to insure the taxing local unit against default, (b) stimulate a search for alternative nonproperty revenues, (c) provide an inducement to attract industry, and (d) encourage examination of which level of government should provide what services. Opponents, on the other hand, suggest that tax restrictions (a) stimulate excessive special legislation to relieve individual communities from certain limitations, (b) encourage establishment of special districts in order to gain yet another taxing jurisdiction, and (c) stimulate the use of short-term loans for operating expenses. As Ecker-Racz suggests

> Although they undoubtedly had an initial dampening effect, if for no other reason than because they provided officials in communities operating close to the legal tax limit with an excuse for inaction, they have not slowed property tax increases. They did necessitate the invention of techniques to circumvent them, often with the acquiescence and help of state legislatures. In the process the structure of local governments and property tax systems was distorted, and the integrity of public business impaired.[11]

Therefore, depending on the predisposition of local officials when these limits have been reached, they may accept them as absolute or as barriers that can be circumvented. Those who choose to accept them will hold constant or reduce expenditures. On the other hand, those who see them as barriers can appeal to the legislature for category exemptions from the limit, raise assessed valuation by reassessing property, or hold local budget elections to exceed the limits.

Public officials are accustomed to watch for the public reaction to increased taxes in order to minimize dissatisfaction among taxpayers. Voters are generally reluctant to support a constant increase in taxes, let alone

taxes that exceed some state-imposed limit. Taxpayers, when given an opportunity to vote directly in budget and bond elections or indirectly for local
public officials, have expressed their resistance to increased taxes as they
reach or go beyond their threshold of support. For example, school-bond elections have been meeting a "tax revolt" throughout the country since the latter half of the 1960s. In 1965, 25 percent of the bond elections were rejected and by 1969, 43 percent were rejected.[12]

Horton and Thompson believe political alienation among the relatively
powerless explains protest votes against local budgets.[13] Meltsner has identified three tactics by which local officials attempt to reduce the tax consciousness of the taxpayer: one is to follow the lead of what other cities
do. The second is to focus on indirect taxes, which are "paid but not felt."
The third is to impose a number of small, low-yielding taxes rather than those
that involve one large payment. He noticed that officials seek low-yielding
taxes by imposing taxes sequentially, making public participation difficult,
and justifying all actions in terms of property tax relief. This "keeps the
attentive public small, fragmented, and quiet."[14]

There is considerable competition at the local level for revenues
derived from the property tax among the municipality, the county, the school
district, and other special districts. Each unit of local government generally
has its own taxing authority and sets its own tax rate.

The tax rate, translated into dollar costs to the taxpayer and revenue
dollars to the public officials, also can be used for comparative purposes
provided that the effects of differences in assessment levels (as a proportion of market or full value) and the applicable exemptions are taken into
account. The *Census of Government* distinguishes between a *nominal* tax rate
and an *effective* tax rate. The former, set by local authorities using
assessed value, is the quotient of the total annual taxes levied divided by
total taxable assessed value. The latter is the quotient of the total taxes
levied divided by the *sales price* of the property (as a measure of market
value). Both the nominal and effective tax rates are based on actual sales
of properties and their specific tax bills. These rates are composites and
therefore include all taxes billed, not just municipal taxes. For inter-
community comparisons the effective tax rate should be used. In Table EIV-2
is an example of the data on which the nominal tax rate of 13.7 per $1,000
and the effective tax rate of 3.6 for a city in New York State were based.

Two concerns about property taxation are worthwhile considering, that
of the community as a whole and that of the individual taxpayer. The key
elements for the community are (a) the revenue gap to be made up by property
taxes, (b) the total amount of taxable assessed property in the community,
(c) the equity of assessment between and among similar parcels of property,
(d) the legal limits placed on taxation by the state, (e) the competitive
struggle between local taxing jurisdictions for their share of the property
tax dollar, and (f) the political threshold of support for any given level
of taxation. From the taxpayer's point of view the concerns are (a) the
total tax bill presented by all units of local government, (b) the established tax rate, (c) the amount of assessed value placed on the taxpayer's

TABLE EIV-2. EXAMPLE OF THE NOMINAL AND EFFECTIVE
TAX RATES FOR A CITY IN NEW YORK STATE, 1972

Sale price	$34,000.00
Assessed value	
Unadjusted	12,850.00
Adjusted	8,834.00
Taxes billed	
City, county, sewer	663.32
School	550.21
Total taxes	1,213,53

OPERATIONAL DEFINITION

$$\frac{1213.53}{34,000} = 3.6 \text{ (effective tax rate)}$$

$$\frac{1213.53}{8,834} = 13.7 \text{ (nominal tax rate)}$$

own property, and (d) the relationship among an increase in taxes, the tax-payer's capacity to pay, and the benefits received.

The continued use of property taxation is based on the following ratio-nale: (a) it not only produces much needed revenue, but it is the only method generally reserved for local government, making it difficult to re-place; (b) it provides a stable source of revenue in periods of economic adversity; (c) many governmental services are directed toward benefitting property and its owners; (d) it stimulates the use of nonproductive land and encourages the development of marginal land; and (e) property ownership is considered an index of a person's wealth.

Criticism of the property tax is widespread. There is general consen-sus that the property tax is regressive and therefore places a greater burden on low-income families. In fact, Netzer equates the property tax to a very "stiff" sales tax and says,

> we tax housing more heavily than any other item of con-sumer expenditure in the United States with the excep-tion of liquor, tobacco, and gasoline. I think it is a grotesque social policy to tax something we all agree is a good thing, more heavily than almost anything else a consumer chooses to spend money for.[15]

Furthermore, some critics have expressed concern about the relatively unequal share of property taxes falling upon lower-income rather than middle-income and upper-income families. The Advisory Commission on Intergovernmental Relations estimated that property taxes take 16.6 percent of the income of those with less than $2,000 and only 2.9 percent of those with $25,000 or more income. The spread is higher in the Northeast, 30.8 percent to 3.9 percent, and lower in the South, 8.2 to 1.7 percent. The Commission cites certain "irritating" characteristics of the property tax: "No other major tax in our public finance system bears down so harshly on low-income households, or is so capriciously related to the ability to pay taxes."[16]

Additional criticism of the property tax has focused on the facts that (a) it is an inflexible tax in times of inflation, (b) it discourages improvements to property, (c) it has substantial administrative problems, (d) the growing list of tax-exempt properties produces inequities, and (e) differential property taxes between adjacent communities results in considerable competition. Welch identifies the various critics of the property tax,

> It is under attack from all sides. It is denounced by welfare economists as our most repressive tax, by businessmen as our most inflexible major tax, by farmers as our most unfair tax, by the aged as our tax least related to ability to pay, by guardians of the law as our most dishonestly assessed tax, by students of government as our most ineptly administered tax, and by conscious or instinctive disciples of Henry George as our most regressive tax. Indeed, it is hard to find anyone who will say a good word for the property tax as we know it in this country.[17]

TYPOLOGY

The willingness of a community to tax for public purposes has two aspects which are shown in the following typology. We have determined the per capita taxes for local purposes and the proportion that property taxes comprise of local taxes. The national cutting points for both should be selected by the population size and type of place. Per capita total taxes will of course be higher for those cities with dependent school districts and carrying out county functions and, conversely, those carrying out only municipal functions will be much lower tax communities.

FIGURE EIV-1. TYPOLOGY OF TAX WILLINGNESS
(Relative to the Nation)

PER CAPITA LOCAL TAXES

		Above	*Below*
		High Tax— Property Oriented	Low Tax— Property Oriented
PERCENTAGE PROPERTY TAX OF LOCAL TAXES	*Above*		
	Below	High Tax— Diversified	Low Tax— Diversified

High-tax communities and low-tax communities may be either *property oriented* or *diversified*. One can expect large cities and metropolitan areas to be *high tax* places, whereas small towns are more likely to be *low tax* places. By diversified we mean that the community uses a variety of taxes, such as sales and income as well as the property tax, as sources of local revenues. The diversified tax systems may be found among large central cities as well as newer and growing cities that have determined to avoid placing a heavy burden on property. The property-oriented communities, on the other hand, seldom use other forms of taxation.

SOURCES AND CAVEATS

Assessed value and the assessment-sales price ratio (the closest national measure to a state or county equalization rate) and some tax rate data may be found in the U.S. Bureau of the Census, *Census of Governments*, Vol. 2, *Taxable Property Values*. Other sources for assessed value, equalization rates, and full value are found in state and city financial reports. Local financial reports provide the most complete tax rate data. Tax levies for municipal purposes can be found in the Bureau of the Census, *Compendium of City Government Finance* published annually. A breakdown of taxes levied by purpose can be most readily found in local financial reports. Tax limits and margins can be found in either state of local financial reports.

It should be noted that various reporting units often present different data for a given item. This occurs largely due to interpretation, grouping for comparability, and the projected use of the data. For example, the taxable assessed value in Table EIV-3 differs slightly from that in Table EIV-4 as the former was reported by the state comptroller and the latter by the local assessor.

Refer to Figure EIII-3 to find the size and type of your city for classification. Table EIV-2 and the classification indicators for municipal taxation for Mount Vernon and New Rochelle were computed from data in *City Government Finance* in order to make them comparable with the national figures. In order to provide consistent data on the many aspects of taxation not included in national reporting sources, Tables EIV-3 and EIV-4 are based on state and local data. There are minor discrepancies between the national figures and those appearing in Tables EIV-3 and EIV-4 derived from local and New York state reports.

While assembling financial data, be certain to determine whether there are any provisions to refer municipal budgets to the voters for approval. If so, find out under what circumstances such approval is necessary.

PROFILE EXAMPLE

TABLE EIV-3. INTERSTATE MEASURES OF TAXATION FOR MUNICIPAL PURPOSES
(\$ Amounts in 1000's Except for Per Capitas)

	MOUNT VERNON			NEW ROCHELLE		
	1960	1970	% Change	1960	1970	% Change
Taxes	\$5,501	\$8,675	58.7	\$6,016	\$11,993	99.4
Property	5,280	8,383	58.8	5,745	11,656	102.9
General Sales & Gross Receipts	NA	NA	NA	NA	NA	NA
Selective Sales & Gross Receipts	98	115	17.3	101	148	46.5
Other	123	177	43.9	170	189	11.2
Per Capita Total Taxes	\$72.37	\$119.20	64.7	\$78.30	\$159.09	103.1
Per Capita Property Taxes	69.46	115.19	65.8	74.79	154.62	106.7

TABLE EIV-4. INTRASTATE COMPONENTS OF MUNICIPAL PROPERTY TAXES

	MOUNT VERNON			NEW ROCHELLE		
Tax Base (in \$1000's)	1960	1970	% Change	1960	1970	% Change
Gross Assessed Value	\$211,570	\$238,528	12.8	\$401,323	\$484,825	20.8
Wholly Exempt Value	23,698	37,625	58.8	75,185	99,894	32.9
Taxable Assessed Value	187,872	200,903	6.9	326,138	384,931	18.0
Full Value	293,550	418,548	42.6	388,260	566,075	45.8
Equalization Rate (%)	64	48	-	84	68	-
Tax Rates (per \$1000)						
Municipal	25.93	39.20	51.2	16.93	30.18	78.3
State & County	9.75	19.23	92.2	6.74	11.33	68.1
Special District	2.00	3.17	58.5	3.13	1.73	44.7
Total Tax Rate	37.68	61.60	63.5	26.80	43.24	61.3
Taxes Levied (in \$1000's)						
Municipal	4,876	7,875	61.5	5,519	11,616	110.5
State & County	1,831	3,914	113.8	2,200	4,362	98.3
Special District	376	636	69.1	1,012	803	68.2
Total	7,083	12,426	75.6	8,741	16,781	92.0
Tax Limits & Margins (in \$1000's)						
Tax Limit	4,906	7,704	57.0	6,722	10,238	52.3
Tax Margin*	402	103	-74.4	1,659	643	-51.9
Margin as % of Limit	8.2	1.3	-84.1	24.7	6.3	-66.4

*Tax margins are not always the difference between limits and levies since parts of tax levies may be excluded from the limit.

OPERATIONAL DEFINITIONS

Full Value = $\frac{\text{Assessed Value}}{\text{Equalization Rate}}$

Municipal Taxes = Taxable Assessed Value x Municipal Tax Rate

State and County Taxes = Taxable Assessed Value x State/County Tax Rate

Special District Taxes = Taxable Assessed Value x Special District Tax Rate

Margin as % of Limit = $\frac{\text{Tax Margin}}{\text{Tax Limit}}$

PROFILE EXAMPLE

TABLE EIV-5. CLASSIFICATION OF ASSESSMENT ROLLS, 1960 and 1970.

MOUNT VERNON

	1960			1970			
	Number of Parcels	Assessed Value (in 1000's)	% of Total Taxable	Number of Parcels	Assessed Value (in 1000's)	% of Total Taxable	% Change in Value 1960-70
Vacant Land	1,427	$ 3,934	2	900	$ 3,725	2	-5.3
Residential Property (1-3 Family)	7,926	76,618	41	8,037	79,836	38	4.2
Apartments (4 or more families)	467	35,598	19	462	41,635	20	17.0
Combination & Commercial	848	26,947	14	816	26,006	13	-3.5
Industrial	307	17,361	9	318	26,633	13	53.4
Miscellaneous	96	7,078	4	278	8,207	4	16.0
Utilities & Railroad	24	11,457	6	11	9,085	4	-20.7
Special Franchise	3	10,157	5	3	12,832	6	26.3
Total Taxable Properties	11,098	189,152	100	10,825	207,958	100	9.9

NEW ROCHELLE

	1960			1970			
	Number of Parcels	Assessed Value (in 1000's)	% of Total Taxable	Number of Parcels	Assessed Value (in 1000's)	% of Total Taxable	% Change in Value 1960-70
Vacant Land	2,041	$ 7,194	2	1,543	$ 6,262	2	-12.9
Residential Property (1-3 Family)	10,709	187,036	56	11,194	206,035	53	10.2
Apartments (4 or more families)	353	48,438	15	358	64,223	16	36.7
Combination & Commercial	817	43,007	13	714	54,291	14	26.2
Industrial	113	9,318	3	129	17,100	4	83.5
Miscellaneous	339	14,462	4	343	20,042	5	38.6
Utilities & Railroad	34	9,542	3	39	6,775	2	-29.0
Special Franchise	-	12,547	4	-	17,797	4	41.8
Total Taxable Properties	14,406	331,544	100	14,320	392,526	100	18.4

OPERATIONAL DEFINITIONS

$$\% \text{ Change in Value, 1960 to 1970} = \frac{(\text{Value, 1970} - \text{Value, 1960})}{\text{Value, 1960}}$$

CLASSIFICATION INDICATORS

Municipalities in 1970-71 with	*1,000,000 or more*	*500,000 to 999,999*	*300,000 to 499,999*	*200,000 to 299,999*	*100,000 to 199,999*	*50,000 to 99,999*
Dependent School Districts and County Functions	N=1*	N=3	N=2	N=1*	N=8	N=4
Per Capita Total Taxes	$413.30	$390.21	$174.60	$284.00	$232.27	$240.31
% Property Tax of All Local Taxes	61.7	60.4	68.2	60.6	84.7	75.8
Dependent School Districts	N=0	N=1*	N=3	N=3	N=15	N-47
Per Capita Total Taxes	0	$ 86.53	$175.70	$226.02	$219.04	$252.01
% Property Tax of All Local Taxes	0	70.4	72.2	86.6	96.2	97.6
Independent School Districts and County Functions	N=1*	N=7	N=0	N=1*	N=1*	N=0
Per Captia Total Taxes	$192.92	$176.76	0	$113.97	$64.94	0
% Property Tax of All Local Taxes	30.9	63.6	0	45.2	59.9	0
Municipal Functions Only	N=4	N=10	N=16	N=12	N=64	N=178
Per Capita Total Taxes	$127.03	$96.72	$85.86	$85.42	$80.55	$58.37
% Property Tax of All Local Taxes	58.6	56.7	59.2	59.9	63.2	52.2

Mount Vernon

Per Capita Total Taxes $119.20
% Property Tax of All Local Taxes   96.6

New Rochelle

Per Capita Total Taxes $159.09
% Property Tax of All Local Taxes   97.2

* See Note Exercise EIII, *Classification Indicators*

FINDINGS AND SUGGESTED IMPLICATIONS

In 1970 Mount Vernon and New Rochelle were *high-tax, property-oriented* communities. Per capita taxes of both cities were considerably above the national level for cities of their size and type, and New Rochelle's were substantially higher than Mount Vernon's. Both communities raised a higher percentage of local taxes from property than the average of comparable cities. The 1970 per capita taxes in Mount Vernon were $119, with virtually all of it (97 percent) from property taxes. New Rochelle data reveal even higher per capita taxes—$159 with a similar heavy reliance on property.

The distribution of assessible property upon which taxes fall differs somewhat between Mount Vernon and New Rochelle. Homeowners property in Mount Vernon constituted slightly more than one-third of the taxable property, whereas in New Rochelle it comprised more than one-half of such property (see Table EIV-5). Apartment holdings were the second largest proportion of assessible property, 20 percent in Mount Vernon and 16 percent in New Rochelle. Both cities experienced increases in their industrial property, 53 percent for Mount Vernon and 83 percent for New Rochelle. However, industrial property still only constituted 13 percent of assessible property in Mount Vernon and 4 percent in New Rochelle. Although New Rochelle increased its commercial assessibles by 26 percent, Mount Vernon's decreased by 3.5 percent.

During the decade per capita property taxes in Mount Vernon rose by nearly 60 percent (see Table EIV-3), while those in New Rochelle more than doubled. This property-tax rise occurred in Mount Vernon despite a relatively constant amount of assessibles thereby increasing the tax burden on existing properties (see Table EIV-4). By contrast the new assessible property in New Rochelle (increased 18.0 percent) allowed not only increased revenues but also spread the financial burden.

One factor affecting the amount of assessibles is the proportion of property exempt from taxation because of special status. In 1960 Mount Vernon exempted $24 million worth of property, about 11 percent of all its property, and by the end of the decade exempted $14 million more or 15.5 percent of the 1970 gross assessed value. New Rochelle, on the other hand, began the decade with considerably more tax-exempt property, including two college campuses, (18.7 percent of gross assessed value) and exempted $25 million more by the end of the decade, increasing the proportion of tax-exempt property to 23 percent of gross assessed value. It is interesting to note that during the decade one-third of the added gross assessed value in New Rochelle fell into the tax-exempt category as did more than one-half of that of Mount Vernon.

Both communities chose to increase tax rates rather than reassess their properties as is indicated in their declining equalization rates. During the decade from 1960 to 1970 Mount Vernon's property tax levy for municipal, county/state, and special districts increased by 75.6 percent (from $7.1 million to $12.4 million). In 1960 almost $4.9 million was for municipal purposes, and by 1970, $7.9 million was. The largest percentage increase was in county/state taxes, mainly because of the transfer of the city health function to the county and to rising public welfare costs—a county, state, and federal responsibility. New Rochelle increased its total taxes 92.0

percent, from $8.7 million to $16.8 million, with the largest increase (110.5 percent) for municipal purposes. By 1970, although Mount Vernon's tax limit increased by 57 percent, its tax margin decreased by 74 percent (see Table EIV-4). Similarly, New Rochelle's tax limit increased and its tax margin decreased, but less so than in Mount Vernon.

New Rochelle's greater willingness and ability to generate property-tax dollars put considerable pressure upon Mount Vernon's leaders and citizens in their struggle to keep up with their neighbor. The fact that Mount Vernon raised $3.8 million less in property taxes for municipal purposes probably yielded lower levels of public services, which placed it at a disadvantage in its attempt to maintain a suburban character. Given its lack of open space for new housing and commercial development as well as its lagging aggregate income (see Exercise EII), Mount Vernon will have to reassess its properties, replace old structures with new ones, attract high-yield industrial firms, seek alternative forms of taxation (sales and/or income taxes), and/or seek additional state and federal aid to keep abreast with New Rochelle.

As the perceived need for additional revenue increases, Mount Vernon's as well as many other communities' heavy reliance on property taxation is being questioned. This has encouraged the consideration of alternative forms of taxation at the local level. A shift in tax policy should be evaluated in terms of potential dollar yield as well as in terms of the political costs such as voter resistance, controversy, and even the defeat of elected officials. Generally, local officials have learned that high-yield taxes, for instance an income tax, are associated with high political costs. Therefore, the prevailing practice has been as Meltsner suggests, "the selection of low-yielding taxes which involve minimal political costs and only a small segment of the environment."[18] We offer the following speculations to illustrate some political considerations as various kinds of taxes are proposed for initiation or at increased rates. We attempt to delineate who (not including public authorities) would be most affected, how they might react as constituents in the community, and what other options they might perceive beyond the community.

FIGURE EIV-2. SPECULATIONS ON PERSPECTIVES ON AND REACTIONS TO VARIOUS TAXES AND TAX RATE CHANGES

TAX	Constituents	Limited To Community	Beyond the Community
I. PROPERTY			
A. Remove tax exemptions	Religious, educational, governmental institutions	Mobilize to resist.	Those with obsolete facilities or small operations will move.
B. Increase tax rates	All property owners	Taxpayer associations mobilize to (1) replace authorities, (2) constrain to incrementalism. Landlords raise rents or allow property to run down.	The cost/benefit conscious will seek better value elsewhere.
II. SALES			
A. Impose a sales tax	Merchants	Organize economic sector to oppose. Try to influence authorities.	Fight to keep lower than surrounding communities for competitive advantage.
	Consumers	Organize antisales tax group.	"Shop around" for lower prices and taxes
B. Increase sales tax	Merchants	Business coalition against increase. Prefer increase in sales tax to progressive tax.	Keep increase within competitive range.
	Consumers	Accept.	Consume in lower tax areas.
III. INCOME			
A. Introduce	All income earners	Make an issue of it.	Upper income families move if costs exceed benefits.
B. Increase rate	Middle and working class earners	Turn to conservative expenditure policies emphasizing traditional "housekeeping" practices and rejecting support of dependent populations.	Middle class moves in resistance to supporting dependent populations.
IV. USER CHARGES			
A. Introduce	Users	Small mobilized publics will oppose a specific kind of charge based on vested interest while supporting other kinds of charges.	Accept as universal and minor nuisance.
B. Increase rate	Users	Accept as preferable to more direct taxes.	Make more of an effort to circumvent.

DISCUSSION

1. What is your community's tax-willingness classification?

2. What is your community's (a) gross assessed value, (b) exempt property, (c) taxable assessed value, (d) true value, (e) tax rates? To what extent have these factors changed from 1960 to 1970?

3. To what do you attribute your community's level of tax-willingness: (a) residents' wealth and income, (b) level of needs and government responsiveness, (c) attitudes of citizens and public officials toward taxation, (d) inflation, recession, boom, (e) new forms of taxation, (f) changing requirements of external governments, or (g) level of external government aid?

4. Speculate on the ways your community's taxation policy affects the following major areas of public life: (a) education, (b) housing, (c) crime, (d) health, (e) welfare, (f) economic opportunity, (g) cultural activities, and (h) social tensions.

5. Do you think it is important to change your community's tax policy? If so, in what direction? What social, economic, and/or political strategies might be employed to bring about the desired change?

NOTES

1. Arthur D. Lynn, Jr., "Property-Tax Development: Selected Historical Perspectives," in *Property Taxation & USA* edited by Richard W. Lindholm (University of Wisonsin Press, 1969), p. 17.

2. Report of the Temporary New York State Commission on State and Local Finances, *The Real Property Tax,* Vol. 2, March, 1965, p. 16.

3. Donald Phares, *Metropolitan Fiscal Indicators* (Center of Community and Metropolitan Studies, University of Missouri-St. Louis, 1969), p. 45.

4. L.L. Ecker-Racz, *The Politics and Economics of State-Local Finance* (Prentice-Hall, 1970), p. 81.

5. John Shannon, "Conflict Between State Assessment Law and Local Assessment Practice," in Lindholm, p. 47.

6. *Ibid.,* p. 50.

7. Oliver Oldman and Henry Aaron, "Assessment-Sales Ratio Under the Boston Property Tax," *National Tax Journal,* March, 1965, p. 35. For additional examination of the major cities, see Table A-20, Advisory Commission on Intergovernmental Relations, *Financing Schools and Property Tax Relief— a State Responsibility,* June, 1 73, pp. 154-57.

8. Robert M. Brandon, Jonathon Rowe, and Thomas H. Stanton, *Tax Politics: How They Make You Pay and What You Can Do About It* (Pantheon, 1976) p. 189.

9.   Shannon, p. 53.

10.   Irving Howards, "Property-Tax-Rate Limits," in Lindholm, p. 169.

11.   Ecker-Racz, p. 83

12.   *U.S. News and World Report,* October 20, 1969, p. 37.

13.   John E. Horton and Wayne E. Thompson, "Powerlessness and Political Negativism: A Study of Repeated Local Referendums," *American Jounral of Sociology* 67 (March, 1962), pp. 485-93. See also Clarence N. Stone, "Local Referendums, an Alternative to the Alienated-Voter Model," *Public Opinion Quarterly* 29 (1965), pp. 213-22.

14.   Arnold J. Meltsner, *The Politics of City Revenue* (University of California Press, 1971), pp. 102-107.

15.   Dick Netzer, "Property Taxes," *Municipal Finances* 44:2 (November, 1971), p. 36.

16.   Advisory Commission on Intergovernmental Relations, *Financing Schools and Property Tax Relief--A State Responsibility,* January, 1973, p. 36.

17.   Ronald B. Welch, "Property Taxation: Policy Potentials and Probabilities," in *The Property Tax and Its Administration* edited by Arthur D. Lynn, Jr. (University of Wisconsin Press, 1969), p. 203.

18.   Meltsner, p. 102.

COMMUNITY DATA PROFILE EIV-A

GENERAL MUNICIPAL REVENUES

(EIV-3) INTERSTATE COMPONENTS OF MUNICIPAL PROPERTY TAXES

	YOUR COMMUNITY			COMPARISON CITY		
Taxes	1960	1970	% Change	1960	1970	% Change
Property						
General Sales & Gross Receipts						
Selective Sales & Gross Receipts						
Other						
Per Capita Total Taxes						
Per Capita Property Taxes						

(EIV-4) INTRASTATE COMPONENTS OF MUNICIPAL PROPERTY TAXES

	YOUR COMMUNITY			COMPARISON CITY		
Tax Base (in $1000's)	1960	1970	% Change	1960	1970	% Change
Gross Assessed Value						
Wholly Exempt Value						
Taxable Assessed Value						
Equalization Rate						
Full Value						
Tax Rates (per $1000)						
Municipal						
State & County						
Special District						
Total Tax Rate						
Taxes Levied (in $1000's)						
Municipal						
State & County						
Special District						
Total						
Tax Limits & Margins (in $1000's)						
Tax Limit						
Tax Margin						
Margin as % of Limit						

COMMUNITY DATA PROFILE EIV-B

(EIV-5) DISTRIBUTION OF ASSESSMENT ROLLS

YOUR COMMUNITY

Type of Property	1 9 6 0			1 9 7 0			% Change in value 1960-1970
	Number of Parcels	Assessed Value (in $1000's)	% of Total Taxable	Number of Parcels	Assessed Value (in $1000's)	% of Total Taxable	
Vacant Land							
Residential Property (1-3)							
Apartments (4 families or more)							
Combination and Commercial							
Industrial							
Miscellaneous							
Utilities and Railroads							
Special Franchise							
Total Taxable Properties							

COMPARISON CITY

Type of Property	1 9 6 0			1 9 7 0			% Change in Value 1960-1970
	Number of Parcels	Assessed Value (in $1000's)	% of Total Taxable	Number of Parcels	Assessed Value (in $1000's)	% of Total Taxable	
Vacant Land							
Residential Property (1-3)							
Apartments (4 families or more)							
Combination and Commercial							
Industrial							
Miscellaneous							
Utilities and Railroads							
Special Franchise							
Total Taxable Properties							

CLASSIFICATION INDICATORS (TABLE EIV-3)

	Your Community	Comparison City
Per Capita Total Taxes, 1970		
% Property Tax of All Local Taxes, 1970		
CLASSIFICATION		

EV. MUNICIPAL EXPENDITURES

WHAT DO THE EXPENDITURE PATTERNS REVEAL ABOUT THE PRIORITIES GIVEN SELECTED MUNICIPAL FUNCTIONS?

CONCEPT

The other side of revenues, of course, is expenditures. That is, monies are raised to be spent. Although expenditures receive only moderate attention from citizens (see Figure EIII-1), they are key to understanding a community's order of priorities. A host of decisions are made by elected officials (mayor and city council members) and appointed officials (city managers and department heads) on how much should be spent for what set of public goods and services. As crime rates increase, should more money be spent to deter or prevent crime, and how is this best done? Or, should the community spend more for teachers and recreational programs as a part of crime prevention? Should the community spend more money on modernizing the equipment of the police department or professionalizing its personnel by upgrading the educational and training requirements of policemen? Should the community increase the direct take-home pay of policemen or add fringe benefits such as health insurance and pensions?

Heilbrun, using Musgrave's[1] division of the functions of government into allocation, redistribution, and stabilization has classified specific activities as (a) allocations (police and fire protection, highway and street maintenance, sanitation and sewage, and parks and recreation); (b) redistribution (public assistance or welfare); and (c) joint allocation and redistribution (education, health, and hospitals, and housing and urban renewal). Thus, the function of allocating public goods and services develops when the private sector cannot or is unwilling to provide these services at prices and in quantities that are optimal and local citizens agree that they want and are willing to pay for them. If a redistribution of income from those more affluent to the disadvantaged is desirable, a transfer in cash rather than service is generally made. This is most directly observed in the provision of public welfare or assistance to families with dependent children (AFDC) or to disabled persons. There are other local policies in which allocation and redistribution objectives are more or less deliberately joined to insure the wider distribution of services at less than full cost or entirely free. Heilburn states, "Where benefits are received by rich and poor families in equal amounts per child, but the rich pay far higher school taxes than the poor . . . Local governments provide the poor with more service benefits than they pay for in taxes and the rich with less."[2]

We offer a taxonomy of public services that focuses on the charges for and access to specific governmental functions.[3] Most municipalities provide *distributive* functions in that the charges for services are relatively unequal in their impact, as those who own more property, for example, pay more but

339

all residents have potentially equal access to their delivery. Of course, the administration of the property tax system may exacerbate the unequalness in charges, and the potential bias in the administrative delivery of services may lead to inequality in their access. *Fee-for-service* functions are generally provided upon a set charge uniformly applied for, say, garbage collection or the rate for a bus ride; those who pay these fees should expect to receive equal amounts of goods and services. It should be pointed out that some rates, such as for electricity, are charged on a sliding scale—the more the customer uses the lower the rate. During the energy crisis, the Gainesville, Florida, municipal electric utility considered reversing the rate structure to discourage consumption.

FIGURE EV-1.   TAXONOMY ON THE CHARGES FOR AND ACCESS TO PUBLIC
GOODS AND SERVICES

Function	Charges	Access	Goods and Services
Distributive	Unequal	Equal	1. police protection 2. fire protection 3. streets and highways 4. parks 5. planning and zoning 6. building and health inspections 7. libraries 8. civil defense 9. general control/financial administration
Fee-for-services	Equal	Equal	1. sanitation, refuse collection 2. utilities, water, gas, and electricity 3. parking lots 4. sewage disposal 5. transportation
Redistributive	Unequal	Unequal	1. public assistance (welfare) 2. education 3. recreation 4. low-income housing 5. downtown redevelopment 6. day care centers 7. hospitals 8. public health
Preferential treatment	Unequal	Unequal	(discriminatory practices)

Redistributional functions are provided to selective target populations who have demonstrated at least to the public and their officials a special need, and the charges are applied to others more able to pay. For example, education directly benefits the youth and indirectly benefits the community in the long run. Public assistance is also redistributive in that it is a cash transfer from the taxpayers of the federal, state, and local governments to the recipients who meet specified criteria of need. *Preferential treatment,* of course, is not supposed to occur in charges for and delivery of public services. However, to the extent there are discriminatory practices in either the charges for or access to distributive, fee-for-service, and redistributive functions, favoritism operates. For example, those who live in deteriorated neighborhoods may not receive equitable services. An attempt to measure variations in services in the Washington metropolitan area found that rougher roads occurred in black neighborhoods than in white neighborhoods.[4]

Most municipal functions are distributive, and a growing interest is being expressed in fee-for-services, while redistributive functions have become most controversial. This may be because most of the focus has been placed on the provision of services to the poor. A more comprehensive view would examine the public goods and services going to all strata of the community. For example, the relative gains and losses of two different but related community projects, one public housing for low-income families and the other downtown redevelopment, illustrate the many trade-offs that occur in local politics.

FIGURE EV-2. EXPECTED GAINS AND LOSSES
FOR TWO URBAN RENEWAL PROJECTS

Cost/Benefit	*Public Housing*	*Downtown Redevelopment*
Direct gains	builder suppliers banks tenants	downtown business financial institutions city government builders
Indirect gains	neighborhood merchants	consumers tourists
Negligible gains	middle class	lower class
Net loss	former landlords developers of private housing	dispossessed tenants neighborhood shopping centers

Mitchell points out the perplexity of determining who benefits and who is burdened by differing projects and explains that

> First, they [government] simply do not know the distributive consequences of specific policies and activities. The economic processes have not clearly been defined. Second, governments may not want people to know who benefits and who pays. If a large number of voters found out they were supporting a small number of other citizens they might well vote against the party in power.

> Third, they would face almost insurmountable problems
> of research because many public goods are such that
> they are available to all; no one can trace the values
> each acquires. . . . Finally, citizens do not always
> want to know about inequities, because of our tradition
> that everyone is equal before the law and that each man
> has but one vote.[5]

One should note which government is engaged in which public function.
The *distributive* functions are generally confined to municipal governments
with an occasional use of special districts. The *redistributive* function
is primarily a federal and state responsibility with the county government
as the local partner, except in some large cities where the city performs
many of the county functions. Often special governmental units have been
created to provide utilities and the *fee-for-services* for those public goods
and services that are believed best developed outside or beyond the normal
activities and responsibility of municipal governments. To examine a municipal budget alone may obscure the full picture on how much a local community
is spending for various public functions. Nonetheless an examination of municipal budgets should provide a sense of what functions the mayor and other
municipal officials believe are important.

The budget of local government reflects the relative priorities among
public choices, as Beard suggests, "the history of urban civilization could
be written in terms of appropriations, for they show what the citizens think
is worth doing and worth paying for."[6] An examination of the expenditures
of the nation's cities in 1970-71 indicate their priorities (see Table EV-1).

Although education and welfare are two of the top three priorities of
municipal expenditures for the nation's cities, as a whole they are not functions of most municipalities, as most often education is a function of independent school districts and welfare of counties. For the vast majority of
cities, police protection is the single largest budget item (10.0 percent),
followed by highways (8.3 percent), fire (6.3 percent), hospitals (5.6 percent),
sewerage (5.5 percent), housing and urban renewal (4.5 percent), parks and
recreation (4.1 percent), and sanitation (3.9 percent).

Municipal costs increased significantly during the 1960s (170.3 percent),
in large measure because of inflation (see Exercise EII, *Sources and Caveats*
for implicit price deflators and Table EV-3), with less than one-third due to
an increase in the scope or quality of public services rendered. The increases
between functions is very noticeable. From 1960 to 1970 (see Table EV-1) the
redistributive functions increased most: public welfare (342.1 percent),
housing and urban renewal (210.8 percent), education (191.1 percent) and
hospitals (179.2 percent). The distributive functions showed the next highest
increases: police (172.2 percent), parks and recreation (161.2 percent),
highways (69.2 percent), and fire (125.5 percent). The fee-for-service functions increased the least, yet more than doubled: sewerage (129.5 percent)
and sanitation (121.2 percent).

One item of growing importance in the local expenditure budget is the
amount paid for interest on debt outstanding. Not only has it more than

TABLE EV-1. SUMMARY OF THE FUNCTIONAL DISTRIBUTION OF MUNICIPAL
GOVERNMENT'S GENERAL EXPENDITURES IN 1970-71, AND CHANGE, 1960-70

Function	Amount (millions of dollars)	Percent	Per Capita Amount (dollars)	Percent Change 1960-1970
Total General Expenditures	31,947	100.0	240.02	170.3
Education	4,242	16.4	39.71	191.1
Police Protection	3,471	10.9	26.29	172.2
Highways	2,664	8.3	20.18	69.2
Fire protection	1,996	6.3	15.12	125.5
Sewerage	1,767	5.5	13.39	129.5
Public welfare	2,688	8.4	20.36	342.1
Hospitals	1,780	5.6	13.48	179.4
Parks and recreation	1,439	4.5	10.90	161.2
Sanitation other than sewerage	1,243	3.9	9.42	121.2
Housing and urban renewal	1,442	4.5	10.92	210.8
Interest on general debt	1,308	4.1	9.91	203.5
General control	876	2.7	6.56	45.0
Financial administration	515	1.6	3.90	NA
General public buildings	489	1.5	3.70	NA
All other functions	5,036	15.8	38.15	169.6

Source: Adapted from *City Government Finances* (1970-71)

doubled (212 percent) from 1960 to 1972, but it comprised more money ($11.57 per capita) than is being spent by cities for sanitation ($10.00) or sewerage ($5.60). In the New York City fiscal crisis of 1975 the city's massive debt service was seen as contributing significantly to the loss of investor confidence. In fact, debt service was projected to be $1.9 billion in 1975 and to consume "14 cents out of every expense budget dollar, or more than the city spends for police, fire, the City University, sanitation, and the environment combined."[7] Thus the greater such interest payments become, the less the amount of money generally available for the day-to-day operation of the government.

It should be noted that the expenditures discussed here report both those involved in the day-to-day operation of local government and capital outlays. The latter include expenditures for facilities (buildings) and equipment (police cars and fire trucks). Those functions wherein the census reports distinguish capital outlays from operating expenditures include

education, highways, hospitals, sewers, and housing and urban renewal.
Those for which no distinction are made are welfare, police, fire, sanitation,
and parks and recreation. It is important to make this distinction, as a
capital outlay in some instances may be a one-time expenditure that will dis-
tort the spending for that function in a particular year. Also, one should
note that included in the expenditure budget are a number of general items.
These involve financial administration for accounting purposes (comptroller),
general control for carrying out the activities of the mayor's office and
the city council, and other expenditures that are a bundle of small miscellaneous expenditures.

Scott distinguishes between two sets of factors that influence municipal expenditure patterns, the internal and the external.[8] The internal factor is one of a problem-solving sequence within an organization that focuses
on conflict between various subunits of the municipal bureaucracy.[9]

The external factors influencing expenditure patterns are environmental
and center around the demand for services and the availability of resources.
Muller believes that public services cost proportionally more in the largest
cities as well as in those with declining populations. He indicates that
older cities " . . . also tend to have proportionally larger low-income populations that have above-average need for public services, a situation that
worsens with the continued outmigration of middle-income families from older
cities."[10] Pettingill and Uppal cite population size, density, and growth
as well as the proportions of transients, foreign-born, and blacks, as associated with levels of crime that require high levels of per capita police
expenditures. High demands for fire protection were related to high density
and an aging city.[11] On the other hand, in a study of metropolitan Milwaukee,
Curran found that high expenditures for police and fire protection were
closely related to available resources, whereas sanitation was related to
population density. He found no clear relationship between spending for
highways and demographic or resource variables.[12]

Another consideration is the effect that the federal and state governments have on local spending as they provide both demands (such as requiring
that a sewage system be installed) and opportunities (such as providing monies
for redevelopment). These external governmental demands and opportunities
affect local spending priorities as local officials respond to the demands
and take advantage of the opportunities.

One should note that the governmental functions with the greatest increases involve activities generally encouraged and supported by the federal
government, which has had its influence upon shifting local budgetary priorities (see Table EV-1). Brown and Gilbert, for example, found that in Philadelphia federal-funded and state-funded projects are given preference, which
may have influenced resource allocation.[13] This has led Meltsner to point
to the disjunctions in the budgetary process itself between the "budget
spenders," the departments concerned about service, and the "budget cutters,"
the mayor, council, and financial officers, who worry about adequate revenues.
This dichotomy leads to latent conflicts as the latter "seek to hold down
costs while operating officials seek to improve service and indirectly to
expand costs."[14]

In an effort to reconcile the internal and external factors, Scott indicates these differences are more a difference in degree than in kind. She states

> The fact that demographic changes in New Haven in the
> past decade appear to have had an impact on the supply
> of services and that the supply adjustment varied among
> departments within the city are observations which are
> consistent with theories derived from both internal
> and external views of the budgetary process. While the
> variation in expansion of supply from various departments
> may be considered evidence of the greater power of cer-
> tain subunits in the organization, the increases in the
> supply of services from several of the departments may
> be said to be the result of the increased demand for these
> public services by New Haven residents. It seems reason-
> able to suppose that the speed with which supply adjusts
> to meet demand in the area of public goods is a func-
> tion of the nature of the services provided. An increase
> in the demand for education, i.e., more public school
> enrollments, usually implies an increase in the number
> of teachers, given a fairly rigid pupil-teacher ratio;
> however, a greater degree of utilization of public parks
> does not necessarily result in the purchase of more park
> land. The greater the extent to which provision of a
> service resembles provision of a pure public good, the
> smaller will be the impact upon supply (and upon public
> expenditures) of an increase in the demand for the ser-
> vice.[15]

Many analysts believe that budgetary decisions reflect "incremen-talism." That is, the size and nature of a budget is principally determined by the size and nature of the previous year's budget. Lineberry and Sharkansky cite four factors that contribute to incrementalism and retard programmatic decision-making: (a) *complexity* of budgets, (b) *imperfect information and incommensurable goals,* (c) the *uncontrollable* budget, and (d) *revenue constraints.*[16]

In fact, in the midst of the New York City's fiscal crisis, the myth was dispelled that municipal finance is an exact science as, "Politicians, labor leaders, bankers, and a range of free-lance fiscal critics have all joined in the running arguments, all of them awash in technicalities and filled with conflicting remarks on matters that the public might have thought were beyond dispute."[17] Wriston, president of the First National City Bank, put it succinctly when he said, "You must understand, the whole city account-ing system was designed to prevent anyone from finding out what was really going on."[18]

TYPOLOGY

We have chosen to classify the expenditure patterns by examining
total expenditures and each major function. We include the latter because
an important consideration is to determine the relative priorities of the
community as expressed through its budget. We offer the following typology
to identify local preferences relative to other comparable size communities
throughout the nation by recording per capita expenditures for each function
in 1970 and the degree of change in spending during the decade 1960-70.

FIGURE EV-3. TYPOLOGY OF EXPENDITURE PATTERNS FOR COMPARABLE
SIZE CITIES (Relative to the Average)

PER CAPITA EXPENDITURES BY
FUNCTION

	Above	*Below*
PERCENT CHANGE IN PER CAPITA EXPENDITURES *Above*	Progressively Big Spender	Catching-up
Below	Leveling-off	Continuously Frugal

First we will consider the classifications in terms of total general
expenditures. A *progressively big spender* is a city with a higher per capita
expenditure in 1970 for all functions and that has increased its spending
more than the average of comparable cities. *Progressively big-spender* cities
with municipal functions only are more likely to be affluent communities
demanding traditional services. Also, among the big spenders are those
cities carrying out county functions. These are generally large central
cities that are effective in obtaining substantial amounts of state and
federal aid. If a city has a greater than average per capita expenditure
but has not increased as much as other comparable places during the decade,
we describe such a place as *leveling-off*. These communities are found among
the mature and decline cities facing lagging revenues and fiscal constraints.
They may also be big cities shifting to a more conservative administration,
cracking down on welfare or with a reactionary constituency defeating "liberal"
candidates who support social and racial change. Our *catching-up* places
spend below the average per capita but have increased their expenditures
more than comparable cities. These are growing cities facing rising expectations and increased demands for public services. They may also be places
that are responding to a changing demography. Finally, a *continuously frugal*
city has below-average per capita expenditures that have increased less during
the decade than those of their counterparts. These are smaller stable

communities favoring a minimal scope of government. With limited resources they have little interest in competing with other cities on the basis of the level of public services.

Considering classifications by individual functions, it should be noted that a city may have different classifications for different functions. That is, it may be a *progressively big-spender* for police but *continuously frugal* for parks and recreation. From these differences a sense of priorities may be discerned.

SOURCES AND CAVEATS

Expenditure data for cities with populations of 50,000 or more can be found in the U.S. Bureau of the Census, *Compendium of City Government Finances,* published annually. This report also includes per capita expenditures of selected functions. Expenditure data for municipalities and townships with populations of 10,000 or more can be found in U. S. Bureau of the Census, *Census of Governments,* Vol. 4, *Government Finances,* No. 4: *Finances of Municipalities and Township Governments,* published every five years, that is, 1962, 1967, 1972.

Note that the classification indicators in this exercise are based on cities by size only, not by school type or county function, so that you may compare the expenditures for any function that your community assumes with those of all communities of comparable size carrying out the same function.

PROFILE EXAMPLE

TABLE EV-2. GENERAL EXPENDITURES FOR MUNICIPAL PURPOSES, 1960 and 1970
            (Amounts in 1000's)

	MOUNT VERNON			NEW ROCHELLE		
	1960	1970	% Change	1960	1970	% Change
General Expenditures, All Functions	$6,484	$16,014	147.0	$7,251	$19,089	163.3
Capital Outlay	491	3,948	704.1	748	4,413	490.0
Other	5,993	12,067	101.4	6,503	14,676	125.7
Education*	NA	NA	NA	NA	NA	NA
Other than Capital OUtlay	NA	NA	NA	NA	NA	NA
Highways	528	884	67.4	718	1,414	96.9
Other than Capital Outlay	326	738	126.4	431	1,091	153.1
Public Welfare*	14	NA	NA	31	51	64.5
Cash Assistance Payments	NA	NA	NA	NA	NA	NA
Hospitals*	50	NA	NA	86	NA	NA
Other than Capital Outlay	50	NA	NA	86	NA	NA
Health, Other than Hospitals	170	59	-65.3	186	471	153.2
Police Protection	1,178	2,762	134.5	1,042	2,394	129.8
Fire Protection	823	1,567	90.4	1,007	2,100	108.5
Sewerage	94	80	-14.9	421	1,390	230.2
Other than Capital Outlay	56	80	42.9	123	257	108.9
Sanitation, Other than Sewerage	609	870	42.9	777	1,031	32.7
Parks and Recreation	374	609	62.8	437	2,489	469.6
Housing and Urban Renewal**	219	1,341	512.3	270	1,393	415.9
Other than Capital Outlay	208	657	215.9	250	562	124.8
Libraries	NA	664	NA	NA	508	NA
Financial Administration	NA	307	NA	NA	241	NA
General Control	501	503	0	619	573	-7.4
General Public Buildings	NA	135	NA	NA	259	NA
Other than Capital Outlay	NA	125	NA	NA	256	NA
Interest on General Debt	180	679	277.2	224	1,189	430.8
All Other	1,774	5,553	218.4	1,433	3,585	150.2
Total Expenditures for Personal Services	4,436	7,323	65.1	4,452	9,154	105.6

*Both Mount Vernon and New Rochelle carry out only municipal functions, therefore
 expenditures for education, public welfare, and hospitals are either not in these
 budgets or appear in only nominal amounts.

**In 1960, this item was named "Housing and Community Redevelopment."

PROFILE EXAMPLE

TABLE EV-3. DEFLATED SELECTED EXPENDITURES FOR MUNICIPAL PURPOSES, 1960 and 1970
($ Amounts in 1,000's)

	MOUNT VERNON			NEW ROCHELLE		
	1960	1970	% Change	1960	1970	% Change
General Expenditures, all Functions	$6,123	$9,700	58.4	$6,847	$11,562	68.9
Total, excluding Capital Outlays	5,659	7,309	29.2	6,141	8,889	44.7
Gen. Expenditures, Selected Items						
Education	NA	NA	NA	NA	NA	NA
Highways	499	535	7.2	678	856	26.3
Excl. Capital Outlays	308	447	45.1	407	661	62.4
Public Welfare	13	NA	NA	29	31	6.9
Health & Hospitals	208	36	-82.7	257	285	10.9
Police Protection	1,112	1,673	50.4	984	1,450	47.4
Fire Protection	777	949	22.1	951	1,272	33.8
Sewerage	89	48	-46.1	398	842	111.6
Excl. Capital Outlays	53	48	-9.4	116	156	34.5
Sanitation Other Than Sewerage	575	527	-8.3	734	624	15.0
Parks and Recreation	353	369	4.5	413	1,508	265.1
Housing and Urban Renewal	207	812	292.3	255	844	231.0
Interest on General Debt	107	411	141.8	212	720	239.6

OPERATIONAL DEFINITIONS

$$\text{Deflated Expenditure, 1960} = \frac{\text{Expenditure, 1960}}{105.9} \qquad \text{Deflated Expenditure, 1970} = \frac{\text{Expenditure, 1970}}{165.1}$$

$$\text{\% Change, 1960 to 1970} = \frac{(\text{Deflated Expenditure, 1970}) - (\text{Deflated Expenditure, 1960})}{\text{Deflated Expenditure, 1960}}$$

TABLE EV-4. PER CAPITA AMOUNTS AND PROPORTION OF BUDGET OF SELECTED MUNICIPAL EXPENDITURES

	MOUNT VERNON				NEW ROCHELLE			
	1960		1970		1960		1970	
	Per Capita	% Budget	Per Capita	% Budget	Per Capita	% Budget	Per Capita	% Budget
General Expenditures, All Functions	$85.30	-	$220.04	-	$94.40	-	$253.22	-
Gen. Expenditures, Excl. Cap. Outlay	78.84	92.4	165.81	75.4	84.66	89.7	194.68	76.9
Selected Functions								
Education	NA	NA	NA	NA	NA	NA	NA	NA
Highways, total	6.95	8.4	12.15	5.5	9.35	9.9	18.76	7.4
Excl. Cap. Outlay	4.29	5.0	10.14	4.6	5.61	5.9	14.47	5.7
Public Welfare	0.18	.2	-	-	0.40	0.4	0.68	0.3
Health & Hospitals	2.89	3.4	0.81	0.4	3.54	3.7	6.25	2.5
Police Protection	15.50	18.2	37.95	17.2	13.57	14.4	31.76	12.5
Fire Protection	10.83	12.7	21.53	9.8	13.11	13.9	27.86	11.0
Sewers, Total	1.24	1.5	1.10	0.5	5.48	5.8	18.44	7.3
Excl. Cap. Outlay	.74	.9	1.10	0.5	1.60	1.7	3.41	1.3
Other Sanitation	8.01	9.4	11.95	5.4	10.12	10.7	13.68	5.4
Parks and Recreation	4.92	5.8	8.37	3.8	5.69	6.0	33.02	13.0
Housing & Urban Renewal, Total	2.88	3.4	18.43	8.4	3.52	3.7	18.48	7.3
Interest on Gen. Debt	2.37	2.8	9.32	4.2	2.92	3.1	15.72	6.2

OPERATIONAL DEFINITIONS

$$\text{Per Capita Expenditure} = \frac{\text{Expenditure Each Function}}{\text{Total Population}}$$

$$\text{Percent of Budget} = \frac{\text{Expenditure Each Function}}{\text{General Expenditure, All Functions}}$$

CLASSIFICATION INDICATORS

	1,000,000 or more	500,000 to 999,999	300,000 to 499,999	200,000 to 299,999	100,000 to 199,999	50,000 to 99,999	Mount Vernon	New Rochelle
General Expenditures, All Functions								
Per Capita (1960)	$192.67	$142.85	$109.27	$114.82	$109.11	$98.51	$85.30	$94.40
Per Capita (1970)	$568.58	$350.28	$270.73	$263.20	$243.50	$189.10	$220.04	$253.22
% of Change (1960-70)	195.1	145.2	147.8	129.2	114.9	92.0	158.0	168.2
General Expenditures, Excluding Capital Outlays								
Per Capita (1960)	$148.86	$111.28	$80.45	$84.65	$83.44	$76.55	$78.84	$84.66
Per Capita (1970)	$483.09	$279.70	$205.20	$198.88	$182.43	$148.46	$165.81	$194.68
% Change (1960-70)	224.53	151.35	155.07	134.94	118.64	93.9	110.1	129.96
SELECTED FUNCTIONS								
Education								
Per Capita (1960)	$30.89	$19.17	$16.44	$20.91	$19.83	$18.23	NA	NA
Per Capita (1970)	$107.57	$50.85	$57.33	$44.93	$48.66	$34.98	NA	NA
% Change (1960-70)	248.2	165.3	248.7	114.9	150.4	91.9	NA	NA
Highways, Total								
Per Capita (1960)	$18.08	$16.34	$11.43	$14.07	$13.27	$13.22	$6.95	$5.61
Per Capita (1970)	$19.64	$25.20	$20.80	$26.77	$20.53	$20.08	$12.15	$18.76
% Change (1960-70)	8.6	54.2	82.0	90.3	54.7	51.9	74.8	234.4
Public Welfare								
Per Capita (1960)	$17.73	$10.26	$4.38	$2.56	$3.91	$4.03	$0.18	$0.40
Per Capita (1970)	$108.79	$30.66	$5.58	$6.76	$4.77	$2.53	NA	$0.68
% Change (1960-70)	513.6	198.8	27.4	164.1	22.0	(37.2)	NA	70.0
Hospitals, Total								
Per Capita (1960)	$14.04	$9.17	$4.10	$5.31	$5.64	$3.52	NA	NA
Per Capita (1970)	$47.17	$22.25	$6.97	$4.91	$7.20	$5.56	NA	NA
% Change (1960-70)	236.0	142.6	70.0	(7.5)	27.7	58.0	NA	NA

CLASSIFICATION INDICATORS, Cont.

	1,000,000 or more	500,000 to 999,999	300,000 to 499,999	200,000 to 299,999	100,000 to 199,999	50,000 to 99,999	Mount Vernon	New Rochelle
Health								
Per Capita (1960)	$3.09	$2.84	$1.81	$1.79	$1.51	$1.10	$2.24	$2.42
Per Capita (1970)	$14.27	$9.62	$3.94	$3.41	$2.83	$1.53	0	$6.25
% Change (1960-70)	361.81	238.73	117.68	90.5	87.42	39.09	-	158.26
Police								
Per Capita (1960)	$20.70	$16.62	$11.99	$11.55	$10.88	$9.73	$15.50	$13.51
Per Capita (1970)	$55.40	$40.75	$27.69	$26.26	$24.33	$20.94	$37.95	$31.76
% Change (1960-70)	167.6	145.2	130.9	127.4	123.6	115.2	144.8	135.1
Fire								
Per Capita (1960)	$9.80	$10.91	$9.73	$9.74	$9.99	$9.04	$10.83	$13.11
Per Capita (1970)	$23.12	$22.27	$20.15	$19.84	$19.84	$17.01	$21.53	$27.86
% Change (1960-70)	135.9	104.1	107.1	103.7	98.6	88.2	98.8	112.5
Sewerage								
Per Capita (1960)	$6.39	$7.53	$6.50	$8.41	$6.86	$7.44	$1.24	$5.48
Per Capita (1970)	$13.99	$18.10	$17.77	$16.04	$14.63	$11.65	$1.10	$13.44
% Change (1960-70)	118.9	140.4	173.4	90.7	113.3	56.6	-11.3	145.3
Other Sanitation								
Per Capita (1960)	$9.33	$6.40	$5.29	$6.28	$5.14	$4.71	$8.01	$10.12
Per Capita (1970)	$18.77	$12.45	$9.93	$13.25	$8.79	$7.99	$11.95	$13.68
% Change (1960-70)	101.2	94.5	87.7	111.0	71.0	69.6	49.2	35.2
Parks and Recreation								
Per Capita (1960)	$6.73	$7.42	$7.64	$5.87	$6.49	$5.21	$4.92	$5.69
Per Capita (1970)	$13.48	$18.03	$20.06	$15.56	$13.76	$12.02	$8.37	$33.02
% Change (1960-70)	100.3	143.0	162.6	165.1	112.0	130.7	70.1	480.3
Housing and Urban Renewal, Total								
Per Capita (1960)	$15.88	$4.65	$3.89	$3.24	$4.05	$1.78	$2.88	$3.52
Per Capita (1970)	$35.37	$16.23	$10.81	$20.89	$14.67	$6.94	$18.43	$18.48
% Change (1960-70)	123.0	249.0	193.0	544.8	262.2	289.9	539.9	425.0
Interest on General Debt								
Per Capita (1960)	$9.14	$4.56	$3.91	$4.59	$3.22	$2.93	$2.36	$2.92
Per Capita (1970)	$19.49	$13.56	$12.79	$14.37	$10.17	$7.56	$9.32	$15.72
% Change (1960-70)	113.2	197.4	227.1	213.1	215.8	158.0	294.9	438.4

FINDINGS AND SUGGESTED IMPLICATIONS

Mount Vernon and New Rochelle both were *progressively big-spenders* in that their total expenditures with or without capital outlays were substantially higher than cities their size and increased more in the decade. This was to be expected, of course, given the fact that they were both *advantaged* in their revenue patterns (see Exercise EIII). As cities with independent school districts and carrying out few or no county functions, their expenditures were overwhelmingly distributive, with a much smaller proportion of expenditures going for redistributive and fee-for-service functions. Mount Vernon, however, was a *progressively big-spender* on three of the seven primary functions it performs, that is, for police, fire, and housing (see Figure EV-4). These functions made up the largest proportions of the budget (see Table EV-4), and compared to other cities its size Mount Vernon had nearly twice the per capita expenditures for police and nearly three times the per capita expenditures for housing and urban renewal.

FIGURE EV-4.   EXPENDITURE CLASSIFICATIONS, TOTALS AND BY SELECTED FUNCTION

	MOUNT VERNON	*NEW ROCHELLE*
General expenditures, all functions	Progressively big spender	Progressively big spender
General expenditures without capital outlay	Progressively big spender	Progressively big spender
SELECTED FUNCTIONS		
Education	NA	NA
Highways	Catching up	Catching up
Public Welfare	NA	NA
Hospitals	NA	NA
Health	NA	Progressively big spender
Police	Progressively big spender	Progressively big spender
Fire	Progressively big spender	Progressively big spender
Sewerage	Continuously frugal	Progressively big spender
Sanitation	Leveling off	Leveling off
Parks and Recreation	Continuously frugal	Progressively big spender
Housing and Urban Renewal	Progressively big spender	Progressively big spender
Interest on the General Debt	Progressively big spender	Progressively big spender

For two of its functions, Mount Vernon was *continuously frugal,* that is, for parks and recreation and sewers. In the case of sewers, a special sewer district had been established, leaving Mount Vernon with only a minimal responsibility. Mount Vernon was classified as a *catching-up* place in highway spending. As a geographically small area with its streets and highways long established, recent redevelopment in urban renewal and local adjustment to a major county parkway reconstruction increased its expenditures for this function.

Sanitation expenditures were *leveling-off,* probably as a result of a decreasing population. In addition, Mount Vernon was a *progressively big-spender* for interest on the debt. It spent more for interest than it spent on parks and recreation.

New Rochelle was a *progressively big-spender* on six of the eight primary functions its performs, three more than Mount Vernon (health, parks and recreation, and sewers). New Rochelle still operated its own health department, while Mount Vernon transferred this function to the county. Its miles of waterfront on Long Island Sound stimulated per capita expenditures on recreation that were nearly three times as much as comparably-sized cities spent and four times more than Mount Vernon spent. The shape of the city, long and narrow, requires an extensive fire protection system, and therefore it spent one and a half times as much as other cities of its size. New Rochelle spent $6 more per person on fire protection and $6 less per person on police than Mount Vernon. Sewers, the responsibility of the city, were an expense Mount Vernon did not directly incur. New Rochelle's classification for highways is the same as Mount Vernon's *(catching-up)* and sanitation *(leveling-off).* As a *progressively big-spender* for interest on the debt, it spent twice as much per capita as comparably-sized cities and more than it spent for sanitation.

In 1970, Mount Vernon's general expenditures for all functions amounted to $16 million, a 147 percent increase from the $6.5 million it spent in 1960. New Rochelle, on the other hand, spent $19 million or 163 percent more than its general expenditures of $7.3 million in 1960 (see Table EV-2). Greater increases in expenditures during the decade occurred in capital outlays, housing and urban renewal, and interest on the debt for Mount Vernon (see Table EV-2). Similar increases occurred in New Rochelle, which also substantially increased its expenditures for parks and recreation.

Generally speaking, Mount Vernon's budget merely kept pace with inflation (see Table EV-3). The few exceptions were housing and urban renewal and interest on the debt. Sanitation did not quite keep pace nor did sewage. Parks and recreation remained constant. As a matter of fact, during the decade Mount Vernon added only 16 employees for common municipal functions (see PII-4). In New Rochelle housing and urban renewal, sewage, parks and recreation, and interest on the debt all increased significantly even when controlled for inflation. Expenditures for other functions increased incrementally (see Table EV-3). New Rochelle, in fact, decreased its number of municipal employees by 22. This decrease in personnel was not an across-the-board reduction but reflected a shift in priorities. For instance, decreases occurred in highways and sanitation but were accompanied by an increase in employees in police, fire, and parks and recreation.

We offer the following speculations on some factors that may be associated with increased expenditures for specific functions.

FIGURE EV-5. SPECULATIONS ON SOME FACTORS ASSOCIATED WITH
HIGH PRIORITY GIVEN TO EXPENDITURES BY FUNCTION

Function

EDUCATION

City has a dependent school system
High proportion of youth
High SES of community residents
Organized demands, i.e., PTA and teachers' unions

HIGHWAYS

Previous administration commitments
Poor conditions require repairs/replacement
External priorities (state) force construction
Growth of community necessitates additions

WELFARE

Governmental organization includes county functions
Interest in minimizing civil disorder
Responsive to client (poor) needs
Meet external standards
Responsive to national economic trends/events
Responsive to social service bureaucracy

HEALTH
AND
HOSPITALS

Governmental organization includes county functions
Responsive to constituent demands
Aging population
Responsive to medical-economic elite

POLICE

Responsive to constituent demands for law and order
Need to minimize civil disorder
Technological changes
Influenced by professionalized bureaucracy
Degree of density, transients, minorities

FIRE

High density or large area to cover
Standards set by insurance companies
Growth of community, population, and/or area
High property value
Large proportion of older and/or substandard property

SEWERAGE

New housing developments
No special sewer district
Building developers pressure for installation
Need to meet external health standards
Need to meet guidelines for external matched grants

SANITATION

Demands by constituents to increase/improve service
Growing population
High cost disposal sites

PARKS
AND
RECREATION

Large proportion of youth/aged
Constituents demand more recreational facilities
Trends increase awareness of value of open space

HOUSING
AND
URBAN
RENEWAL

Public authorities secure external grants
Deterioration of the central business district and/or
    residential areas
Need and demand for slum clearance, decent housing
Need to stimulate and/or complement economic development
Large proportion of low-income and/or aged population

INTEREST
ON
THE
DEBT

Increase in new public facilities due to growth
Replacement of facilities due to obsolescence
Previous administration commitments
Deferred-payment ideology of authorities
Economic elite prefers publically supported redevelopment
Accidental occurrences such as fire or flood require
    rebuilding of facilities
Poor credit rating results in high interest rates

DISCUSSION

1. What is your community's expenditure classifications for
(a) general expenditures, (b) education, (c) highways, (d) public welfare, (e) health and hospitals, (f) police protection, (g) fire protection,
(h) sewerage, (i) sanitation, (j) parks and recreation, (k) housing and
urban renewal, and (l) interest on the debt?

2. What proportion of the budget is allocated for each of the above
functions? How have these proportions changed from 1960 to 1970?

3. To what do you attribute the expenditure patterns in your community: (a) the responsibility for county functions, (b) having a dependent
school system, (c) population size and density, (d) level of social dispari-
ties (different kinds of people with different kinds of needs), (e) external
set of priorities and regulations, (f) past commitments and future expectations, (g) campaign promises (electoral options) and citizen preferences
(electoral patterns), and (h) electoral influence reflected in the budgetary
decisions of the authorities?

4. Speculate on the ways your community's expenditure patterns affect
the following major areas of public life: (a) education, (b) housing,
(c) crime, (d) health, (e) welfare, (f) economic opportunity, (g) cultural
activities, and (h) social tensions.

5. Do you think it is important to change your community's expenditure
patterns? If so, in what direction? What social, economic, and/or political
strategies might be employed to bring about the desired change?

NOTES

1. R. A. Musgrave, *The Theory of Public Finance* (McGraw-Hill, 1959),
Chapter I.

2. James Heilbrun, *Urban Economics and Public Policy* (St. Martin's
Press, 1974), p. 321.

3. For an earlier attempt to classify governmental activities, see
Bert E. Swanson, *The Concern for Community in Urban America* (Odyssey Press,
1970), p. 72.

4. Andrew J. Boots, III, Grace Dawson, William Silverman, and Harry
P. Hatry, *Inequality in Local Government Services: A Case Study of Neighborhood Roads* (The Urban Institute, 1972), pp. 31-43.

5. William C. Mitchell, *Public Choice in America* (Markham Publishing
Co., 1971), p. 69.

6. Charles A. Beard, *American Government and Politics,* 4th ed.
(MacMillan, 1924), p. 727.

7.   *New York Times,* October 27, 1975, p. 33.

8.   Claudia D. Scott, *Forecasting Local Government Spending* (The Urban Institute, 1972), pp. 109-116.

9.   Four concepts have been identified——(1) quasi-resolution, (2) uncertainty avoidance, (3) problemistic search, and (4) organizational learning——in Richard M. Cyert and J. B. March, *A Behavioral Theory of the Firm* (Prentice-Hall, 1963), pp. 116-25.

10.   *New York Times,* October 11, 1975.

11.   Robert B. Pettengill and Jogindar S. Uppal, *Can Cities Survive?* (St. Martins Press, 1974), pp. 27-30.

12.   Donald J. Curran, *Metropolitan Financing* (University of Wisconsin Press, 1973), pp. 85-97.

13.   W. H. Brown, Jr., and C. E. Gilbert, *Municipal Investment* (University of Pennsylvania Press, 1961), p. 270.

14.   Arnold J. Meltsner, *The Politics of City Revenue* (University of California Press, 1971), p. 270.

15.   Scott, p. 116.

16.   Robert L. Lineberry and Ira Sharkansky, *Urban Politics and Public Policy* (Harper & Row, 1971), p. 233.

17.   *New York Times,* October 11, 1975.

18.   Richard Reeves, "Will Congress Save New York?" in *New York,* Vol. 8, No. 44 (November 3, 1975), p. 46.

COMMUNITY DATA PROFILE EV-A

(EV-2) GENERAL EXPENDITURES FOR MUNICIPAL PURPOSES ($Amounts in 1,000's)

	YOUR COMMUNITY			COMPARISON CITY		
	1960	1970	% Change	1960	1970	% Change
Gen. Expenditures, All Functions						
Capital Outlay						
Other						
Education						
Other than Capital Outlay						
Highways						
Other than Capital Outlay						
Public Welfare						
Cash Assistance Payments						
Hospitals						
Other than Capital Outlay						
Health, other than Hospitals						
Police Protection						
Fire Protection						
Sewerage						
Other than Capital Outlay						
Sanitation other than Sewerage						
Parks and Recreation						
Housing and Urban Renewal						
Other than Capital Outlay						
Libraries						
Financial Administration						
General Control						
General Public Buildings						
Other than Capital Outlay						
Interest on General Debt						
All Other						

(EV-3) DEFLATED SELECTED EXPENDITURES FOR MUNICIPAL PURPOSES
1960 and 1970 ($ Amounts in 1,000's)

	YOUR COMMUNITY			COMPARISON CITY		
	1960	1970	% Change	1960	1970	% Change
Gen. Expenditures, all Functions						
Total, Excluding Capital Outlays						
General Expenditures, Selected Items						
Education						
Highways						
Exluding Capital Outlays						
Public Welfare						
Health & Hospitals						
Police Protection						
Fire Protection						
Sewerage						
Excluding Capital Outlays						
Sanitation Other than Sewerage						
Parks and Recreation						
Housing and Urban Renewal						
Interest on General Debt						

COMMUNITY DATA PROFILE EV-B

(EV-4) PER CAPITA AMOUNTS AND PROPORTION OF THE BUDGET OF SELECTED MUNICIPAL EXPENDITURES

| | YOUR COMMUNITY | | | | COMPARISON CITY | | | |
| | 1960 | | 1970 | | 1960 | | 1970 | |
	Per Capita	% Budget	Per Capita	% Budget	Per Capita	% Budget	Per Capita	% Budget
General Expenditures, All Functions								
Total, Excluding Capital Outlays								
General Expenditures, Selected Items								
Education								
Highways								
Excluding Capital Outlay								
Public Welfare								
Health and Hospitals								
Police Protection								
Fire Protection								
Sewerage								
Excluding Capital Outlays								
Sanitation, other than Sewerage								
Parks and Recreation								
Housing & Urban Renewal								
Interest on General Debt								

COMMUNITY DATA PROFILE EV-C

CLASSIFICATION INDICATORS

| | | INDICATORS | | CLASSIFICATIONS | |
		Your Community	Comparison City	Your Community	Comparison City
General Expenditures, (All Functions)	Per Capita, 1970				
	% Change 1960-1970				
General Expenditures, Without Capital Outlays	Per Capita, 1970				
	% Change 1960-1970				
Education	Per Capita, 1970				
	% Change 1960-1970				
Highways	Per Capita, 1970				
	% Change 1960-1970				
Public Welfare	Per Capita, 1970				
	% Change 1960-1970				
Hospitals, Total	Per Capita, 1970				
	% Change 1960-1970				
Health	Per Capita, 1970				
	% Change 1960-1970				
Police	Per Capita, 1970				
	% Change 1960-1970				
Fire	Per Capita, 1970				
	% Change 1960-1970				
Sewerage	Per Capita, 1970				
	% Change 1960-1970				
Sanitation	Per Capita, 1970				
	% Change 1960-1970				
Parks & Recreation	Per Capita, 1970				
	% Change 1960-1970				
Housing & Urban Renewal	Per Capita, 1970				
	% Change 1960-1970				
Interest on General Debt	Per Capita, 1970				
	% Change 1960-1970				

EVI. MUNICIPAL DEBT

HOW MUCH PUBLIC DEBT HAS YOUR COMMUNITY INCURRED?

CONCEPT

Most communities borrow money for the acquisition of land and the construction of public facilities such as streets and sidewalks, police and fire stations, and parks and playgrounds. In this way the building projects are paid for on a deferred payment plan with varying lengths of time and are justified on the grounds that future generations of inhabitants should pay for them as they too will benefit from their use. This spreading of public costs over a longer period, of course, incurs some additional costs as interest on the debt paid to the private investors. The rate of interest is in part determined by the credit rating of the city and the availability of funds in the money market.

Unfortunately, local governments generally enter the market during prosperous times when interest rates are higher; during recessions and depression, rates are down but officials are reluctant to borrow with voters feeling the economic squeeze. During wartime they are also restrained from expanding public facilities because materials are less available. Thus, local governments enter the bond market and compete with other borrowers for scarce money which, of course, generally increases interest rates. Interest rates on municipal bonds, for example, rose dramatically during the decade from 3.18 percent in 1960 to over 6.5 percent in 1970.

The pattern of public debt has shifted considerably. State and local governments entered the depression of the 1930s with a debt equal to that of the federal government. During the depression, however, the federal debt increased rapidly while that of state and local governments declined somewhat. World War II, of course, brought a sharp increase in federal debt and an even sharper decrease in local debt. Since the war local debt has grown rapidly in the prosperous postwar era. Local debt grew from under $20 billion in 1950 to over $100 billion in 1970 and is expected to reach $250 billion by 1980. Municipalities incurred less than half of this amount as schools and other special districts funded their growth through bonded indebtedness and deferred payments also. The full extent of governmental debt ($2,531 per capita in 1970) includes that of the federal, state, and all local governments.

The rapid increase in the levels of outstanding local debt has raised concern about the purposes of borrowing. How much debt can be safely incurred? What means should be used to control the authorization of debt? What are the best instruments of borrowing?

The instruments of borrowing can be classified according to their length of term, the security pledged, and their ratings in the bond market.[1] Cities borrow on both a short-term and a long-term basis; some 85 percent is long-term debt (see Table VI-1). Short-term borrowing for periods not exceeding one year is generally used to meet an anticipated receipt of revenues from taxes and other sources, as well as to meet unforeseen budgetary emergencies and in anticipation of bonds used for capital outlays. A growing number of communities have begun to rely on these short-term obligations as a means of supplementing their operating revenues. In so doing they risk unbalancing their budgets and living beyond their means, as becoming dependent on these additional funds makes it more difficult to return to a balanced budget. In addition, short-term loans increase the annual payments of interest on the debt. Communities continually resorting to short-term loans and accumulating large interest obligations also run the risk of lowering their credit rating.

Long-term debt, on the other hand, has usually been incurred for general improvements, for revenue-producing enterprises such as water, gas, and electric utilities, and for industrial development. Although the use of long-term debt to cover budget deficits is frowned upon, there is some allowance given to meet emergencies. The security pledging repayment is either general obligation or nonguaranteed bonds. The former, the most widely used (56 percent of long-term debt in 1970), involves the pledge by local governments of their full faith and credit and financial resource and is taken to mean that the city has the right to levy an unlimited property tax. The latter is any obligation that is payable from pledge-specific sources, such as earnings from revenue-producing activities, from special assessments, or from specific non-property taxes. Since they are not full-faith-and-credit debt they tend to carry higher interest rates.

The *Census of Governments* reports gross debt outstanding figures for both long-term and short-term debt outstanding. It records the debt not only for the municipality but also for any dependent agencies and authorities such as an urban renewal agency, housing authority, or parking authority. Interest on the general debt reported by the census also reflects municipal and agency interest.

Ratings of municipal bonds are provided by several private firms. Moody's ratings and definitions are:

Rating	Moody's
Aaa	Best quality
Aa	High quality (somewhat larger long-term risk)
A	Upper-medium grade (possible susceptibility to impairment)
A1	Strongest upper-medium (maximum quality in group)
Baa	Medium grade (speculative characteristics)
Ba	Speculative
B	Lacks characteristics of desirable investment
Caa	Poor standing
Ca	Speculative in a high degree
C	Lowest-rated class

Generally, the better the credit rating, the lower the interest rates. Some municipal officials have begun to question the reliability of those who provide the credit ratings while others question the objectivity. Ecker-Racz has summarized a variety of factors regarded as favorable to a good credit rating:

> A long record of responsible and prudent financial management free of political machination.
>
> An expanding local economy, backstopped by an affirmative public policy to encourage economic development.
>
> The presence of a fair amount of trade and industry, preferably diversified, with a record of stable growth and the prospect of future growth.
>
> A growing population with a good level of family income.
>
> A low debt in relation to the size, wealth, and income of the population, and to a community's tax resources.
>
> A good debt-service record, free of defaults.
>
> A diversified tax system, including a well-administered property tax.
>
> A minimum of state-imposed restrictions on the taxing and borrowing powers of the community.
>
> Relatively limited future borrowing needs.
>
> Enlightened political leadership supported by professionally competent staff and serving a citizenry interested in and proud of its community.[2]

Just as many state legislatures have established tax limitations (see Exercise EIV), so too have they imposed *debt limits*. Four states—Alaska, Connecticut, Nebraska, and Tennessee—have no limitations. Some use of the referendum to authorize bond issuance is required by nearly all states. Less than half of all states require that municipalities obtain the consent of their citizens by referenda before issuing bonds for public improvements, some require simple majorities and others require as much as a two-thirds vote. The constitution of New York state, for example, provides a debt limit of 7 percent on the average full value of real property for the preceding years (not all debts, however, are subject to the limits; such excluded debts are issued for water, sewer, and self-supporting projects as well as tax and revenue anticipation notes and budget notes). If the bonds exceed $750,000

for municipal purposes, they must be referred to the electorate; if they
are for ten years' duration or longer and for educational purposes, they
also must be referred. Because each state has different debt limits, one
should determine what these limits are. The debt *margin* is the difference
between the debt *limit* and the amount of outstanding debt incurred by the
community.

Characterizing the current practices of states in limiting municipal
debt as too restrictive, Ecker-Racz states that "the principal safeguard
that a state or municipality will not engage in excessive borrowing is the
unwillingness of the market to buy its securities, except at prohibiting
high interest rates." His suggestions for a "meaningful" debt limitation
include a prohibition against the payment of interest rates above some multiple of the prevailing interest rate paid on prime obligations of a comparable maturity, or a limitation on debt as a proportion of the aggregate
annual personal income of the population represented by the borrowing entity.[3]

It is important to point out that the payments of debt service—principal and interest on the local debt—are part of the current annual operating
budget. The greater the debt, the larger is the proportion of the operating
budget diverted to the retirement of the debt. Debt service generally ranges
from 10 to 20 percent of total expenditures. This, of course, means that
the accumulation of a high debt affects not only the amount diverted for
deferred payments on debt service but obviously reduces the flexibility and
the expansiveness of the operating budget for years to come.

There have been few studies on the factors that affect the amount of
community debt. From the point of view of local officials the amount of
debt that can safely be incurred depends on the numerous factors cited by
Moax and Hillhouse:

> the purposes for which the debt is incurred; the
> community's economic characteristics; the community's
> prospects for economic stability, growth, or decline;
> the adequacy of the municipality's revenue system;
> the competence with which debt is planned and managed;
> the amount of debt that overlapping governments incur;
> and the intangible factor of the people's willingness
> to support the debt issue.[4]

They go on to indicate the danger points of a debt policy in trouble:

> A mark-down in credit rating; two or more unsuccessful
> bond referenda; a banker group's refusal to extend
> large temporary loans; a succession of peak years in
> debt service requirements with outcries from property
> taxpayers over steep increases in rates, or a temporary
> bond default.[5]

TYPOLOGY

The following typology provides a framework for classifying communities according to their municipal indebtedness for the funding of public facilities. We have distinguished between cities which do or do not operate public utilities. Two elements of debt have been dichotomized for cities by size and type. One is the per capita amount of gross outstanding debt. The national average of per capita debt in 1970 for municipal purposes was $370.91. Big cities have incurred generally more debt than smaller cities. The other dimension is the per capita amount of interest on gross debt, which includes the interest on utility debt. The national average per capita interest on the debt is $13.64.

FIGURE EVI-1. TYPOLOGY OF DEBT OBLIGATIONS BY SIZE AND TYPE OF CITIES

(Relative to National Average)

PER CAPITA LONG-TERM DEBT

		Above	*Below*
PER CAPITA INTEREST ON THE GENERAL DEBT	*Above*	Expensive Debtor	Costly Borrower
	Below	Prudent Debtor	Cautious Borrower

Four patterns of local debt policy are evident. The first is the *expensive debtor,* in which the community has not only an above-the-national-average per capita indebtedness for cities of its size and type but has also obligated itself to a larger than average interest on its debt. These communities have been improving themselves and have chosen to "buy now" (public facilities) and in doing so have obligated future generations. They may also be cities that have assumed considerable short-term debt. The second type, the *costly borrower,* includes those communities with less than the national per capita debt for cities of their size and type but a higher than average payment of interest. The high interest payments may be due to considerable short-term debt and/or to high interest rates because either the community has a poor credit rating or the debt was incurred during a period of high interest rates. The third type is the *prudent debtor* community, wherein per capita debt is above the national average for cities of its size and type but the level of interest payments are below the national average. These communities may have a good credit rating that results in lower interest rates, or they may have borrowed during periods when interest rates were low. The final type is the *cautious borrower* community, which simply has chosen to incur little debt and is therefore obligated with less than the national average of debt and interest for its size and type of city. This

kind of community could vary from the very affluent to one with a low spending pattern. An affluent one may either provide few public facilities, relying instead on the private sector for goods and services, or have enough
slack in its operating budget to purchase preferred facilities on a pay-as-
you-go principle. Communities with an ideology of low spending prefer a
minimal scope of government, as there may be voter resistance or leadership
reluctance to incur obligations and/or to pass on present costs to future
generations.

SOURCES AND CAVEATS

Data on municipal debt and debt service can be found in the
Compendium of City Government Finances published annually by the
Bureau of the Census. Debt service is a compilation of interest and
debt retired. Note that we include interest on the general debt and
interest on all utility debt in our classification indicators on
interest. However, only interest on the general debt is included as
a current operating expenditure. Debt limits, debt subject to limits,
and debt margins can be found in state reports or in local financial
reports or budgets. Data on debt ratings and the like may be obtained
from private firms' publications such as Moody's Investor's Service,
Inc., *Moody's Municipal and Government Manual*.

It should be noted that discrepancies in debt amounts may
occur between the Bureau of the Census reports and state and/or
local reports because of differences in definitions of municipal debt
(see Tables EVI-1 and EVI-2). The Bureau of the Census includes in
its figure of gross debt outstanding the debt issued by utilities, by
various agencies and authorities affiliated with cities, and that
incurred by the municipality itself. The debt figure quoted in the
city budgets and state reports often includes only the debt issued
by the city itself.

PROFILE EXAMPLE

TABLE EVI-1. INTERSTATE MEASURES OF MUNICIPAL DEBT ($ Amounts in 1,000's Except Per Capitas)

	MOUNT VERNON			NEW ROCHELLE		
	1960	1970	% Change	1960	1970	% Change
Gross Debt Outstanding	$8,161	$19,005	132.9	$8,417	$32,523	286.4
Long-Term	7,789	8,802	13.0	8,076	12,453	54.2
Full Faith and Credit	3,253	5,513	69.5	3,708	5,773	55.7
Utility Debt Only	332	160	-51.8			
Nonguaranteed	4,536	3,289	-27.5	4,368	6,680	52.9
Utility Debt Only						
Short-Term	372	10,203	2642.7	341	20,070	5785.6
Debt Service	760	1,823	139.9	913	1,841	101.6
Interest	186	684	267.7	224	1,189	430.8
On the General Debt	180	679	277.2	224	1,189	430.8
On the Water Debt	6	5	-16.7			
On Other Utility Debt						
Long-Term Debt Retired	574	1,139	98.4	689	652	-5.4
Per Capita						
Gross Debt Outstanding	107.37	261.10	143.2	109.58	431.43	293.7
Long-Term	102.48	120.93	18.0	105.14	165.19	57.1
Full Faith and Credit	42.80	75.74	77.0	48.27	76.58	58.6
Utility Debt Only	4.37	2.19	-49.9			
Nonguaranteed	59.68	45.19	-24.3	56.87	88.61	55.8
Utility Debt Only						
Short-Term	4.89	140.17	2766.5	4.44	266.23	5896.2
Debt Service	10.00	25.05	150.5	11.87	24.42	105.7
Interest	2.45	9.40	283.7	2.92	15.77	432.0
On the General Debt	2.37	9.33	293.7	2.92	15.77	432.0
On the Water Debt	.08	.07	-12.5			
On Other Utility Debt						
Long-Term Debt Retired	7.55	15.65	107.3	8.97	8.64	-3.7

OPERATIONAL DEFINITIONS

Debt Service = Interest + Long-Term Debt Retired

Interest = Interest on General Debt + Interest on Water Debt + Interest on Other Utility Debt

TABLE EVI-2. INTRASTATE MEASURE OF MUNICIPAL DEBT, LIMITS, AND MARGINS* ($ Amounts in 1,000's)

	MOUNT VERNON			NEW ROCHELLE		
	1960	1970	% Change	1960	1970	% Change
Average Full Value	$268,035	$411,341	53.5	$348,904	$490,340	40.5
Debt Limit	17,994	27,767	54.3	24,670	37,903	53.6
Total Debt	3,626	11,421	215.0	6,561	27,367	317.1
Debt Subject to Limit	3,248	8,949	175.5	6,561	22,293	239.8
Debt Not Subject to Limit	378	1,142	202.1	-0-	5,074	-
Debt Margin	14,746	18,818	27.6	18,109	15,610	-13.8

*The amount of total debt in this table does not correspond to gross debt outstanding in Table EVI-1 in that the census includes debt from all agencies and authorities in the city (not just municipal debt).

CLASSIFICATION INDICATORS

	1,000,000 or more with Utilities	500,000 to 999,999 with Utilities	300,000 to 499,999 with Utilities	300,000 to 499,999 no Utilities	200,000 to 299,999 with Utilities	100,000 to 199,999 with Utilities	100,000 to 199,999 no Utilities	50,000 to 99,999 with Utilities	50,000 to 99,999 no Utilities
Dependent School Districts and County Functions									
(Per capita)	(N=1)*	(N=3)	(N=2)	(N=0)	(N=1)*	(N=4)	(N=4)	(N=3)	(N=1)*
Gross debt outstanding	$1,287.38	$639.54	$678.15	–	$978.61	$550.20	$525.55	$482.77	$392.02
Interest on debt	43.24	22.65	25.60	–	39.89	18.85	22.62	14.50	13.46
Dependent School Districts									
(Per capita)	(N=0)	(N=1)*	(N=3)	(N=0)	(N=3)	(N=12)	(N=3)	(N=34)	(N=13)
Gross debt outstanding	–	$650.49	$498.66	–	$415.24	$424.76	$396.99	$337.49	$347.64
Interest on debt	–	22.63	19.05	–	22.03	17.50	15.13	14.12	12.21
Independent School Districts and County Functions									
(Per capita)	(N=1)*	(N=6)	(N=0)	(N=0)	(N=0)	(N=1)*	(N=0)	(N=0)	(N=0)
Gross debt outstanding	$571.35	$456.94	–	–	–	$148.29	–	–	–
Interest on debt	22.89	16.56	–	–	–	5.83	–	–	–
Municipal Functions Only									
(Per capita)	(N=4)	(N=10)	(N=14)	(N=2)	(N=12)	(N=55)	(N=9)	(N=139)	(N=41)
Gross debt outstanding	$443.95	$368.59	$392.78	$255.47	$366.64	$305.20	$175.57	$308.10	$111.66
Interest on debt	15.19	14.37	14.21	10.17	13.91	11.31	7.74	11.32	4.10
Mount Vernon									
(Per capita)									
Gross debt outstanding								$264.14	
Interest on debt								9.39	
New Rochelle									
(Per capita)									
Gross debt outstanding								$431.43	
Interest on debt								15.77	

*See Note Exercise EIII, *Classification Indicators*

FINDINGS AND SUGGESTED IMPLICATIONS

Mount Vernon, which has a water utility, was a *cautious borrower,* with a per capita gross debt outstanding of $264.14 and interest on that debt of $9.39 per capita, both below the average for comparable size and type cities. Mount Vernon's bonds were rated by Moody as A, upper-medium grade, in 1970, which was a drop from its Aa (high quality) rating in 1960. The city more than doubled its debt during the 1960-1970 decade from $8 to $19 million (see Table EVI-1). Virtually all of this increase took the form of short-term loans, which included those of the Urban Renewal Agency. Approximately two-thirds of the long-term debt was full faith and credit. The enormous increase in outstanding debt, of course, was reflected in a substantially increased debt service that heavily burdened the operating budget. Mount Vernon's debt service increased from $760,000 to $1,830,000, which included one-third for interest. In fact, debt service payments exceeded expenditures for any other single function except police.

New Rochelle, on the other hand, with no utilities was an *expensive debtor,* with a per capita gross debt of $431.33 and interest on that debt of $15.77 per capita. The amounts were four times greater than those of comparable size and type cities. Like Mount Vernon's, New Rochelle's bonds were rated A by Moody's in 1970, the same as its rating in 1960. Although both cities began the decade with similar debts ($8 million), New Rochelle's had quadrupled ($32.5 million) by the decade's end. Of the $24 million added debt, $20 million was short-term, twice the amount of Mount Vernon's. More of New Rochelle's long-term debt is nonguaranteed (54 percent) than is Mount Vernon's. By 1970 debt service in New Rochelle doubled from $913,000 to $1,841,000, largely a result of a $1 million increase in interest payments.

It is important to note, however, that both communities remained with considerable leeway to incur additional debt obligations (Mount Vernon had a $18.8 million debt margin and New Rochelle's was $15.6 million). Despite the increased amount of debt, Mount Vernon's margin increased during the decade partly as a result of the increase in its average full value of property and partly because of a change in those items that could be excluded from the constitutional debt limits (see Table EVI-2). Nearly one-half of the debt was excluded from the limit in 1970. New Rochelle's debt margin, in contrast, decreased, because its fourfold increase in debt outpaced the increase in its average full value of property.

The fact that both communities could incur more long-term debt but chose not to do so probably is related more to the effect of increased debt service on current expenditures than on the debt obligation itself. To pay for increased debt service would mean increasing taxes. As both communities were virtually at their tax limits, such costs would be indefensible. However short-term debt can be used to purchase equipment and the like, and thus frees up other funds for current operating expenses. Although interest would still have to be paid, it would be less than the expense of buying equipment. Short-term debt therefore can be seen as one means of civcumventing tax limits.

One can expect certain support for and resistance to a prevailing debt strategy from various sectors of the community. We offer the following speculations as an illustration.

FIGURE EVI-2. SPECULATIONS ON SUPPORTERS OF AND RESISTERS TO DEBT STRATEGIES

Strategy	Supporters	Rationale	Resisters	Rationale
Expensive debtor	Families with rising incomes	Prefer improvements and can afford them	Fixed-income and low-income taxpayers	Cannot afford extra costs in budget
	Community boosters	Improve community at any cost to stimulate business	Taxpayer associations	Tax consciousness
	Pro social service persons	Social benefits outweigh the costs		
	Elected officials supported by progressive consensual elite	Must maintain competitive position vis-à-vis other communities		
Prudent debtor	Commercial interests	Civic improvements to stimulate business but on fiscally conservative terms	Taxpayer associations	Tax consciousness
	Upper-class residents	Prize civic amenities but cost-conscious, seeing themselves as major taxpayers		
	Professional managers	Focus on impact of debt service on operating budgets		
	Officials in fiscally sound communities	Progress means investment but only on favorable terms		
Costly borrower	Elected officials who fear defeat	Seek support thru symbolic achievements	"Watchdogs"	Cost-consciousness
	Groups with specialized needs	Urgent projects		
Cautious borrower	Working-class, fixed-income residents, and small merchants	Fearful of growing debt and unable to pay increased debt service charges	Community boosters	Fear decline in community attractiveness
	Low-risk political officials	Do not want to risk political career by losing support of fiscally conservative constituents		

DISCUSSION

1. What is the municipal-debt classification for your community?

2. What are the per capita amounts of (a) long-term debt, (b) short-term debt, and (c) debt service? To what extent have these amounts changed over time?

3. Of your long-term debt what proportion is (a) full-faith-and-credit debt or (b) utility debt? To what extent have these proportions changed over time?

4. To what do you attribute the debt policy in your community?
(a) new community with need to build public facilities, (b) boosterism, (c) spendthrift public officials, (d) conservative ideology on spending, (e) pay-as-you-go attitude, (f) the community's credit rating, or (g) interest rate levels at the time of borrowing?

5. Speculate on the ways in which the debt policy affects the following major areas of community life: (a) housing, (b) education, (c) health, (d) welfare, (e) economic opportunity, (f) cultural activities, and (g) social tensions.

6. Do you think it important to change the debt policy in your community? If so, in what direction? What social, political, and/or economic strategies can be employed to bring about the desired change?

NOTES

1. See Chapter 15, Lennox L. Moax and Albert M. Hillhouse, *Concepts and Practices in Local Government Finance* (Municipal Finance Officers Association, 1975), pp. 309-328.

2. L. L. Ecker-Racz, *The Politics and Economics of State-Local Finance* (Prentice-Hall, Inc., 1970), pp. 126-27.

3. Ecker-Racz, pp. 132-33.

4. Moax and Hillhouse, p. 270.

5. *Ibid.*, p. 307

COMMUNITY DATA PROFILE EVI-A

(EVI-1) INTERSTATE MEASURES OF MUNICIPAL DEBT

	YOUR COMMUNITY			COMPARISON CITY		
	1960	1970	% Change	1960	1970	% Change
Gross Debt Outstanding						
Long-Term						
Full Faith and Credit						
Utility Debt Only						
Nonguaranteed						
Utility Debt Only						
Short-Term						
Debt Service						
Interest						
On the General Debt						
On the Water Debt						
On Other Utility Debt						
Long-Term Debt Retired						
Per Capita						
Gross Debt Outstanding						
Long-Term						
Full Faith and Credit						
Utility Debt Only						
Nonguaranteed						
Utility Debt Only						
Short-Term						
Debt Service						
Interest						
On the General Debt						
On the Water Debt						
On Other Utility Debt						
Long-Term Debt Retired						

(EVI-2) INTRASTATE MEASURE OF MUNICIPAL DEBT, LIMITS, AND MARGINS
($ Amounts in 1,000's)

	YOUR COMMUNITY			COMPARISON CITY		
	1960	1970	% Change	1960	1970	% Change
Average Full Value						
Debt Limit						
Total Debt						
Debt Subject to Limit						
Debt Not Subject to Limit						
Debt Margin						

CLASSIFICATION INDICATORS

	YOUR COMMUNITY	COMPARISON CITY
Per Capita Gross Debt Outstanding		
Per Capita Interest on Debt		
CLASSIFICATION		

Part V
THE COMMUNITY DISCOVERED

COMMUNITY DISCOVERED

We have collected and assembled hundreds of bits and pieces of information about our congruent communities in implementing this natural experiment. A number of broader patterns have been discovered that can be explored comparatively for a similar time period. A set of patterns can be discovered within each of the three dimensions—social, political, and economic. That is, we have prepared a brief summary that uses the classification to discover what our two communities have in common and in what ways they may differ, compared to the averages for the nation's cities (see Figure 1). We have concentrated on the differences, even noting the degree of variation within a common classification. We also have recapitulated most of the variables, in terms of differences in amounts and in degree of relative change, so that Mount Vernon is contrasted to New Rochelle (see Figures 2, 3, and 4). The variable condition is expressed so that in the first column appears Mount Vernon's position in 1960 relative to New Rochelle's (Mount Vernon's population size was smaller than New Rochelle's in 1960), the second column contains whether the variable changed more or less in the decade than New Rochelle's (population size decreased more in Mount Vernon than in New Rochelle), and the third column states the relative condition of the specific variable in 1970 (Mount Vernon's population in 1970 remained slightly smaller than New Rochelle's). We also draw upon the conceptual materials and knowledge developed by the various traditional disciplines such as sociology, political science, and economics to guide our analysis.

Another pattern explored is the linkages between the social, political, and economic dimensions. Political sociologists, for example, attempt to discover the social basis of politics, while political economists believe there are important connections between economics and public policy. It is difficult, however, to discern how a particular social fact such as population size causes a specific political decision that in turn results in a given pattern of public finance. We will, however, attempt to draw out some of these linkages, especially in the areas where our two communities differ. This process will help us highlight several major differences between Mount Vernon and New Rochelle.

SUMMARIES

SOCIAL

As expected by our criteria of selection, Mount Vernon and New Rochelle had much in common as two comparably sized *established suburbs* located next to each other (see Figure 1). By 1970 they both experienced *out-migration, increasing heterogeneity,* and *slipping higher status* (family income). They also both had a *voluntary female participatory* labor force. There were,

FIGURE 1

COMPARISONS OF THE SOCIAL, POLITICAL, AND ECONOMIC
CLASSIFICATIONS OF TWO COMMUNITIES

SOCIAL	*MOUNT VERNON*	*NEW ROCHELLE*
I. Community location	Established suburb	Established suburb
II. Population size, density & change	Out-migration	Out-migration
III. Ethnic diversity	Increasing heterogeneity	Increasing heterogeneity
IV. Sex, age & family characteristics	Voluntary female participatory	Voluntary female participatory
V. Socioeconomic status:		
a. Income	Slipping higher status	Slipping higher status
b. Education	Declining lower status	Slipping higher status
c. Occupation	Slipping higher status	Increasing higher status

POLITICAL		
I. Governmental magni-complexity	Areal complexity	Areal complexity
II. Government form and reform	Traditional	Professional reform
III. Electoral participation	Civic duty of select	Efficacious
IV. Party potential:		
a. Republican	Slipping with organizational edge	Slipping with organizational edge
b. Democrat	Aspiring with organizational slack	Aspiring with organizational slack
V. Electoral options	Optimal	Restrictive but competitive
VI. Electoral patterns:		
a. Executive	Locally competitive	Consensual
b. Legislative	Generally competitive	Generally competitive
VII. Party effectiveness		
a. Republican	Effective but inefficient	Prevailing
b. Democrat	Efficient but ineffective	Low viability

ECONOMIC		
I. Economic Function		
a. Activity	Manufacturing	Diversified manufacturing
b. E/R ratio	Employing	Balanced
II. Wealth and income	Affluent	Affluent
III. Municipal revenues	Advantaged with support	Independently advantaged
IV. Property taxation	High tax, property reliant	High tax, property reliant
V. Municipal expenditures		
General expenditures, all functions	Progressively big spender	Progressively big spender
VI. Municipal debt	Cautious borrower	Expensive debtor

however, some noticeable differences in kind and degree. Mount Vernon's
heterogeneity increased substantially, while New Rochelle's was slight.
In addition, Mount Vernon's occupational structure was of *slipping higher
status,* and New Rochelle's was of an *increasing higher status.* While
Mount Vernon's educational structure was *declining lower status,* New
Rochelle's was *slipping higher status.*

Despite the leveling off or even slight decline of total population
in both communities, Mount Vernon remained with a substantially greater
density, nearly 17,000 persons per square mile, compared to 7,000 for New
Rochelle (see Figure 2). Mount Vernon experienced a net out-migration
of one-fourth of the whites (15,199) and a net in-migration of one-half
that number of blacks (7,437). In New Rochelle, on the other hand, the
net out-migration of whites and blacks was roughly equal (8 percent).
Accompanying this great difference in racial change as reflected in the substantially higher heterogeneity index in Mount Vernon were some other important demographic consequences that distinguish one community from the
other. By 1970 native whites of native white parents comprised only 28
percent of Mount Vernon's population but 45 percent of New Rochelle's,
and blacks comprised 35 percent of the population in Mount Vernon but only
14 percent in New Rochelle. This created a dramatic change in the comparability of the racial composition of the two communities, as blacks had
constituted 10 percent in both places in 1950. In addition, Mount Vernon
ended the decade with a substantially higher proportion of attenuated
families and children not living with both families.

Within Mount Vernon whites and blacks differed substantially from
each other, as blacks were substantially younger, a larger proportion of
black women than white women were of childbearing age and in the labor force,
and nearly three times as many were heads of households. The black birth
rate was double the white rate, and black infant mortality was nearly twice
as high but not so high as in New Rochelle. Some two-fifths of the black
children under 18 years of age did not live with both parents, three times
the proportion of white children in that status. On the other hand, in
New Rochelle black and white women were approximately the same age. Black
women of childbearing age were not a discernibly larger proportion of the
population than others. On other demographic factors the black-white differences paralleled those of Mount Vernon. The greatest demographic differences were those between whites and blacks in general. The difference
was greater in Mount Vernon than in New Rochelle. The blacks were more
like each other in the two communities than were the whites.

While the residents in these two suburban communities were of higher
socioeconomic status than the average of the nation's cities, the SES of
those in New Rochelle was considerably higher than in Mount Vernon. Mount
Vernon's families had a lower median income ($10,993) than New Rochelle's
($13,183), there was a smaller proportion of upper white-collar workers
(21.5 percent to 34.4 percent), and a smaller proportion of adults who were
college educated (18.5 percent to 32.4 percent). In fact, the major social
strata changes during the decade that may affect the future of these two
communities were that New Rochelle increased its proportion of upper white-
collar workers and its college educated and decreased its percentage of

FIGURE 2
SOCIAL VARIABLES OF MOUNT VERNON CONTRASTED
TO THOSE OF NEW ROCHELLE (1960 to 1970)

Variables	In 1960	Change 1960 to 1970	In 1970
Population size (number)	<	>	remains slightly smaller
Density (number)	>	>	remains substantially more
Net migration	<	>	slightly more out
White	<	>	becomes substantially more out
Black	>	+>	becomes substantially more in
Native white (%)	<	-VS+	becomes substantially less
Foreign born (%)	>	->	becomes slightly less
Foreign stock (%)	>	->	becomes slightly less
Italian (%)	>	+<	remains somewhat more
Blacks (%)	>	+>	becomes substantially more
Heterogeneity index	>	+>	becomes substantially higher
Segregation index	<	+VS-	becomes slightly higher
Median age	>	->	remains slightly older
Under 18 years (%)	<	->	remains slightly less
Over 65 years (%)	>	+<	remains slightly more
Female child-bearing age (%)	<	-VS+	remains slightly less
Cumulative fertility rate	<	+<	remains slightly lower
Birth rate	>	-<	remains slightly higher
Death rate	>	+VS-	remains slightly higher
Infant mortality rate	<	+VS-	remains slightly lower
White	<	-VS+	remains substantially lower
Black	<	-<	remains substantially lower
Females in labor force (%)	>	+>	remains slightly more
Whites	>	+>	remains slightly more
Blacks	<	+VS-	becomes slightly less
Nonworker-to-worker ratio	<	->	remains slightly lower
Attenuated families (%)	>	+>	remains substantially more
White	>	-VS+	remains slightly more
Black	<	+>	becomes same
Children not living with both parents (%)	>	+>	remains substantially more
Whites	>	+>	becomes substantially more
Blacks	<	+>	becomes slightly more
Median family income	<	+<	remains substantially less
Income upper quintile	<	+>	remains substantially less
Income lower quintile	>	+>	remains slightly more
White collar (%)	<	+<	remains substantially less
Occupation upper white collar (%)	<	-VS+	remains substantially less
Occupation lower blue collar (%)	>	+VS-	becomes substantially more
Median education	<	+>	remains slightly less
Education college (%)	<	-VS+	remains substantially less
Education less than 5th (%)	>	-<	remains slightly more

Key:

< Mount Vernon less than New Rochelle   > Mount Vernon greater than New Rochelle
+> Mount Vernon increased more than New Rochelle +< Mount Vernon increased less than New Rochelle
-> Mount Vernon decreased more than New Rochelle -< Mount Vernon decreased less than New Rochelle
VS Mount Vernon changed in one direction and New Rochelle in the other

lower blue-collar worker residents, while Mount Vernon lost some upper status persons, gained some lower blue-collar workers, and actually fell behind the national trends.

During the decade Mount Vernon's population began to decline in size, became more racially diverse, and showed signs of slipping socioeconomic status. New Rochelle's population, on the other hand, remained relatively stable both in size and racial composition, with some improvement in its socioeconomic status, especially in occupation. If the social trends of the 1960's continue, it is likely that New Rochelle will remain stable in its racial composition and improve or at least maintain its high SES, whereas Mount Vernon will experience increasing heterogeneity and a further declining SES.

POLITICAL

One would expect that the common location of the two communities in New York State and in Westchester County would produce very similar governmental forms and political dynamics (see Figure 1). In fact, their common location in the New York SMSA did provide both an *areal complexity* governmental setting. Their political parties displayed similar potential in that the Republican party was dominant with a *slipping organizational edge*. The electoral patterns for legislative office in both communities were *generally competitive*.

There were, however, considerable differences in their forms of government and electoral participation as well as in their electoral options and competitive electoral patterns for mayor (see Figure 3). Mount Vernon's *traditional* form of government placed an emphasis on a strong mayor system, whereas New Rochelle's *professional reform* relied on the city manager. The two cities, however, both retained partisan and at-large elections with staggered terms for city councilmen. Mount Vernon's leadership pattern was pluralistic—representing more diverse segments—compared to New Rochelle's consensual elite pattern—dominated by business interests. Electoral participation differed between the two communities in that Mount Vernon's was the *civic duty of the select* while New Rochelle's was *efficacious*. Mount Vernon had a smaller proportion of eligible citizens registered (62.6 percent) than the nation, whereas New Rochelle had a larger proportion (71.4 percent). However, both had higher proportions of those registered who actually voted than the nation. It appears that in Mount Vernon registration screened out newcomers. Nonetheless, in socially diverse Mount Vernon an overwhelming proportion of those who did register turned out to vote (95.7%), perceiving high stakes especially in local elections. This perceived self-interest combined with a system headed by a strong executive produced a *locally competitive* pattern; the average winner's margin for the mayoralty was 10.1 percent. On the other hand, the more homogeneous population in New Rochelle along with the more ceremonial nature of the mayoralty provided a *consensual* electoral pattern (for the mayor the average winner's margin was 21.0 percent).

Both communities engaged in vigorous two-party competition. In Mount Vernon the *aspiring* Democratic party, constantly challenging Republican

FIGURE 3

POLITICAL VARIABLES OF MOUNT VERNON CONTRASTED
TO THOSE OF NEW ROCHELLE (1960 to 1970)

	In 1960	Change 1960 to 1970	In 1970
Public employee rate	<	+VS-	remains slightly lower
Teacher rate	<	+VS-	becomes substantially higher
Turnout mayoralty election %			
manifest	>	-VS+	becomes substantially less
active	<	-<	becomes slightly more
mobilized	<	->	becomes substantially less
Political party registration %			
Republican	>	->	becomes slightly less
Democrat	>	+>	remains slightly more
Form of government	different	none	remains substantially different
Leadership	NA	NA	substantially different
Evictions % (mayor and city council)	NA	NA	substantially higher (average for the decade)
Republican control	same	none	same

Contrasting representativeness between:

	Candidate Options	Winners
Italian-Catholics	slightly over	substantially over
Jewish	substantially under	slightly over vs. under
Protestants (white)	substantially over	same
Blacks	substantially under	substantially under

Contrasting margin (competition) between:

	Winner over Loser	Republican over Democrat
President	slightly wider	slightly wider
Mayor	substantially closer	substantially closer
Congress	slightly closer	slightly closer
City council	slightly wider	substantially wider
Incumbents (mayor/ city countil)	substantially closer	

Interparty contrasts:

	Republican	Democrat
Balanced tickets	substantially less	substantially more
Use & need 3rd parties	substantially more	substantially more
Use of primaries	substantially less	somewhat more
Victories	slightly more	slightly less
Proficiency:		
Mayor	somewhat less	somewhat more
City council	slightly more	slightly less
Representation:		
Mayor	slightly more	substantially more
City council	slightly more	substantially less

incumbents, was able to control the mayoralty for 4 years during the decade. The vigorous party competition in Mount Vernon not only produced closer margins in mayoralty contests but also resulted in many more evictions of elected officials than occurred in New Rochelle. Mount Vernon's Republican party was *effective but inefficient* while its Democratic party was *efficient but ineffective*. New Rochelle, however, had a *prevailing* Republican party and a Democratic party that was of *low viability*. New Rochelle's Republican party's proficiency for the mayoralty was greater than its counterpart's in Mount Vernon and produced large margins for their candidate. However, the proficiency of the dominant party for city council contests was less than in Mount Vernon.

Reformers within the Democratic party of New Rochelle increase their activity to make their party more responsive to changes in the electorate as well as to the policy issues of the 1960s. They challenged party regulars at the precinct level and in primaries with a reform slate of candidates. Voters supported both intraparty challengers and independent reform movements. There was less reliance on third party coalitions.

Mount Vernon's political parties were able to resist any internal reform, as they relied instead on using third parties to enhance their relative positions in the competitive struggle. The more the Democrats grew in strength (proportion of registered voters) and used the Liberal party, the more threatened the Republicans became, especially since a Democratic mayor and two city councilmen were elected only with the aid of the third party. This stimulated the Republican party to seek the endorsement of a third party, the Conservative Party. The use of third parties contributed to Mount Vernon's *optimal* electoral options. New Rochelle's electoral options with fewer city council positions were *restrictive but competitive*. However, Mount Vernon's electoral options were less representative of its Jewish and black population segments than were New Rochelle's. Italians and Jews were more overrepresented and blacks more underrepresented among winning candidates in Mount Vernon than in New Rochelle.

In Mount Vernon, the decade witnessed reduced electoral participation, a slipping Republican registration, a growing and aspiring Democratic party offering more electoral options, continued vigorous competition, and a greater turnover of public authorities; yet the Republicans regained their dominance over the mayoralty and retained their control of the city council. New Rochelle's political dynamics, while similar to Mount Vernon's, differed in that its electoral competition and turnover of public officials was not so high during the 1960s.

Democratic party leaders and constituents in Mount Vernon undoubtedly will experience growing frustration if their party continues to lose local elections despite an increasing party potential (a plurality of registrants in 1972). The Republicans, on the other hand, will probably continue their success if they maintain their effective strategies such as the cooptation of moderate black spokesmen, coalescing the white community against racial change, and modifying their own fiscal policies sufficiently to seek and obtain substantial amounts of federal funds for urban redevelopment. In the last analysis, party distinctions will become less significant if both parties continue to put forward conservative candidates—encouraging the turnout of conservative voters while discouraging many liberal and moderate Democrats from voting. The political dialogue of the 70s is more likely to be to the right of center, with Republicans continuing their control of the decision-making centers. Modification of these dynamics may occur if there is a successful Democratic party reform movement; or if the Democrats can find an issue that increases the registration and voter turnout of the poor and the black, draws their registrants out to vote, and also attracts the independent voters to their candidates; or some national political (change in the federal administration) or economic (recession) trends sufficiently affect the local scene.

New Rochelle's political future, on the other hand, seems to be inter-twined with the reform thrust of its Democratic party. Should this reform dynamic pick up momentum, the system may see a growing proficiency in the Democratic party.

ECONOMIC

As established suburbs with a dominant Republican party in 1970, Mount Vernon and New Rochelle, compared to the nation, had in common *affluent* residents, a taxation policy that was *high tax, property reliant* and were generally considered to be *progressively big spenders* (see Figure 1). However, within these common classifications, New Rochelle had con-siderably more wealth (more than twice as much per capita full value of property—$19,116 compared to Mount Vernon's $8,568) and greater per capita income ($5,029 per capita compared to $3,860). This differential in turn affected their relative ability to sustain high property taxes with New Rochelle having the greater advantage ($159 per capita compared to $119 per capita).

The two communities differed in their main economic function: Mount Vernon's primary economic function was *manufacturing,* with 52.0 percent employed in manufacturing, and it employed more people in the basic business activities than there were residents in the labor force engaged in these activities. Mount Vernon's location on two major railroads and a barge canal, bordering New York City, enhanced it as a manufacturing place. On the other hand New Rochelle's economic function was *diversified manufacturing,* with nearly equal proportions employed in manufacturing and retail trade (37.1 percent in manufacturing and 34.6 percent in retail trade). There was also a balance in New Rochelle between those employed on a place-of-work basis in the major facets of business activity and those engaged in these same activities on a place-of-residence basis. Mount Vernon's business activity generated more dollars, especially from manufacturing and wholesale trade, than did New Rochelle's (one-half billion compared to one-third billion). During the decade, however, New Rochelle increased its wholesale and retail trade substantially more than did Mount Vernon, whereas Mount Vernon increased its receipts from services more (see Figure 4).

In these suburban communities, business activities and business property did not generate the largest proportion of municipal revenues. As *high tax,*

FIGURE 4
ECONOMIC VARIABLES OF MOUNT VERNON CONTRASTED
TO THOSE OF NEW ROCHELLE (1960 to 1970)

	In 1960	Change 1960 to 1970	In 1970
Full value property $	<	+<	remains substantially less
Aggregate income $	<	+<	remains substantially less
Per capita income $	<	+<	remains substantially less
Value added by (mfg.) $	>	+<	remains substantially more
Wholesale trade $	>	+<	remains substantially more
Retail sales $	<	+<	remains somewhat less
Service receipts $	>	+>	becomes substantially more
General revenues per capita $	<	+<	remains substantially less
Intergovernmental revenues per capita $	<	+>	becomes substantially more
Property taxes per capita $	<	+<	becomes substantially less
Assessed property value $	<	+<	remains substantially less
Municipal tax rates $	>	+>	remains substantially higher
Municipal taxes levied $	<	+<	remains substantially less
Tax margin $	<	->	remains slightly less
Residential property assessment %	<	->	remains substantially less
General expenditures per capita $	<	+<	remains substantially less
Highways	<	+<	becomes substantially less
Health & hospitals	<	-VS+	becomes substantially less
Police protection	>	+>	becomes substantially more
Fire protection	<	+<	remains substantially less
Sewers	<	-VS+	remains substantially less
Sanitation	<	+>	remains somewhat less
Parks & recreation	<	+<	becomes substantially less
Housing & urban revewal	<	+>	remains slightly less
Interest on debt	<	+<	becomes substantially less
Personal services	<	+<	becomes substantially less
Gross outstanding debt per capita	<	+<	becomes substantially less
Long term	<	+<	becomes substantially less
Short term	>	+<	becomes substantially less
Debt margin $	<	+VS-	becomes substantially less

property reliant fiscal systems they raised more than three-fourths of their local revenues from property taxes. Residential property provided 58 percent of the assessed value in Mount Vernon and 69 percent in New Rochelle. Mount Vernon, however, had substantially less taxable assessed value, which also increased less in the 1960-1970 decade. Although its municipal tax rate was higher because of its lower assessed value, its tax levy was substantially below New Rochelle's ($7.9 million compared to $11.6 million).

With respect to municipal general revenues, Mount Vernon was *advantaged with support,* receiving $59 per capita of intergovernmental transfers, while New Rochelle was *independently advantaged.* Mount Vernon's external aid was a substantial proportion of its budget, comprising 28.9 percent compared to only 17.6 percent for New Rochelle. Despite greater federal aid Mount Vernon had substantially lower per capita revenues ($203.99) than did New Rochelle ($239.72).

Both communities engaged in primarily distributive expenditures, wherein they were *progressively big spenders* except for highways, in which case they were *catching up,* and in parks and recreation where Mount Vernon was *continuously frugal.* In the fee-for-service functions, both were *leveling-off* for sanitation. In the one redistributive function, housing and urban renewal, both communities were *progressively big spenders.* As New Rochelle operates its own sewer and health systems its expenses for those functions were obviously greater than Mount Vernon's. New Rochelle had also a greater commitment to provide such suburban amenities as parks and recreation ($33 per capita compared to $8 per capita). In all functions except for police New Rochelle spent more per capita than did Mount Vernon. As for expenditures for personnel, Mount Vernon spent considerably less than New Rochelle ($7.2 million compared to $9.1), and its increase for the decade was substantially less (65.1 percent compared to 105.6 percent).

Whereas both communities were *progressively big spenders* for interest on the general debt, New Rochelle's interest was significantly higher ($16 per capita compared to $6). This reflected, of course, their different debt policy, whereby Mount Vernon was a *cautious borrower* and New Rochelle an *expensive debtor.* That is, for cities of their size carrying out similar functions, Mount Vernon had less per capita debt ($26) and interest ($9) than the average in the nation, and New Rochelle had more (debt of $43 per capita and interest of $16 per capita). The largest share of debt for both cities was short term, and it constituted the major part of the debt increase. Long-term debt increased about $1 million in Mount Vernon, whereas short-term debt increased to $10 million from virtually zero in 1960. In New Rochelle long-term debt increased by $4.4 million during the decade, whereas short-term debt increased by $20 million, also from virtually nothing. Although the emphasis placed on short-term debt left both communities with comfortable debt margins (margins are based on long-term debt), Mount Vernon's margin was substantially greater. Obviously New Rochelle had an expansive debt policy in the 1960s with urban development in full swing, which at a time of increasing interest rates became an expensive venture.

Mount Vernon, despite being an affluent community by national standards, experienced a much more rapid increase in expenditures than in its economic resources, especially its taxable property. This, in contrast to New Rochelle's greater affluence and growth in its resources (allowing it to spend more on public services), placed considerable fiscal stress on Mount Vernon to keep up with its neighbor. To a certain extent this gap between the two communities was alleviated by the greater amount of external aid granted to Mount Vernon.

If Mount Vernon should continue to pursue a fiscal policy with the objective of keeping up with its more affluent neighbors, this could induce greater stress by placing too great a burden on its residential property. On the other hand, if Mount Vernon's interest is to reduce or at least not to increase the burden on its residential property, it would have to supplement its tax base by increasing industrial and commerical properties or decrease its expenditures. This strategy, however, would change the suburban character of the community, making it even less attractive to middle-strata and upper-strata families and individuals.

New Rochelle, by contrast, made a choice in the 1960s to keep up with its more affluent neighbors by incurring considerable debt for extensive urban renewal and commercial development. The greater affluence of New Rochelle allows it more leeway to maintain its suburban character.

SPECULATIVE LINKAGES

Our discovery process has revealed that our two congruent communities have in fact many dissimilarities. The basis of the divergence, among other dynamics, was the difference in racial change that was well under way by the 1960s. Mount Vernon apparently was more vulnerable to the social and economic forces of New York City than was New Rochelle. Figure 5 describes some major relationships between the social, political, and economic dimensions of Mount Vernon, the components of which differed between Mount Vernon and New Rochelle. The statements within the matrix are stated in terms of Mount Vernon's contextual linkages and are contrasted with New Rochelle's in terms of "more" or "less."

These linkages should highlight some different dynamics that suggest different futures for the two communities. They suggest that Mount Vernon and New Rochelle will remain different places for some time to come. The question is not whether Mount Vernon can regain its suburban character, but what it will become. Perhaps the best strategy for leaders and citizens of both communities is to carefully discover not only the contemporary community characteristics but also the dynamics of change that they are experiencing. These should be evaluated in the context of preferred futures and reasonable expectations. If undesirable futures seem likely, a policy agenda should be set to establish priorities for community action so that the community as a whole can affect the direction toward preferred outcomes.

FIGURE 5

MOUNT VERNON'S SOCIAL, POLITICAL, AND ECONOMIC
LINKAGES COMPARED TO THOSE OF NEW ROCHELLE

	SOCIAL	POLITICAL	ECONOMIC
SOCIAL	As the net out-migration of whites and in-migration of blacks became substantially more, SES slipped considerably more.	As the social heterogeneity increased more, Italian and Jewish residents were more overrepresented among elected officials and blacks were more underrepresented.	As the SES slipped more, the growth of the private economic sector did not increase as much, especially in retail trade and service activities.
POLITICAL	As the ethnics won more of the elected positions, more native whites of native white parents left the community.	As voter registration decreased more (especially for Republicans) and the Democratic party used third-party labels and balanced tickets more, Republicans maintained the same control.	As a competitive pluralistic leadership resulted in less consensus, public officials found it more difficult to obtain new rateables or to increase taxes on existing properties, but were more successful in securing external aid.
ECONOMIC	As the property tax base increased less and tax rates increased more, the upper and upper-middle strata residents moved elsewhere.	As the tax base increased less accompanied by increasing expenditure, more political stress was placed on the mayor, leading to greater competition for the office and more incumbent evictions.	As the community was less able to increase revenues from local sources, it became more dependent upon external aid.

AUTHOR INDEX